DANGEROUS CURVES

THE TERRI O'CONNELL STORY

"Where there is danger, there is drama"
-- Martin Scorsese

Registration Number: 1271181

ISBN: 1-4392-0138-2
ISBN-13: 9781439201381

Visit www.booksurge.com to order additional copies.

This is the most compelling autobiography in our time, and the first tell all in NASCAR history. National champion race driver and model Terri O'Connell positions her self as the most unique, controversial and dynamic athlete in the world.

This is the speed secret the power players in motorsports and big name politicians don't want told . . . but the story that millions of fans around the world can't wait to read.

By Terri O'Connell

Meeting Terri and traveling with her on the NASCAR circuit was like sitting in a rocket car blasting through the American night. The force of her speed, the mastery of her self-determination, left me wobbly-legged at the end of the ride.
Keven Gray, Senior Writer, Conde Nast Portfolio magazine

"Terri O'Connell is Mario Andretti, Cindy Crawford and Rosa Parks all in one person ... she has a once in world history story. This book is intense and frank, it is simply fantastic."
Maer Roshan, Editor Radar Magazine

"Terri's life story is one of the most incredible stories I have ever worked on ... She is going to be a star at whatever she does."
Judy Tygard, Producer for *CBS - 48 Hours* ... formerly with *20/20 ABC*

"Jackie Robinson, Erin Brokovitch, Jeff Gordon and gorgeous ... those are the names I use to describe Terri O'Connell. She is a social trailblazer and she is a very courageous living piece of history. This book is simply amazing."
Paul Weber, Weber Casting and Independent Film Producer

"Terri's race driving skills and accomplishments rivals any racing champion out there. She has won in virtually every type of race car like so many of the hall of fame drivers in the past, she is a racer. It's amazing that she was so successful while dealing with so much danger and drama in her life, her life is manual for how to beat the odds."
Jan Roland, Winning Race Team Owner

Since Terri O's first in world history story broke in the international press back in 1998, her amazing story has played in the media all around the world more than all the other gender

related stories combined. She has also become the most important social and pop culture event in motorsports over 110 year
history. Her media exposure continues today more than ever
before and with the release of this book she is clearly raising the
bar for the next athletic autobiography coming down the pike.
Maer Roshan, the executive editor of *Radar Magazine* makes
an additional bold statement by stating, "Terri O'Connell is
the most dynamic, the most unique and the most controversial
athlete in the world simply because of her female and first in
motorsports status. *Terri O'Connell transcends motor sports and
the gender identity issue, she is one of the Great American Stories
of our time.*"

ACKNOWLEDGMENTS

It took a lot of dedicated and strong-willed people to get me to this point in my life. For sure, there have been many amazing people who have not only helped me get this book in proper order, but also helped me survive my life and make it to victory lane. All these amazing people deserve to be in the Human Being Hall of Fame. It ain't been easy knowing me or helping me get it all done.

Patricia Nell Warren is an angel sent from the literary heavens. Without her direction, inspiration and extreme guidance, this book would still be a 1000-page convoluted rant about my life. Patricia is an icon within the literary community, but she is much more than that. She is a damn fine human being, a woman of impeccable integrity and vision for what the heart really stands for – which is kindness, inclusion, perseverance and awareness. She pushed me to excel, she inspired me with constructive criticism and lifted me up when I was down and out. She supported me when so many did not, and for that, I put her at the very top of my fave five.

Salute to you, Patricia Nell Warren, you deserve only the very best in your life.

Eileen Stewart. . . the Blond Rocker and all-around kick-ass chick, I take my hat off to you. Big-time thanks for catching my back, helping out with my bills and keeping my self-esteem in good working order. Eileen gets it. She understood me from the very first time I met her sitting out on the Starbucks patio at the Glenn Center. From the first time we met, we were pals. Eileen, I will always be indebted to you for all you did to keep me ticking while all of this incredible journey played out. Rock on, girl -- E. C. luvs ya.

When my best bud Randy Mottsinger passed away, I was a lost puppy. I did not know what to do with myself. My sense of purpose, especially on getting this story told, seemed to have wrecked itself against some invisible wall. Then came along Paul Weber, a good-looking sharp-as-a-tack California boy whom I drove crazy for the first year that I knew him, as I was trying to position my story with the right people. Paul hung in there with me. We both kept plugging any way we could with just the right producer, or a publicist that could take the story to the next level. He listened to me rant and rave to the top of my lungs about all the a-holes I was having to deal with, and he always held my heart close to his and never let anyone run over me. I owe ya big time, Paul Weber, you movie mogul you.

Gil Toff is the most interesting person I have yet to encounter. He is clearly a one-of-a-kind cosmic dreamer. As a back-in-the-day liberal and free spirit, Gil played soccer internationally for the U.S. soccer team, toured Europe lecturing on mental health, and found himself consumed with the tragic death of President John F. Kennedy. He made documentaries, rode motorcycles along Mulholland Drive at three in the morning, and argued passionately for what is right on this earth with anyone he could get to engage him. Gil, you're my partner, my mentor and my damn fine friend. You offered up your friendship unconditionally and let me in on Charlie O's and the fabulous Patrick Toselino, the coolest crooner on the planet. Thanks for everything you do for me... I'm a better person for it.

Now for Jan Roland. If anyone would have told me back in 1985 that we would be best friends or girlfriends and keeping the dance floor lit up at BB King's in Memphis, I would have told them, "You're crazy!" Jan is a hoot, she is my BFFL and I could not fathom living on this planet without knowing her. She deserves only the very best in her life, and if it's in my power to do it, I'm going to make sure she gets it.

Thanks, Jan, for the moral support, the fried eggs on Sunday mornings and a place to hide out when my life came crashing down around me. Oh yeah, and thanks for letting me drive your race car back in the day, and I do want to apologize once again and tell you I am deeply sorry for wrecking that baby over in Little Rock, even if it did make us famous. Luv ya, baby!

Maer Roshan came into my life quite by accident, or maybe it was preordained destiny, back in 1998. He saw my interview on "20/20" and made the decision right then that he wanted to be a part of my story. Since then he has become one of my brothers, he has helped nurture this story through the press, gave me damn good advice and supported me with absolute commitment in getting the book to market. Maer is a free thinker, he is outside the box and his *Radar Magazine* is one of the finest celebrity news outlets going. He positioned my story with the right people and backed it up with unyielding support.

You're my buddy and you're family, Maer. I take my hat off to ya and wish you a Pulitzer Prize or more importantly, a hot date.

Donzaleigh Abernathy is just one more destined friend that changed my life. She opened my eyes to the real adversity on this earth. Donseleigh is beautiful, both physically and spiritually, and one fine actress. She also wears her literary skills well by publishing fine books about her father, Dr. Ralph David Abernathy, and his best friend Dr. Martin Luther King. But more than that, she is someone who loves me without boundaries. She pushes me to be my best and to never let anyone stand in the way of telling my life story or getting back out on the race track. Thanks for the bed and the Beverly Glen coffee breaks, babe, you're a star that shines brightly and a friend who shares passionately.

Robert Wilford is absolutely the most cosmic person I have ever met. I love him with all of my heart. Robert and his partner Mark Flanders took me in, gave me a place to land my crashing plane and allowed me time to heal my broken heart. I first met Robert when he was a fabulous make-up artist at Barney's out in Los Angeles. He took me out line-dancing at Oil Can Harry's and I knew right then that Robert was a contradiction in terms.

Then Robert took that contradiction one step father when he worked his tail off and became Dr. Robert Wilford, board-certified psychologist. Thanks, Robert, for letting me vent and get the weight of the world off my shoulders and more importantly, thanks for the fab make-up tips. Thanks for the laughter that released our stresses, and the opportunity to step up my cultural experience. You and Mark are the greatest.

Stewart Rigby, aka Tom, is another friend to whom I have to pay homage in this book. Stu came from the motherland to seek his dream of being a movie star and that is exactly what he should be. He does have one character flaw, though -- he is way too nice a person to be a movie star. Thanks, Stu, for the couch, the lovely conversation over scrambled eggs at the Glen Deli, and the moral support in getting this book finished and just loving me as a friend. "You got it," my friend, so let your star shine brightly and never give up on your dream. You're smart, talented and caring – and a lot better-looking than Tom Cruise.

I have been incredibly fortunate to meet a lot of really cool people in my life. But Barry Pullman touched my heart as much as anyone, with awareness, openness and a whole lot of intelligence. He is a fine man, a fine screenwriter and all-around good human being Thanks, Barry, for the loan of your couch and the way-out conversations up at the Glen Center. Thanks for breaking bread with me at Fabrocini's, and for letting me hold court and analyze the world while we snickered at the world passing by. Thanks for the advice in getting this book to fruition and for sticking to your craft when your chips were down. You have talent, buddy, use it up!

I have to give a big shout-out to all my Beverly Glen friends. Everyone from D.A. Dave, Nick and Armon to Mort, Fiona and Jack have been my California coffee-drinking buddies. Salute to Vladimir, Mike, Granny, Joy and Dr Miller and all of the Starbucks crew at the Glen Center for giving me a neighborhood full of intelligent conversation and friendship to hang with. All of you made my time in Los Angeles very special. All of you opened my life up to bigger and better possibilities.

I also want to thank all my home-town friends who have sparkled friendship dust over me for most of my life, especially when the pressure was on them to not associate with me. They deserve a big ole Corinth acknowledgment for showing courage and perseverance in surviving the Terri O' hurricane. Here's to the two Wanda's, Lynn, Rene, Lisa, Judy, Debbie, Patty, Dale, Nathan, Ernie, Neil, Flat Top, Dan, Tracy, the two David's, Vic, Bobby W., Lynn W. Bob, Jan, Brent, Cindy, Hal, Melanie, Cheryl, Scottie, John D. and Rob. And of course I have to give my buddy Ken a big thumbs up for palling around with me and helping me with all my crazy projects. You're my buddy, Ken, and I love ya for it big time. Also, I want to give a special thanks to Christine White for all her support, and for being a great friend to my mom. Christine, you're family.

If not for Lake and Rice' Speed, I most likely would not be alive. They looked after me when no one else would, and made sure that not only was I safe and fed, but also that my soul was being nurtured. I have to thank them with all of my heart for believing in me, for understanding me and for giving me a chance. Lake and Rice,' I will always love you and respect you for all that you did for me; both of you are my guardian Angels.

I also can't leave out a big hug for my North Carolina buddy Harpo Ruttman. She supported me, laughed and cried with me and let me vent about my life when I most needed to do it. Harpo, you go, girl.

When I became a businesswoman I was taking a big step off into unknown territory, but Wanda Edwards Miller embraced my dreams and helped me -- through her support and encouragement – to bring those dreams to fruition. Big thanks, Wanda Edwards, for giving me a chance to prove myself and for believing that chicks can compete with the big boys in the business world. Thanks for the power lunches, the free meals and a place to present my talents to the big leagues. Wanda, you have class, you have heart and you're a real nice person. P.S., thanks for giving me the opportunity to know Doris and Betty.

I also want to give a big shout-out to my old friend Russ Thompson for chasing down news articles and stats about my racing career and getting me reacquainted with my old Karting buds, Theresa Gammons and Tommy Crosby. I've known and been friends with Russ for longer than both of us want to admit. Russ is a kick-butt race-car driver, a genius at compiling race statistics that he has turned into a very successful business. We share motorsports history, and we love talking about it. Russ, ole buddy, you're a good person, a fine dad and someone I'm glad to have back in my life. Salute to you!

Throughout the years there have been many who have made my racing career possible and I want to express my gratitude to as many of them as I can.

First, the Haines Brothers jump-started my Karting career and gave me that professionalism I need to take my racing to the top. Charles Toler inspired me and made me see that the details meant something. Bill Bagwell pushed me to excel, and Gene Calvary believed in me no matter what. Steve Clark gave me a chance to be a professional and took heat by doing so. Duce Turrell pushed me to the right people and Rich Lovell gave me a second chance that allowed me to reach victory lane. Al Leist welcomed me into his home and let me have a race car to drive when I needed it most. Don and Nancy O'Brian took me in, gave me culture and supported me in my NASCAR quest and then supported me at my darkest moments in life. Junnie Donlavey graciously let me live my NASCAR dream and then lived up to his reputation for being a really nice person when he went on the record saying that I had talent right there on "20/20." I have to give a shout- out to Shand Tillman over at Riverside Speedway for catching my back and to all the crew guys who ever helped me get my car on the track. Without any of these fine people, my career would have been less than it was. I owe all of them a real debt of gratitude. Thanks guys and gals, you all made it worth the effort.

Last but not least, there's Mom and Dad. They deserve a special place in heaven. They worked their tails off to make sure I was fed, that I was healthy and that I had a roof over my head. They also sacrificed unbelievably trying to help me race and to keep me alive while I tried to work all of the Gender Identity business out. They took almost as much heat as I did in our hometown and struggled to make sense of it all. But as a family, we hung in there, rode out the speed bumps and loved one another in spite of the obstacles put before us. I can never thank my mom and dad enough for loving me, for keeping me safe and for allowing me a place to come home whenever my life came crashing down on top of me.

Mom. Especially deserves to live on the Riviera with servants at her beck and call, because of everything that she did for me. I love you, Mom. We finally made it, didn't we?

Thanks!

INTRODUCTION

The Great American Story
By Patricia Nell Warren

Back in that 20th-century yesteryear when fiction still dominated our literary skyline, we used to hear a lot about the Great American Novel. Many an American writer dreamed of writing it...had tried to write it. Depending on which literary critic you believed, some writers succeeded in that try...and others had failed.

Yet defining the Great American Novel has proven as challenging as actually creating one. In late 2007, writing in *The Independent* about Norman Mailer's death, literary critic John Walsh wondered if the GAN has even survived into the post-millennial era. Walsh came up with a definition that is as good as any, in my opinion. He said: "It was an ideal that brought with it a holy grail: that of a single perfect work of fiction that would encapsulate the heart of the U.S., interpret its history through the light of a single, outstanding consciousness, unite the private lives of the characters with the public drama of its politics. It would be the *War and Peace* of the great plains and the Manhattan skyline. ...Mailer believed in it utterly. He called it 'the big one' and dreamed of bagging it one day."

As the ghastly realities of World War II lingered on, and pushed America to deal with real-life human fact around the world, nonfiction emerged as a real genre, challenging the primacy of fiction. Mailer and some other American authors turned away from the Great American Novel and pushed further in the direction of writing directly and unflinchingly about real-life American people and American events. Critics called it the "New Journalism."

During my 16 years as a book editor at The Reader's Digest, from 1964 till 1980, I watched the emergence of the celebrity autobiography as a type of provocative new nonfiction. "Memoirs" had been around for a couple of centuries – an 18th century model that was usually genteel, polite, witty, penned by a court lady or a statesman in a powdered wig. But the New Autobiography was anything but genteel. More often it was rowdy, rebellious, impolite, angry, and in your face. Often it cut loose from any self-conscious concerns over "fine literature." The celeb biog was all about plain speaking, naked soul-searching and cantankerous questioning.

For around 16 years, I read many of those autobiographies as they came through RD's Book Department or Condensed Book Club in the form of manuscripts or galley proofs, to be considered for condensation by the Digest. With America tearing itself in half amid cultural and social conflict, the Sixties and Seventies were a big break-through time for the explosive and controversial "tell all" bestseller -- whether it was Jerry Rubin's *Doing It!* or Eldridge Cleaver's *Soul on Ice* or Jim Bouton's *Ball Four* or Loretta Lynn's *Coal Miner's Daughter.*

Frequently, at the Digest, I worked on the actual condensations of intense personal nonfiction stories. They ranged from Alex Haley's *Roots* to Coretta King's *My Life with Martin Luther King, Jr.* to Stanley Brock's *Jungle Cowboy.* Brock was the action guy on the "Wild Kingdom" show in those days.

The power of those take-no-prisoners personal stories really sank in with me. In 1973, when I finally started working on my second novel *The Front Runner,* I felt that the story would be most effective if I wrote it in a voice more typical of those celebrity autobiogs that came storming across my desk. So when TFR was done, it read as if a real-life gay track coach named Harlan Brown had sat down to his typewriter, some years after the fact, and painfully poured out his own perspective on what he'd gone through.

Today, as television and the Internet become ever more powerful forces that bend the way we define reality, autobiography has gotten as searingly frank and unpretentious as a few minutes of YouTube video footage showing a train wreck or an armed robbery at a 7-11. Tru TV's log line says that television is stepping beyond "reality" into "actuality," because so many so-called "reality" shows are scripted and faked to some degree, while "actuality" programs are crafted from raw video and news and security-camera footage. I think that "actuality" is a trend in books as well.

What this means, with nonfiction -- and especially provocative autobiography – dominating our national skyline more than ever, is that we don't hear much about the Great American Novel any more. Indeed, the GAN is rapidly being replaced by the autobiographical Great American Story.

What is the difference between the Great American Novel and the Great American Story? Possibly the writers of GAS's are not too worried about what the critics will think. Their chief passion is to tell the story, to get their experience across to the reader with as much force as possible. As a result, provocative autobiography is bigger than ever, with stories like Eric Clapton's *Clapton: The Autobiography* sitting high on last year's list of unapologetically vivid bestselling memoirs. Daniel Tammet's *Born on a Blue Day* challenges the reader to step into his personal actuality of what it's like to be an autistic savant.

As I write this, Barbara Walters' *Audition* has everybody oh'ing and ah'ing with shock. But nobody should be surprised. Her book is entirely within that tradition that was launched so noisily and necessarily in the Sixties.

Yet Walsh's definition of the Great American Novel fits the Great American Story too, as neatly as a wing fits on a race car. And Terri O'Connell's *Dangerous Curves* is definitely a Great American Story.

First of all, Terri's narrative of her life has what Walsh called that "light of a single, outstanding consciousness." It shines its merciless beam, like a police detective's flashlight, into the basement of the American mind, onto a vast pile of dusty steamer trunks and battered retro furniture that constitutes our taught notions about sexuality and gender.

Dangerous Curves certainly has what Walsh terms "private lives into public drama" – namely, a national champion race-car driver becoming one of the most controversial figures in American sports history. The drama is rooted in a region that is terra incognita for many Americans -- the Deep South, and its small-town life, its own ways of socializing, its own humor, its loves and loyalties, its biases and judgments, and its deep-dyed evangelical religion. There, in the South, the drama centers on America's biggest spectator sport, auto racing – on the immense crowds, the heroes, the screeching wrecks, the reek of danger and threat of death that must rival chariot racing in the Circus Maximus of ancient Rome.

Last but not least, Terri's story does what Walsh calls "encapsulating the heart of American history." Our notions of gender, and what our country expects from each gender in terms of personal performance, form the very bedrock of American history, from the Founding Fathers to the 2008 Presidential campaign with its woman candidate. Terri's story puts a large earthquake crack through that bedrock, revealing how little grounded in scientific fact is the attitude that most Americans have about gender – how far many of us are from understanding what gender really is, and how it should or could be expressed.

Indeed, Terri's portrait of her own parents, and their private struggle to understand and support their child in spite of hostile public pressures from many in their home town, goes to the very heart of the history of American family.

Since the 19ᵗʰ century, the South has been cultivating its own riches of autobiography. My own family's Virginia and West Virginia ancestry has led me to read many of its literary classics. They often focused on painful old issues of history, family, racism and social class, from *Mary Chestnut's Civil War* to Richard Wright's *Black Boy.* By the 70s, the national trend in personal stories was hitting the South, with Tennessee Williams' controversial *Memoirs.* Willie Morris's *North Toward Home* wrestled with a Southerner's uncomfortable sense of finding himself viewed through an unfriendly and unappreciative lens by Northerners. Theodore Rosengarten's *All God's Dangers: The Life of Nate Shaw* was veering towards post-millennial "actuality" with its oral history of a sharecropper.

Today the South's all-time list of celeb biogs includes unconventional spirits like Dolly Parton and Paula Deen. But it's safe to say that Dangerous Curves is – and will be for a long time – a new and startling benchmark of Southern autobiography.

With gender issues now frequently in the news, a spate of recent autobiographies have approached the subject from more of an academic and political point of view. In the sports world, one book that takes a real Great Story approach is the 1988 autobiography of Olympic and world-champion downhill skier Erik Schinegger, titled *Mein Sieg über mich. Der Mann, der Weltmeisterin wurde.* But it's a European Great Story and came out only in German. Schinegger's epic struggle with gender, and his successful fight to go on making a living in his beloved sport, has as its backdrop the somewhat more liberal and accepting approach of Europeans to the question.

Unfortunately, many Americans still refuse to "get it" about gender challenges, especially those that are inborn, as Terri's was. They take an appallingly simplistic, judgmental and narrow stance that is now hardwired into American culture, owing to the influence of evangelical Protestantism in our national history. Because the Old Testament banned cross-dressing by both women and men, many American believers today still view gender questioning as a "sin" and a "disorder" – as a mere urge to masquerade as the opposite gender that can supposedly be cured by sermons and will power. Unfortunately this religious belief is now masquerading as science and finding its way into the psychotherapy field – as I write this, the APA has put its imprimatur on "reparative therapy" by appointing Kenneth Zucker Ph.D., chief advocate of religion-based "repair"school, as chair of its Sexual and Gender Identity Disorders work group.

Thus American denialism about gender variants and gender questions is creating the screaming need for Great Stories like Terri's to be told.

I first met Terri in 2007 when I was researching an article on motorsports and ran across her massive listing of media mentions on Google. In an age when people come and go from the news in a few days or a few weeks, Terri's story had continued to make news for 10 years. She didn't even have a publicist – in fact, she didn't need one. The big talk shows and the major magazines kept calling her. For the media, O'Connell had become a festering question that wouldn't go away -- that nobody had an easy answer for.

The media often mentioned her book -- she had been writing it off and on for a number of years.

After my article was done, Terri and I stayed in touch and I finally asked if I could read the book.

From her Mississippi office with its shelves crammed with racing trophies, she emailed me the still-incomplete Word files. As I sat in my Los Angeles office and read them, my hair was standing on end, and I knew I was looking at one of those Great American Stories. And yes, I am a pushover for a good sports story too. The raw power of *Dangerous Curves* was unmistakable, even in the book's unfinished and unedited state.

I offered to give Terri some professional Digest-style help with organizing and polishing. But the material and the writing, not to mention the perspective and the expressiveness, is 100 percent the creation of Terri O'Connell. Indeed, I was careful to respect the conversational Southern flavor of Terri's writing style, and its rich sprinkle of racing slang. The book wouldn't be "actual" if it were written any other way.

Terri told me, "A whole lot of people have had their say about me. Now I get to have my say."

Patricia Nell Warren is author of several bestselling novels, including the 1974 New York Times bestseller *The Front Runner*. A veteran of publishing with big mainstream houses like William Morrow and Ballantine, she went independent in 1993 and started her own publishing company, Wildcat Press, with business partner Tyler St. Mark. Her editing career at the Reader's Digest ended in 1981, when she left to pursue full-time writing and research her Western history novel *One Is the Sun.*

Warren also writes provocative nonfiction, including political commentary and sports analysis – her most recent title, *The Lavender Locker Room,* was an Amazon topseller and won an Independent Publishing Gold Medal in 2006.

Her web pages are at www.wildcatpress.com and www.patricianellwarren.com.

DANGEROUS CURVES
CONTENTS

1) Getting Here Early – Barely ...
Close Calls & Southern Snapshots.............25

2) Hanging With the Boys –
Watching my step ... Getting
My Race Face On......................................59

3) National Champ – The Pivot
Point (Facing Gender) 85

4) What was I Thinking –
Wrecking in the Astro Dome 117

5) March 1982 – The Chase 141

6) Now What ... Living as a Girl
– First Time 157

7) Life is Hard – Racing is Easy 189

8) The Sprint Car Experience
– Fighting With Rattlesnakes..................205

9) Meet Blackie Fortune –
Go Racing...223

10) Mom and Christine . . . Pit Crew
and Marriage 251

11) Next Stop ... California – Re Start
(More Drama)..275

12) Back Home – A Place of My Own
– Praying for Answers 303

13) Edge of Despair – Pivot Point #2.............331

14) Going Home – NASCAR? 365

15) Dad Comes Through – Let's Race 383

16) Big Wreck – Goodby JT –
Hello Terri . . . Pivot point #3 401

17) NASCAR or Terri – Drama
in a Small Town 427

18) Feminine Snap Shots –
Get on With It 461

19) Get to Charlotte – Birth of a
Businesswoman – Hello Congress.............481

20) Word Gets Around – I Need a
Partner – Playing With the
Big Boys 513

21) Life Goes on – But for How Long
– Lost Innocence...545

22) Who Can be Trusted – Chance
Meeting - Country Crooners 571

23) Breaking the Story – Pivot Point #4..........593

24) The Next Dangerous Curves –
The Media – Home Again..........................631

CHAPTER 1

Getting here early – Barely

Close calls and Southern Snapshots

After sixteen blood transfusions, constant bed rest and two near-death experiences, my mom brought me into this world kicking and screaming, at four in the morning, July twenty ninth, half a generation past the baby boomer revolution. It was a hot sultry dawn in Corinth, Mississippi. I got to Earth on a wing and a prayer, two months early – blue, gasping for air and barely weighing three pounds. Doctor Sweat and the hospital team worked like hell to get me breathing normally.

The first few days were touch and go, but two months later my mom was holding me nervously tight as she sat in the grandstands watching my dad risking his life as he raced his midget racer down in Birmingham, Alabama. I surely could feel her anxiety for my dad's life, the danger was always looming. From the very beginning I had danger, motor oil and the sounds of high-horsepowered engines running in my veins. My destiny was set -- I was born to race.

Jim and Nellie Kate Hayes had waited for ten long years to have a baby, and now they thought they had a bouncing baby boy to carry on the Hayes racing legacy. They named me James Terryl Hayes, after my dad and my mom's dad who had passed away when my mom was ten. The Hayes clan had family and friends scattered all across the South, and they gave me the secret handshake the minute I came into this world, the one that only the bravest and most talented race drivers get and give. There was a destiny to fulfill, but first I had to survive premature birth and all its after-effects.

My dad was the coolest cat in town -- a World War Two vet, a bonafide kamikaze race-car driver and a mechanical genius. He was born in Pocahontas, Tennessee, a little blip on the train tracks not unlike Whistle-stop in the movie *Fried Green Tomatoes*. He was the youngest of seven, two older brothers, Herman and Garner and four older sisters, Catharine, Eva, Dee and Vera. His mom and dad, John and Lilly, were hard core rural Tennessee folk who just barely scraped by but always provided their family with love and enough to eat. They had all lived in a three room shack with a dirt floor and plenty of chickens around laying eggs to feed the family.

When the Hayes clan moved to Corinth in the late 1930s, papa Hayes got a job working at the local sawmill and finally could afford a big modern house. Of course, my dad always had his own personal cachet, both with things that went fast, and with the girls. He was James Dean before James Dean made his mark out in Hollywood, a handsome and charismatic daredevil with a genius for everything mechanical. Everyone who ever crossed the path of Jim Hayes, both men and women, fell in love with him. But it was my mom who had snagged him away from the hundred girls chasing him, and got him off his tricked-out Harley Davidson.

Mom and dad looking very much in love around 1954

Mom, at 5'2" and barely a hundred pounds, was drop-dead gorgeous and a bit of a fireball. I guess that fireball thing was what got to my dad. Next thing he knew, he and Kate had eloped and got married all to the horrors of my mom's mother Sarah Jane. Voila, the first Brad Pitt and Angelina Jolie high-profile relationship of Corinth was born. Nellie Kate's dad had died when she was only ten, and she and my Granny had managed to somehow keep going on their own through World War II. Granny worked several jobs, Mom helped out around the house and they were always worshiping at West Corinth Baptist Church only fifty yards from their back door. A church, by the way, that my mom's dad and his dad had helped build back in the 1920s.

This is my granny, Sarah Jane Tankersley around 1954

Not long after my mom and dad got married, Granny re-married again -- a kind, gentle and handsome man, Parker Tankersley, a well-known carpenter who had had his eye on this beautiful widow for some time. Parker and his three brothers had worked for the big nuclear plant project in Blue Ridge, Tennessee during the war, and all were highly respected throughout the community. Mom and Dad made a beautiful couple, and everyone loved them. They soon steered into an idyllic life in Corinth, and all seemed to be perfect with the world. Dad worked at Berry Hydraulics, which built hydraulic pumps for all types of industrial purposes, plus he had a small engine-repair business he ran out of the race shop behind the house. Mom worked at the nearby ITT factory which manu-factured telephones. On the weekends, they took off to the dirt track stock-car races either down in Birmingham, Alabama or up in Nashville Tennessee.

But all was not perfect at the Hayes household. My granny had been against the marriage at first because she thought my dad was a roughhouse biker who was corrupting her precious little daughter. Problem was, my mom was just as wild and crazy as my dad was in the early years. In the beginning, the battles between my granny and my dad were legendary around town.

That's dad and his stock car down in Columbus, Mississippi in 1952 looking sharp as a tack.

Then, in the third year of their marriage, Dad almost lost his life in a stock-car crash down in Tupelo Mississippi. He was thrown from his racer, then run over by another competitor and dragged down the track for over a hundred yards before the officials could rescue him. Dad broke almost every bone in his body, the major injuries being a a broken pelvis, a broken leg and several internal injuries. He almost died several times in the first week in the hospital. At one point the doctors wanted to amputate his leg at the hip but my mom yelled at them, "You're gonna do that over my dead body."

Dad had to recuperate for almost a year.

That's when all his buds, especially Dexter Bumbas and Ben Singleton, got my dad interested in midget racers. Their reasoning was that if daredevil Jim Hayes didn't get out of those dangerous dirt-track stock cars, he was going to get himself killed. He would be better off racing the midgets. Not that midgets were safe as God's pocket...but at the time, in the mid 1950s, they were safer than stock cars.

Mom and Dad's house became the Mecca for local and regional racers to come and work on their race cars, and to just hang out for some hard-core alpha-male bench racing. During the winter, they socialized with their closest friends by playing cards at one another's houses, or heading off to the Cat Fish Hotel on the Tennessee River twenty miles up the road for sure-fire down-home fried catfish and a very good time.

Up in Nashville, Dad raced at the infamous Ewing Lane Speedway near where Opry Land is today. He became the track's most popular and winningest driver. All the fans would swarm out to meet Jimmy Hayes, who always stood out among the other drivers. He was a class act in a black polo shirt, black slacks, white socks and deck shoes. That along with his wayfarer sunglasses and his calm and gentlemanly personality, endeared him to fans and racers alike.

In fact Ewing Lane Speedway was where many of the day's top country-music entertainers hung out. A few even competed on the track with my dad. Hawkshaw Hawkings and his wife Gene Simmons, and even Patsy Cline and her husband Charlie Dick, often showed up to kick back and let their hair down from time to time, watching my dad and the other drivers kick up some major dust in their little high-tech lightning-fast midget racers.

But the most famous of the country stars who raced with my dad was Marty Robbins, and he and my dad had become pretty good friends. Marty looked up to my dad as somewhat of a hero, and actually tried to buy Dad's purple-and-white car that had won for him for three or four years. Legend has it that Marty drove my dad crazy trying to buy that exotic-looking little racer and even made a special trip down to Corinth to persuade my dad to sell. But Dad wouldn't part with it. So Marty bought a car from someone else and painted it purple just to get at Dad a bit.

During one of Marty's Grand Ole Opry appearances, which most of the Ewing Lane Speedway clan always attended, Marty made my dad stand up in the audience and introduced him as the best race-driver he had ever seen. While my dad stood there red-faced and embarrassed at first, the crowd gave him a standing ovation. But finally, Mom said later, Dad relaxed and ate up the applause.

So over the first few years of my life, that was the routine. Socializing with our friends, hanging out down in the race shop with Dad and the guys, going to races up in Nashville, and then driving back late at night with me sleeping across the laps of my dad and his buds in the front seat while the womenfolk slept in the back seat. I knew myself to be unconditionally loved, the holder of the Hayes legacy. We all attended church as much as possible to make sure that Jesus approved of and protected our lives.

Even more important than racing and church, however, everyone was working overtime trying to keep me alive.

My dad's friends had their opinion about my premature birth. They liked to say, "Little Hayes had to get here and get busy…he's going to win the Indy 500 someday and he needed a head start on the competition."

Bacon and Homemade Biscuits

My early life did have its idyllic moments. By the time I turned two, my mom had gone back to work at the telephone factory there in town. She had to be at work by seven a.m. So at 6:15 she would bundle me up in my favorite blanket, take me over to Granny's and put me in Granny's and Granddad's warm bed, then head off to work.

By that time in the morning, my grandparents were already up cooking a full-fledged country breakfast. Half awake I would lay in bed waiting anxiously to feast on the tastiest array of country cooking this side of the Mason-Dixon line. The magic smell of home-grown country sausage, homemade biscuits and sawmill gravy blended with fried eggs and Granny's homemade pear preserves was almost more than one person could handle.

At the table I would sit right by my granddad, watching every move he made peppering his fried eggs and pouring saw-mill gravy over those biscuits that melted in your mouth, while Granny prepared my plate exactly like Granddads. As we ate, we listened to the radio -- ole Buddy Bain, a local and iconic morning DJ giving the local farm reports and playing some sure-fire down-home country music over station WCMA.

My granny cooked breakfast like this every single morning. She and Granddad were Southern, had grown up in the rural country and this was their heritage. Now it had become mine. It was warm, family focused and heartfelt, and full of love.

After breakfast, Granny would clean the table and wash the dishes, while Granddad would put on his carpenters overalls and head off to work. I would run back to their bedroom to watch "Captain Kangaroo" and "I Love Lucy" reruns.

Later in the day, at least four days a week, we ate supper up at Granny's, and it was always another feast. Just like her morning breakfast ritual, she made supper a Southern extravaganza filled with fresh vegetables she had grown in the prize garden behind our houses.

Every spring, she and Granddad plowed and tilled that 100 by 100 foot garden and planted it with corn, green beans and black-eyed peas and butterbeans along with squash, cucumbers and the biggest tomatoes you would ever see. She nurtured that garden like it was a newborn child and throughout the summer we feasted on every bounty that fertile piece of Corinth soil could provide. Granny and Mom canned green beans, peas and pickled cucumbers for all of us to eat upon through the winter. It was all organic, the flavors were rich, mouth watering and delicious. Those organic meals clearly made all of us healthier.

That garden defined my Granny -- it was her prize possession. She got up early in the summer mornings, grabbed her hoe, and removed the weeds trying to choke her baby veggies. However, she could be obsessive about it all, and would drive us crazy especially my granddad, with wanting us to help her keep it in fine order. If you did not get out there and help her hoe and pick just when she wanted you to, she could get pissy about it. She would jump your tail saying, "If you want to eat those green beans, you're going to have to help me pick them."

Of course, we would jump to help her with a pout on our faces. But since we loved the bounty that garden produced, the pout didn't last too long and soon turned to smiles.

But those early idylls faded. The wheels of my life were starting to turn in a different direction than my mom and dad had hoped.

Trying to survive

At five years old, I was fragile and small for my size. My appearance was so androgynous that most people couldn't tell if I was a boy or a girl. Often I was convulsed with chronic asthma. My parents were constantly fighting off my chest and ear infections, and my nose bled a river at least twice a week. They took me to every allergy doctor between Memphis and Birmingham. I was stuck with a thousand unmerciful needles as I screamed in horror for my mom and dad to please make the doctors and nurses stop hurting me. By age five, I felt old already... worn out from the drama of just trying to catch a good breath of air into my fragile lungs.

And something else was getting my parents worried. I was showing a growing affinity for girl clothes... slipping into my mom's and my granny's chest of drawers, especially their lingerie drawer and dressing up in their clothes. By age five, I loved the feel of silk and lace women's undergarments on my body.

On top of that, I was identifying more with the women-folk in my family than the men, even though my role models were my dad and his buds at the race shop -- the kings of the Corinth alpha-male kingdom. There wasn't a sissy among them. In fact, my dad, who carried himself with the aura of a real-life Clint Eastwood, had the only boy kid in the bunch. All his best buds, Dexter Bumbas, Hobert Patterson, Ben Singlton and John Jourdan, all had girl children.

To top it off, Dexter Bumbas had given my mom his blood several times during her dangerous pregnancy. So I had Dexter's blood running through my veins and he considered me his godson. He loved me almost as much as my mom and dad did, and was damn sure that I was going to carry on the Jim Hayes legacy. In fact he and the guys were already telling me that I was going to be the next AJ Foyt and win the Indy 500 when I grew up.

Even though I was eating up all the attention they were giving me up, deep down inside my heart, I longed to dress up with all of their daughters.

Whenever they caught me dressing up in my granny's clothes, my granddad Parker teased me about it, and my mom scolded and humiliated me. My dad never put in his two cents' worth, but I'm sure he shared my mom's concern. The message was abundantly clear -- acting like and dressing up like a girl was a bad thing to do. I did not know why because it seemed so honest and natural to me. So I started hiding my desires to have femininity in my life.

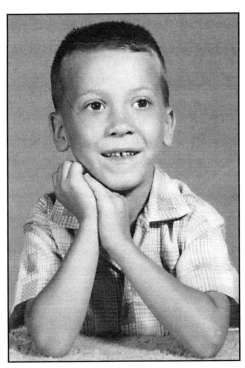

Me at four, the tone is already set.

A dryer climate

That summer was one of the hottest summers in recent history. The heat and 90% humidity was just about to kill me. Topping it off, the asthma medicine I was taking made me sick to my stomach constantly. I was allergic to everything, even cold water broke me out into huge whelps and no one could figure that one out. I was miserable, always in constant pain and my parents were freaking out, but it didn't stop us from going to races in Nashville every weekend. That year, Dad had decided to run for the track championship there at Ewing Lane Speedway and by the end of October, he had wrapped the championship up.

But I was sicker than ever. On the last trip to Nashville, at two in the morning Mom and Dad had to rush me to the emergency room where I desperately gasped for breath before the attack finally eased off.

It scared the hell out of me when I overheard Mom say, "Jim, Dr. Sweat says we might have to move to a dryer climate . . . probably to Arizona. He might die if we don't get him out of this climate."

As we drove back down Route 100 at four in the morning to our home, the sense of urgency and concern was thick and somber.

Three weeks later, on a cold gloomy day in late November, Mom dropped me off up at Granny's early that morning, as usual, and headed off to the telephone factory. Dad was at work as well, and Granny and I were hanging out watching "I Love Lucy" reruns on TV when little by little I became violently ill. My fever jumped up to 102, and my side was so sore that I could not stand for anyone to touch me. Granny called my mom, and my mom called Dr. Sweat, who said to get me to the emergency room right away.

When Dr. Sweat examined me, he said, "His appendix is rupturing, we have to get him up to surgery right now." The doctor turned to my dad and my mom and said, "You need to call your minister. We're going to need prayers to help him pull through this."

When my dad heard that, he went white as a sheet -- I was his pride and joy, the holder of the legacy. Like his own stock-car crash, this was another prophetic reminder that we are all human, and vulnerable.

Our minister, the Reverend Warford, got there in just minutes, and prayers filled the waiting room near the OR. My mom and dad, most of their friends and my grandparents franticly sat there worried out of their minds. Brother Warford earnestly prayed with all of them, while my mom cried her eyes out and my dad paced the room and chain smoking cigarettes in fear that he just might lose his only child.

"Dear heavenly father, watch over this child as these doctors fight to save Terry's life…"

Thirty minutes later all seemed to be going well – Dr. Sweat had removed the appendix and was busy trying to clean the infection when in the blink of an eye, right out of no where, all hell broke loose. Suddenly I began to flatline, my frail little body convulsed – I was having an asthma attack right there on the operating table with a big gaping hole in my side and infection still oozing. Dr. Sweat and his team worked frantically to stop the attack but then, adding to the drama, my heart stopped beating and I was turning blue.

Dr. Sweat was frantic. He had brought me into the world and fought to keep me healthy over the past five years. Now he had to pull some magic out of his hat, he needed a miracle.

"I can't go back out there to the waiting room and tell that momma her baby is dead," he shouted at his OR team. "We have to save this child's life!"

Dr. Sweat and his team pulled every trick in the medical book out of their hats and finally, after a few frantic and emotional minutes, my heart was beating normally again.

When I came out of the anesthesia, one of the first things I saw was my dad bending over me, looking emotionally devastated but happy.

"You get well now," he said, "and I'm going to get you a go-kart. We're going to go racing."

Over the next few weeks, as I recuperated there in the hospital, all of my dad's friends spoiled me rotten, as if I wasn't already rotten to the core. Every day they brought me presents, mostly toy cars and army stuff, trying to cheer me up and calm my parents' frazzled nerves. Everyone knew it was a miracle that I was alive. Just about once a week, my dad repeated the promise about the go-kart, which he said we'd buy at Sears in Memphis.

I couldn't resist bragging to Mom. "Daddy is going to buy me a go-kart at Sears where uncle T.K. works," I told her.

Mom frowned. "No, he isn't. You're just making that up. And you're too little to go racing."

I paid no attention to Mom, and bragged about it to my Cousin Theresa who was ten years older, my Aunt Vera's daughter. Cousin Theresa told me that my daddy was pulling my leg, that he wasn't going to buy me no go-kart. A couple of times she had me in tears, but I had always kept the faith that my dad was good for his word.

My parents still had to decide whether we had to pack our bags and move to Arizona, where the air was warmer and drier, and my life depended on it! The clock was ticking.

Dr. Sweat, shaken up by how close he'd come to losing me, had got busy researching every doctor in the country who specialized in asthma and upper respiratory illness in children. He knew full well that my parents did not want to move away from Corinth, away from their families and their close circle of friends and racing.

Finally, with relentless pursuit and a bit of luck, he found an asthma specialist right there in Mississippi, in Biloxi. Dr. Gray, a middle-aged upper-respiratory doctor, had come up with a new medicine that had helped over a hundred kids throughout the South East. Dr. Sweat called him, gave him the get-go on my situation and booked us an appointment for that next week.

Finding Dr. Gray was a godsend. Even though he didn't cure my asthma completely, he helped to get it under control. We did not have to move to Arizona, and my parents were very relieved.

*Me and mom wading in the Gulf of Mexico
while on a doctors visit in Biloxi*

Macho Christmas mornings

As my health improved, my dad's buds kept plying me with toy cars and toy trucks. They aimed to keep me going in the right direction – away from androgynous frailty and towards being a lusty little southern boy like others in the town.

That Christmas after the appendix emergency, I'd been pestering for a slot-car set and my parents decided I was finally old enough to get one. They had ordered it from the Sears and Roebuck catalog.

On Christmas Eve, after I went to bed, my dad and his buds stayed up till two in the morning putting that darn slot-car set together. Mon made coffee, and after they all ate Christmas cookies and cake, they argued over who would get to play with racing those two slot cars around the little track.

"You're acting like a bunch of five year olds," my mom growled at them. Finally she made Dad's buds go home to put their own kids' toys under the tree.

On Christmas morning at around 7:30, Mom and Dad woke me and told me that Santa had come -- I should go see what he had brought. Wildly jumping out of bed in my P J's with race cars printed on them, I rushed into the living room. There it was -- that racing toy I'd been wanting, with cool-looking little sports cars made for speed. One was bright red with the number 1 on its hood, and the other one was British racing green with the number 5, which was my dad's racing number as well.

With my heart about to jump out of my chest, I grabbed the triggers that operated the cars and started racing them. Santa had been very good to me!

Just a few minutes later, there was a knock on our back door and in burst ole Dexter and Hobert, along with Larry Killough. They could hardly wait to see me racing my slot cars! They were all smiles as they gathered around to watch me compete in a death match. Then they got so carried away that they grabbed the triggers and started racing each other -- you would have thought it was the INDY 500.

Finding myself pushed aside, I went to the kitchen and tugged on my mom's robe with my bottom lip stuck out and tears rolling down my cheeks.

"Mom, they won't let me play with my race car set."

That's when my mom's wrath fell from heaven on the 30-year-old babies reliving their childhoods. She went in the living room and roared, "All right, yawl are hogging his toys. Don't you have kids at home too? Go home and let Terry play."

For a moment, the living room was dead silent. All the men sat there staring at my mom, afraid she was going to kill them. Then they all burst into laughter. Larry grabbed me and put me back down by the slot-car set. Dexter and Hobert gave my mom a hug and headed out the door laughing their tails off with Christmas spirit and joy. More than reliving a bit of childhood, they had just done some quality male bonding around me.

All was peace on Earth, good will towards men... except for one thing. I hadn't gotten that Barbie Doll that I wanted as much as the slot-car set.

The need for feminine things had solidified. Not only did I want girl toys but I also snuck peeks at my mom's Christmas Sears Catalog with all the beautiful girls' clothes between the pages. Even at this early age I felt like I was in the CIA maneuvering a covert operation against the Russians.

When I turned six and entered first grade at West Corinth Elementary just two blocks from home I was mesmerized by how cute the girls were in their clothes. I loved their wonderful little dresses and shoes, and craved to let my hair grow so I could wear a bow in it.

But nothing I saw at school could compare to the apricot angora sweater worn by Rene McQuery. She was an olive-skinned beauty, tall and slender, with the face of an angel. When she wore that sweater, which was every two weeks, mostly on Fridays, I turned to mush when I saw it. At night, after my regular prayers, I'd make a separate prayer that God would turn me to a girl for Christmas, and give an apricot angora sweater

just like Rene's. For the next two years, I stealthed through
each new Sears catalog in hopes of finding that sweater or one
like it. But I never did.

Years later, when she married my best friend's brother, I
would wonder if Rene remembered that sweater and if she had
the same reverence as I did for that masterpiece.

That Go-Kart at Sears

By the summer I was six, I was hyper as a cat on a hot tin
roof from Dr. Gray's asthma medicine. But whatever the ingre-
dients were, it was working, and my health was getting better
by the month.

One weekend around the first of June, Mom, Dad and I
were over in Memphis visiting my dad's sister Vera and her
husband T.K. Dad and I headed to the Sears store on Popo-
lar Avenue where uncle T.K. worked as a department manager.
Going to Sears was a magical experience -- the store was alive
with action and customers, and they had everything under the
sun in there, including go-karts.

Dad had kept telling me he'd get me a go-kart ever since
that fateful November day when my appendix burst. The great
day had finally come. Dad and I were on a mission to buy a
go-kart. Everyone was going to have to eat their words; I was
going to rub it in their faces.

That afternoon, while Dad and uncle T.K. made the deal, I
picked out the one I wanted. It was a cool-ass white one with a
3-horsepower Brigs and Stratton four-cycle engine, and it was
clearly built for speed -- a sure-fire Indy 500 winner. To be
honest, Dad and uncle T.K had schmoozed me in the direction
of that one with their wit and charm. But at least they let me

think I had made the monumental decision to buy the right one.

I was a cocky little shit and couldn't wait to get over my aunt Vera's to drive that puppy. My dad was grinning from ear to ear -- beaming with pride for his son, proud that I was happy about the kart and getting stronger -- though I wasn't out of the woods just yet.

When we got back to aunt Vera's, I was all over everybody. "Guess what, daddy bought me a go-kart . . . I told you he was going to get me a go –kart! I told you, I told you!"

Over the next few months, I wore that go-kart out, going around and around our house and my grandparent's house next door. My dad's buds were always egging me on to make it go faster and faster. Especially the two Larry's. Larry Roberts and Larry Killough were the young bucks of the race- shop clan, both in their early twenties. But the fact was, my dad had the kart governed down because he had realized I had a kamikaze streak. I might be a little shy of other physical activities like baseball and football, but put a helmet on my head and a steering wheel in my hands and I got my crazy bone cranked up.

One Saturday afternoon at the end of September, Dad and the guys were down in the race shop working on their cars, getting them ready for a Sunday race up in Nashville the next day. I was on my kart making kamikaze runs around and around my grandparent's house. You could get a high speed run going when you came around Granny's back porch and took a right hand turn between the two houses. The two Larry's were standing out side the race shop with shop towels in their hands and every time I came around the back porch they would get those shop towels a-flying egging me on to go faster and faster.

Lap after lap I got braver and braver as I rounded the turn and had begun to get that little ole kart up on two wheels at each turn. I was on my game, I was winning the Indy 500 and all the glory would be mine, I would not be denied.

Then just when I thought I'd turned the fastest lap to date, I lost control and flipped upside down with the kart landing on top of me. As the engine screamed out of control, everybody in the race shop came hightailing it to the crash scene to see if I was dead or alive. Inside her house, my mom knew by the sound of my super-duper engine that I was in trouble and she was racing to the rescue as well.

When everyone turned the little Brigs and Stratton engine off and got me out from under that kamikaze machine, they realized that I barely had a scratch on me.

I looked up at my dad out of my cool-ass race helmet, through my aviator goggles, and said, "Daddy, that was fun, I want to do it again."

All the men burst out laughing. But my mom put her foot down. She said, "No sir young man, you have overdone it and it's time to go in the house and calm down." All while she was picking the grass and dirt out of my clothes from the crash.

Then she lit into my dad and the two Larry's.

"It's all your faults, you're always egging him on," she yelled. "No wonder he is so darn rotten. When yawl get him killed, you're going to be sorry, I ought to smack all of you for making him the way he is."

Of course all the guys took a stiff upper lip. But legend has it that, after Mom marched me into the house with me pouting, they went back down to the race shop and laughed their asses off. They were all very proud of me. I was living up to the Jim Hayes legacy with miles to spare. I was a Darc Devil.

That's me, dad and Larry Killough and the infamous first Go Kart. Like most racers, I'm already a primadonna.

Racing was cool

Over the next few years our family kept to our routine. We raced, we went to church, we socialized with friends, and my parents worked their tails off to make us an upper middle class living and keep me healthy.

But even though our lives seemed idyllic and rooted in a strict small-town moral culture, they were anything but boring.

By now, every night after the races were over, Dad took me on his lap in his midget race car and we would do ten or twelve hot laps. He would really stand on the gas, broadsliding that little racer while I held on for dear life. I lived for it! Every chance I got, I was sitting in his racer at the track or down in the race shop, with my helmet and goggles on, dreaming about the day I would actually get to race a grown-up car like that puppy.

By the time I was seven, Dad was letting me take a few hot laps by myself, with the help of an overstuffed pillow so I could see over the steering wheel. My dad's buds loved it, but my mom was horrified.

Me at seven years old.

"Jim, please don't let him do that. You're going to get him killed. He is too little to be doing this."

Of course, deep in her heart Mom was beaming with pride that I was walking in my dad's footsteps, especially since my girl issue was still rearing its head almost on a weekly basis.

By the age of ten, my life had taken on three different and distinctive angles. One -- I wanted to become the greatest racing driver of all time. Two -- I still suffered sometimes from asthma attacks and upper respiratory ailments -- they drove me crazy because it limited my physical activity with all the kids in the neighborhood. Three -- my desire to have girlness in my life was all-consuming. I came to the conclusion that somehow God had gotten things all mixed up with me.

Most importantly and most tragically, I was afraid to talk about it to my parents. If I actually told them that I thought I wanted to be a girl, my mom would either shoot me dead or die from a heart attack.

Dad was a different story. We clearly had that father-son bond going, but he always kept a level head concerning this girl stuff. Somehow he just thought I would grow out of it, especially if he kept me busy with racing and the guys in the race shop. A steady dose of alpha male bonding would surely transform me magically into a macho puppy to beat all macho puppies.

To make things worse, I had not grown much. By age ten, I barely weighed fifty pounds and I could pass as a boy or a girl at any given moment. Because of that, some of the older boys in the neighborhood and at school had started picking on me unmercifully. As they taunted me with "sissy Terry this" and "sissy Terry that," the anger and hurt just burned me up inside. Hell, I couldn't help what I looked like.

And by now, my mom had had as much of the bullying as I had.

So when I turned eleven, she got me involved with the local YMCA program there in Corinth. It was the smartest thing she had ever done to help me get along socially. The teasing didn't stop, but the Y experience opened me up to new friends from the right side of the tracks. I got active in all the sports.

By the time I was twelve, Coach Wroten, the Y's executive director, had given me a summer job there. I helped out at the baseball games, running the concession stand and helping out at day camp.

The irony about the teasing was, I was a good athlete and my front yard was the hangout for most of the kids in the neighborhood. Every day after school, everyone congregated to play football, chase or even army. We had some kick-ass touch football games while my mom threatened all of our lives if we broke her picture window in front of the house. We came close more times than we could count -- everytime a football or a baseball would hit the window or just get close, we all ran for the hills knowing that my mom was going to skin us alive. The sad part was -- I was roughhousing with all those boys just trying to fit in. But I had a lot to prove, and many days I just got the shit kicked out of me.

At night, I sometimes cried myself to sleep, praying that when I awoke the next morning I would be a girl and this nightmare would be over.

Let's go racing . . .

While the YMCA experience was cool, the most important thing in my life was that I finally started racing. My dad had bought me a real racing go-kart, and I was out there kicking butt on all the little kart tracks scattered through the Mid South. I had won my first Junior Kart race right there in Corinth at a track that Dad and his buds had built just outside the city limits.

The second time I raced, I had a big crash when another karter crashed into me and we flipped upside down several times. I flew off the track at about 60 miles per hour and slammed into a parked Mustang sitting there. It knocked me clean out. This was not baseball at the Y, this was damn dangerous stuff and my mom was not sure that she wanted her baby doing it.

However, I was soon winning kart races on a regular basis. My destiny was chiseled in the mud and grease of motorsports, I was living up to my dad's legacy with every brave move and win.

Soon we were making regular trips down to Saltillo, Mississippi, about five miles north of Tupelo, to race on a lighting-fast asphalt track. On Labor Day weekend we made a regular pilgrimage down to Columbus, Mississippi to race in the JC's annual 100-mile Kart race. The first two years I finished third and by the time I was fourteen, I had figured out the tricks of the trade for asphalt Kart road racing and wanted to take it to a higher level. That meant heading out to Memphis or down to Jackson, Mississippi to compete in International Kart Federation events -- racing with the best karters in America.

That's me sitting in my Kart and dad right behind me in his classic black thirty seconds before my first big Kart race in Columbus, Mississippi

There I am getting my second place trophy
after the Columbus race, this was a very big deal

During this period, the early and mid 1970s, is when I met Lake Speed. He was probably the most successful Karter in America at the time and he was from Mississippi too. I had also gotten hooked up with that crazy bunch of Kart racers from up in the Chattanooga and Nashville area. Lynn Haddock, the ringleader of the bunch, was just as successful as Lake and he had an entire clan of Tennessee boys helping him out. Tommy Crosby and Russ Thompson were closer to my age and from the early '70s to end of the decade we became good buds. We were all winners in our own right, and we looked after on another when we were out on the road. Our dads hung out together, we all dined together and we all bullshitted together while we continued to advance our careers.

There was one girl racer from Nashville that we were always infatuated by. Theresa Gammons was lightning fast and she kicked our asses as many times as we kicked hers. Sometimes though, I felt for her because some of the red-neck racers had a hard time accepting her talent. But I always did. Over the years, we became friends and I always pulled for her to kick every one else's butt but mine.

The Church Next Door

In the meantime, my life was getting more complicated by the day.

Under my boy clothes, I always wore women's underwear which I had managed to filch or buy when nobody was looking. I was not maturing physically into a boy at the same rate as other boys were. In fact by now, my body could have been that of a young girl's and I was frightened out of my mind that people were going to figure it out and expose me, especially the boys at the YMCA and – even worse -- the boys I was competing against on the karting circuit.

By my junior year in high school I was a nervous wreck, I could barely get out of bed at times and I dreaded with every beat of my heart having to go to school. Even though I had become popular at school, mostly because of my YMCA experience and because I was pretty damn cute, I still felt like an outsider.

The only real escape was racing. It gave me a macho cachet – and it prevented most of the teasing. That, and the fact that Dad bought me a Honda 50 motorcycle which I rode to school, kept me somewhat safe there. Still, I was depressed. For the first time, I started thinking about suicide.

What held me back – and paradoxically what added to my fear and depression as well -- was the little old church I had grown up in. They had taught me that suicide is a sin. Ever since I had been saved at the age of twelve I had tried to maintain the true Southern Baptist and Christian spirit of living up to Jesus' expectations and standards. The religious standards only made me feel worse about myself, and the day would come when I'd see them as bigotry.

But right now I was doing my level best to be the kind of Christian they talked about.

After all, I had been raised in the church, which was located right near our house. I did every Bible study class you could possibly do right there at West Corinth Baptist Church. I was saved there, I was there virtually every time the doors were open. I ate and socialized with all the preacher's kids.

The preacher of the moment was always down at our race shop hanging out, and I loved being a part of the entire church experience.

The people of West Corinth Baptist were my friends. The elders had halfway raised me and I respected each and every one of them. Some of my fondest memories as a kid were when I would be up at my grandparents house early on Sunday mornings having my breakfast back in their bedroom while my granddad -- who was a deacon and the Sunday School superintendent -- would be dressing for church while the Sunday morning Southern gospel music shows played on their television. I remember fondly the music and showmanship of the Happy Goodman Family, The Dixie Echoes and The Florida

Boys. All of those music groups infatuated me. They were part of a way of life for our family at the time. In short --God, Jesus and the true Christian spirit and lots of prayer lived in our households, and I embraced it as much as anyone.

So my life there in Corinth was surrounded by churches, good Christian people and lots of positive and moral direction.

At first my gender issue seemed to have no connection to religion. It was just about biology and Mother Nature had screwed up. At the most, God had let it happen to me.

But as I grew towards being a teen, I knew beyond any shadow of a doubt that if I uttered one word about my issue, the church would go nuts and most likely burn me at the stake. That was the ugly part about right-wing religion. For all the love and tolerance that they preached, there were limits on their tolerance. They were selective on social and biological issues.

Heck, this group barely had any respect for women, so they were not going to have any respect for me. On this issue they were nothing but a bunch of hypocrites and I knew it.

Southern Bigotry

My Dad stood out in this church crowd -- there was not a bigoted bone in my dad's body. He saw everyone equally. Thanks to his example, that same inclusive and compassionate feeling lived within my heart as well. Since the late 1960s I had been a part of the desegregation process throughout the South. From the first day I got to junior high school, I went to school with blacks and that was not a big deal to me on any level. The African American kids I studied with and sat in the cafeteria with were just my friends.

My dad had hired a black boy named Jimmy to help out at the tool and die shop in the afternoons after school. Jimmy and I were around the same age and I thought he was as cool as any one I knew. He and I worked our asses off deburring and cleaning up parts for my dad.

By the time I had begun to race, Jimmy was helping us load up and going to the races with us almost every weekend. He was a great help and my dad would reward him by letting him drive my kart or take a lap or two in his midget. My dad and a few other men around town were running their own track right outside of Corinth and we would usually meet out there on a Thursday or Friday night to prepare the track and the concession stands for the next night of racing. Most times Jimmy would be with us.

But not all of those hard-ass white boys at the track were socially aware and inclusive. For most of my life I had heard the talk that blacks weren't equal and shouldn't be assimilated into white society. Not from my parent's closest friends, but from others around our shop and the race tracks.

Then one Friday night after we got the track ready, racism finally reared its ugly head for me to see first hand.

My dad, Jimmy and I, along with five or six sure-fire country boys, were all standing around shooting the bull, just about to get into our vehicles and head back home. That's when one of the rednecks, Ole Harvey, slowly and purposely walked off over to his truck, opened the passenger door and got out his shotgun. I was watching him out of the corner of my eye because ole Harvey was always joking around but sometimes he went too far, so I didn't want to be the brunt of his sometimes belligerent humor.

Then, just like lightning, Harvey sprinted towards our group. He was yelling. "Nigger, you better run for your life, I'm gonna shoot your black ass dead and then string you up on court square."

Then he pointed the shotgun up in the air and pulled both triggers with a deafening boom. We all ran for cover, not knowing if ole Harvey was kidding or not. He was rumored to be in the KKK, but who really knew. Jimmy did not hesitate. I guarantee you he was running twenty miles per hour as he took off toward the back straightaway fence.

All the while Harvey was yelling after him. "When I reload this shotgun I'm coming after your black ass. You better run and not look back 'cause I'm coming after you."

Harvey reloaded and fired the gun once again, upward but in the direction of poor Jimmy as he dove over the wall. I could not believe what I was seeing.

Dad looked utterly disgusted and cussed ole Harvey out. That was the first time I ever heard my dad cuss.

"Go put that fucking gun up, Harvey," he barked. "I got my kid out here. What you do when you leave here is up to you, but this is not funny. You just scared the hell out of all of us, especially little ole Jimmy. You have just given him a heart attack. He is just a kid. I know you thought this was cute but it is not. Now go put that fucking gun up before you get all of us in trouble."

Harvey had a lot of respect from my dad, so he obeyed. It took us twenty minutes to get Jimmy to come back over that fence. My dad made Harvey apologize, but Jimmy was still reluctant to come back over to our truck so we could all go home.

That night, I lay in my bed thinking about it. I had lost all respect for Harvey, and felt sorry for my friend Jimmy. He didn't deserve to be treated that way, and he would probably remember that night for the rest of his life.

The experience sank deep with in me. I knew beyond any shadow of doubt if any of those good ole boy Mississippi types ever figured out that I thought I was a girl, that shotgun could be pointed at me, or worse. The thought was daunting.

CHAPTER 2

Hanging With the
Boys – Watching My Step

Getting My Race Face On

When I turned fifteen, my dad bought me a 1964 baby-blue Chevy Nova station wagon. It had about a hundred thousand miles on it and a perky little old straightline six cylinder engine with a three speed column shift. It was perfect for driving back and forth to school not to mention hauling my kart equipment all over the Mid South during summer racing. I had never gotten into any legal trouble while riding my motorcycle, so dad thought I was ready to handle the responsibility of a car.

My high-school buds and I were elated over my having some wheels to cruise around town, in especially on Friday nights out on the Shiloh Road Strip. Right out of *American Graffiti,* Shiloh Road was the Mecca for teenagers around Corinth and the surrounding communities. We kept that strip lit up every weekend, chasing the cute girls around and cranking up the radio to WLS out of Chicago to the hot sounds of the 70s.

My co-conspirators were Robert Martin, Kevin Brawnier, Jimmy Whitaker, Lance Floyd and crazy-ass Andy Ayers. We would all ante up three dollars a piece for gas and that would be enough to keep that Baby Blue Nova purring like a lion all night. We terrorized the local bowling alley, ate hamburgers at the Dixie Queen, and parked on Frailey's parking lot hurling water balloons and eggs at whomever we wanted to get at. We were not bad kids, but we pushed the limits every chance we got. In fact, we liked the reputations of being "a little dangerous." Especially me, because it deflected the bullying off to less popular kids and gave me some badly needed feelings of machismo.

Eventually we cut a deal with some of the older guys from high school to nab us a six pack of beer. That made us feel as if we were the Hell's Angels themselves. That's Hells Angels wearing preppy clothes. We never got drunk…hell we were afraid to because our parents would kick our tails if they caught us. But we did have a good time splitting those six beers between the four of us. Pot never entered our equation. The real bad asses in high school were lighting up, but my baby-blue posse had not crossed over into Pot Nation just yet.

That winter, we came up with a cool scheme. On Friday nights, I would tell my folks that I was spending the night with my bud Robert. Robert would tell his folks he was spending the night with me, and Kevin and Whit would pull the same plot on their parents. Then the four of us would stay out all night, cruising the streets and back roads, hitting a few slumber parties. The next morning we would head on home like little angels.

One Friday night, a few weeks after Valentines Day, Sheryl Williams, one of the hot chicks at Corinth High, was having a monster slumber party for all the other hot chicks at her grandmother's house a few miles out of town down highway 72. My hoodlum friends and I did our usual scheme on our parents and headed out to the slumber party. We each had a chick there that we wanted to hook up with. I was making sure that all my buds thought I was hot to trot for my main squeeze Cindy Spears, when in all reality, I was not that interested.

At first everything went according to plan. Then around eleven p.m. we discovered that we were starving to death and almost out of gas. Plus my left rear tire seemed to have a slow leak. So we decided to head for Charlie's Truck Stop about five miles up the road. We would grab a cheeseburger, fill up with gas and put some air in that tire and then head back to the party for the better part of the night. Who knew, we might even score some good make-out time.

So we jumped in the station wagon and hightailed back toward the city limits and the Truck stop. It started to rain, so I was darn careful to not speed, especially with that low tire. About a mile and a half down highway 72 with me, we saw a big 18-wheeler looming at us out of the rain. He was going about a hundred miles an hour and damn near on my side of the road.

Kevin, who was riding shotgun and helping me watch the road, yelled out, "Watch that bastard, he is trying to run us over."

I got as far over on my side of the road as I could. The 18-wheeler roared by without hitting us, but his wind draft caused my little station wagon to swerve. Then that low rear tire rolled off the rim and my baby blue Nova was suddenly all over the road as I fought to keep control. If another vehicle had been coming at us, we would have hit them head on.

My buds were screaming, "Hayes, hold onto this baby… you can do it…you're a race driver…"

Then, in a blink, that car took a hell-raising right and drove off the highway, down a 10-foot bank and into a little creek that was flooding with water. After we caught our breath, we realized we didn't have a scratch. Scrambling up the embankment, we were horrified to see that we had missed ramming head-on into a concrete bridge by only inches.

Then, out of the dark and rain, came another car full of buds—Dave Norman in his souped-up American Motors Hornet. Dave was a few years older and a bad-ass who was notorious for hot-rod antics. But at the time, we were glad to see him.

How were we going to get ourselves out of this mess? When our parents found out, we would be grounded for the rest of our lives.

"I've got this good friend, Ricky King," Davey said. "He has a wrecker, and he'd probably come and pull the car out...if we can find him at this time of night."

So we all piled into Dave's Hornet and took off to Ricky's house just a few miles down the highway. Davey was going 130 miles per hour in the middle of a Mississippi downpour, and my buds and I belatedly realized that we had made another mistake to ride with him. There was dead silence in the car except for the scream of that big ole engine and the sound of the tires hitting water pockets in the road which caused us to hydroplane almost out of control. I was praying my ass off that if God got me safely back home, that I would take any punishment my parent would dish out.

John Hora yelled out, "God damn it Dave, slow your ass down, you're going get all of us killed."

Dave got the message, and backed off the gas. Still, no one was saying a word, we all were about to mess in our pants.

Ricky King got out of bed and we all headed back to the creek. When we got there – surprise! There sat the highway patrol with his blue lights flashing investigating the scene. The trooper was Red Browning, one of my dad's good friends. He recognized me and scolded my ass for being out on the highway late at night in that rain storm. That's when I knew our little scheme was over. My dad was going to kill me. And my mom would kill me all over again when Dad was done.

Quickly I told Red what had happened to make my car skid, hoping he would go light on me. But he told us to meet him back there the next morning at eight o'clock and we could pull my car out of the creek. He said that the creek would not rise any more than it had. So Davey took us all home to our different houses.

The next morning, I had to tell my parents the whole sorry tale. My mom was mad as hell – not about the wreck but about my lying to her.

Dad stayed pretty calm and let Mom do all the drama stuff, but I could tell he was not a happy camper. He quickly called his best friend David McLemore up who owned a garage and wrecker service in town and told him to meet us out there with his wrecker.

I had told my dad about the low tire and how I saved us from wrecking. He believed me. So when we got out to the car, I was pretty sure he was not going to kill me, just ground me for a whole miserable year. But when the wrecker hauled the car out of the creek, that left rear tired looked to be in perfect condition, fully inflated. My dad and Red Browning were staring at it with a look of disgust on their faces. They were clearly doubting my story.

Then, as if the heavens had parted the red sea, water began spewing out of that tire. Within two minutes it was completely flat and I was breathing a whole lot better.

Dad quickly changed the tire, put five gallons of gas in, and we headed on back to our house with water sloshing in the bottom of the Nova. Dad never said a word, but I was heartsick that I had let him down, and knew the punishment was coming.

Back at the race shop, he calmly handed me a small coffee cup that held about six ounces.

He looked directly in my eyes and said, "You're grounded indefinitely. Now take this cup and scoop every drop of water out of your car. Don't use anything else. I'll be back after lunch and I want to see it all done."

He walked out to his truck and drove off. I got to work with that little ole coffee cup counting my blessings, knowing that if I did not do as he said, he probably would just kill me and bury me in the back yard. His face said it all.

That morning, as I scooped creek water out of the car, I pondered my deeds. For sure I shouldn't have lied to my parents about spending the night with my friends. But worse than that, my best friends and I could have been killed. We all had lost a few friends since we got to Junior high school. Just a year ago, Mike Roberson had been killed in a tragic car accident not two miles up from where we dove in the creek. We had been spared to see another day.

With my gender issue now bothering me more than ever, I pondered what my future might hold.

For almost two years now, I had thought about killing myself. Our accident made me open my head up to living. But would that life be happy and joyous, or hard and sorrowful?

Three weeks later, my mom and dad removed the grounding penalty and gave me back my car keys. My buds and I were right back on the Shiloh road strip raising hell. Only this time we stayed off highway 72 and we made it home to our parents' houses each and every Friday night.

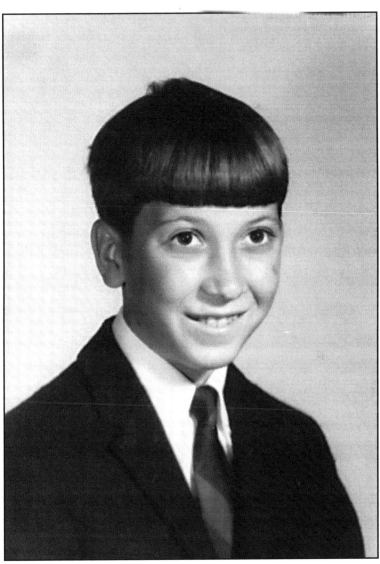

*Me at fifteen, I'm still a runt, but I'm brave
and hiding a big secret*

Taking racing to the next level

The only way to stay alive was racing. If I stayed 100% focused on that, I could keep my sanity—at least that was what I was hoping. As far as girls, I really didn't want to date but because of the peer pressure there at Corinth High, I did the girl stuff as best I could. However, I couldn't have been a very enthusiastic date or boyfriend. Girls must have felt let down.

For the summer I had been living with my Aunt Vera while I worked for the Haines brothers at their go-kart shop on Broad Avenue there in Memphis. The Haines brothers owned a successful electrical contracting company and were hard -core karting fanatics who had opened up a retail store to support their own racing needs and support karting there in the Mid South area. They were also heavily into professional off-shore power-boat racing and had actually won a few national championships with their Mr. Kilowatt race boats.

I had met those guys at the kart races out on Summer Avenue and their professionalism and class had always impressed me. I wanted to emulate them as much as I could. Dad had taken me over to their Kart Shop a few times and we had become good friends. Through that friendship and the fact that I was pretty darn fast in outdated equipment, they realized I had potential to do something on the national scene and wanted to help me out with my racing.

So when their current manager, Charles Toler, quit because of the brothers' internal politics, they gave me the job. Ironically, Charles was a bit of a hero of mine and I had learned a lot from him about building engines and karts. My dad had taught me well over the years but his background was in midgets and stock cars. These racing karts, especially outside the local dirt tracks where I had been winning everything in sight, were a different animal.

Over the last year, I had ventured to more of the International Kart Federation (IKF) events in Memphis and Jackson. Charles and Lake Speed were the fast guys and they inspired me to take karting to the next level. Especially Charles, whom I saw more than Lake simply because he lived only an hour from Corinth. Every time I got a chance, I would head over to Charles' house a few blocks from my aunts. Till the wee hours of the morning, he was always camped out in his race shop, tinkering with kart engines, trying to make those little two-stroke powder kegs faster and more durable. He drove a cool tricked-out hot-rod Ford van that he had painted metallic purple, with chrome wheels and shag-rug interior that he kept spotless. That was how Charles did things – and it rubbed off on me.

So taking Charles' job was bittersweet. The very afternoon he quit the company, I had seen his meltdown. He was so pissed off at A.B., the older Haines brother, that he had taken a two by four and beat the crap out of one of A.B.'s beautiful candy-apple-red Margay Karts. It was a fit of rage over something A.B. had asked him to do that evidently seemed really stupid and insulting. His intensity scared the hell out me.

Ten minutes later, Charles had loaded his tools into his tricked-out hot-rod van and was gone!

But I was young and eager and naïve about what I was getting into so I jumped into the job with both feet.

Being in Memphis at my aunt Vera's during the summer was a normal occurrence for me. I had almost grown up there on Weymouth street, right in the backyard of Kingsbury High

School and a ten-minute walk over to Gysman Park where I hung out with my Memphis pals Norman and Steve Brazer on most summer afternoons, playing pick-up games on the basketball courts and eating snow balls at the Rebel Dairy Queen up the street. So I loved Memphis and actually felt more like a Memphian than a Corinthian.

But this summer, instead of hanging out, I had more important fish to fry. The Haines brothers were helping my racing efforts. Normal teenager stuff was done and over with forever.

However, all was not well with my pursuing this opportunity. My dad felt as if I had turned my back on his plans for me, not only in racing but at his tool and die company. Plus he never really liked those Haines boys. He was always saying, "They think they're better than everyone else." I did know them better than he did – the middle brother David had a heart of gold. But I got where Dad was coming from: they were a bunch of country clubbers who had stepped in and taken me down a different path.

But to me, the Haines' opportunity there in Memphis, in a bigger and more urban setting, was sexy and hip. Whereas the tool and die business there in Corinth, a small rural community with me stuck in the shop welding and deburring parts, was pure torture. Like most teenagers, I was wanting to stretch my wings and fly out of Corinth. Even though Dad was my hero and I worshiped the ground he walked on, the pressure of trying to live up to the Jim Hayes legacy helping him run his new company, along with going through puberty and dealing with the gender situation, had us both cranky and temperamental.

Dad had also started drinking more, and could get mean at the drop of a hat… which always led to us mouthing off at one another. During a pro race a week before the Nationals there in Memphis that year, he and I had had a tense moment when he accidentally let some cigarette ashes fall into my engine after the first heat race. I had smarted off to him about it, with all the Haines brothers gathered around.

Dad just blew up at me. "You're nothing but an arrogant little prick!" he shouted.

Then he stormed off into the pits leaving us standing there in shock.

That was out of character for my otherwise cool dad. Sure, I had let my smart mouth go off over something that was not a big deal. However, if he hadn't been drinking, he would have never let the ashes fall into the engine.

However, the first time I realized he was beginning to drink heavily was a month or so before that. We were going to a kart race down in Tupelo and stopped to get soft drinks and snacks. Ever since we'd left home, he had been riding my ass over my not having a trick set of carburetors on my engine like some of the other guys had.

"You're going to get your skinny ass beat like a drum," he said.

Several times I told him not to worry, that I had modified the one big carburetor on the engine – it was better than having two and a lot easier to make work. But he kept on drilling me about it. "You're gonna get your ass beat…"

When we pulled away from the convenience store to get back on the highway, the red light by the store turned yellow. Instead of gunning the truck and making the light, I chose to wait for the green. We were in no hurry, and I didn't want to sling the tool boxes and parts around in the back of the truck.

My dad yelled out, "What are you waiting on? Gun it . . . get on through the light! You could have made the damn light!"

Well, I had had enough. But instead of yelling back at him, I just slammed the truck into park, walked around to the passenger side, and looked my dad square in the eye.

"If you can do it better," I said, "get your ass over there and drive."

Of course, he did, and we headed on to Tupelo. We never spoke a word to each other until halfway through the night of racing. I ended up winning the 75-lap race, even lapping the entire field. I never said one word to Dad about how he had been such an ass over the carburetor. I just put my trophy in the truck and we went home. Oh, he was proud of me for winning, but the damage was done, and it was all over alcohol.

When he got like that, I couldn't stand to be around him. But the day I told him I wanted to work for the Haines brothers and live in Memphis for the summer, I felt like I was breaking his heart. At one point we both teared up and I had to turn away to keep him from seeing me cry.

However, Dad knew he had to let me spread my wings. Hell, he and Mom would let me go off racing by myself all over the Mid South because they knew I could handle myself. In a lot of ways, I was mature for my age, considering the fact that I had been through so much, both physically and emotionally, as well as growing up in the highly charged, dangerous and challenging environment of auto racing. That was why the Haines brothers had hired me to look after their karting business at such a young age—they saw something in me that told them I could pull it off.

All I had heard since I could remember was that "you're going to be just like your daddy, your dad is the greatest." I needed to go where I was not being measured by my dad's successes.

By the last week of August, I was on overload with all the work but somehow I managed to qualify third and finish sixth with a faulty fuel system causing my engine to lean out in my first International Kart Federation Grand National Championships, which were held there in Memphis. In addition I had finished 10th in the first United States professional kart race the week before which was a big accomplishment. I was competing with the best in the United States, Prutt, Dinsmore, Haddock and a whol lot more of soon to be super stars in Indy Cars and NASCAR. But by the end of the summer, I was toast. Though I was already skinny, I had lost weight and had a summer cold that was kicking my ass. Because of my frail health and chronic asthma, I needed to give myself a break. But I ignored the warning signs.

The irony in my finishing sixth at the Nationals was, I was so damn tired and emotionally rundown that I failed to notice a malfunctioning carburetor part until the last heat race. Ignoring my condition was another way of avoiding the unavoidable—sooner or later, my gender issue would force me to deal with it.

Then…disaster. My Aunt Vera found some of my girl clothes under my bed at her house. She ratted me out to my parents.

Mom and Dad showed up at the kart races on Summer Avenue and told me I had to move back home and get into counseling. As usual my mom was pissed. As usual Dad was quiet and elusive about it all.

As I stood there listening to Mom ranting, my memory went back to the year before, when Dad and I had a long talk…our first. He and Mom had just found some of my girl clothes stashed behind the race shop.

That night, Dad and I had driven around Corinth in his tricked-out red-and-white '59 Chevy El Camino just trying to hash the craziness out. Only the glow from his cigarette and the dash gave any light in the cab. To my surprise, Dad was trying to be understanding and supportive, and offered to help me any way he could to get over my desire to dress up in girls' clothes.

I was frightened out of my mind at discussing my most daunting and embarrassing secret with my dad. Deep in my soul I felt that I couldn't let my dad down again, nor tell him about my suicidal thoughts. That would surely break his heart. Worst of all, he and Mom might decide to have me committed. Legally, they had the right to do it.

So I manned up and told him with a stone-cold poker face, "I'll try. I'll really try and not do the girl stuff."

It was a hopeful lie to get me out of a tough spot. In the end, we both just wanted the girl thing to go away.

That night, I cried myself to sleep after begging God to give me some sort of reason for my feminine desires and my feminine appearance. It just seemed as if this would live with me until the day I died. Which, if things did not change, would be much sooner than later. I really didn't want to kill myself, but the self doubt, the teasing and bullying, the secrecy I had built around my life, the loneliness and the fear of discovery, had me at a breaking point. Suicide would take all this doubt and stress away. But my religious convictions, that fact that I had been saved only two years before, always prevented me from going through with it.

On that frightening night a year ago, dealing with my mom was a different deal. She was a diva, temperamental, demanding and prissy, and could rip you up with her smart tongue. But she was also a doting mom who got her butt out of bed every morning at five AM and went to work in order to give me the things I needed and wanted. I loved her, she was my mom, my flesh and blood. But at times, she frightened the hell out me and I resented her for it.

But, now everything was different, one year later…a broken promise and and another pile of newly discovered girl clothes later.

So, that afternoon at the Summer Avenue track, I agreed to move back home, start helping my dad at his tool and die business again, and get into counseling. My parents said they would go with me. They were determined to get this girl thing under control.

Seeing the First Doctor

Seeing a psychologist scared my parents as much as it scared me. We were proud Southern Baptists who would rather die than talk about our troubles with a perfect stranger, let alone our neighbors who my mom and dad were praying to almighty God would never find out. Just the fact that my mom and dad had actually contacted a psychologist was cutting-edge stuff in Corinth, Mississippi. It took courage and tons of guts to make that phone call.

For the first time in my life I would have to be honest with my parents about my gender challenges... and would have to spill my guts out to a doctor about how I really felt deep in my heart. Ever since I was three years old I had been hiding behind a wall of secrecy that kept me safe from all that ridicule and humiliation that made me feel so dirty and unworthy.

And so, at 10 a.m. on Tuesday, three weeks after I finished sixth in the karting Nationals, I was sitting in the doctor's office.

"Hello, Terry, I'm Dr. Martin, I want you to feel at ease here . . . we all just want to help you figure all of this out."

Dr. Martin stood there looking at me. He was an Errol Flyn look-a-like – six foot, slender, with graying hair and a pencil-thin mustache. He smoked a pipe, and had a commanding but calming baritone voice much like my dad's. His office was located on the second floor in an office complex next door to Macy's in East Memphis...and right across the street from the Sears where I got my first go-kart. How ironic!

As I stared back at him mistrustfully, my insides were churning. But I had my poker face on and I looked cool as a ice cube.

Dr. Martin took my parents into his office and closed the door for their first little chat. I could hear the murmur of their voices as I sat alone out in the waiting room.

My mind was going 500 miles per hour wondering what they were telling him about me, but more than that if that was possible, I was more worried about what in the heck I was going to say when he ask me why I wanted to wear women's clothes. I had no idea how in God's name I was going to tell him that the clothes were just the tip of the iceberg—that this reproductive maleness I had to look at every day was some sort of mistake. He was going to think I was nuts, quite possibly have me committed to a mental hospital.

By now I had read about transsexuals in my best friend Robert's older brother's *Playboy* a year or so back, and I had seen a few of them on the "Tom Snider Show" back in the summer. The concept of a transsexual – being "trapped in a man's body"—didn't seem to apply to me. I thought my situation was deeper than that. My body was that of a young girl, and my psychology was also aligned with most of the girls I knew, even though I did think some girls were a bit silly…but some of the guys I knew were pretty silly too. So, I was searching for a word or a condition that fit me, but I damn sure was not going to mention the word "transsexual" to this doctor. Right wing southern religion was playing the biggest role in making all of us miserable.

After about 20 minutes of torture in the waiting room, mom and dad emerged from his office. They looked depressed, gloomy and a bit aloof.

Dr. Martin was standing in his office door and looked over at me with a very pleasant but manly smile.

"Come on back to my office," he said.

Without looking over to my parents, I made my way toward his office door. My hands and knees were almost shaking out of control, and I actually thought I was going to black out.

Dr. Martin quickly noticed that I was having a hard time.

"Can I get you a Coke or some orange juice?"

"No thanks," I said.

"Are you all right? Can I get you anything to calm your nerves?" he persisted.

"I'm okay," I said. "A Coke would be fine."

Suddenly I lost control and broke down weeping in front of him and for the next ten minutes that was all that I could do. Every time I thought I was going to be able to tell him I was all right, I would begin to cry again. Over the past two years, I had cried myself to sleep more times than I could count but never like this. The emotion that flowed from my eyes that day was ripping at my very core.

Dr. Martin just let me weep. He held my hand, rubbed my back and never told me to stop. He just let me cleanse my soul. Finally after what seemed like an eternity I slowly got my act back together and we began to talk about what was making me feel so hurt and scared.

At the time, I still was not willing to utter the words, "I'm a girl, I want to be a girl." But, we were making progress. While he calmly smoked his pipe, he was just roaming around inside my head with a lot of questions about my life.

"What do you like to eat?'

"Why do you obsess over you hair and clothes so much?"

"Your mom and dad say you're having a tough time in school, why is that?"

"Do the older boys pick on you?"

"It seems that you have stopped dating, is there any particular reason why?"

Then Dr. Martin hit me with something that my mom and dad must have said. He commented, "Your parents don't think you're aggressive enough when you race. They think you're holding back. They wonder if this gender issue has something to do with you not being as aggressive as the other boys."

I sat there dumbfounded. It was hard to believe my mom and dad saw me that way, considering what I had accomplished. My Irish was up.

"Heck," I blurted angrily, "I always thought I was a damn kamikaze pilot. Maybe I didn't wreck my competitors, but I won almost all of the time. Doc, I just finished sixth in the nation, and I just won the southeastern championships. How could I not be aggressive and do that? This girl stuff has nothing to do with my racing. I drive just like my dad."

Dr. Martin leaned back in his seat with a big grin.

"Well, Terry, maybe your mom and dad just misread the situation," he said. "I can see that the aggressive thing is something we are not going to worry about."

From that point on, I was more open and honest with him. He had unlocked my soul by getting me riled up. Pretty smart when you think about it.

Five minutes later, he had my mom and dad come back into his office and laid out his plan. I was to see him twice a month for a few months, and then he would see where we ended up. He assured my mom and dad that he could help us get to the bottom of this little issue, and assured me that he would not do anything that would scare me, or cause me any more stress than I already felt.

"I also want to schedule a series of psychological tests," he said, "just to see where I need to go. It's standard procedure."

Who is he kidding? I thought. I knew what this was about. He wanted to see if my brain worked like a girl's brain or a boy's brain. I hated having to do it, but didn't have any other choice.

By the time we left the doctor's office, Mom was calming down a bit and dad, seemed to be less pensive. For me, it was the most humiliating thing that had happened to me since the first time I had gotten in trouble for dressing up in my mom's clothes almost fourteen years ago.

I did know, down deep in my soul, that I was girl. Yet this life I had been given—this life in Corinth, Mississippi, this life as the only child of Jim and Kate Hayes, this life lived in the midst of a legacy that I could never live up to, this life lived in the midst of right-wing Southern Baptists and hard core macho racers—was diametrically opposed to who I was and who I ultimately wanted to be. I was fortunate to have all that I had, namely two parents who had done everything in their power to keep me alive and happy, the opportunity to race and win against the best racers in America. For sure, my troubles could have been much worse. I knew that, and thanked God every day for my gifts and opportunities. I also asked God every day to tell me why I struggled so mightily with my identity as a human being.

This was strong stuff for a teenager. I would be the one who got the blame for the family's demise, not my mom, not my dad and his alcoholism, but me; I would surely be blamed for it all. Figuring all of this out would be on my shoulders.

Ironically, seeing the doctor didn't relieve my stress, it actually made the stress worse. By the time we all got back to Corinth, I was a frikin' wreck, but I just sucked it up and put on a happy face to keep my mom and dad from having a complete meltdown. The wall of secrecy I had built over the last fourteen years was mighty and very high. Now this wall was about to get stronger and higher, though they didn't know it yet.

A haunting dream

Over the next month and a half, I saw Dr Martin six times. Instead of having me visit him twice a month, he had decided we needed to dive into this situation hard and heavy for at least the first month or so.

During this six-week period Dad and I made a few trips over to a testing facility run by the University of Tennessee in downtown Memphis, on Front Street, just a block off of the Mississippi River. Those tests drained the life out me. They were long and repetitive, and reminded me of the achievement tests we took in school, which were just a waste of time.

During one of the appointments at the testing facility, they dilated my eyes without telling me why they did that. It was almost 24 hours before I could see a damn thing again.

"I've had enough of this," I told Dad.

By then, Dad had had enough too. He was seeing first hand how hard I was trying to get my life back on track. Plus, these doctor's visits conjured up old and painful memories for him, from my days of seeing allergy and asthma doctors throughout the South. Doctors and nurses had pulled and poked me with needles and stethoscopes to the point where I screamed at the top of my lungs to please stop hurting me, while my parents looked on in horror. After that came the pneumonia, when I damn near died. As a family we had suffered through enough doctors and hospitals and medical tests for three lifetimes.

However, as bad as I hated taking those tests, I didn't hate seeing Dr. Martin so much as I thought I would.

In fact, by the end of September, I had begun to open up somewhat and was revealing a few things to him – not the "I want to be a girl" part, but bullying and teasing. That bullying was still eating at me. Plus I had developed some pretty strong compulsive behaviors. For example, my hair which was now cut in a shag like David Cassidy's on "The Partridge Family" had to be just right—not one hair could be out of place. My clothes had to be perfect, my shirt had to be tucked in just right. At times I couldn't leave the mirror in fear that my hair and clothes would somehow get ruffled up before I could get out the bathroom door at school. That compulsive behavior caused me to always be late to class. So, Dr Martin and I were steadily pulling a little of that pent-up fear and frustration out into the open.

However, the most dramatic thing I was dealing with was a reoccurring dream that I've been having for over two years—ever since I had gone to my first Junior High dance out at HIlllngdalc Country Club

In the dream, I would sit right up in the middle of my bed and feel as if I was sitting in the middle of the country club floor. Kids, all of my friends and more importantly, the older boys who were bullying me danced around me, gawking and teasing me. Some of the kids in the dream just ignored me, some laughed at me and teased me about my girly legs. Some just stared at me as if to wonder why I was wearing a girl's nightgown. That dream was so real that I felt I could reach out and touch these people. Every time it popped up, I could not escape having it. In the morning, it was all I could do get up out my bed after a night of fighting through that dream.

The people in my dream were the same people I had to see and deal with every day, once I left the safety of my house and went to school, church or to work. That dream was killing me little by little. I cannot count the times after a night of having that dream that I would just drive straight by my high school and head out to the back roads of Corinth and just drive around until I mustered up the courage to finally make it to my classes. At times I did think about driving out in the country somewhere and killing myself.

Ironically—by my senior year I was not being teased any more. I had become one of the popular kids in school and was excelling in my racing. Yet, that damn dream kept up its steady pace, as real and as hurtful now as it had ever been. Its impact and the stress it caused was actually stronger than ever.

When Dr Martin heard about the dream, he was sure he was onto something.

"It we could get to the source of this fear, the dream will stop haunting you," he said. "And we could possibly resolve your feminine desires."

I sat there in my chair listening to him but in the back of my head, I actually thought he was full of crap. To me, that dream was not the key that unlocked my feminine soul. That dream was a defense mechanism which my heart and soul had kicked into gear. For sure, I wanted it to stop haunting me. I was almost at the point of not wanting to sleep just to avoid it.

Later, looking back on that time, I realized what a big influence the dream had on a habit I started that winter—staying up all night in the race shop at home and at the Haines Brothers Kart shop and working until the sun rose the next morning. Not only could I get a lot of work done, but I wouldn't run into that dream.

So far, the doctor visits were not making the dream disappear. However, I was hopeful, and so was my mom and dad who were taking time to go to the doctor and to the testing with me. They were pinning their hopes and dreams on me getting better, getting on with my life like most boys do. I was feeling the pressure to not disappoint them.

It scared me half to death to have any of them know the truth—that somehow something had gone drastically wrong at birth, in my moms womb. Hell, I had been born two months premature and my mom had almost lost me at least six times during her pregnancy. She had over twenty blood transfusions while carrying me, I had been sick since the day I was born. There had to be cause in all those circumstances, other than just me conjuring up these perverted thoughts in my head.

There had to be more to this than the devil trying to take over my life.

I was living in the midst of the male kingdom where men ruled the den and women submitted to their Southern Baptist husbands. The words "gay" or "lesbian," and "transgender" or "intersex," seldom came up. If it did, it was in the form of a joke or spewed out as a venomous mist, ensuring that those words and those people were exorcised into oblivion. In other words, people from my neck of the woods hated gays and lesbians and they thought transgender people were foolish clowns who were all headed straight to hell. These perverted souls were clearly riding shotgun with the devil himself on a sightseeing tour of Hell.

So I had to fix this gender issue and get on with my life as a race driver and the heir to the Jim Hayes legacy. My mom and dad, as well as my dad's best buds, were depending on me taking all of them to the Indy 500. For sure, I had the talent and the charisma to get there, I just needed a pile of money and an end to the girl stuff. If I did that, I could be racing at Indy or Daytona with in five years.

By the middle of October, I had completed all those stupid psychological tests and was declared sane and not a threat to society. I never knew exactly what those tests revealed. Dr. Martin just told me that he was very pleased with how I had hung in there with him.

We had hashed out some of the pressure I was feeling from my parents to fit in with the community, and we had put that aggression issue to rest. But, the issues that lay deeply imbedded in my soul over that dream still haunted both of us. That scene in the dream with kids staring and gawking at me had made me gunshy about trusting people. For someone who desperately needed trust and acceptance, the bullying had damaged my ability to let my guard down for fear of being judged and ridiculed.

So, with all my might, I was holding back my truest feelings from shining through the fog of my life. I totally shut down the flow of information going to Dr Martin that could have resolved my dilemma. If I did let my guard down, I would lose every single bit of respect and dignity I had fought for over the past few years. Worse yet—if any of those boys in my neighborhood or at the YMCA or at school found out what was going on in my life, they would beat the crap out me instead of just picking on me.

Somewhere between that summer day when my parents intervened, and the middle of October, I missed the first real opportunity to fix my life.

CHAPTER 3

National Champ – Pivot Point #1

Facing Gender

The second weekend of October, my best high-school friends Robert and Whit ramrodded me into a date with Judy Hines, one of the cutest girls within a hundred miles of Corinth. They had the idea that she was interested in me. My steady girlfriend since the tenth grade, Cindy Spears, had broken up with me back before the summer, and I hadn't been interested in dating anyone since then.

But the pressure was on from Robert and Whit, and another friend, Curtis Potts.

Curtis told me, "Terry, if you don't hurry up and ask her out, it's gonna be too late. Lamar Benjamin is hot on her trail and she likes him."

That date, which happened at my high school's homecoming football game, turned out to be the pivot point in my information shutdown.

Asking Judy out seemed like a logical thing to do. It was our homecoming, and I had just won my big karting victory. It would be cool to strut into the grand stands at Warrior Stadium with a hot chick on my arm, knock down a few Dr. Peppers with a spike of bourbon to get the juices flowing, and watch my best home-town bud Robert quarterbacking the team. Then finish the night off at Hillingdale Country Club dancing our asses off celebrating the football victory. The whole thing might be good for my self-esteem.

When I asked Judy, she said she'd go.

By half-time on that crisp fall night, everything looked to be going perfect. Our team was winning by two touchdown passes Robert had thrown. The Warrior Band, headed by another one of my buds, Victor Dixon, rallied their horn section in a bad-ass rendition of the "Mexican Hat Dance." Judy and I were sitting in the student section. She seemed to be glad I had asked her out, and was nestled close to me. Even though I was enjoying myself more than I thought I might, I was still nervous and knew that I was acting. It would be nicer to be Judy, nestled against this cute guy who was sixth in the nation driving race karts.

Then, five minutes before the third quarter, life hit me with a bombshell. Two girls sitting near us were whispering out loud to each other, and one of them hissed, "Are those *girls* sitting that close together?"

Shocked, I immediately slid away from Judy a little. My David Cassidy shag cut and my cool-ass Reid Brothers clothes right out of *Saturday Night Fever* were not the buzz cuts and blue jeans seen on guys around Corinth. So my cool androgynous hip was throwing those girls off.

Then, off to my left, about five or six rows below us, I noticed a group of kids who were the geeks, the outcasts of our high school. Through the band music, the yells of cheerleaders and spectators suddenly became deafening and strange. It felt like I was having an out-of- body experience as I focused on one geek, Roy. He had been teased and treated like dirt for years. I had been teased too, but had struggled on to become one of the most popular kids in town. Thanks to the YMCA program, and people seeing I was a good athlete, I had been allowed a better place in Corinth society. This, in turn, allowed me to make the country-club scene and date cute girls whose dads were doctors and lawyers. Yet there sat ole Roy, still stuck in the abyss of geekdom, hated and reviled by most of the kids at the game.

It struck me that Roy was a human being who deserved to be treated with respect. His worth and grace was not valued to the heavens above because of his looks, or his ability to conjugate a sentence, or the side of the tracks he lived on. He was as human as every popular kid in that school. Yet, he was considered a second-class citizen no matter what lay in his heart. Worst yet—if any of those kids in the grand stands were to find out what lay buried within my heart, even ole Roy would reject me.

That thought ran cold chill bumps down my back, and tears welled dangerously close to my eyes. Knowing I could never let my date or anyone else see me crying, I managed to look at her calmly and asked, "Do you need anything from the concession?"

"No, I'm fine," she said, smiling sweetly.

"Okay, I'm going to the rest room," I said. "I'll be right back."

Casually heading out of the stands, I passed Roy and his band of geeks, and gave ole Roy a pat on the back as some sort of acknowledgement of friendship. He looked up at my *Saturday Night Fever* threads, then at me with bewilderment, as if asking me, "Why in hell are you being nice to me?"

Somehow, I made it to the dark, lonely back of the stadium where I tried hard to gain my composure. Deep breaths of the cool crisp fall air helped to pull me out of the panic attack. After about ten minutes, I manned up and cruised by the concession stand for yet another Hot Dr Pepper, then made my way back to Judy and sat as close to her as I could for the rest of the ball game, as if nothing had ever happened.

That was the pivot point, when I decided to shut down the flow of information coming out of my soul. This way, I would never be rejected or bullied ever again.

Men being asses to women

About that time, I was wrestling with the way men view women. Could I step into a girl's shoes and live her life? Was it in me to compromise and be submissive?

All my female role models were submissive—the complete Southern Baptist package who saw themselves as beholden to their husbands and boyfriends. The guys who hung out at my dad's race shop were demeaning and downright hateful to women at times. My dad never went that far, but he did have his chauvinistic ways. All my high-school buds had their male-kingdom attitudes, and I always wondered why girls put up with it.

Hell, at times I boiled over with those chauvinistic attitudes myself, and got pissed off when I caught myself doing it. After all, I was living in the midst of the male kingdom. Because of my motorsports gifts and accomplishments, I had the golden key to the most dominant, macho and dangerous brotherhood on earth. Race-car drivers were the 20th century version of Old West gunfighters…the sports answer to astronauts. So being a male allowed me to have incredible privileges that others would kill their grandmothers to have. By being a girl, I would be taking a seat in the back of the bus. My ego would surely suffer some major damage.

So I was wrestling with this social stuff, and wasn't ready yet to download my thoughts on the issue to Dr. Martin.

By the end of October, my cure looked complete. I never wanted to wear women's clothes again . . . at least that was what I let Dr Martin think. But, in my heart of hearts I was aware that I was only fooling myself.

On my last visit at Dr. Martin's, the girl thing wasn't even mentioned. He and I only talked about my racing and an upcoming pro event in Chattanooga. He encouraged me to go after the win, made a quick adjustment to the crick in my neck, and sent me on my way.

My dad was in the waiting room. When we walked out of that office building on the corner of Popular and Perkins I felt as if I had been let out of jail. As we drove out of the parking lot, I could see that the weight of the world had been lifted off Dad's shoulders too. He suddenly seemed happier than he had been in a while and, his happiness made me feel at ease.

A new vision . . . an old problem

Dad and I were starved so we hightailed over to the Krystal Hamburgers diner and ordered up a heap of those little pint-size burgers and tore into them. As we ate, Dad and I chitchatted about the upcoming races in Chattanooga. After he paid the bill, we headed out to the car. Instead of me driving like I always did, Dad wanted to drive so, I got in the passenger side and we took off. However, instead of making a left on Poplor Avenue and heading toward Corinth, he took a right and headed back toward town.

"Do you…uh… know where you're going?" I asked him.

"Oh," he said casually, "I want to go by Al's Cycle Shop to see I can find some Honda parts I need."

But when we got to the Honda shop's driveway he went on by. I was bewildered, but before I could say anything he took a left into the Chevy dealership just one block up on the corner of Summer Avenue and Tillman and parked.

"Get on out," he said. "I want to look at a van here."

By now, I was beginning to wonder what the hell he had up. We took a stroll to the front of the lot where several new Chevy vans were parked and looked inside all five of them. Then we went back to the show room and Dad asked a salesman if he could drive that bright-blue long-wheel-base Chevy van out there. I just about had a damn heart attack. Was he looking for a van for the family, or was it for his now successful tool and die business? Whatever it was, having a van was pretty damn cool.

We took a test drive to Perkins Road a few miles down the road, then came back. Inside the show room, Dad asked the salesman to make us a deal. After thirty minutes of haggling, Dad pulled out four one-thousand- dollar bills and paid cash. I was about to pee all over myself. Never had my dad done anything so extravagant! In a few minutes, the dealership had that baby polished up, full of gas and ready to go.

Dad pitched me the car keys to our Chevy Impala and told me to follow him home. Of course, that entire 90 minutes to Corinth was torture as I tried to figure out what he was up to.

We made it home around 6:00 p.m. in time for him and Mom to head out with friends to the Catfish Hotel for some kick-ass fried catfish. So Dad was in a hurry to jump in the shower. He parked the van in the front yard, and I headed towards the race shop to work on my kart.

As he turned towards the back door, Dad called out, "Turn around."

I did, and he pitched me the keys to the van.

"I'm proud of you," he said. "You really put the work in over the past few months. You deserve this. Now you have something you can haul your karts in. Be careful and take care of it."

Holy crap, he had planned it all out without spilling the beans one single time. I was speechless and humbled. Even though he and I had been going through growing pains for years, he was still my most beloved hero, and I was his only child whom he worked his fingers to the bone for. As exciting and full as our life was, it had been hard and heart- breaking at times. As a family, we had been through hell over my asthma and my gender situation. Now I was being rewarded for making our lives more normal again.

So when he pitched me those keys, Dad shared his love the only emotional way he knew how, and I wasn't going to let him down no matter what. I just had to stay focused on racing and keep those feminine demons locked down somewhere.

Right now, I was going to take a drive down Shiloh Road to Frailey's Drive-In, where all the kids hung out on weekends. It was show-off time. Working on my karts would have to wait for an hour or so.

The next day I just had to drive over to Charles Toler's place and show off the van again. Inspired by his style, I tricked that van out to the max with Mag wheels, wide tires and a killer stereo system. Yeah, baby!

I was fully aware of the sacrifices my mom and dad had made for me—not only over the Dr. Martin ordeal, not only to keep me alive and healthy, but for me to have a nice life. Fortunately, as a family we were now doing okay. Dad's business was going better and we were reaping the benefits. We were not rich, just upper middle class but we had earned it. So it was up to me to make the most of my second chance.

Working to perfect my racing, I began to build and trick engines for other karters around the Mid South. Like my dad, I had a knack for making engines run fast and because of my success on the track, nine or ten customers were counting on me to keep their engines running at top song. My little business was called Terry Hayes Engines. When it made me money, I put it back into my own engines, and it was paying off with more wins. One year after my final encounter with Dr. Martin, I had managed to win the World Karting National Championships held in Memphis. I had finished fifth at the International

Karting Federation National Championships in Quincy, Illinois, second at the IKF spring Nationals in Oklahoma City, second at the IKF Winter nationals in Jacksonville, Florida. And I won the IKF South Central Winter Nationals held in Memphis. In short, I was on a roll, and meeting some cool folks from all around the country.

Karting legend Lake Speed and I had come to be good friends. He was promoting a European form of karting and invited me to participate in that incredible program. It took my racing to a whole new level.

But my best karting buds were that bunch of rebels based in Lynn Haddock's Kart Shop up in Chattanooga. Russ Thompson and Tommy Crosby, who were actually from the Nashville area but were Lynn's top posse, had become my hanging-out buds when we were at the races. No matter where we were—in Memphis, Paducah, Chattanooga or down in Jacksonville or Barnesville—we were hanging out. All of us were at the top of our game, and we shared a sense of humor that kept us laughing. Even our dads, who were with us most of the time, were hanging buds. Today I can close my eyes and still see those indelible images of us at the track on practice days when we were fine-tuning our karts for qualifying. I can see Pop Haddock sitting out on the starting grid with four or five stopwatches, and all of us rushing up to him after a practice run to get our time. Pop Haddock would always tell you whether or not you had the speed to win.

That was a priceless time in our lives and I miss it like crazy even today. I had total focus and was thinking about moving on towards the big time by the next year or so.

Winning the World Karting Association National Championships

However all was not well on the home front. Dad's drinking had escalated and it was wearing on me and Mom. Dad was a handful when he drank and he was drinking a lot.

"You're lyin' Eyes"

Lynn Haddock and a few guys in Chattanooga had built a new kart track just south of the city and had decided to promote a big-money pro race a few weeks before Thanksgiving. I couldn't wait to get there and see if I could win that baby.

Over the past month or so, I had designed some engineering innovations into my Burton Kart and was ready to test them out. I had built some new trick front spindles that lowered the front of the kart by one half of an inch, along with 2 more degrees of camber that would add more aggressive grip to the tires. Some work to my exhaust system gave me a wee bit more power. I had also lowered the rear of the Kart by making new bearing hangers for the real axle. So when race weekend came around, I was ready to go.

Early Saturday morning Dad and I piled into my van and headed out to Chattanooga. With us was one of his engineering friends, Roy Williams, one of the guys who had actually grown up hanging out at Dad's race shop back in the day. We were hoping to get there by mid afternoon for a few hours of testing and practice—the race was on Sunday. The trip was actually enjoyable, Dad didn't get snookered, and he and Roy reminisced about when they raced in Nashville at Ewing Lane Speedway and just how much racing had changed over the past twenty years.

By around 2:30 p.m., we rolled in the pit gate at the track.

I had never raced here before, so I got busy working out my gearing and tuning my engine and the handling on my kart. Plus it was important to memorize the lay and the turns of the track. When practice ended at 6 p.m., I had turned in the seventh fast time out about 40 of the fastest kart racers this side of the Mississippi. In fact, I was only a few tenths off Lynn Haddock's time and he had turned the fastest lap of the day. Besides this was his home track so he had all its little speed secrets worked out.

I was not happy with my time, but I had a pretty good idea what to do with my engine and gearing to make my speeds go up the next morning for qualifying. To win or even finish in the top five, I had to get it worked out. I was confident I could do it.

That night, Dad and Roy got us a motel room just up the road, and we caught a bite to eat at a local seafood restaurant. Dad got smashed and was a little snarly about my being seventh on the practice timing sheet.

"If you don't get it going," he said, "you're going to get beat tomorrow."

It was all I could do to not smart off at him but Roy was sitting there so I kept my mouth shut.

Later, in my room, as I tossed and turned trying to sleep, I wondered where all this was going to end up. I was managing to keep my gender demons buried, but Dad was drinking more and more. I hated him nipping at me when he knew very well that I never left any stone unturned when it came to racing. Even though we were winners, national champions now, something deep inside my dad—especially when he was drinking—led him to have no confidence in my racing. Yet on another level he would turn me loose to travel all over America by myself to race, and depended on me for many things that no other parents of teenagers would ever trust their kids to do. Dad had his own version of the fear and fearlessness thing going on, and he was playing it out on me.

So I wondered how long before everything would blow up on us.

A gloomy day to race

The next morning by 8:30, I was out on the track running laps and working on my set-up. The sky was dreary and overcast, and the weather man was calling for rain by late afternoon. But we would have to get out there in the elements and get the job done. One thing was for sure—this cool weather would make my engine run really well.

By the end of morning practice I had managed to get my lap times down by a tenth and a half, which could put me anywhere from second to fifth on the starting grid. Haddock was still fastest. Dad had been drinking vodka and bugging me about my time. If I was going to beat Haddock in the race, I would have to pull a rabbit out of my helmet.

So I just kept my mouth shut, ignored Dad and made one more gear change to the kart. Then, driving my ass off, I managed to qualify fourth.

However, instead of Dad being happy, he was still riding me about Lynn out-qualifying me. Ironically, for two years I had out-qualified Lynn more than Lynn had out-qualified me. But Dad had a short and selective memory. Plus he didn't like Lynn, calling him arrogant and cocky. Like I wasn't just as arrogant and cocky as any driver out there including Lynn! Hell, that was the redeeming quality for racers. If you didn't think you were invincible, you had no business being out there because you were going to get your ass beat. Racing ain't no poetry reading in the Village.

In the race that day, with both Lynn and I driving like crazy people, I finished second right behind him. I hated getting beat, but he was a friend and after all, he was one of the best in the country. So in the end, we had a pretty damn good day.

In fact, after a day of browbeating me, almost to the point of me telling my dad to go screw himself, Dad was suddenly patting me on the back. He had been drinking all day, but now, just as the rain was starting to pour, he seemed to enjoy the moment. But I was fuming. Over the next 20 minutes or so, we all hung out in the technical inspection building and Lynn and I waited to do interviews for the local radio station. Lynn did his interview first, and then they went to break. I took my place next to the sports reporter and was waiting for the commercial to end.

Suddenly I realized that the song they were playing in the background was "Your Lying Eyes" by the Eagles. The meaning of those lyrics cut right into me, and one of my panic attacks started coming on.

My dad and Roy were over there laughing it up with Pop Haddock and my good Buddy Russ Thompson who had actually kicked all of our tails the rear before driving for Haddock, and it was getting to me. I had had enough of trying to be perfect, to control my gender issue, of not disappointing my parents, of just about everything. I was burned out from two years of 24-hour days trying to run my engine-building business and keep my own karts running at the front. I was over my dad's drinking, and that damn song, "Your Lying Eyes" was eating at my very soul. It had me on the brink of bursting into tears right there as I prepared to go on the radio. But if I cried in front of this bunch of hard ankles I would never live it down.

Then, the song stopped, the reporter did his intro about my race and then stuck the microphone in my face. I pulled myself together, talked about my run and thanked him for giving us the coverage.

When it was over, I bolted for the rest room, locked the door behind me and wept for ten minutes like a broken child with no hope for the future. When I came out, I had washed my face and looked like nothing ever happened.

Thirty minutes later, we had our five hundred dollars and a big ole trophy.

With a quick stop at a filling station and a local Krystals for a bag full of those little morsels, we were on our way back to Corinth. Dad was in the back sleeping off a hangover, and Roy was talking to me about the race.

As it got dark, and the white center line of the highway came streaming at me in the headlights, I was pondering the future. I had been there, done that with karts, and was thinking about getting into midgets next year. Dad and I had even talked about a sprint-car deal at some point. I also had to do something about education; I had left high school early and gotten my GED in the spring. My dad wanted me to go to engineering school and then help him run his tool and die business. But because of his drinking, because I hated Corinth and didn't like the tool and die business, I was looking for something else to do. For sure I wanted to have a pro career in motorsports. But to do that, I had to get a plan. Plus if I didn't get a grip on the gender issue, I was going to lose my mind.

That night, traveling down I-40 at eighty miles per hour and listening to my Allman Brothers tape I asked myself the familiar questions. Would I go on to become one of America's greatest race drivers? Would I pursue my feminine desires and live as a female till the day I died? Or would I just kill myself and get it over with?

If I chose to live, I had to get it right.

The Haines Brothers Deal

Two weeks after that race in Chattanooga, Dad and I headed down to Jacksonville, Florida, for the IKF Eastern Winter nationals. But before we left, I made a quick run over to Memphis to pick up some racing fuel at the Haines Brothers.

While I was there, David Haines had cornered me in his office.

"What are your plans for school?" he asked. "Are you going back to work for your dad full time?"

He knew that I hated the tool and die business, and we had already had some talks about how redneck Corinth was getting. At first I thought his questions were a bit meddling.

But David finally quit beating around the bush and asked me, "Would you like to come back to work for us? At our electrical contracting firm instead of the Kart Shop?"

He said they would send me to school to study electrical engineering which would ultimately take me to an electrical estimator position with in their company. Plus he made it very clear that I could and should continue my racing, and they would help me with that.

I listened with that poker face that I had perfected over the years, but inside I was blown away by his trust and belief in me. Hell, I was barely eighteen at the time, and he was making me the offer of a lifetime.

"Hell," he said, "you could be making eighty grand a year in just a few years."

He clearly had my attention. "Can I have a few days to think it over…at least till I got back from the races down in Jacksonville?"

"Hell, Terry, think it over, talk to your dad about it," he said. "You can wait to start at the first of the year if you like. But we would really like to train you and help you get a good career going. You don't belong in that hick town. You have what it takes to make it here in the city and we want to help make that possible."

I shook his hand and told him I appreciated the opportunity and would be back after Jacksonville to discuss it further. I was running a bit late so after telling him good buy, I took off for the parking lot. Then suddenly, as I was pulling the van out, I said to myself out loud, "What the hell, I'm not missing out on this opportunity."

Re-parking the van, I ran back inside to find David.

"I've already thought it over. If you want me to start the day after I get back from Florida I'll be ready to get going."

David almost burst out laughing said, "Damn Terry, it didn't take you long to think it over. Are you sure you're ready to make this commitment? Is you dad going to be okay with this"

I looked him straight in the eye. "I'm positive."

"Okay," he said. "We'll see you in a week. Now go on down to Florida and beat those guys."

Driving back to Corinth, I was almost in shock about what had just happened . . . and started feeling a little torn. After all, my dad was giving me virtually the same opportunity. At some point the tool and die business would be mine; I would not just be an employee. But because of his drinking, working for him full time plus racing with him would be a recipe for disaster. I was also feeling a bit unappreciated by the country clubbers I had been associating with since I first got to High school. These "clicky" snobs had no idea what I had accomplished in Karting over the past few years. My national championships and the fact that I was competing and winning against the nations future super star racers meant nothing to these people. The local golfers and tennis kids were much more appreciated than my national talents. This love hate relationship I had with these people, was as much of the reason I had accepted the job with the Haines Brothers as any thing.

By the time I got back home, I had resolved it. Going to work for the Haines Brothers was the right thing to do.

I also had started seeing this hot Corinth babe who could pass as Stevie Nicks' twin. Once again my best bud Whit had hooked me up with this girl… he and his aunt, who was only a few years older than we were. Over the past few weeks, I had had a few dates with Jimmie and it looked as if it might go somewhere. We had gone down to Ole Miss for a couple of frat parties, and she had actually gone to one race with me in Memphis and didn't seem to mind it at all. I felt like I had the gender thing under some control, and having a hot chick and a new high-powered job opportunity would surely help me with that control.

The one thing that did bother me about working for the Haines Bothers was that I might be giving up my dream to be a professional race driver in the Indy or the Daytona 500. But for right now, I had made the commitment to do the responsible thing—go back to school, get a good job, date a hot chick, be a part of mainstream society and keep everybody happy. By submitting to this pressure to fit in, I was hoping that it would somehow help me keep a grip on my gender demons.

Dr Martin had told me over and over that if I found a new focus for my life and re-directed all my energies towards a more normal set of circumstances, I could overcome those feminine desires. Now, I had to fight like hell to make sure it did.

At Jacksonville, I had a good weekend and finished second overall. All of us hot shoes got our tails beat by some cat from Wisconsin no one had ever heard of. However a second-place finish at the Winter Nationals was pretty damn good.

All was not perfect though. I had caught the flu on the way down there and Dad had gotten pissed off at me when I wouldn't let him go with me into the technical inspection building. The rule was, only one person from each team could come in, so there wasn't a thing I could do about it. But Dad had a buzz on, so he took it as a personal attack.

The next day, we headed back to Corinth where I was going to drop Dad off, unload the kart and tools, then head to Aunt Vera's in Memphis so I could be at work at Haines Electric by eight a.m. sharp the next morning. On the way home, Dad and I got along quite well—he actually seemed excited about the opportunity with the Haines group. As usual, we never discussed his piss-off the day before.

At speed down in Jacksonville during the IKF Winter Nationals

A big move

In Memphis I quickly settled into my new job, and a new apartment just a mile from work.

Over the next month I went out with David and his brothers on jobs all around town, and studied my ass off learning all the little symbols and tricks of the electrical trade. The plan was that I would enroll at State Tech after New Year's. David and his family took me under their wing and tried to make me feel as comfortable as possible. I really applied my self and worked at learning all I could with all my might. On the weekends I would cut out of the office at six p.m. and head to Corinth to spend the weekend with my girlfriend Jimmie and her four-year-old son.

So everything seemed to be rolling along fine…except I could not get a handle on the gender demons no matter what I did. I tried growing a mustache, but it was thin and looked awful. Prayer wasn't helping either.

Inevitably my boss could see the growing strain on my face. David even asked me, "Are you working too hard? It's a lot to learn in a short time. I don't want to put too much pressure on you."

A week before Christmas, on Friday night, he and I were working a little overtime finishing up on a bid and he could tell that my mind was not on my work.

"Are you all right?" he asked with real concern. "Is there anything you… want to talk about? Are you okay with money? How is your girlfriend? Yawl are not fighting, are you? I'm worried about you."

"I'm all right," I answered quickly. "Don't worry…I'll get it all worked out."

From my tone, you wouldn't know I was on the verge of a breakdown.

Wrapping up our work, we headed out the front door. I stood there in the glassed-in entrance waiting on David as he shut off all the lights and set the alarm system. Suddenly I caught my reflection in the glass walls. It was daunting to see myself all stressed out. I now had a hell of a job and the opportunity with the Haines Brothers. I had a beautiful and loving girlfriend who worshiped the ground I walked on, and my relationship with my parents had never been better. I was still able to race. The world was my oyster.

Then just at that moment, I realized that the muzak over the intercom in the office was playing "Your Lyin' Eyes" by the Eagles. My eyes teared up and I dried them with my sleeve, hoping that David wouldn't notice. That damn song had shown up one more time, in little more than a year.

When David came out, I said quickly, "See you Monday!"

Then I made a mad dash to my new Mercury Cougar and got the hell out of there. I was already late getting back to Corinth. Jimmie and I had a Christmas party to attend.

All the way home, my mind was going 200 miles per hour. If I did not put this gender situation behind me at all cost, my life was going to come crashing down. I had to make a big bold new move of some kind. Maybe I should get married. That would really force me to put the girl stuff in the closet for good.

At the Christmas party that night, Jimmie and I were having a good time. I had made up my mind to bite the bullet and had a few drinks to get my courage up. At about ten o'clock, she and I were sitting on a couch alone and away from the rest of the party when I looked right into her eyes and point-blank asked, "Will you marry me?"

Then I wanted to add that I was just kidding.

But Jimmy met my eyes with a big smile and said, "I'd love to marry you."

What had I just done? Was I crazy? Sometime in the next couple of months, I was going to be a husband and a step dad to a four-year-old boy. A tidal wave of sensations washed over me. First I wanted to go and throw up. Next I thought I would pass out from the terror that was rushing through my mind and my body.

Recovering quickly, I gave her a big ole kiss and told her that everything was going to be wonderful. We immediately told everyone at the party. There were shouts and shrieks of excitement, and everyone congratulated us like crazy. After she and I left, we drove to Junior's Bar and Grill on the state line and got smashed. My old buddy Danny Irvin (Irv) happened to be there and was cool enough to drive us home.

The next day she and I cooked some breakfast, laughed about the night before and then drove to my parents' house and told them the news.

Of course, my folks were elated. Hell, every one was. But I knew I had just sold my soul to the devil.

Next came some hard decisions

First, Jimmie had a good job there in Corinth, at the hospital, and her son's dad and grand parents lived in Corinth as well. I didn't want to uproot Jimmie and her family, at least not right now. For sure I could have her move to Memphis and my apartment. It would be a tight fit for all of us. Or I could just continue to commute back to Corinth on the weekends. That would actually work.

But to be honest, I missed being down in Corinth and around my race shop. And by now, the office politics among the Haines Brothers was beginning to get to me. David was my immediate boss, but his brother A.B always wanted me to be doing something for him and their dad, Armie, always wanted me to be in their shop building him something for his cabin up on Pick Wick lake. I was confused on what my job description was and I hated being pulled in three different directions.

So by New Years, I made up my mind that I would move back to Corinth and go to work for my dad. When I gave my notice to the Haines Brothers, they were disappointed, but understood that marriage made a difference in my future.

Right after New Year's, Jimmie and I made our plans. We decided to keep it simple. First we went to Clausel Jewelers (who were distant cousins, by the way) and I bought two wedding rings. Then we headed to the courthouse, where another cousin of mine was the circuit court clerk, and got our marriage license. Finally we quickly found a justice of the peace and got married on the spot.

That weekend, Jimmie and I, along with my bud Dewayne McLemore and his wife Nell, went to Memphis to get my stuff. On Saturday night, we all went out on the town celebrating our marriage. On Sunday, we emptied out my apartment and came on back to Corinth. That Monday, I was at my dad's tool and die business bright and early, ready for work. I was now a married man—if you could really say that. Hell, I was barely able to grow a pitiful little mustache so being a man was the last thing I was. And I had responsibilities—a family to look after.

Over the next month Jimmie and I got into our new routine—went to work, went to church, socialized with our friends. My mom and dad were elated over us getting married and for a while, I was too. After all, I was giving it my best shot. But deep in my heart, I was mourning the loss of my truest self.

Then the sky fell in.

About a month and a half after we got married, on a bitter cold February weekend night, Jimmie and I were lying in the bed snuggled up to one another after we made love. I had my back to her and she was curled up around me, slowly and gently sliding her hand up and down the side of my body. She slid her hand across my hips and my waist, and I noticed that she repeated this move several times.

Then, as if she had seen a ghost or been struck by lightning, Jimmie jumped up into the middle of the bed and began to shout almost in a panic.

"My God, Terry, your body is shaped just like a girl's! I never noticed it before but…your body is better than mine! Oh my God, that is so weird. I can't believe I never noticed that before . . . I don't know if I like this . . . it's really weird."

She was freaking out, and by now I was too. She had just discovered the reason why I had quit going to PE class in high school … why I went out of my way to hide my form, always wearing pants low on my waist, trying not to show my girly legs and small feminine feet. By now, she had rushed into the bathroom and locked the door.

I lay there wondering nervously how the hell I was going to explain this. At that time there were no rumors about me around town. I had been nothing but a good boyfriend, and was doing my damnedest to be a good husband.

Finally she came out of the bathroom, but spent the rest of the night on the far side of the bed, while I panicked for hours on how this would turn out the next morning. Something in her had clicked, and not for the better.

Three days later, we separated. One month later we were in the process of getting a divorce. Just like that, it was all over, and there was not one damn thing I could do about it.

My parents were in shock, and so was I—shell-shocked and embarrassed over the whole sorry affair.

A Bottle of Wine

While Jimmie and I were separating, I almost went crazy with wondering who all she was telling. One night I drove over to our apartment intending to give her a real cussing out. When I drove up the driveway, out walked her old boyfriend Roger. He arrogantly walked right past me and gave me a look as if to say, "Screw you, ya little fag, I got the chick now."

Not wanting to get in a fight, I sucked it up and left before I drove my van into the apartment and killed all of us.

That was when I thought to myself, I've got to have someone I can talk to. But who? I racked my brain on whom I could call up and have them listen to my pitiful tale. Then I thought of my old friend from back in the day, Stephanie. She was back in Corinth regrouping after a whirlwind failed marriage that had left her with a beautiful three-year-old boy. Her pregnancy and shotgun marriage had been a big deal back in high school and Stephanie's dad Ben, who was a hard-core Church of Christ elder, was having no part of his little girl embarrassing the family. Stephanie and her new husband Ron had joined the military and got the hell of Corinth. But that marriage had fallen through and there she was, right back in Corinth trying to pick up the pieces and raise a little boy. It had to be hard for her.

In fact, back in the fall, I had run up on Stephanie down at an Ole Miss frat party when Jimmie and a few other friends had invaded Oxford for a weekend of partying. That night down she and I had connected, almost like two soul mates. Jimmie had picked up on it and got pretty damn jealous. Ever since then, I had thought about Stephanie.

So I decided to give her a call, play it cool – just tell her that I'd like to grab a bottle of wine and come over to catch up on old times.

When she answered the phone, she was glad to hear from me. "Hey," she asked me, "do you want to get a bottle of wine, maybe grab a pizza and come on over?"

I got over there as fast as I could. Stephanie was as beautiful as ever, and it hit me how much I liked her. She had long thick auburn hair, the best body this side of L. A. and she was dead ringer for the movie star Connie Selica. She was a hottie of the first degree. Besides, she came from a racing family, so she loved race cars.

The Winter Nationals

In spite of the marriage crisis, I was still racing. That March, I headed down to Barnesville, Georgia for the Winter Nationals. I loved racing there and this year, I was the reigning national champion so my bravado was up.

Lake Speed was still bringing in the European karting and I was helping to push that along. I had picked up a new Birel Kart made in Italy and was chomping at the bit to try that baby out. When I made my first practice runs I was a full three tenths of second faster than everyone in my 125cc light class.

Scott Pruitt, the California hot shoe, was second fastest, followed closely by the track owner's son, Dickey Wilson

The day for qualifying, the temperature dropped thirty degrees and we were all freezing our asses off. To make things worse, that new tricked-out Birel Kart was a handful. The cold weather had made it very loose and I was on the verge of spinning out at any moment. In the warmer weather the day before, it had been a rocket ship.

So I picked Lake's brain on what to do. He was having the same problem and pulled out a couple of mounted-up supersticky Dunlap rear tires for me to throw on.

When it came time for my qualifying run, I hauled it onto the track not knowing if those tires would do the trick or not. But they made up most of the difference that the cold weather had taken away. I qualified second fastest, right behind Pruitt by about three one hundredths of a second.

The day of the race, it had warmed up a bit so I felt better about my chances.

During the race, I was running a strong second to Pruitt with Dickey Wilson only a few kart lengths behind. If anyone made a mistake, the other one would grab their position. Then, on the last lap, just two turns from the checkered flag, Pruitt clipped a tire marking the inside of the turn, causing water that was inside that tire to squirt onto the track. I hit the water and tried not to spin out, but the second I hit the brakes, Dickey slammed into my rear bumper, knocking me out of the way. He motored on by me never looking back and took second place. I followed up with a close third.

When we got back to the pits, I was mad as hell at Dickey for slamming into me like that. He could have avoided hitting me.

But Lake kept me from escalating to something more serious.

"Just let it go," Lake said. "You had a good drive. His time will come."

Since I really looked up to Lake, I bit my tongue.

That night, there was a big super-cross motorcycle race going on in Atlanta at Braves Stadium about forty miles away. So Lake and his kick-ass wife Aurora and I, along with the California Flash Kyle Atkins, piled into Lake's bright green Dodge van and high-tailed it to the motorcycle races. We still had our racing leathers on, but we were running late and needed to get in the road.

Lake was driving, Aurora was riding shotgun and Kyle was in the jump seat behind Lake. Me, I was sitting in one of Lake's karts in the back of the van. We had several bottles of wine and a few beers so we were set. As we headed up the road, I was venting like hell about Dickey Wilson. The more we drank, the braver we got. I was going to kick that little s.o.b.'s ass and Kyle was egging me on, saying, "Fucking A, I'll help you do it." Aurora was laughing her head off, and Lake was grinning like a three-legged frog up there driving, knowing full well that we were not going to do a thing to Dickey the next day. But he let us raise hell. Kyle and I got snockered, and we raised a ruckus at the super-cross.

Aurora drilled me unmercifully over my soon-to-be-ex wife. She kept saying, "You do not need to be married; you need to focus on your racing. Terry, you're too young to be married. Tell him, Lake... he is crazy for doing this."

The next day, we went home all hung over but glad we had had the Winter National experience once again.

For me, though, coming home was melancholy. Aurora was right, I had been crazy to get married. But on the entire trip back to Corinth, all I could think about was re-connecting with Stephanie.

Over the next three months Stephanie and I saw one another almost daily, except on the weekends. She and I had the ever-loving hots for each other. We were killer in bed, we had the same vision for life, and we had a lifetime of history with one another. I could let my hair down in front of her without any judgment. At times she probably thought that I was a very emotional boy, but she just hung in there with me.

I would park on the street behind her garage apartment and then race through the back yard and into the apartment as if we were running a covert love operation for the CIA. Over those few months, we were fully aware that in the summer she was going to get married. Her husband-to-be, Bob, was an automotive executive. That was the plan, and her dad was adamant about it. I felt sorry for Stephanie because she felt so much pressure to please her parents.

By May, she was beginning to put me on the spot as to what my interest in her really was. Would I be willing to make a real life commitment to her? If I was, the deal between she and Bob might be left on the side of the road. Even though I felt she was a soul mate, I was not willing to make another marriage commitment. She had no clue about my gender issue. I

was doing good to just get through every day without emotionally crashing.

In fact our relationship was both good and bad for me.
On the one hand, the times we shared filled my heart with
love and joy that I desperately needed. On the other hand,
the relationship confused me… it pushed my gender issue into
a boiling pot of water and cooked the living daylights out of
it. With Stephanie my heart got nurtured, but my soul still
thirsted for my femininity. I was still attracted to men. So I was
in a pickle.

Besides, Stephanie's little boy needed a strong male role
model. So by June, she and I agreed that she would go ahead
and marry Bob, and get on with her life.

In the meantime, we continued our shadow relationship up
to the night before she was married. That night we made sweet
love for what we thought would be the last time in our lives.
Later that night, we lay in the middle of her den floor holding
on to each other with only the light of the stereo casting a glow
across our faces. We talked about life, our futures and hope that
we both would find peace and love. We also both vowed to get
the hell of Corinth and to never come back.

Two weeks later, Stephanie was in Memphis, married. She
and Bob set up house at an apartment complex there in Ger-
mantown a suburb just outside of Memphis. Two days later,
she and I spent the day together. We made love and wept like
babies knowing full well that we had probably made a big mistake for not marrying each other.

As time went by, we drove one another crazy. We could not
walk away from one another. Bob was an asshole and several
times Stephanie left him, always going back to him because of

the pressure from her parents and because I could never make the commitment to marry her. But I kept trying to convince myself that she was another way to keep my gender issue under control. Besides I was totally, completely devoted and in love with her.

Another big move was needed.

One day during this time, I took all the girl clothes I had collected for years, and all the makeup, and threw them in the trash can beside my race shop… and burnt them. At times the fire was ten feet high as all of my precious garments went up in roaring flames—the cute sweaters and tops, the lacy underwear. The last thing I threw in, reluctantly, was a favorite pair of girl's pajamas, white, with little red hearts and anchors printed all over them. With a huge lump in my throat, I watched as that final and sorrowful plume of smoke rose towering into the sky. You could see it from all over Corinth.

When nothing was left in the trash can but smoking ashes, I stood there feeling stupid and empty.

The next step was going to be testing and hard—possibly the hardest thing I had ever done in my life!

CHAPTER 4

What was I Thinking?

Wrecking in the Astro Dome

By January 1980, my racing had taken on a whole new life and I was looking to move on up the racing ladder. NASCAR and the Indy 500 were on my list of things to do. In my mind, because of my extraordinary life experiences—complications with asthma, my stupid failed marriage and the looming dysfunction and depression over my gender issue—I had a lot to do in a very short period of time. If I did not get busy, I might not be around long enough to achieve the dreams!

I had won just about everything in Karting over the past five years . . . the Grand Nationals, the Winter Nationals, The Spring Nationals and everything in between. I loved Karting, and missed the people I had come to know all across the country, especially that bunch of nuts up in the Nashville and Chattanooga area. But a little over a year ago, I had decided to focus on those little racers my dad had driven over the past 30 years with incredible success. By this time, I had a good feel for midget racers and was a force to be reckoned with on the national level, just like in Karting. On top of my wins, I had the mechanical ability and the gift for designing and building race cars that gave me an edge on my competition.

However, my desire to be a girl was stressing me to the point of no return. It was playing Russian roulette with my life. On one side of the wheel I wanted to race in the Indy 500 and on the other side, I held all the hopes and desires any other girl in the world held in her heart. So I was skidding back and forth between emotional highs and lows, and could sense a big wreck of some sort looming around the corner—not a racing accident but something deeper and more hurtful. Worst of all, I had convinced myself that I could not talk about this to anyone. Rightly or wrongly, I had always felt that my parents looked down up on me because of the gender issue—that if any one in the racing community—or worse, any one in my home town—were to know my deepest desires, my life would be over.

The week after New Years Eve, there was this big midget race down in Houston, Texas. Dad and I had spent the last few weeks working on our cars getting them ready to race in the Astro Dome. As usual, we had come up with one more project over and above the usual workload before heading out on a big racing trip, so I was busting my butt putting a stereo system in our new Dodge van so we could have cool tunes to get us through the long nights on the highway. At about seven AM I finally got that little jewel hooked up and working and was worn slap-dab out – but now it was time get all the cars loaded on the trailer. We planned to leave about 10 a.m.

About then, a part-time employee of my dad's, Irv (Danny Irvin) showed up out of the blue and decided he was going with us. That was cool with me, I liked him. He was probably the funniest person I had ever known in my life and a great bodyguard when other racers thought they wanted to start a fight over something that happened on the track. He and I had gone down to Bike Week in Daytona the year before and thought it would be hilarious to ride a little Honda 90

What was I Thinking?
Wrecking in the Astro Dome

119

rice-burner around in the midst of all those Harleys. We were a sight, with my 5'6" 115 pound ass driving and his 6'2" 200-pound hulk on the back wearing his John Deer hat with Irv embroidered on the bill. So we were buds and he'd be a lot of help driving. I would need some sleep in three or four hours.

As it turned out, my dad had to deal with something at work, so it was darn near 3:00 pm before we left Corinth. I hit highway 45 south driving like a maniac, with my mom raising hell at me about driving too fast. By the time we got down to Tupelo, Mississippi, only 50 miles down the road, my dad was hell bent on stopping and getting some junk food to put in his cooler. My mom had packed her famous pimento cheese sandwiches and tasty fried chicken, but as usual my dad just had to have some pork rinds and beer. So, I spotted a local convenience store on the outskirts of Tupelo, and everyone but mom went inside in search of our own personal junk food treasure chest.

It was only about 4:30 in the afternoon but for some reason, the place had some unsavory late-night characters hanging out inside the store. My dad had his courage up so he just pushed his way through the crowd and proceeded to get his beer, while Irv and I grabbed some bags of chips and Gummy Bears, and headed on back out to the van. Suddenly my dad rushed out of the store and jumped in the van. He was white and actually frightened.

"Jim, what's wrong?" my mom asked, all panicky. "Are you all right?"

I was about to burst out laughing because I had never seen my dad, who was the coolest cat I had ever known, get in that big of a hurry.

After he caught his breath, Dad told us that some whore inside the store had propositioned him back at the beer cooler. Her pimp, who ultimately was her husband, came back there and threatened him with a knife for messing around with his wife. Then, the pimp made a big slice across his wife's chest, and that was when my dad decided to exit the building.

Dad looked at me with sweat beads all over his forehead and said, "What in the hell are you waiting on? Let's get the hell out of here."

As we exited the premises, Irv and I were about to die from laughing while my mom was chewing my dad out for wanting to stop in the first place.

At around one in the morning we were a few miles outside of Baton Rouge, Louisiana, right smack in the middle of a hurricane that had blown up from the Gulf of Mexico. It was raining so hard you couldn't see ten feet in front of the van. Those big eighteen wheelers we were sharing the interstate with were causing me all kinds of trouble seeing where I was going. We didn't have time to stop and let the storm pass us by, because we had to be in Huston next morning at 11 for practice. Irv was helping me watch the road while mom and dad were sound asleep in the back. I had everything in control, baby, and when one of those big rigs blew by me at 80 miles per hour I tucked in right behind him. That took us out of the wind turbulence and water spray that blew off those trucks that was causing me so much trouble in the first place. I followed that guy for ten or fifteen minutes like I was drafting Richard Petty in the Daytona 500. Everything was going perfect, the new stereo was pouring out tunes, and all was good on planet earth. Then, in the blink of an eye, the big rig's right mud flap and metal frame attaching it to the back of his trailer broke off. In a hail of unbelievable sparks, it hit right in front us, then proceeded to ricochet under

What was I Thinking?
Wrecking in the Astro Dome

121

us. It sounded like we were crashing a 747 and as it careened, ripped and slammed its way from the front of the van to the rear of the trailer. In the mean time, we had blown a rear tire out and I was all over the road trying to keep all of us alive. Finally after a few daunting seconds, I slowed and pulled onto the shoulder, as close to the guard rail as I could. But we were still very close to passing rigs on the interstate.

Irv quickly said, "Boy, Hayes you did a hell of a job. We better see what the damage is before one of those big sons a bitches runs over us."

Of course, by now, my mom jumped up in a total panic and I told her just to sit tight.

Irv and I quickly jumped out into the thunder storm. Right away we saw two blown tires, one on the van and one on the trailer. But that was the least of our worries. The mud flap had also knocked a hole in our gas tank about the size if a quarter. Gas was spewing out at a pretty good clip; we had to fill that hole in a hurry before all our gas ran out. My dad was just waking up and Irv yelled out, "Big Hayes, don't light no damn cigarette, you'll blow all of our asses up."

I remembered we had a few pieces of bubble gum up in the van so me and mom began chewing that stuff like crazy and sticking it in the puncture. Irv found a big half-inch bolt in a parts box, and rammed that baby into the hole with all that bubble gum sealed up around it. It did the trick.

But we were still in a hell of a mess. As we tried to fix the flats, those big 18 wheelers were about to blow us off the shoulder every time one of them zoomed by. One damn near ran over Irv's feet which were protruding from under the van within inches of the road. When Ole Irv felt the rush of the eighteen wheeler barely miss his feet, he quickly jerked them back …and banged his head on the undercarriage of the van.

"You damn #x%# truckers," he yelled, "you don't have no courtesy a-tall."

Finally, after about a hour, we got that baby fixed and headed on down the road. We were soaked to the bone. It was the second near miss of the night and I was wondering if we needed to turn around and head back home. Something just didn't feel right about this trip. It was almost like it was doomed from the start. If we had left on time, we would have missed the rain storm and the flying mud flap. But what the hell, we had a race to run!

FRIDAY 10:45 AM

Racing in the Astro Dome was going to be cool . . . fifty thousand people tomorrow night for the main event. Tonight, twenty thousand people for practice and some preliminary events, including some guy who was going to jump a bunch of cars on his motorcycle. While we unloaded our cars and rolled them down into the Dome, Mom and some other wives drove down the road to get us a motel room.

My car was fast as hell and I was elated at how everything was going. Maybe our luck was changing! However, with twenty minutes left in our test session, my engine blew up. In a split second, all of my hard work and effort had gone down the drain. To say I was disappointed would be an understatement but what are you going to do—that's racing.

Dad quickly came over to me and said, "I want you to drive my car."

What was I Thinking?
Wrecking in the Astro Dome

123

"No," I told him. "I'll just help you for the weekend."

I was young, so I'd have more opportunities to race in the Astro Dome, and he might not. But the uncanniness of my engine blowing, along with the other dark moments of the past 18 hours, did not pass me by.

Then, just as I put a tarp over my car to keep competitors from seeing some of my trick chassis engineering, a good friend, Gene Calvary from back home came over and asked me if I'd drive his car the next night.

"I'd love to drive your little rocket ship," I said. Screw the bad karma. His car was damn near as fast as mine. But we'd have to make a bunch of changes to the cockpit—I was 5'6" and weighed less than 120 pounds and he was over 6' tall and weighed at least 200 pounds, so we needed some padding for the seat. Practice was about to close in fifteen minutes so we had to get it going. We managed to find enough padding and foam rubber to get me comfortable in the car and I got in a few hot laps before the track closed down. One was the fastest lap of the test session—I was going to be hard to beat the next night.

Back at the motel, I could barely hold my eyes open—after all, I had virtually not slept for three days. I felt like I was catching a cold from standing out in the rain, and my gender issue was on my mind like crazy. Even though I was energized to be driving my friend's little racer the next night, down deep in my bones I had a bad feeling.

Dad, Irv and some other racing guys headed off to the bar to drink some beer and raise a little hell. I was not up for the fun that night so I sent that bunch of hard legs off to do some bench racing, and took a long hot shower. Mom was just as tired as I was, so she just ordered us room service and we settled in for the night. After our meal, I dozed off while laying worrying about my life. All while my mom massaged my back which was killing me.

Saturday morning, the wind was blowing and it was cold as hell. We all had to get out in the motel parking lot in that cold-ass wind and work on Dad's car. What the hell, I owed him, he had done everything on earth for me so I really didn't bitch too much. After three miserable hours, Dad and Irv and I finally got his little racer fixed. At around 3:00 that afternoon, I took a hot shower and we headed over to the Astro Dome to get our pit passes and practice around 5:00. Luckily, practice went like clockwork, and we had a few hours to kill before our main event.

So Mom and I cruised the Astro Dome for a while, ate some junk food and I looked over the race car, double checking everything one more time. I still felt eerie… like I was walking around outside my body.

"Are you all right?" Mom asked me a couple of times.

"I'm just fine," I told her.

Mom knew I could get a little pensive before I raced. As a racer, I was used to fighting through adversity and uneasy circumstances. This sport is the most unpredictable of any sport… it will challenge your will to stay in the game . . . it will kick your ass at every turn and if you take it for granted it will hurt you worse. Thirty years earlier it had come within a millisecond of killing my dad, and he still suffered from that stock car wreck down in Columbus, Mississippi. I knew this was my life. I loved it. I accepted its challenges and its dangers. But I was also fighting another battle just as dangerous and just as challenging. My entire identity was in question and it was eating at me like never before. When I got back home, I would need to get some help – my home town doctor maybe, who could help me find a way through.

*Here I set strapped in and ready for practice at
the Astro Dome Race*

8:00 PM . . . time to race.

The Astro Dome as packed. The National Anthem had been played and the fans were going crazy with anticipation. They love watching us crazy-ass drivers get out there and do battle just like we are gladiators back in the days of the Roman Empire. The hard-core fans love the competition, but the casual fans really like the wrecks, if the truth be known. Of coarse these little midget racers almost never disappoint them.

When the pit steward gave the word for drivers to get in our cars, I quickly slid down inside, slipped my helmet and gloves on, and got buckled in as tightly as I could. The car still did not fit me that well, but at the time it seemed good enough. Once I was ready to go, the push truck got behind me and gave me a shove out to the track. I took a few quick hot turns and then found my assigned place at the front of the pack and got ready. We made a few pace laps, and then the flag man waved the green flag and the race was on.

As the fans jumped to their feet and cheered, I immediately took the lead. I could win this thing! Heading out of Turn Two down the back straightaway, I hauled that little throttle rocket into the third turn, right up next to the wall at about 100 miles per hour. But in a split-second life changing moment, the steering mechanism broke and the damn car did not make the next turn. Instead it went straight forward, slamming head on into the concrete wall so hard that my body stretched almost twelve inches. My head hit the upper cross-member of the roll cage and the entire right side of my body careened against the cockpit of the car. The entire wreck seemed as if it had happened in slow motion but in a flash, I was right back to reality. From reflex I immediately tried to get out but realized that I was hurt.

Within seconds the emergency crew was there. I knew something was wrong with my right leg and ankle, and my neck and right hip were killing me. But at least I was alive. When they got me out, I laid flat on my back looking up at the ceiling and those huge lights beaming down into my eyes seemed foggy and far way. I felt like I was in a dream state, fighting like hell to stay awake and the paramedics were talking to me trying to get me to respond.

My mom was screaming like crazy. "My baby's hurt! Let me through!"

What was I Thinking?
Wrecking in the Astro Dome

127

I was glad to see her even if she was screaming like a wild woman. She had just sprinted a hundred yards to get to me, knocking everyone in her path out the way. In just a few more seconds my dad showed up, still wearing his racing helmet with the letters BIG HAYES painted on the front, and got Mom under control. He then leaned over me and in his cool and calm manner asked me, "Are you all right?"

I slowly nodded. "Yeah, I'm all right . . . yeah, but I think my ankle is broken . . . my hip feels weird too . . . "

Once again, in his usual calm way and with Irv looking over his shoulder and grinning like a big ole goober from Mississippi, he tried to assure me that I hadn't broken my ankle.

"If my ankle isn't broke," I said, "I've grown another foot . . . because, the one I'm looking at is turned completely sideways . . . kind of like me and him racing around a dirt track together."

The emergency crew cracked up when I said that. But I was starting to turn white as a sheet, possibly be going into shock. What I didn't know was, I had knocked a big gash out of my helmet and split my visor right in two when I hit my head on the roll cage. In all likelihood a head injury was involved. Getting me to the hospital in a hurry was imperative. When the ambulance finally got there, the paramedics gently loaded me into that red and white monster. Then, with Mom and the car-owner's wife Linda riding with me, we took off to the Texas Medical Center with the lights flashing like crazy.

About half way to the Hospital, I realized foggily that I had a bigger problem than my injuries. Under my driving suit, I was wearing women's underwear, and there were traces of red nail polish on my toenails. How was I going to explain that to the nurses and doctors. Or even worse, to my mom? I could just see the headlines: "RACE DRIVER DISCOVERED TO BE WEARING WOMEN'S UNDERPANTS, STORY ON PAGE FIVE."

Three hours later, the doctors thought I had a concussion and a possible head injury so they wouldn't give me anything for pain. I was living in a nightmare. I had known some physical pain in my life but this was different. My ankle was killing me, but my hip was causing me the most trouble—any little movement drove a knife into me. My mom and Linda were telling me to just hang on, assuring me that doctors would give me a painkiller as soon as they knew where my head injury was.

Linda, who was like a second mom to me, was crying and apologizing about the steering breaking. Through the pain, I told her it wasn't their fault, just a racing accident. As for Mom, her cup was half empty, as usual. She loved me like crazy but she will always see the worst in anything. So she leaned over and told me that I would never be able to walk the same after this.

The head nurse overheard this and hustled Mom out of my little cubicle, telling her to never tell me or anyone anything like that ever again. I could tell that it hurt my mom's feelings—she was just scared and trying to help in her own way. But I needed to hear that I was going to be as good as new!

Finally, at around 11:30 the head nurse gave me a shot of morphine which immediately began to subdue the pain. She told my mom that they were taking me up to ICU—that the surgeon wanted to do surgery on my ankle first thing the next morning and they would access my other injuries at that time. She said I must have had a dislocated hip but somehow it had

What was I Thinking?
Wrecking in the Astro Dome

129

gotten itself back in the socket but they were going to re x-ray me to find out. By then, that morphine had me going to sleep like a new born baby.

The next day I wake up about three in the afternoon. There was a cast on my right leg all the way up to the hip, and a neck brace around my neck, and a syringe without the needle taped to my chest. The night before I was wearing my driving uniform and women's underwear. Now they were gone. I wondered where in the hell they were . . . but I wasn't bringing the subject up.

For the next two weeks the Texas Medical Center was our home. Because of my asthma and frail lungs, I developed a touch of pneumonia and a fever. But finally I got well enough to be released, and we all headed back to Mississippi. Dad and Irv made a special bed in the back of the van, the doctors gave me some really good pain pills and we took off, back to our home and an uncertain future. Thank God, Ole Irv was down there with my parents to help us out. It had not passed me by that my guardian angels had sent him over our house the day we left. And thank God, no one ever mentioned the fact that I was wearing ladies undergarments when I wrecked. Thank God I was alive and would race again soon.

One thing was for sure though—as soon as I could get back on my feet, I was getting into counseling and I was going to figure out what to do about my gender quagmire. Clearly, I was one hell of a race car driver, and could design and build virtually anything, but down in the core of my soul, I was a girl, and every day that passed I came to know it more. I had a woman's heart and a woman' s desires for life, plus I looked like a girl almost from the top of my head to the bottom of my feet. I did not have a male's body, except for my reproductive biology, yet I had always wanted to race in the Indy 500.

AJ Foyt and Mario Andretti and of course my dad were my racing heroes but I also looked up to women like Cheryl Tiegs and Chris Evert. The racing accident had given me a wake up call, and I had to hear it!

By the time we got back to Corinth I knew it was going to take longer than I thought to get over this.

For the first two weeks I lived on my mom's and dad's couch, and all I did was sleep and throw up. Finally the local doctor gave me something for my nausea and after that I began to get better. Once I stopped sleeping all the time, my mind raced into building that new car. I had some new ideas that would make that baby really fast. My dad brought my drafting instruments and pins from his tool and die business so I could work on sketches. Within a few weeks I had the new car all worked out and talked my dad into ordering all the raw materials to build that baby once I was healthy enough to start building. I was just trying to fill up my time and keep my mind occupied.

In the meantime, all of my best buds, Nathan, Victor and Flat Top, had been coming by pretty regularly to check on me. My on again and off again girlfriend Stephanie had also been by a time or two, but I was at a point that girls really did not interest me that much.

Two months later, the second week of March, I got a shorter cast that only came up to my knee.

That same day, all my racing buds from Corinth were leaving to go to Daytona for Bike Week. My dad's best friend David McLemore had two sons, Dewayne and Dan, who owned the local Honda and Yamaha dealership in Corinth and Starkville along with Terry Vetrono, a bad-ass Cajon who played fullback for the Mississippi State Bull Dogs. They were loaded up and

What was I Thinking?
Wrecking in the Astro Dome

131

getting ready to leave the next day. Dewayne and Dan had a cousin, Dennis Mclemore, who was going too. Dennis was a good friend of mine—his family owned all of the Mclemore convince stores and grocery stores in Memphis. Dewayne's crazy live-in girlfriend Nell was going too.

Dan and Dennis wanted me to go to Daytona with the group – they said they would look after me on the trip. However Dewayne and Nell clearly did not want me dragging along stinking up their good time. Well, when I found out that they did not want me to go, I was hell-bent on going. I loved Dan like a brother but Dewayne and I rubbed each other the wrong way. He was too cocky. To add fuel to the fire, we were racing rivals and he always had a hard time beating me, so he tried to needle me all the damn time trying to get under my skin. So I packed my suitcase, drove over to the Honda dealership where the motor home was ready and we all took off to Daytona.

I was still very fragile and weak, and my mom had pitched a fit about my going, but I had been cooped up and needed a break!

When we got down to Daytona we found a place to park the motor home at Orange Park. The other guys unloaded the motorcycles and we all took off for the beach with me riding on the back of a brand new 750 Honda with Dan driving. He did not like Dewayne's needling me all the time, and he really did not like Dewayne's girl friend Nell.

The next day everyone wanted to go to Disney World for the day. Dewayne and Nell were bitching about how much trouble I was going to be, that I would just hold every one up. But my buddy Dan and Dennis said, that once we got there, they would get me a wheel chair and push me around. Well, once we got there, we found out that any one in a wheelchair and their group got to go to the front of any line at the park. Dewayne and Nell became my new best friends . . . it wasn't long before ole Dewayne himself was pushing me along. Needless to say I milked it to the bone. For the rest of the trip I managed to hold my own, steadily regaining some of my strength and confidence and I never once held any one up.

Back home, I got busy building the new race car. I was still on crutches, but that didn't hold me back. My goal was, get the second cast off in three months. The midget nationals would be coming up the first of July in North Carolina and I intended on being there. Over the next three months I went to races around the area with my dad, but mostly I would sit on the floor of my race shop and weld on that baby, or sit in a chair and make all the parts. Little by little, I managed to get that yellow and blue racer built and by the middle of June the cast came off. Just a few more parts and the car would be ready to test.

My gender issue was driving me crazy ... by immersing myself in getting that car built I had neglected my personal happiness. In all reality, I knew deep in my heart that once I started confronting the issue with total honesty all hell was going to break loose.

The weekend the cast came off, I was itching to take a few laps in my dad's car. I was hanging around the pit area at a race right outside of Corinth helping my dad fuel his car up and shooting the bull with friends. I was still hobbling around on crutches and my ankle was very tender. I had no business driving a race car. But that night, after the main event I hunted down Gene Calvary, the guy I was driving for down in Texas when I got injured. He was just getting ready to load his car up, and asked me if I could take it for a few laps just to see how I could do.

What was I Thinking?
Wrecking in the Astro Dome

133

He had a new young buck by the name of Bobby Davis Jr. driving for him and he was pretty damn fast. I liked Little Bobby and had no problem with him, he was actually a really nice kid. However, he and his dads posse were a bunch of braggers and Gene and I both had had enough of them putting everybody down, including how Little Bobby could kick my ass on the track. So when Calvary pitched me his helmet, I immediately slapped that puppy on and gingerly slid down into his racer. He and my dad quickly pushed me out to the track, the push vehicle got behind me, gave me a shove and I was on my way.

I took it pretty slow for a few laps, just to get my right foot to feel the gas pedal, and then I turned that baby loose. I had my ego up pretty good and I was hammer down Gene was standing right off of the first turn wall holding a stop watch and timing every lap I ran. Little Bobby's posse were gathered along the front stretch wall watching in absolute anticipation what I was about to do. Which in my mind was to give them a driving lesson. After about ten laps, as I flashed by him, he held up his hand signaling to run one more lap and then pull it in. I ran that lap virtually wide-ass open and then pulled back into the pits. My dad and Gene had a big smile on their faces and all of little Bobby's posse were not smiling at all, which put a smile on my face. It seems that I had driven around that little dirt oval three tenths of a second faster than Bobby had all night.

Suddenly everybody ran for the hills. Even my dad left me sitting inside the car unable to get out. My mom had just shown up and she was pissed off big time. She had my crutches in her hands and she looked as if she was ready to take someone out with those aluminum weapons. There wasn't anything to do sit but there and take my beating.

So I said, "Mom, be nice to me, it's not my fault . . . Gene and dad made me do it!"

She lit into me anyway. "You just got your cast off, you could re- break that ankle in a flash! You and your daddy are going to be the death of me. I can't take this! You have no business driving that car; you don't even have your driving uniform on. What if you had turned that car over? You're just like your daddy . . . I just want to beat you up."

That's when she took my crutches and slung them as far as she could, and then turned around and stormed away. There was total silence throughout that racing facility. Not a bad-ass redneck in the joint was willing to cross my mom.

By the time we got back home that night, she was over it. And it was worth every threat that I'd heard from her. I had conquered the beast that had hurt me back in January and I had given Little Bobby and his posse a driving lesson.

Three days before we were scheduled to head to the Nationals, I took my car to the track a few times to work the bugs out of it. When it came time to go, I had that yellow and blue racer hauling the mail. All my pain and suffering and sacrifice looked as if it was going to pay off. So Dad, Mom and I hit the road . . . pimento cheese, fried chicken and a cooler full of beer for my dad. There would be no stopping for beer until we got to North Carolina. Mom was not taking any chances on this trip.

At the races, I set fast time and a new track record. Dewayne Mclemore, my arch rival, qualified twenty-fifth. I felt really good about that!

That night after qualifying, my dad got smashed as hell. When some guy told him that I had done a hell of a job by taking the pole, he responded by saying in a drunken slur, "Yeah, he may not be good for nothing else but he can build and drive a race car . . . that's all he's good for, driving race cars."

When I heard that, it tore my heart out. I knew he was drunk, but I had been a pretty good kid, had not gotten into much trouble at all. I did a lot of things well, not just racing. I had always worked, in fact all through high school I had held down two and some times three jobs at a time when none of my friends worked at all. I had excelled at my racing and I had just braved my way through six months of extreme pain. What the hell was going on in his head to talk about me like that? There sat Dewayne, who had been a womanizer, got a girl pregnant and had to marry her, drank like a fish and treated me like shit, but my dad thought Dewayne hung the moon. Give me a break.

Later on that night, at the waffle shop just across the parking lot from our motel, Mom and I and one of our best friends Randy and my surrogate brother Larry Roberts were having a bite of late-night breakfast. Dad was over in the motel room passed out from drinking too much, and Mom and I were pissed off about it. The restaurant was packed with racers from all over America and most of them had come by our table and congratulated me on my new track record and fast time for the event. It was nice to get all those pats on my back but the one person I really wanted to be there enjoying the moment with me was my dad. After a while I just couldn't take it any more and rushed outside to the parking lot and began to weep.

Ten seconds later Larry came outside to console me because he knew full well what I was feeling. He had seen my dad's drinking get worse in the past few years and this was not the first time I had felt slighted. Dad had treated me virtually the same way when I won the Karting Grand National Championships in Memphis. He was not a bad man, in fact, he was an exceptional human being but now, he had become a full-blown alcoholic and it was killing me. In fact, one night about a month after my accident, when he'd had too much to drink, he had dropped me when he was trying to help me get into the house one night. That had scared the hell out of all of us, especially him, and he had eased off on drinking since then but now, it was catching up to him again.

"Your dad does love you," Larry insisted over and over.

After a few minutes of pep talk, I managed to get myself back together and we headed on back to the motel. Tomorrow I hoped that everything would somehow get back to normal.

The next night, during the 100-lap National Championship main event, I took off from my number one starting position and grabbed a commanding lead for the first twenty-five laps. The car was fast as lighting and I had virtually lapped the entire field but taking the victory was not in the cards. On the twenty-sixth lap my engine broke its crank shaft and I was finished for the night. It was very disappointing to not win, but I was back and I was better than ever. In fact, I actually thought I was a better driver than before the accident, smoother yet more aggressive.

Dad came over as I was getting out of the car and gave me a pat on my back.

"I'm proud of you," he said. "You did a hell of a job coming back like this." That pat on the back and words of encouragement meant more to me than winning that damn race.

The next day, we got in our Dodge van and headed back to Mississippi.

What was I Thinking?
Wrecking in the Astro Dome

137

I had high hopes for the remainder of the year but I was not completely focused on my racing. The gender issue was always lurking in the corner, ready to pounce at any moment. I dreamed about being a girl every night; the need to be feminine was stronger than ever and that was on my mind the entire trip home. Getting into counseling as soon as possible would now become my number one priority.

When we got back to Corinth, I unloaded my new race car and rolled her in the race shop without even washing the dirt off.

Three weeks later, I had found a new psychologist in Memphis and already seen him twice. I was dressing up as Terri and doing everything possible not to get seen that way by my parents and the rednecks in Corinth. However, I had found out that I could go over to Memphis and hang out at the malls and no one had a clue that the cute and skinny brunette was actually a boy. I looked so much like a girl that it was even amazing me. But even though I was glad to be finally expressing and embracing my femininity, I felt like I was on a desert island with it. It's one thing to talk to your doctor but I was dying for a friend who could share in my feminine life.

Susan was a girl in town that I knew—a raving beauty and the girlfriend of one of my racing buds. She and I were all ways ribbing each another about something. I felt a strong connection to her. After thinking about it for a few weeks, I was sure she would understand—she had a good heart and wasn't a gossip.

So, one afternoon around 4:00 I finally got the courage to call her up and ask her if I could talk to her about something that I needed some help on figuring out what to do about it. She immediately told me to come on over and we would drink a beer and talk about it. When I got to her apartment, I was so damn nervous that my hands were trembling.

We plopped down on the sofa. She handed me a beer and said, "Terry, I know what you want to talk about. I know you want to be a girl!"

I was stunned, amazed.

"How did you firkin' know that?" I burst out. "What in the hell tipped you off to my situation?"

She told me that she had always suspected that I was gay or something, but the more she got to know me she realized that it was more complicated than that.

"Just look at you," she said. "You're a girl. Your face, your little ole curvy body. Your hands are so small I don't know how you hold onto the steering wheel. Mother Nature really fixed you right up, didn't she? What are you going to do about it? Don't your parents have a clue?"

I told her that my parents were aware to a point but they did not really know just how serious this really was. If they found out what I really wanted, which was to have sex realignment surgery, it would take them over the edge. Then it dawned on me that if she had suspected I wanted to be a girl, who else had? Especially some of the guys we both ran around with and, I ask her that very question.

"Hell, no," she said. "The guys don't have a clue."

She did mention that Jack, her good looking macho boy friend, had made the comment that I had a cute girl's butt.

But people were not looking for it, because I was such a good racer.

It was a relief to have some one like Susan I could at least be open with about all of this. She let me come over to her place and get all dolled up, even laying out in her back yard in a bikini catching a sun tan. I kept it tight though, I was real darn care full not to get caught by any one there in Corinth. Finally having the opportunity to express my femininity with a lot more flexibility helped to calm my nerves just a bit but I knew there would soon come a day when I would need more than just catching some rays in a bikini and cute little hair cut to get me through my life. Then just to complicate my life even more, My old flame Stephanie came creeping back into my life, and this time we seemed to be more attached to one another than ever before. I guess I was just trying to hold on for a while longer to my old life, the need to fit in and to please my parents, jut to be normal. So by that fall, Stephanie and I had heated up our relationship to a fever pitch but I was also enthralled in my gender quest as well. I had a double life going on like never before, it as just a matter of time before this would blow up in my face.

CHAPTER 5

March 1982 – The chase

My life was spiraling out control . . . and I could feel the walls closing in on me.

All winter, as I worked at rebuilding my racecar, I was working on another plan—the plan to change my sex, if you want to call it that. I was looking for a doctor who would fix my sex, which I considered to be very badly broken. To me it was just a matter of a scientific adjustment to my already feminine body. But most everyone else was not going to see it in a scientific manner. They were going to take a hard-core and ugly view, and that was what was scaring me!

Thursday evening . . . 6:00 pm . . . once again, I was playing Russian roulette with my life there in Corinth and with my parents, and with my girl friend Stephanie. I had begun to express my feminine side more and more—getting all dolled up and riding around out on the county roads or cruising over to Memphis to the mall to shop. I was being very careful to not slip up and have my parents find my girl stuff like they had in the Seventies, I had a secret hiding place down in my race shop and behind the seat in my truck. I even had my schedule planned to the last second so I could avoid being seen by my parents or the fine citizens of my home town. My dad always took about an hour nap after supper, then went back down to his tool and die business to work a few more hours. So I figured out that when he was napping, I could slip down to the tool and die shop and get dolled up and head out, and no one would know. The back of the shop was facing a back street so I could park there and no one could see me as I cruised away to my little two hour drive to heaven. I had been doing it for a few months. But sometimes you get lazy and complacent because it's working for you.

So that Thursday evening right after supper, I headed off to the tool and die shop to continue my weekly routine. When I got there, I unlocked the front door and went inside, straight to the big sliding back door and slid it back just enough to squeeze through. Then I walked back out the front door, locked it behind me, and drove it around the building and parked behind a bunch of used machines dad was storing there. Then I slipped through the back door and went inside. But before I started my beauty transition, I walked back up to the front door and padlocked it just to make sure that someone with a key—several employees had them—didn't walk in on me while I was getting my girl face on. Then I headed to the bathroom and proceeded to get into the Terri Zone. On that night it was a cute little baby blue sundress and a pair of Bass sandals I had purchased only the day before—I couldn't wait to get them on and cruise off to Memphis.

I was just about finished putting my make-up on when I heard a faint thud at the front of the shop. It wasn't a loud thud but because my senses were at a heightened level—because I was living in the danger zone and my racing skills were always on alert—the thud got my attention. I walked halfway to the front of the shop to check every thing out. I had to be careful wearing those sandals though because of all of the metal slivers and machinery scattered all along the floor, which could slice open my bare toes in a flash.

Suddenly there was a huge bang on the door. Someone was trying to get in but because I had the door pad locked from the inside they couldn't get the darn thing open. Immediately I made a mad dash for the rest room to get all of my stuff and get the hell out of there. Just as I stuffed everything inside my back pack I heard a huge crash and the sound of breaking glass. Someone, most likely my dad, had broken in through the office window and was headed my way. He would be drinking and if he caught me in drag he just might shoot my ass with that .38 he kept in his van up under the dash.

So I sprinted out the back door, high stepping and dodging milling machines, scrap metal and unfinished saw mill parts sitting out on the back loading dock. Slinging my backpack into the truck bed, I virtually dove into the driver's seat like the Dukes of Hazard, shoved the key into the ignition and slung gravel for 50 yards as I backed that baby out to the street. Then, as I put her into 1st fear, I looked in my rear view mirror and was horrified to see my dad peeling around the corner in his big Dodge van with tires squealing. He had fire in his eyes and liquor in his belly, and was hell bent on catching whoever had been in his shop.

I took off as fast as I could, towards the highway, but he was right on my tail pipes. The race of the century was on. It could have been a scene right out of the Steve McQueen blockbuster movie "Bullitt." But this high-speed car chase was on the streets of Corinth, Mississippi and, instead of a tricked out Mustang and Dodge Charger, this one was between a big ole Dodge van and a yellow Nissan pickup with a little bitty person dressed up in a baby blue sundress. We were weaving in and out of traffic as we hauled ass down Highway 72, 90 miles per hour right through the middle of Corinth and my dad was right on my tail. My dad's damn van had a 400 cubic inch engine so my little Nissan pick up was not going to out run that big piece of iron. So if I wanted to escape, I had to take evasive action. Plus, if we didn't watch out, the cops were going to catch both of us and that would be the worst thing that could ever happen. I could just see the headlines the next day in the *Daily*

Corinthian . . . "Father and son caught in a dramatic car chase through the streets of Corinth, the son was wearing a dress and the father was driving under the influence of alcohol . . . entire family dies from embarrassment."

So when we were approaching the last red light before heading out of town, I made the decision to try and escape out into the county where the roads were tight and twisty . . . my road racing skills and my little yellow truck would give me the advantage. At the light, I hung an out-of-control right on two wheels, crossed over to the other lane and damn near into the ditch, then kept on mojoing down the wrong side of the road for at least a hundred feet before I could get back into the right lane. Meantime I flipped off my headlights, so Dad couldn't see me heading out in to the county.

He completely missed the turn. By the time he got his ride turned around, I was long gone!

My hands were shaking and I was on the verge of bursting into tears. For the moment, I was safe. But eventually I would have to go home and face him.

For the rest of that night I rode around on the back roads of Corinth . . Towards morning, with no sleep, I finally conjured up the courage to go home. But to be safe and avoid a confrontation, I waited until my dad went to work. That day, I didn't go to work down at the tool and die business, I just stayed there at my race shop and worked on my race car.

That, afternoon, when dad got home from work, he never said a word to me about the night before. Not one word about the car chase or shop fiasco. Not even a dirty look.

That night, he and mom took off to the Elks Lodge and me and my girlfriend Stephanie socialized with our friends there in Corinth. Just like nothing had ever happened. But the clock was ticking. It was going to be either suicide or altering my sex.

I have to confront Mother Nature

It was May 1982. My girlfriend Stephanie and I had been driving one another crazy for four years and now, it looked as if we were finally going to get hitched.

For the 10th time she had finally left her myopic husband, whom she only married for security and to please her dad, but this time she actually filed for a divorce and we were on go to get married as soon as the divorce was final. Our love seemed doomed from the beginning, but we came to the conclusion that we would end up together even if it meant her over-religious dad might hate and reject us. What should have been a joyous time had turned out to be a gut-wrenching affair for me. I was realizing that my gender issue would never go away. I was a woman to the core of my being, both emotionally and physically. If I didn't do something about it, I could wreck Stephanie's life. She had a five-year-old kid and a husband who actually loved her. I wanted to be a girl and a wife, not a husband. Somehow I had to back out of my commitment to her.

It took a few weeks of driving myself crazy about how I was going to break the bad news to her, but finally I got a desperate plan together that I hoped would let Stephanie down easy and help me move forward with transition and surgery. To do this, I had to get out of Corinth if I didn't want my parents to get humiliated and myself maybe killed by all those rednecks.

By the first of May, I had found an apartment and a job over in Memphis. But I had no extra cash flow to get my sex realignment under way. Psychologist, surgery, clothes . . . all the girl stuff was going to take some serious cash. So I decided to sell my midget racer, the one I had set a new track record with at the National Championship only the year before. It was worth at least five or six thousand dollars but the engine belonged to my dad. So I quickly found a guy in Memphis who wanted get in the racing business, He bought my yellow and blue jewel without the engine, and within a week I was living in Memphis and beginning my transition.

My parents and Stephanie thought I had moved over there to work for a tool and die company. I was finding it hard to get up the courage to tell Stephanie. But I did make a fatal mistake by coming clean with my three best buds, Victor, Nathan and Flat Top . . . something I regret to this day. At the time, I felt like I could confide in them – they were open minded and I felt they would keep the secret. If I got into trouble over all of this I would need them to lean on. I told Victor first because he was a biology major from Ole Miss and, he would know more about the biological implications, plus he was the most open minded. I told him to tell Nathan and Flat Top but please, please not to tell any one else. Victor assured me that the secret would be kept.

Now, I had to tell Stephanie. That day was a Tuesday, the night after Memorial Day weekend. I got in from work at the tool and die company some time around 5:30 p.m. She was at home. Her soon-to-be-ex was out of the house and off on a month long training program for his new employer Xerox. The time had come to give her the news, but suddenly I couldn't face her so I decided to call her and do the dirty business over the phone. Looking back I could kick myself for not looking her in the eye when I told her but at the time I was scared out of my mind. I was giving up my only true love and I knew once I told her I could never return.

So around 7·00 I finally mustered up the courage to call her.

"Hi, baby it's me," I said. "Are you there by yourself"

In a voice as sweet as an angel's she said, "Well, yes, you know I am. Are you coming over? I'm starved. Let's go get a bite to eat."

There was a long silence on my end, and then I mustered up the courage.

"No," I said. "We need to talk over a little problem before we see one another. I have something really important to tell you. Do you have a bottle of merlot opened? If you don't you might do that before I go any further."

"Damn it, JT," she burst out. "What are you up to? You better not be backing out on me. What is going on with you… why can't you come over here?"

"Well, baby, I've got a little issue I need to take care of before I can see you. I've had something going on in my life ever since I was three years old and if I don't take care of it right now I don't think I can survive the summer. It has nothing to do with anything you've done, and I don't know how to tell you except, just to tell you. Ever since I can remember I've felt like and wanted to be like you, in other words, uh . . . I've always wanted to be a girl . . . In fact, if you're honest you will have to admit that I actually look like a girl all except for some of my male biology. I can't live like this any longer, and that I can't drag you into the chaos. You have a kid, for God's sake, and he doesn't deserve to have a step dad who is always hiding something. You know, we're actually like a couple of lesbians instead of being like a man and a woman."

Now there was an even longer silence on the other end of the line. For a moment I thought Stephanie had hung up on me.

Finally she said, "But you're a race car driver and a very good lover. I don't care if you're small and a little feminine, you're still cute as hell and when you have that small mustache you look very masculine, I don't understand...you better not be messing with me. If you are, it's not funny. This is scaring me. . . I'm in love with you, I always have been. Please tell me you're kidding me."

"All those things are true, but I'm not messing with you here...I wouldn't do that to you. I'm being honest with you here. It's better to break our relationship off right now before we go too far and I really mess your life up. Please forgive me, but this is all for the best."

We continued to banter back and forth for almost an hour. I have to give her a lot of credit—even though she was extremely hurt, she was actually very calm. That was Stephanie's nature anyway, so I didn't expect her to go off on emotional rampage. However, I could tell that she was not happy about the little bombshell I had thrown into her lap. If she could get her hands on me she probably would break my neck.

Anyway, we agreed to get together in a few days to break some bread and really get into my gender issue. She said that she wanted to know about everything I would be going through, that she actually wanted to help me get through this if she could.

When I hung up the phone, I was appalled. Not only had I broken up with my only true love but I also told her that I was going to have a sex change. This was the craziest thing I had ever done in my life, and the nightmare was just beginning . . . now I was going to have to tell my parents! The reality slammed me to the ground in a sense of absolute lonely ness. For most of that night, my emotions flowed from my eyes.

Fathers Day, 1982

With the wisdom of a piss ant and the hope of a fool, I thought I would go back down to Corinth and see my folks on Fathers Day weekend.

Basically, my intention was to get them up to speed on my life changing plans, and of course to see my dad on Fathers Day. If I got there in time, I could go to the races with him at the local dirt track right outside of Corinth. I needed a racing fix and who knew, dad might want me to drive his car. It just might turn out to be a pleasant weekend, if he wasn't drinking too much. So I decided to slip into town as quickly and quietly as possible, and then get back over to Memphis without too many people seeing me.

Unfortunately I looked a little bit different than when I left. Not only had I lost a lot of weight but I had been taking hormones for almost three months, so I had a nice little feminine glow about me. Even without makeup, I now looked like a skinny girl. So when I put on just a wee bit of eye liner and lipstick on and fluffed up my little shag hair cut, I could pass for Pat Benatar without any trouble. In fact the first time I walked into the gay club in Memphis, everyone there thought I was a lipstick lesbian. It took some convincing to make them believe that I was a boy and wanted to be a girl. All those lesbian girls were hitting on me which was flattering and gave me a lot of confidence about how I looked, but I wasn't interested in hooking up with a chick.

It was around 2:00 in the afternoon when I got to Corinth. I was low on gas, so I stopped at the Dixon brothers' service station. Dixon's was a place where my family had done business for twenty years. Bill, the younger brother, rushed out to wait on me but instead of carrying on with me with a few jokes and asking me about my racing, he was very formal and almost patronizing. His attitude confounded me for a few moments.

Then all of a sudden he leaned into my window and blurted, "Damn, Terry, is that you? I thought it was your girl friend. Are you all right? You're not sick or nothing, are you?"

Holy shit . . . did I look that different? I was caught off guard by what Bill had said and it made me wonder if I should actually go to my mom and dad's. For almost an hour I drove all around Corinth, trying to get up some courage. After all, it wasn't like they hadn't had some clues for years – since I was a small child. Finally I reached deep into my stupid yet grand and hopeful illusion that my parents would deal with this "minor" adjustment in my life, and pulled into their driveway with my heart about to explode out of my chest. I wished I was on another planet . . . hell, I was, and that planet was Corinth.

I quietly tapped on the back door and slowly walked into the kitchen. To my surprise, my mom was standing right there. I could tell by the look on her face that she was not a happy camper. She immediately put her finger up to her mouth to signal me to be quiet and pointed over to my dad who was sleeping on the couch. Then she motioned me to go next door to my grandparents' house and she would meet me there. I got the feeling that they probably already knew. Who had told them?

Granny met me at the door, and gave me a hug.

"Let me fix you something to eat," she said. "How about a BLT, it won't take me any time to fix you something. You've got to eat, you're just too skinny . . . I'm worried about you, are you all right?"

I nodded.

"Your mom and dad know what you're up to," she went on. "Jim is really mad at you."

"How do they know, I mean . . . who told them? There is no way they can know."

Granny looked me right in the eye and said, "Dewayne McLemore told your dad. But I have to tell you, it's all over town. Your mom even heard it down at the factory."

Holy crap, I couldn't believe what I was hearing. The whole damn booger eaten' town thinks I'm a silly little fag. I'm screwed. I will never be able to show my face here again. I couldn't believe someone ratted out on me . . . who would do that?

When my mom came charging through the door, she lit into me just like I knew she would. "Are you really crazy? We've spent all that money on your doctors and you told that last doctor you were cured and that you would never do this again. You better not let you dad see you, there is no telling what he will do. You need to get on back over to Memphis . . . don't let anyone see you looking like this!"

Granny finally told Mom to sit down and cool off, that this shouting wasn't helping anything. I hadn't said a single word yet, but Mom was pushing my buttons like she always did. I did not want to say something I would regret later on. After about five minutes, we began to try and communicate. Granny had my sandwich ready and I dove into that thing like I hadn't eaten in a week. But after two bites, the back door slammed open and my dad blasted into the house with a look of a killer in his eyes. He was drunk and so pissed off that I actually feared for my life . . . he always carried a little .22 caliber handgun in his pocket and from the look on his face I figured he was angry enough to use it.

He lunged for me but he was too drunk to catch me. I wanted to run but he was standing between me and the door. So I just stood there frightened out of my mind.

"Get the hell out of here," he roared. "I never want to see you again…God hates you, you might as well be dead. Here, take all my money and never come back!" He slammed his wallet on the kitchen counter. Then, he glared at Granny and my mom and shouted, "It's your entire fault that he's the way he is."

Then Granny stepped between us and yelled at my dad herself.

"Jim, this is not your house, and if you don't leave I'm going to call the police. Now get on out of here, and leave Terry alone. He can't help this and you know it, so leave him alone. You're saying things you don't mean." Suddenly, as if an angel had come into the room and grabbed him by the back of his neck, Dad seemed to calm down. With tears running down his face he just turned around and left.

I was shaking so hard I couldn't stand, and just fell to my knees and began to weep. By this time Granny was bawling her eyes out and to our surprise Mom was crying too. This was the worst thing that had ever happened to us . . . my dad and my mom had just ripped my heart out, and I knew I had broken theirs. How could I have been so stupid to think this would turn out any other way than it had.

"Dad's right, I might as well be dead!" I screamed out.

Then I ran out the back door, jumped into my truck and sped off. I was virtually hyperventilating, and tears were rolling down my face so badly I could barely see but I never looked back. I just stood on the gas and got the hell out of there. Who had told them? I wanted to kill Dewayne McLemore; but how had he found out? This was Corinth, Mississippi, not New York City; there was no place to hide. I was famous; everyone knew me and my parents. These fine Southerners were not going to accept my change in any shape, form or fashion.

I managed to get out to highway 72 without running into anyone and headed back over to Memphis. For the first thirty miles I continued to run all of the chaos through my mind. Then I barely missed having a head-on collision with a car in the east-bound lane. The close call scared the hell out of me so I quickly pulled off to the right side of the road, fell over into the seat and cried for a while in safety. When it started to get dark, I realized I had better get the heck out of there before some macho good old boy Tennessee state trooper found me sitting there.

So I drove on into Memphis like a crazy person, back to my apartment, and called Stephanie to tell her what had happened. I had to talk to someone. This was a very sad day for me, and for my parents . . . our lives had taken a dramatic and profoundly ugly turn.

Thank God Stephanie was home. She told me to get myself over there as fast as possible. She was alone and said she had a bottle of merlot opened. I didn't drink much but she was right, I need a good stiff drink.

I have to give Stephanie a lot of credit—she was really concerned and she didn't have to be. But once I got over to her house she tried to tell me that in a few months it would all die down and my folks would come around. That night, she held me close, caressed my neck and let me cry like a child who was lost in the wilderness; I could not have made it through without her compassion.

Over the next three weeks, she and I repeated that scene over and over and over. I was crying for hours at a time, she crying with me. I was cleansing my soul . . . relieving twenty years of stress over my gender issue, chronic asthma, racing, my mom's controlling and volatile personality, my dad's alcoholism. I had walked away from my best girl, lost my parents' love, didn't have a race car to drive, my reputation was toast in my home town, and I had no idea where I would go from there.

Stephanie was actually impressed with how naturally feminine I was. She said I looked like Marlo Thomas instead of Pat Benatar, which was all right with me. In fact I was comfortable being Terri around her, which really surprised me because she had been my main squeeze for almost four years.

The macho deal was totally thrown out the window. Her seeing me in a little peasant dress and a pair of sandals took care of that. But a little spark was still there. We both felt it, and it scared the hell out of both of us.

One night during the week, she and I planned to cook dinner at her place. I picked up a bottle of wine and paid a little more attention to my make up than usual, as if we were on a date or something. I was feeling weird about the emotions I was feeling. When I walked into her kitchen and she put a huge passionate kiss right on my lips, I knew we were in big trouble. Hell fire, I wanted to be a girl, not kissing and hugging on one. Stephanie told me I was an awesome kisser, which made me wonder how she actually knew how a girl kissed.

Anyway, dinner and candlelight and the wine took me and Stephanie directly into the bedroom! That night was amazing; we made love as two women. There was no intercourse, only passion and caressing, only warm sultry enduring kissing and holding each other like we had never held one another before. It was the most incredible sexual experience of my life—my entire body melted into the softness.

But the next day I didn't quite know what to think, and wondered if she was trying to convince me not to go through with the realignment surgery. Even though I had thoroughly enjoyed the experience, I knew I wasn't going back for a return engagement. We needed to be friends, not lesbian lovers.

CHAPTER 6

Now What ... Living as a Girl – First Time

I hadn't found a job and was two weeks late on my rent. Stephanie's husband, Bob, came home and they had reconciled. She was covering her bases and I totally understood the situation so I stayed away.

Meanwhile I had found some new friends at Georgie's, the biggest gay bar in Memphis. The first time I graced the front door of that fine dancing establishment everyone in there thought I was a lipstick lesbian and it took some mighty big persuading to convince them I was actually part of the gender identity family. But, I finally did, and palled up with a couple of the female impersonators, Michelle and Veronica, who were drop dead gorgeous.

I had also been blindsided by a tall curly-haired drink of water by the name of Mike. The first night I walked in there, he had spun me around and pulled up my dress and said, "Lesbians don't need to be wearing dresses in here, it's too easy for girls to get to your privates."

Damn, that was bold, I thought. So I told him my story right off and he and I became buds. It was good to meet people who never made any type of a judgment call on you whatsoever. They were in the same boat as me—their families had rejected them as well.

But I was not altogether comfortable being there. That environment was just a wee bit different from the ones around Corinth and out on the racing circuit. I had never been a big partier and this bunch lived to party. It definitely was not Juniors, a hard-core road house in Guys, Tennessee about five miles from my mom and dad's. Up at Juniors, if you didn't have a gun, they gave you one when you came in. Juniors had hard-core bikers and certified Lynyrd Skynyrd types jamming to the best damn Southern rock in America and the men almost never danced. Georgie's played disco and techno and, all the men danced . . . with each other!

I had not been home since that crazy day at my grannie's, but I was feeling the itch to maybe mosey on back down there over the weekend. It would be my birthday on the 29th of July, and my mom's two days before and my grannies two days afterwards. Which was way too many Leos in one city block to ever work out. I figured I could at least slip into Grannie's without my dad knowing and have a visit with her. I missed her, and I figured she missed me too. I also figured my mom was calming down and there might be a small possibility that I could see her as well.

Meanwhile I needed money fast. I hadn't eaten but one meal a day (one Krystal with cheese $.72, a small fry $.49, water no charge . . . result, skinny ass person) for a solid week. Plus I needed gas money to get to Corinth. So I was job-surfing big time. But I looked like a girl, walked like a girl, and my ID read James Terry Hayes, male. That was a problem. So I asked my new bud Mike if he knew of any one in the gay community that could help me out with a job, real fast.

"Why don't you do a drag show like Michele and Veronica?" he suggested. "They make five hundred a week in tips."

That seemed mighty tempting, but not for me.

"Hellfire," I said, "I'm a National Champion race car driver, I can't perform in a drag show. Plus I don't want to be a drag queen or a female impersonator . . . I want to be a girl."

"Okay, so TGI Fridays down on Madison Avenue is hiring bussers and waiters. I've got a lesbian friend that works there. She might be able to get you on."

I went right over and put my application in. The very next morning Fridays called me back and told me to come to work as a bus boy that afternoon. At the end of the night, all the waiters and bus boys split their tips, which meant I had some cold hard cash. Even though my poor ankle that I had broken at the Astro Dome was killing me, I made a beeline to the Exxon station down the street to put some gas in my little truck.

However, when I got to work the next morning, my supervisor came back to the time clock and asked me to come into her office.

"What's up?" I asked.

"Well, Terry, I've heard some very disturbing information about you. Someone told me you're a drag queen and that you do a drag show over at the gay bar. This is a family restaurant and we can't have that here. I'm sorry but you need to go on your way."

I told her that whoever told her that was a big damn liar. No matter, she was done with me, so I told her to go to hell and stormed out the back entrance mad as hell. A family place, my ass. There were kids in there sitting right next to the bar with men and women getting hammered and they fired me over a unprovable rumor which was a lie, plus 90% of the people working there were gay because I had seen them at the club. Most likely, one of those assholes ratted me out without having the facts.

I was so pissed off that I got into my truck and drove around the mid-town area for a hour. Just like clockwork, the depression began to set in. I had just crossed Perkins Road when I began to tremble and shake. Not wanting to have a wreck, I quickly pulled into a small shopping and office parking lot. Jumping out, I leaned up against the right front fender and tried to catch my breath. Was I having an asthma attack? It took a few minutes to pull back the tears and regain my composure but I finally got back in my truck before someone saw me acting like a crazy person and called the cops.

How was I going to pay my rent and car payment? In four days, it would be my birth day. If things didn't change I might not make it to see another one.

So I sucked it up—drove down to Corinth and went to Granny's house. Granny fixed me a quick bite to eat, and then I headed over to Hotel Hell #1, which was Nathan's, Victor's and Flat Top's house. I had not seen or talked to them since I had left in May almost three months ago, so they didn't have a clue about the journey I had been on.

They were actually glad to see me.

Victor said, "Hazer, where in the hell have you been? We all thought you were dead. Ha, ha, ha . . . well, you sure look like a girl. Matter of fact, it I didn't know you I would be asking you out. Damn, you look stressed out, are you all right?"

Tears started welling deep down, but I was damned and determined to not cry in front of those guys so I choked the tears back.

"I'd go out with you too, if I didn't know your nasty reputation," I shot back.

Victor laughed his ass off and then looked me right in the eye.

"Well, Hayes, you're big news here in Corinth. I mean big news! Everybody knows what you're doing. It ain't good, but you know all of us love ya. Ole Flat Top is a little sideways over all of this but he will come around. But I have to tell ya, those boys up at Lake Hill Motors, Dewayne particularly, they are really fanning the fires. Dewayne can't tell people fast enough. I had words with him over you last week but there ain't nothing you can do about it. Whipping his ass ain't gonna stop the damage he has already done."

Dewayne, one of my dad's best friends, was a scrappy 5' 10" 175-pound country boy whose family owned the motorcycle dealership in Corinth and he hated my guts. His claim to fame was that he was a bonafide kamikaze flat-track motorcycle racer who now raced midgets on the Southern circuit along with me. He was the most arrogant human being I had ever met. He was always bragging about how good he was and I hated that with every ounce of my soul. He was my racing nemesis, an all- around prick. So now he and his womanizing gang up at his speed shop where I bought my racing supplies were adding fuel to the fire of rumor and gossip about me every chance they got. I was heartsick over those guys having fun at my expense and I could just imagine what people were saying. This was not Soho or the Sunset Strip. This was booger-eatin' moron redneck Corinth . . . the land that time forgot.

For a few hours, I hung out there at Hotel Hell #1 drinking a few beers and giving Vic all the gory details of the last three months.

Back at Grannie's, Mom came over, and I told them enough details for them to realize I was in trouble. The ordeal with my dad never came up, but that was typical of our family…we never talked about the tough stuff. The weekend was very uneventful—we made homemade ice cream and ate birthday cake and never discussed my situation again until Sunday night when my mom told me she wanted me to move back home where she and granny could look after me.

"You can stay with your grandmother," she said, "and we can get you back up on your feet. Your dad will be all right. It will take him a while but he will come around. You just can't prance around town like a girl; you can't do that in Corinth. But we will get through this."

I didn't know if I could endure the humiliation. People in Corinth were going to be mean to me. But I had to find a solution to my financial needs. In fact, I was so depressed that I could barely get out of bed, let along find a job. Through all of the damn drama, one thing had remained constant. My passion to be female had never wavered. It was who I was and it was my destiny, I felt it deep within my soul. Giving that up just might drive me over the edge.

Only one solution…at least at the moment

I needed to talk to someone who knew both me and my dad, so I decided on Larry Roberts, my surrogate brother and one of my dad's oldest friends. He, and several other of my dad's buds, had practically raised me and he knew my dad as good as anyone. It would be hard facing him with all of these rumors swirling around but I had to talk to someone with a clear head, and I trusted his judgment.

Larry owned an engine machine shop just down the highway. I parked my truck in front of the big garage door and went inside. It wasn't even 9 a.m. yet, but the temperature was already about 90 degrees and the humidity was so thick you could cut it with a knife. I never sweated but on this day I was sweating like crazy, emotionally and literally. There was this huge fan setting in the back of the shop, and that baby was blowing so hard that when I walked in front of it, it damn near blew me down and really messed up my hair which had grown down to my shoulders. I quickly fluffed it back into place and stuck my head in his office to let him know I had come in to see him.

Larry was on the phone but motioned for me to wait just outside on an old bus seat. When he finished up his call, he came out, and there was a look of utter disgust on his face.

"You need to get your act together," he said right away looking me dead in the eye. "This girl thing you're doing is a bunch of nonsense. You've hurt you parents and they don't deserve that. Your dad loves you more than life and you need to stop all of this stuff, and get back to racing and working at your dad's shop. You're too talented to be doing all of this. Look at you; you don't weigh a hundred pounds. If you come home and do what your dad wants you to do you can have anything you want. He would give you anything! You're his son. You need to act like it!"

I had just got reamed out like I've never been reamed out before. I sat there in total shock wondering what else he was going to say to make me feel like shit.

Larry seemed taken back to see tears falling off my cheeks. Then he sat down beside me and gave me a quick hug.

"You need to go down to your dad's shop and talk to him right now. He will talk to you. He wants you to get it together. He will forgive you if you do what I say. Now, go on... get out here and be responsible."

That was not what I'd been expecting to hear. His eyes told me that he was pissed. He had my dad's best interest at heart, not mine. He thought he was looking after me but he didn't have a clue about what I was going through since I was three years old. But he was right! If I did all the things he told me to do, my dad would forgive me, I would get a new race car to drive, and I would inherit his successful business. I would also be selling my soul to the devil. But Larry didn't know that. He was a product of this piss hole of a town, Corinth, Mississippi. Gender issues didn't happen here and they damn sure didn't happen to Jim Hayes and his buds. No matter what those damn biology books said, they weren't having any part of it. At the moment I might as well have been Darwin telling everyone we all came from monkeys.

For 17 years people had been picking on me for being small and feminine. They had been telling me to suck it up all of my life. In reality I had been tougher than all those Corinthian bubba boos could ever be, and I was the only one from here to become a National Champion at anything, let alone motorsports. I wasn't that little five-year-old kid any longer, the one who slept across their laps when we traveled to the races. I was a human being who had grown up, and I didn't need tough love, I needed some educated understanding and help. Screw him!

All that being said, the cold hard facts were what they were. So I went to Memphis and hauled my stuff back to Corinth. Next time, I'd make damn sure that no one knew what I was up to.

These people are mean to me!

After about a month, my dad finally began to take me back into his good graces. I went to work at my dad's tool and die shop as much as possible. He and I started going back to the races and I was running the car I had wrecked in the Astro Dome. Gene Calvary, the guy who owned the car, had never rejected me and was actually pissed off at everyone for running my name through the wringer. The car was pretty fast so we had won a race or two but the rumors and the stares were almost unbearable.

You would have thought I had the bubonic plague or worse, and Dewayne was on my ass like crazy. He would make it a point to call me a sissy or a girl-boy right in front of someone. The irony in this entire riff with Dewayne was, he and I had been buds until just a year ago. Even though we were competitive on the track, socially we had been friends. Back when I was in middle school and he was a senior, he had protected me from bullies who were always pushing me around because I was so small and feminine. Almost every day during lunch break, he went to battle for me. But now he had turned out to be the bully.

Another guy getting at me whenever he could was one of Dewayne's employees, Jacky, a 22-year old stud muffin motorcycle mechanic and part time disco DJ at the local dance hall. One afternoon he pulled me aside and said to me, "Hey man, I can't believe you want to be a chick. . . you're a racer man, not some silly ass girl. Girls are dumb and stupid . . . they're frikin' flakes, they're supposed to be making babies and cleaning house . . . and taking care of their man . . . you're crazy if you do this. You're throwing you life away."

A lot of good ole boys were hanging in there with ole Jacky. One guy owned an auto-parts store there in Corinth. Whenever I went into his store to place an order he would say, "What can I get you, mama . . . uh sir?"

The entire gang of bubbas who worked there would laugh like crazy when he did that.

To make matters worse, the bank had repoed my truck and I was driving an old puke-green beat-up Chevy truck that dad used to deliver equipment with down at his tool and die business. I hated being seen in it but felt fortunate to have any type of transportation at the time. I knew I had been financially irresponsible, but when you look back on it, my dad could have prevented the repo from happening by making my payments and taking it out of my paycheck down at the shop.

Worst of all, I was clearly suffering from a hard course of depression and very close to killing myself almost daily. So just getting up in the morning was hard to do. Getting up and going down to the machine shop to work for my dad was even harder—even though all my dad's employees were a good bunch of guys, they still had a hard time not teasing me. At home, there was some tough love going on and I was its focus.

I had never liked doing machine work, even though I had become an excellent designer and machinist, and there wasn't any one within 300 miles who could weld aluminum as well as I could. Dad always had me stuck back there welding up something. I made pretty good money but my heart was not in it and I always wondered why he wouldn't allow me to be more involved with the business end of the company. I had excellent organizational and communication skills and could have helped him develop the business side of the company, but he was hell-bent on having me back there in the shop. That was very frustrating for me but no one else in Corinth was going to give me a job.

So it was what it was, and welding was putting money in my pocket.

By Christmas my mom had gotten me to move back into my old bedroom at their house so she could keep an eye on me and prevent Granny from driving both of us crazy. Granny was the greatest but she was a neat freak and wanted everything just right. I honestly don't know how my grand dad put up with her obsessive neatness at times, but he just handled her with kid gloves and got through her compulsive behavior with style and grace. Even though I was a neat freak too, I wasn't in the same universe with Granny. Plus I was young and pushy and that didn't particularly mesh with the lifestyle of a 70-year-old woman and an 80-year-old man. Granny and I loved one another, but next door was close enough. So it was best that I moved back into my old bedroom.

On Friday nights I started the routine of slipping over to Memphis every chance I got to see my friend Michael and the girls at Georgie's . . . and to be Terri. By now, I had come into my own with the feminine appearance—I was small and petite and had this Marlo Thomas thing going on. Every time I stopped at a gas station or restaurant, guys were hitting on me and I liked it. Then on Saturdays, my routine was racing midget cars. What an oxymoron that was.

Meanwhile I was halfway done building myself a new midget. It was going to be fast. I had figured out some new engine secrets, and my rear suspension system was innovative which would give the car some real traction in the corners. I would have her ready by March and the upcoming racing season. I fully intended to come back with a vengeance and pound the hell out of Dewayne in every race.

Early that January, during the middle of the week, I was in our bathroom with the door locked, taking a bubble bath and just relaxing, reading a Cosmo magazine and shaving my legs. So far I had managed to keep my feminine side hidden from my parents... or so I thought. It was around 8:00 and Mom was in the kitchen making a chocolate cake. Dad was in his recliner watching television and drinking beer. When I had gone into the bathroom he was already drunk. I had been in there for about an hour and had almost fallen off to sleep when there was a huge thump on the bathroom door. Dad was banging like hell and yelling at me.

"Terry, get out here! I know what you're doing in there, you're being a girl. I'm not having that under my roof, I'm not having you embarrass me any more. I hate you for what your doing! I'm getting my gun and I'm going to kill you. I'm going to kill your little smart ass . . . get out here."

I freaked out out. When he was that drunk and that out of control, he could do any thing. He would kill me and mom and himself if I didn't get the hell out of there. I was buck-ass naked and dripping wet but there was no time to be indecisive.

I just grabbed my robe and slung it around my waist and burst out of the bathroom door and hauled it back to my room. Dad was right on my ass—he had his .22 caliber pistol and was waving it in the air.

In my room, I tried to grab a pair of jeans but he came up behind me and tried to hit me in the head with the butt of the gun. I quickly spun around and pushed him to the ground. He was so drunk that he couldn't fight me. Thank God, he fell over between the bed and the wall and couldn't get up which gave me the opportunity to escape his rage. So I jerked my jeans on a fast as I could, grabbed a shirt and hightailed it out the back door and up to Grannie's.

Once I was safely at Grannie's I worried about my mom. She was still down there with my dad and I knew he was just mad enough to take a shot at her. I wanted her to get the hell out of there before he really went crazy. Finally she popped in Grannie's back door, frightened and white as a sheet over what had just transpired. My granddad was so pissed off at my dad that he was going to call the cops but my mom assured him that we would sleep there that night and let my dad cool down. Once he was sober, he was a different person; we would be able to deal with him tomorrow.

The next morning, I knew I had to get out of there, no matter what sacrifices I had to make. So I decided to go back to Memphis and try and find a job. Hell fire, I could get a job working at any tool and die business or as draftsman or engineer. Victors girl friend Susan, who lived over in Memphis, and fortunately she said I could catch her couch while I was looking for a job. That afternoon I went to the local bank and begged the loan officer to please give me another chance to finance a truck.

To my absolute surprise he agreed, but he threatened to kill my sorry ass if I screwed up this time around. Then I drove to the GMC dealer and bought myself a new shiny white pickup truck.

By 5:00 my bags were packed and I headed out to Memphis.

A fresh start

It seemed like my luck was changing—after only a few days I found a job working as a draftsman for Phoenix Manufacturing, a fabricating company out on Mud Island. I have to tell you that it was quite nice to be out from under my family's thumb, and the thumb of Corinth. One of the owners, Ben was somewhat of a know-it-all prick, but he and I managed to get along fairly well. After about a month of living with Susan I made a deal to move in with my cousin Jim who had just moved into a two-bedroom apartment off Elvis Presley Boulevard. He needed a roommate to help with the bills and I needed a place to live . . . it was a perfect match, besides we liked each other. No problem! Or so I thought.

On the weekends, I went to Georgie's as Terri. Jim didn't care what I did, and he damn sure wasn't going to tell anyone what I was up to.

I missed working on my new race car though, and I was still reeling and hurt from that escapade with my dad's pistol. My cousin Jim told me that he knew what had pissed my dad off so much that night. Dewayne had seen me leaving town one Friday night dressed as Terri and he had told my dad. He had been fueling the fire, telling my dad that he should run me out of the house and straighten me out, and all of that bullshit had finally gotten to my dad. I might have figured Dewayne as the trouble maker. That son of a bitch lived in the biggest glass house of any one in Corinth but he didn't have any problem chunking rocks at me.

Things are changing

That March, we all got a big scare when my Granddad fell seriously ill with emphysema and pneumonia and almost died.

Granddad and I had always been big buddies. He would jump in the race truck with me at the drop of a hat and head out to the races. He loved going down the road to a race no matter where we were going he had always hung in there with me no matter what . . . he didn't understand all there was to know about this gender identity ordeal but he never rejected me and he never talked down to me. He and Granny were peace makers in our household and kept everyone focused on the bigger goal of love and family. If I had lost him during this time I don't know what I would have done. Back in Corinth a few times to see him, I found that the riff between me and Dad had calmed down enough for us to be civil with each another again.

Anyway, about a month of intensive care, Grandad pulled through. Everyone said a prayer of thanks and got on with their business, including me.

Back in Memphis, I could tell that things were changing at my job.

Our company was bidding on a huge contract to build the Fedex drop boxes that you see on street corners all around the world. We were working 12-hour days trying to re-design older boxes and build prototypes to present to the Fedex big wigs. My boss, Ben was high-strung and hard-headed, so he and I were butting heads on some design changes. He was constantly changing his approach and not making clear what he wanted me to re-draw or have the fabricators re-build. I was getting stressed out with his attitude plus Granddad's illness and the gender situation. I had been procrastinating on getting into counseling and those old emotions were creeping back up on me. The trips back to Corinth to check on Granddad had proven to be a humiliation fest every time I went there.

Early one morning I had gotten a jump on the work list, when Ben came into my office. He smarted off over a few screw-ups the fabricators had made and then stormed out of the room in a huff. I fell over my drawing table and began to weep. Then I felt a panic that someone would see me in this sorry condition, so I managed to regain my composure. That evening, right at six o'clock, he made his way back to the design area and I could tell that he had been drinking. His eyes were watery and glassed over, a look I had seen on my dad ever since I was 14.

Ben looked over the prints I had worked on for ten hours without a lunch break, then said, "These aren't right."

"What do you mean there not right?" I shot back. "These changes are exactly as per your notes, and your partner Lonnie and I made sure that they were right."

"It's your fault, you little fucker . . . I told you I didn't want that flange on the right hand side . . . I'm tired of fucking with you."

I stood up and got right in his face.

"You go to hell, you can make the next changes yourself, You're a frikin' drunk. No wonder you can't keep help back here in your engineering department. I quit."

I stormed out of the office and lit the tires up on my truck as I exited the parking lot.

Driving straight to the apartment, I picked up Cousin Jim and he and I went clubbing. I was so pissed off that I couldn't see straight. It would have been different if I had really screwed up. But I had been in the business since the day I was born, and knew I was a damn good engineer and design specialist. Putting up with more drunks was not something I was ready to do That night Jim and I went crazy. I wasn't a drinker but we hit every bar in town trying to drown my misfortunes. When we finally made it back to our apartment I proceeded to make wide-ass open laps around the parking lot. I was standing on the gas and sliding my new pickup around like I was driving my midget around a quarter mile dirt oval in a high speed slide. Jim was hanging out the right-side window hollering and acting like a real redneck. It was one of the dumbest things I had ever done, but I had to release the anger.

Once we finally made it into the apartment I thought I would show off my masculine side by challenging cousin Jim to a wrestling death match. Of course I only weighed 115 pounds soaking wet and he was 6'6" and weighted about 275 pounds. So I ended up crashed in the bedroom closet laughing my ass off.

The next morning, reality and a hangover set in. What was I doing to do now? If I didn't make my car payment the banker would run me out of town . . . having two cars repoed within one year was not an option.

Over the next three days I drove all over Memphis putting in job applications but no one was hiring, not even McDonalds. I needed to be Terri so badly that my whole body and soul was aching from the pressure. Jim had traveled down to Corinth for a few days to work for his dad's auto parts company, so I was alone in the apartment and feeling very depressed.

I had reached the point where I despised my maleness. Every part of my body was female except my reproductive areas and for almost fifteen years I had longed for them to be gone. I began to ponder the idea of mutilating myself. Just a few months back I had asked my hometown doctor about surgery to remove them. He, of course had refused and encouraged me to get into counseling as soon as possible . . . well duh!

That night, I was very restless and couldn't sleep, thinking about killing myself. At around three a.m. I had turned the television off and was listening to the stereo when "Your Lying Eyes" by the Eagles began to play. This was the third time this song had shown its face at such a dramatic moment in my life, the first being at a Kart race down in Georgia while doing an interview and the second when I was contemplating my future just before marrying my ex wife Jimmie. Now that damn song was pushing my buttons again. Before I knew it, I had retrieved a butcher knife from the kitchen and was sawing away. Blood was flowing out of my groin like a river. All I wanted to do was get rid of what I saw as causing all of my problems. I was so out of my head that I didn't even feel the pain.

Right in the heat of the mutilation I looked down and was shocked to see that the bed was soaked with my blood. The pain was more than I had bargained for. My whole body was trembling from the fear and even though I wanted to continue, something deep down inside of my soul told me not to do this, to wait and do it properly. "Don't be foolish, you're smarter than this . . . Stop, stop, stop . . . stop this foolishness, what are you doing, you're going to die right here if you don't stop!"

Suddenly it was if my guardian angel swept into the room and rescued me from all the demons. In a moment of panic, I dropped the knife and quickly stood up, trying to gain control of my emotions. I was bleeding like crazy, all over myself, the bed and the floor. In fact, I had cut a huge gash into my body and might bleed to death. I didn't have a clue how to fix the situation. Should I go to the emergency room at the hospital just around the corner? Surely having to explain this to doctors and nurses would bring on more questions, and I could end up in the psych ward and my parents would die from embarrassment. But I had to do something fast, so I quickly ran into the bathroom and grabbed a towel and applied pressure to the big gash. From the cabinet above the sink, I grabbed a bottle of rubbing alcohol and poured it over the wound… which caused me to almost pass out from the pain. Hopefully this would sterilize the wound from the obliviously non-sterile knife. I fumbled around looking for some sort of a bandage, and finally found a huge box of gauze pads and Bandaids. A few were big enough to cover the wound and adhere to my body. Fortunately for my stupid deranged ass, the cut had not quite broken through into my scrotum. If it had, I would surely have to go to the emergency room or even worse, I could have died.

Within the hour the sun began to shine through the bedroom window and I was in so much emotional and physical pain that my entire body was shaking with every breath I took. Fortunately, I had found one of cousin Jim's valiums which I knew he had hidden up under his mattress and it was beginning to take affect, which was allowing me to drift off to sleep and escape the pain and trauma.

I need my family

I hated to admit it to myself but I needed to go home . . . needed to get back into counseling and even though I hated how I was treated in Corinth, I needed to be around my closest friends and around my race car shop. So, I bit the bullet and leveled with my mom.

Just from the way I looked, my mom knew I was in serious trouble. She agreed to let me come home and made me promise to keep my girl stuff hidden from my dad. She said she would handle him in her own way in due time.

"Terry, he will come around if we don't push him," Mom said. "He is not drinking as much and hopefully I can get him to listen to reason. He knows this is not your fault, but Dewayne and his bunch just keep him stirred up all the time. I'm going to have a talk with Dewayne myself and tell him to leave us alone and mind his own business."

Thank you Jesus!

Back home in Corinth, I immediately immersed myself into further work on my new race car, and started working part time at my dad's tool and die shop. Dad agreed to let me subcontract jobs instead of me working for him directly. That was the best thing we had ever done with our working relationship, though as it turned out, it would have been better if I had worked for Dad full time instead of part time.

Fortunately, my self-induced wound had managed to heal up; after plenty of peroxide and alcohol, I was almost as good as new. I found a new psychologist over in Memphis, but I wasn't all together comfortable with this guy. He didn't like the fact that I drove race cars and worked in a machine shop. He wanted me to pursue a more feminine life style. Hell, *Cosmo* magazine was telling us to get out there and do whatever we wanted concerning jobs and life. I did continue to go over to Memphis to see all my friends and be Terri but this time, I would go over to Victor's house and get dolled up, and leave from there . . . I was making darn sure that my folks never caught a glimpse of what I was doing.

By the first of May, I had finished my new racer. The local newspaper had done an article about my racing, which was salt in Dewayne's face. That new car was fast as lighting, and I was racing every chance I got—down in Montgomery, Alabama, up in Nashville and in Corinth where Gene Calvary had built a super fast little dirt track that was a real blast to race on. So that was my life, and through it all I avoided any unnecessary contact with the fine citizens of Corinth.

Then I slipped up. I had ordered a new dress out of a JC Penny's catalog and when it came in, since none of us were at home, the delivery man just left the package on our back door step. My dad got home before I did and when he saw the package with ladies apparel on the outside invoice and my name on the label he was not happy. Once I got home, he brought the package down to the race shop and just dropped it on the hood of my race car and walked out without saying a word. I knew I was in trouble but at least he was not so drunk that he had lost his temper.

About a week went by and Dad had not uttered a word about the package. When I sheepishly asked him if he wanted to go down to Montgomery with me that coming Friday night to race our cars, he quickly snapped back, "I don't have time to go. I have to stay and work and make money so that you can go racing."

The racing and staying there at my race shop was helping me—I could almost bear not pursuing the need to live full time as a girl. But Dad just didn't get how difficult it was for me. He only knew that I was embarrassing him. I was always broke and just the week before I had asked him for fifty dollars so I could make my truck payment. He gave me the money and made me promise him that I would pay him back that next week. However, if I went down to race in Montgomery and he didn't go with me, I was going to need the money for gas. If I had stayed home more and worked with him at the tool and die business, I wouldn't be so broke, but I had felt that if I didn't race I would burst at the seams—it was the only place I had any peace from the drama of my life.

That week had been one of my worst in a while. A redneck construction worker who knew who I was frightened the crap out of me when he threatened to beat my ass after I accidentally bumped into him at the gas station. So I needed to get out of this hate pool for at least a day, and on Friday, I headed off to Montgomery all by myself. I had to get the hell out of town and away from those booger-eatin' morons before I went completely nuts. But, my dad didn't know that, he only knew I wasn't doing my job down at the tool and die business.

Be careful . . . it's all an illusion!

That night, at the main event in the races, their local racing hero Rick Baragrive and I were having a hell of a race. I had managed to get five car lengths on him and it looked like I was going to pull off the win and put a little cash in my pocket so I could pay my dad back. But suddenly my engine locked up and slid the rear tires, which almost caused me to crash big time. The rest of the racers who were hauling ass up behind me managed to barely avoid a big crash. That was it, I was finished for the night and hadn't made a dime, and I didn't have the cash to fix the engine once I got home. Damn!

That night, on the way back to Corinth, a zillion ideas ran through my mind on how I could scrape up the cash. There was another race the next night in Corinth, and I just had to be there!

The next morning at eight o'clock, after getting in from Alabama at daylight, I was in my race shop tearing my engine apart. It had a broken crankshaft, broken rods and pistons. I had some spare pistons but no crankshaft and the only place to get one around Corinth was up at Dewayne's. Shit! I wanted to race so badly that I humbled myself and called him up to make the deal.

At first he quickly and arrogantly said no, then told me, "If your dad will pick up the bill, you can come right on up."

I jumped into my truck and drove down to the tool and die shop. My dad was back in the welding department working on some sawmill parts that his chief fab man had screwed up the day before. I humbly told him my sorry tale and that if he would give Dewayne the green light, I could get the parts and have my car ready by race in time for that night. Unfortunately he was already drinking, so he was in a bad mood.

"I'm not going to help you," he said. "You better figure out how to get the parts on your own."

I needed at least a thousand bucks to fix the engine and there was no way I could raise the cash that quickly without his help. When I got back to the house, I hit my mom up for a loan but dad had already gotten to her and she wasn't helping either. The only thing I could do was get my ass down to the tool and die shop on Monday and earn some dough.

Monday morning 6:00 AM

Bright and early Monday morning I beat my dad down to his business and was going to work on those sawmill parts. Right before Dad got there one of his customers and good friend of his, Tommy, came in looking for my dad but spotted me in the welding department and made a beeline back there to talk to me.

At one time I had liked Tommy but he had chosen to humiliate me in public forums a few times. He wasn't as much of a redneck as Dewayne but he was a real smart ass. He had fire in his eyes and I knew it was going to get ugly.

"Hey sweetie," he said, "you look nice this bright and shiny morning. So tell me when you're going to stop embarrassing your folks and get the hell out of town, your old man doesn't deserve what you've put him through. You ain't nothing but a silly little fag. Look at you, you're a pitiful sight. You need to tighten up and be a man. Thank God you ain't my kid. I would have already beaten the crap out of you. I told your ole man he should kick your ass out of here. You don't belong here. Now, you have a nice day, sweetie."

I was embarrassed the worst I had ever been embarrassed in my life, and had to get the hell out of there so my dad's country-boy employees didn't see the tears rolling down my face. So I just took off running for the front door, and jumped in to my truck and sped off down the road. I didn't know where in the hell I was going but knew I couldn't stand one more day down at the tool and die business dealing with all of those good ole boys. The only thing I could think about was getting back to my race shop where it was safe. No one could hurt me there, that was my turf. Ironically, I met my dad at a stop sign only a few blocks from our house and he motioned for me to stop, but I just kept driving right on by. I wanted to be alone; I wanted to race my midget . . . most of all, I just wanted to be Terri. And I'd had enough of the tough love.

The last week of June, 1983 . . . One month later

Life is such a fickle blink of the eye, it will turn on you right in the midst of a Sunday drive and slam you to the ground with an unrelenting force of hurt and humility and hold you there begging for mercy with every beat of your heart. No matter what you do or how you persevere, it seems like there is only malice standing in front of you laughing at your foolish idealism, your trying to beat back the demons hell bent on destroying your life. Life challenges your faith, your belief in goodness and the American dream, which is supposed to be that you finally make it, you beat the odds, you even make a difference in other people's lives while we all live on this little round ball in the middle of a cosmic explosion.

One second, one moment in time, one conversation with one person or one event will change your life forever. It will leave you and your loved ones either joyous because of something wonderful or sad and broken because of a personal tragedy. Ultimately the one-second test of life belongs to you and you alone . . . for sure everyone gets their one second . . . what you do with it is up to you!

My dad was still pissed off at me, and I hadn't been back down to the tool and die shop since my confrontation with Tommy. He was drunker than ever, and according to the macho bull crap floating around this gossipy red neck community and it was my fault that he was so miserable, an alcoholic . . . a mean ass alcoholic.

My dad was the town's Clint Eastwood, the coolest and most macho man in Corinth, and even though we had been dealing with my gender issue since I was three years old, he had made up his mind that he was having no part of it, no matter the cause or reason. The peer pressure from the good ole boys in town was tearing him apart at the seams. He was trying to run a business in this environment and you know that could not have been easy. At the factories there in town where he did business, I was the talk of the break rooms and by now the gossip had gone to a new level of craziness. There were rumors that I had been working as a drag queen down in New Orleans, that I had been caught at a local rest stop having sex with tourist. I had no way of combating the venom as it continued to spew with every Sunday morning sunrise.

In addition, there was enough Monday-morning quarter backing and back seat driving about my life going on by all of Dad's friends to fill up every seat at the Indy 500, especially from his best running bud Dewayne. Dewayne and the bunch of redneck hard legs up at the local speed shop were my dad's drinking buddies, they all thought he was the greatest man of all time. He was their hero, and they were very protective of him.

So, my dad was making a point to me. Do the girl stuff and don't show up to work, then you don't get to race. Don't do the girl stuff and do show up to work, then I'll buy the parts for your car and we will go racing. The only thing wrong with that approach was that it wasn't working. I was sinking deeper and deeper into depression. The little escapade with Tommy down at my dad's shop had ripped my heart out and I was determined to not go back down there. It was all I could do to get up in the morning, I couldn't eat, and most of my friends were afraid to be seen with me. The only thing that gave me purpose and a safe place to hide – racing—was being kept from me.

Now, it was only one week until the Midget National Championships up in Charlotte, North Carolina and I couldn't believe we were not going. Back in 1980 I had been the big Kat Daddy at those races and of course, I missed going last year because I had sold the race car and was in the middle of this nervous-breakdown situation. Now here I was again. If I could only race, then I could fight my way through this mess, even regain my reputation and my dad's respect, and show those Southern redneck sons of bitches I "STEEL" had it in me to kick their sorry asses. But there didn't seem to be any way out now. Who was I kidding ... I was not even in shape emotionally or physically to drive a 100-lap midget race against the best drivers in the nation.

Monday morning, 9:30 AM . . . four days until the Nationals . . . I managed to get myself out of bed and out to the race shop only thirty feet behind our house. But I just sat there drinking a coke and starring at my car.

This was going to be a day of reckoning, I could feel it in my bones. My dad and I had a shouting match the night before over my inability to get to the machine shop and work. My mom was just as pissed off at me if not more as my dad was. This just might be the day to leave it all behind and let everyone else deal with earth school. It was obvious that I didn't seem to belong down here. Every step of my life had come at an emotional and physical cost, and now, my reputation had been crushed in a quagmire of right wing fundamentalism. All of my racing accomplishments, even my hard-won National Championship, was now looked on as unimportant. No one was worried about me, about the reasons why I felt and looked so feminine or why I was so depressed . . . everyone was worried about my mom and dad and how hurt they were. The amazing part was that I was worried about them too; it was breaking my heart that they were being humiliated.

After sitting there brooding and staring at my exotic racer for a while, I decide that I needed to wash that little H-bomb. The idea just popped into my head . . . I mean, how could I kill myself and have everyone think that I could possibly leave behind a dirty race car? My reputation for clean fast race cars was legend throughout the racing community, so leaving behind a dirty car would be completely out of character for Terry Hayes.

So I tried to summon the energy for this task—turned on the air compressor, aired up the tires and rolled the blue, white and yellow racer out of the shop. Then I rounded up a wash bucket, unrolled the water hose and began cleaning off the caked mud left from the race over a month ago where I had broken my engine. I even went over to the radio in the back of the shop and cranked up the volume to FM100, the hottest rock within two hundred miles, trying to create some positive energy. But the more I tried, the harder it became to control my depression. Little by little I began to weep as I tried to wash my racer. It seemed as if crying was all I had done for the past year, and here I was again, weeping uncontrollably on the last day of June 1982 at 10:30 in the morning, with no hope of surviving this earth mess.

As my knees began to buckle, I realized I was about to pass out from the anxiety. The midmorning heat was already up to 90 degrees and our sultry Southern humidity was so thick that you could cut it with a knife. The Mississippi sun was beating down on my back and all I could think about was getting back to my room, back to my bed and my sanctuary. It was only thirty feet to the back door but it might as well have been a one hundred mile trek. Yet I somehow stumbled through the house, falling on the kitchen floor, then knocking over a coffee table and one of my mom's lamps as I careened through the den.

In my room I fell into my bed, shaking and soaked form the heat and humidity. There were so many uncontrollable emotions rushing through my body that I thought I was on the verge of having an asthma attack. This was about the tenth time in the last year that I had come this close to passing out like this, from the anxiety. Losing it like that always scared the hell out of me every time it happened. But this time I was so far gone all I wanted to do was go to sleep forever. It was twenty years past time to do something about the insanity of my life. Time to let everyone off the hook and let them get back to normal. I had been a burden to everyone ever since I was born; they would be glad to get rid of me.

There was a loaded shotgun in my bedroom closet that belonged to my dad. I knew exactly where it was. In fact, I had opened that closet door more than once over the past year just to make sure it was there.

Now several daunting minutes passed as I lay there analyzing about how to kill myself. I could blow my head off . . . that would be instant and without pain. Or I could go and get one of my mom's butcher Knives, or one of my dad's special hand-made knives he kept hidden in a desk in the den next to my room. Then with a sense of calmness, it came to me. It would definitely be the butcher knife and a couple swipes of the wrist. This would be better for the family, not nearly as messy, God knows that would be important. Being tidy would definitely be easier for my mom.

Now, just as suddenly as the anxiety attack had rushed over me, a new rush of energy careened through my soul. My mind was clear and focused on the task at hand. Getting out of bed, I looked at myself in the mirror over my chest of drawers, picked up a tube of ruby-red lipstick, and starred back into the mirror as if to have one final look at what could have been if things had been different. Softly I applied the lipstick to my lips, then turned and walked to the kitchen, retrieved one of my mom's ten-inch-long butcher knives and calmly walked back to my room.

Without a second thought, I clicked the light off, pulled down the window shade, turned back the covers and laid down in my bed—the bed I had slept in since I was twelve years old. The bed where I had hidden my girl panties between the mattresses like a junkie hiding their drugs so that my mom couldn't find them. The bed where I had passed out while gasping for air from too many asthma attacks to count . . . where I and my goofy Beagle, Slick, had recuperated in after my nearly fatal racing crash down in Texas. This was where my sweet dreams of becoming a woman had played in my head night after night, year after year, where I had cried myself to sleep too many times to count. This was where I had dreamed about being normal and living life to the fullest. Now this was where I would die.

Bam!

Out of nowhere I heard a loud slam of the door, and feet rumbling across the floor. Someone had rushed into the house like they were on the way to a fire. In a flash there was a quick knock at my bedroom door and just as suddenly the door swung open. The light from the den rushed in as if the light of Jesus himself was entering the room. I was completely startled, almost frightened—only seconds before I had been prepared to end my life and now there was this brilliant light consuming the room. Just as quickly, as if I was dodging an out-of-control racer on the track, I jerked the butcher knife out of view under the covers and pulled the bedspread over my face trying to hide my painted lips.

"Terry, hey . . . are you in there?" It was my dad's voice. "If you want to, go up to the speed shop and get the parts you need to fix your car, I called up there and said I would pay for them . . . and, if you want to, we will get your car ready and go to the Nationals up in Charlotte and then go on down to Daytona Beach to the NASCAR races for vacation . . . you need to hurry if your going to have time to get ready to go."

Right out of nowhere, my dad had come home to check on me . . . to offer an olive branch of peace, to bring an astonishing piece of divine intervention. The odds against this occurring were a trillion to one. He never came home during the middle of the day. This cosmic intervention saved my life and obviously, there was more left for me to do on this earth.

Just as quickly as my dad had rushed into my room, he turned, walked away through the den, out the back door and headed back to work.

With the sun shining angelically through the den windows and beaming into my room, I lay there stunned by what had just happened to me.

One second, one moment, one conversation, one act of kindness, one tiny insignificant conversation in an insignificant part of the world had once again changed the course of a life . . . my destiny. Just when you think no one is thinking about you, no one is concerned about your well being, your Clarence, your guardian angel taps them on the shoulder, whispers in their ear and tells them that you're in serious trouble and that they should help you. My dad had felt the tap on his shoulder. . . thank God he paid attention! Blood is always thicker than water, even if it is diluted by alcohol. Dad had finally realized that Dewayne and Tommy and all those other chauvinistic bubbas in town were a bunch of fools. They were all driving a wedge between us for the sake of their own self-serving egos. He had had enough of the Terry bashing. I was his child, his flesh and blood, his one and only child! Once again Dad was attempting to fix the situation in the only way he knew how—to keep me racing.

Now the ball was in my court. I had to get my skinny ass out of bed, take off the lipstick and nail polish and go up to the speed shop. I had to endure the humiliation and trash talk I was sure to get and buy those race car parts . . . and go to the Nationals, and win! Now the ball was in my court.

And it was a whole new ball game now. For sure, when I went to the speed shop, Dewayne and his buddies ragged me unmercifully. But I kept my mouth shut, let it roll off me, bought the parts, and high tailed it out of there as fast as I could.

Back at my race shop, I got busy. With the radio blasting, I worked all night, drinking enough coffee to float a battleship and munching on my Mom's famous pimento-cheese sandwiches. Focused and angry, I tried not to think about what I had endured and escaped over the past year, and only thought about winning. At 3:00 AM I finished the repairs, rounded up my tools and spare parts and loaded everything onto the trailer. At four in the morning, I jumped into the van, plugged in my Marty Robbins tape.

As "El Paso" played on the stereo, my mom and dad, my grandmother and my granddad and me all headed out on our 12-hour trip up to Charlotte, North Carolina. Just like nothing had ever happened. Just like we had done for twenty years.

CHAPTER 7

Life is hard – Racing is easy

We drove all night and all day, only stopping for gas and coffee and rest room and let my grandparents stretch their legs. Completely worn out from the second all-niter in a row and buzzing from caffeine, I rolled us into Charlotte at around 6:00 PM. We found a motel fairly close to the speedway, went for a bite to eat and were bedded down by 9:30. Even though I was needing to sleep, I was reeling from the drive so it was past 3:00 AM before I slipped off to sleep.

At 8 a.m. the next morning, Dad and I headed to the track. We registered the car, passed technical inspection, warmed the engine up and headed for practice. Amazingly I was focused, driving smooth as silk and back in National Championship form within two laps on the high-banked dirt oval. It was clear to us and most of the other competitors timing our practice laps that I was the one to beat. I stayed calm all through practice and kept busy tinkering with my car. After a few more practice runs, we felt good about our chances for qualifying.

That's when Dad and I reached into our bag of speed secrets, made a few fine adjustments to the car and when it came my time to qualify, I set fast time of the event out of the eighty other high strung macho competitors. I only missed breaking the track record I had set there two years before with track conditions far less favorable for making good speed runs by only two one hundredths of a second. I out qualified my closest competitor by half a second. One half of a second measured over 100 laps meant that I could possibly be fifty seconds ahead of my nearest competition at the end of the race . . . if everything went perfectly. Reality being what it is, we knew the word perfect did not exist in auto racing. We were confident that we could win the prestigious event but I knew and my dad knew we had to pay attention to every single detail if I was to survive the 100-lap kamikaze run. I immediately got busy checking every single nut and bolt on the car knowing that detailed work would help me win and also keep my mind off the trauma of my life.

But, at ten that night, the night before the biggest race of the year I was still out there in the pit area, alone and working on my car. I had run out of anything to check but I continued looking for something to ensure my car would be fast, anything to make my car win, even just standing there and looking at the sleekness of the machine and contemplating my next nights run. Finally, my dad, who had left me out at the speedway and took the rest of the family out to dinner, returned to the track to get me to stop the madness.

He came up to me and said forcefully, "Look at what you're doing. You're obsessing over this. Put up your tools and let's get you some food and some sleep. You hardly slept the entire week. I swear, I would give anything to see what you could really do in a race car just once without you being exhausted before you ever start a damn race. You're already the best I ever seen drive anywhere . . . just think about what you could do if you had a little rest. Get your tail in the van and let's go!"

Reluctantly, I did what he said. Needless to say, I slept like a baby.

8:00 Saturday night . . . time to race

The tension floating around in the air always has everyone on edge. This is dangerous work, not some tennis match and a cup of tea at Wimbledon. These little midget racers are H-bombs looking to explode at any second . . . these are man-eating machines, metal sharks, and they're being driven by a group of guys whose egos are so far out of control that Napoleon himself would be afraid to take them on.

That night, thirty of these bombs are going to be thrown together to create a nuclear explosion that could quite possibly suck the atmosphere right out of the sky.

On pit road, there was a group of about ten people that Dad and I knew from all over America. They were hanging around my car and nervously chitchatting about everything from Ronald Regan to A.J. Foyt. But I was staying quiet and focused, sitting on the right front tire, not talking to anyone. My dad was standing right beside me and talking to everyone, because everybody loved him.

Five minutes and counting. I'm waiting to the last minute to get in my car—a ritual of mine I had picked up from my dad when he was the bad boy on the block up in Nashville at Ewing Lane Speedway.

Then the race director made his last call to buckle in. Immediately, as if in a panic, there was a flurry of pit-lane activity as drivers finished strapping in. Crew members checked over the cars one last time. Wives and girlfriends kissed their road warriors good luck.

Then the pre- race hoopla and driver introductions were over, and it was time to go.

I calmly reached down to put on the brace protecting the fragile ankle crushed in the Astro Dome, and slipped my driving shoe on over the brace. Then I strapped on the red-white-and-blue helmet with my name emblazoned on the side. Finally I slipped down into my tiny racer, which was specially built to hug my petite body, as if I was slipping into a form- fitting fighter jet, and buckled the seat belts so tightly that I could hardly breath. A split second later, the local minister prayed to God to look over all of us as we fought for the win, the local high school band played the Star Spangled Banner and the crowd roared with patriotism and defiance.

Then there was that silence, that millisecond of time when your emotions rush out the top of your head, anticipating the most famous words in racing.

"Gentlemen, start your engines!"

With absolute clarity and calmness, I reached up to the on-off switch to cranked the volatile racer's engine. As the push-off truck came up behind me to nudge me onto the speedway, my dad tapped me on top of the helmet with a expression of manly love, and gave me a thumbs up. He and I both were in our element, competitive and geared for the battle as the super- charged race fans and my mom cheered at the top of their lungs, anticipating the start of this violent ballet set in a middle-American dirt fest. The track announcer had them worked into a frenzy of adrenalin. They knew that we would not let them down! This would be a hell of a race and crown a new National Champion!

Down on the track, during our warm-up laps, I never looked over at the driver starting beside me on the front row. I was focused on my job and refused to let him know that he was important to me. I only looked straight ahead and anticipated the start.

In the blink of an eye, the green flag waved.

The cars accelerated with the thrust of a Saturn Five rocket blasting us all toward the moon and into a 100 lap orbit around a quarter-mile meteor- battered dirt planet, that felt like it would explode with every turn the out-of- control throttle jocks would take.

Right away I took the lead and never looked back . . . me, in the exotic blue-white-and-yellow racer I had built from scratch with my two bare hands in the race shop 30 feet behind my folks' house. This was personal. I drove with a pace that was unattainable for the rest of the field, and led for 80 of the 100 laps, lapping most of the drivers...before breaking part of my drive line and ultimately finishing a disappointing fourth place.

But it had been a hell of a race. Only four days before, I had been one second from killing myself. . . now I had come within twenty laps of once again becoming a National Champion in the most macho and dangerous sport on earth, all 5', 6" and 110 pounds of me! I had proved that I was clearly the class of the field.

My dad patted me on the back, my mom gave me a hug . . . and we got our trophy for finishing fourth in the nation.

Then we loaded the trailer and said our goodbyes to all our friends.

It was one in the morning as we pulled out of the speedway. I turned on the radio, and just like clockwork, prophetically, "Lyin' Eyes" by the Eagles was softly playing over the speakers. The inside of the van was dark and gloomy with only the dim lights from the dash providing any sort of light and I felt a prophetic and climatic sense of tragic reality flow through my body as I listened to that song. Once again that song and I had crossed paths, like they were old friends helping one another find comfort and solace in the midst of a world out of control. We were softly telling each another to find the courage to move on, to let our love and passion find our freedom . . . to stop the craziness, to be true to our hearts. That daunting and courageous journey had begun over a year ago and now, I knew I had to find the courage to move past the rejection and doubt . . . I knew I could not survive if I continued down the treacherous path I had just crawled down only days ago, my plan and my approach would have to change.

As I turned onto the highway, the glistening lights and haze of the racing arena and the excitement of the night faded into my rearview mirror and into the history books. Everyone bedded down for the six-hour drive down to Daytona. Like a hundred times before, Mom, Dad, Granddad and Granny trusted me with their lives.

For me, those six hours of listening to the Eagles and Joni Mitchell, while I mystically navigated our van through the night, was a time of soul searching and reflecting back on the last year, the last twenty years . . . my entire life. We didn't win that race, but we had somehow won in life. I didn't know what the future held for me and my parents, but I had learned how profound the effect of what one second could be on a life. The question was, could we survive the next time we were faced with that split-second crisis? Would we be too blinded by the hate and bigotry surrounding us to make the right decisions for our family?

The race of my life that was yet to come was going to be vicious, and the curves would be more dangerous than ever before.

We barely made it to Daytona in time for the 10:00 AM start of the NASCAR Firecracker 400. I pulled off to the side of the road outside the speedway, jumped out and took off to the grandstands like a crazy person to find our seats. Dad drove everyone else who were too tired to watch the race back to the hotel, then came on back out to the track to join me in the stands and enjoy the remainder of the race. We were wore-ass out but what the hell, it was NASCAR, baby, we had to do it!

By September, my life had normalized somewhat. Steve Clark, a cool guy from Memphis that I had met racing around the midget tracks in the Mid South, had shown up on our doorstep one late August afternoon and made me a deal that I couldn't refuse.

Steve was a Vietnam veteran and a paraplegic confined to a wheelchair. But he didn't let that get in the way of his passion for life, which happened to be dirt-track midget and sprint-car racing. I was surprised to see him pull up in our driveway, maneuver his wheelchair out of his van and roll down to the race shop. We shook hands and chitchatted for a few minutes, and I could tell he had something on his mind by the way he was quizzing me on what I wanted to do with my racing career. He probably had heard the rumors about me so I was concerned about where the conversation was going to end up.

Soon he asked me, "Where's your dad?" I could tell Steve really liked my dad just by the way he talked about him

"He's not home from work just yet," I said, "but I figure he'll pop in at any moment.

"Hey man, I would like to sponsor your midget and let's go racing all over the country. I've been watching you, and I believe you got what it takes to get to the big time. I want to be associated with a winner."

Not a word about my little gender issue.

I was dumfounded. Finally I said, "Wow…well, yeah that would be cool. What did you have in mind? I mean, how do you want to help us out with sponsorship? That would really help me and Dad out if I could get some traveling money."

Steve and I came to an agreement for him to pay for all the travel cost and the tire bill. Plus we would use his new enclosed trailer which would be a big luxury allowing us to be much more organized and look sharp too.

When Dad got home and heard the news, he and Steve shook hands. Dad was pretty happy to have someone else help out with the bills. There were quite a few big events out in the Midwest during September and October . . . if we were to win one of those damn things that could put some real money in your pocket and prestige on your resume.

By the first of October, we had been on the road almost every weekend and we were racking up some wins. At the end of the season, Mom, Dad, Steve and I traveled out to Kansas for a huge 100-lap Championship event. I set fast time out of about 150 of the fastest midget racers in the country. During the main event I had a hell of a battle with a couple of Oklahoma boys who were financed by their oil-rich sugar daddies. It looked as if I was going to beat those guys, or at least run a strong second. But at about 70 laps, my engine broke a crankshaft and I was on the sidelines.

Steve was a good guy and we loved being out on the road with him. It felt like he was part of the family. He and my dad, who Steve called Pop Hayes, got to be big buds and drinking pals, which didn't sit very well with me or Mom but I knew there wasn't a damn thing I could do about it.

After Kansas, once we got back home, I got busy making plans for the next season. I had designed two new midgets, one for myself and one for Dad, and had begun to build those babies as well as two more cars for a couple of guys I had met up in Kansas. These guys had seen how fast my car was and had called me up the very day we got home and placed orders. That allowed me to generate some good cash to live on and keep me from having to work for my dad, which I hated with all my soul.

All that time, I was just barely managing to keep the gender thing under control.

Well, maybe not!

Building those new cars had turned out to be more work than I had bargained for. There are just so many hours in a day and I was using all of them trying to make the delivery dates for the Kansas guys as well as Dad's and my cars in time for a big regional event up in Nashville at the end of March. Not only was I feeling the pressure both physically and emotionally but the gender crunch was coming on again.

I was doing everything under the sun to keep my femininity out of sight. Since the first of August I had avoided going over to Memphis. I had been wearing men's boxers for underwear, cut my shoulder-length hair up over my ears (which totally broke my heart),—even tried to grow a beard. But I had received enough electrolysis that my little ole beard, which was never that much anyway, was now sparse and pitiful looking.

My best buds, Nathan, Victor and Flat Top, who were now living in Hotel Hell#2, were hanging in there with me and always trying to get me to go out on the town with them. But I stayed at home and in the shop. Dad and I were getting along pretty well because I was totally focused—or so it seemed—on my racing. Steve Clark and I were settled in with the same sponsorship arrangement for the next season, so the future looked exciting.

On a Saturday night, a couple of weeks before Christmas, most of my friends in Corinth, including Nathan, Victor and Flat Top, had rented a big cabin up at Pickwick Lake and there was going to be a big hoedown of a party all weekend. Flat Top had insisted that I should go.

"Hayes," he said, "you got to get back in the swing of things . . . hell fire you're a frikin' race car driver and you got to let all those good ole boys at this party know they can't intimidate you. You know I'm going to back you up. Let me worry about someone smarting off at you. Me and Nathan and Victor will look after you. Me and Doris [his good looking but crazy-ass girl friend] will pick you up at eight o'clock."

That was refreshing coming from him. Not so long ago he had made it a point to reject me, and only recently took me back into his good graces. He was the consummate mountain man and every chick in Corinth had chased him around the bedroom a time or two. So he had to grow into my situation—it was not as easy for him as it was for Nathan or Victor. So I felt honored that Flat was coming around.

After a few minutes of me hemming and hawing, I finally told him I would go. But instead of him picking me up, I would come by his house and we could ride up there in my truck. I figured that if anything went haywire up there, I could at least leave whenever I wanted to.

Saturday night, 8:45. We made it up to the cabin and, just as I thought the place was packed. There had to be at least 30 people there, and I knew every single one of them. In fact, I knew them all too well because most of them had made it a point to shun me over the last year. The whispers began the second I stepped through the door and it really pissed me off.

Doris dragged me over to the bar, stuck a cold beer in my other hand and told me to not let it get to me. She had always stuck up for me so the moment of reassurance calmed me down just a bit. For the next hour or so I kind of held my own, but no one wanted to talk to me or be around me. By ten thirty my three buds were off in another room playing their guitars and I was alone. I could feel a major anxiety attack coming on, and knew I had to get the hell out of there, so I went outside on the deck to get some fresh air and get a hold of myself.

The cold air seemed to clear my mind . . . the stars were out and the sky was as clear as a bell. A frosty mist sprayed from my mouth with every breath I took. Sitting down behind the stairs and gazed up at the stars pondering my fate. What am I doing here putting up with all this humiliation from a bunch of good ole boys who had never done a damn thing in their life except work at the factory, get drunk and chase redneck women around the dance floors at all the lowlife honkytonks around the Corinth area. I thought about what Flat Top had told me about being proud of whom I was. "Hayes, be a man and tell all those rednecks to kiss your ass." But I was having a hard time doing that. I just wanted to go home and go to sleep.

"Hayes . . . Hayes. Where are you?"

At some point, I could barely hear someone calling out my name. It seemed like I was dreaming but I soon realized that I was cold as hell and shivering like crazy.

"Hey, Doris, he's over here up under the steps . . . damn, Hayes, I've been looking all over for your ass. Are you all right? Let's get the heck out of here; it's one o' clock in the morning."

Flat Top was leaning over me, slapping me gently on the face. I had fallen asleep out there in 19-degree winter weather! It was lucky I didn't freeze to death. Flat Top threw me over his shoulders and hauled me off to the truck . . . put me on the passenger side, and he and Doris jumped into the driver side with him driving. As we hightailed it back to Corinth, they cranked up the heater trying to warm me up.

Doris gave me a hug and asked me if I was OK . I quietly nodded yes but I was about to lose my mind. As we drove on down the highway I slipped down into the floorboard, curled up in a fetal position with pitiful and eerie sounds flowing out of me, yelling uncontrollably, "Why me, oh please God, please help me . . . why are people so mean to me, can't they see, why can't they see that it's just me . . . I can't live like this, I can't live like this . . . please, please help me!"

For almost twenty minutes, Doris tried to help me get a hold of myself. I had burst at the seams . . . it had been almost five full months since my last emotional episode and almost that long since I had last expressed my femininity. Twenty years of the strain of trying to live up to everyone else's standards, to my dad's legacy, had caught up with me once again, right there in the floorboard of my truck… right there in front of my friends.

Flat Top and Doris were worried and acted like they didn't have a clue on what to do with me. Thank God, though, they managed to get me home and into my bed without my parents finding out.

It took me a week to get back to normal. I couldn't eat, talk sleep, and my work was definitely put on the back burner.

All I did was drive around alone on the country roads and think about what in the hell I was going to do with myself. Suicide was back on my mind again. Back in July, I had barely escaped with my life but this time I was actually putting methodical and deliberate thought into how and when I was going to kill myself. Something had to give and give ASAP. I had done everything I knew how to do, to repair my reputation with my friends and family . . . I was fighting with all of my might to fit in, to please everyone. I had tried to date the right girl, to wear the right clothes. I cut my hair which virtually killed my spirit, I tried to grow a beard in hopes that would make people see I was really trying to be a man. But they were rejecting me any way. I felt doomed.

By the next Friday night I had calmed down enough to not be completely suicidal. Dad and I were down in the shop and, I was working on the race cars I was building. Dad was warming himself by the heater in the back of the shop when we noticed that someone had pulled up in the driveway and was just sitting there with their lights on. We didn't pay much attention at first because someone was always coming over to the shop. But this vehicle was just sitting there.

Finally, Dad and I stuck our head out the door and realized that the vehicle was Steve Clark's van.

It wasn't that unusual for him to sit there for a few minutes because it took a little time to get the wheelchair out. But this time, when he saw us, he just blew the horn, so we walked over to see what he wanted. He had a big new trailer hooked up to the rear of the van, and there was a sprint car on the trailer!

Steve stuck his head out of the window and yelled at the top of his lungs.

"Little Hayes is going sprint car racing, by God! We're going big time, baby, and you're going to kick Sammy Swindell's ass."

Swindell was one of the nation's best sprint car drivers. Damn, this was unbelievable. This had been one of my biggest dreams!

Once more right at my weakest hour, God intervenes . . . he gives me a carrot and leaves it to me to make the best of the situation. What an opportunity! Men all over the country would give their left nut to drive a sprint car professionally. No pun intended but I would have given up both of mine without the blink of an eye, and I didn't even have to.

My dad was beaming from ear to ear because he knew that was something I had always talked about wanting to do. To top things off Steve wanted to leave the race car with us and let me begin to find out what made it tick.

So we unloaded that little red white and blue multi colored jewel with its big 800 horse-powered fuel-injected V8 up under the hood, and rolled her into the shop. Then Steve and Dad proceeded to get smashed drinking beer and vodka.

I just sat there silent and reflective, looking at that spectacular high-powered racing machine. My spirit was still reeling from the past week of depression and rejection, but I knew I had an opportunity to beat back the town's attitude if I could become a winner out there on the sprint-car circuit. Sprint cars are the most dangerous and macho thing anyone can do.

Becoming a winner on that circuit would prove I was a man to anyone. Hell, that's how AJ Foyt got his start.

However, it had not passed me by that since my private life had been exposed there in Corinth and had now filtered into the national racing scene; I had lost my benefit of the doubt. Before the past summer, I still had cache there in Corinth as being a kick ass race driver and the holder of my dad's legacy. Now, that all seemed to be gone, I wasn't getting that second chance there in Corinth, anything that I did was either criticize or just dismissed. My negatives went off the scale and my positives were not appreciated. If I made a mistake or was even perceived to have made a mistake it was if I had killed the pope. Whenever I excelled or made a positive move, it now seemed to be not good enough. That was very frustrating and little did I know, this was going to haunt me for the rest of my life.

CHAPTER 8

The Sprint Car Experience –
Fighting with Rattlesnakes

I spent the rest of the winter finishing the two customer cars up as well as the new cars I was building for myself and Dad—plus learning everything I could about sprint cars.

Steve had bought the car from Bobby Davis JR. over in Memphis who was now running on the World of Outlaws national tour. Little Bobby, as everyone called him, was being somewhat of a friend to me, and pretty helpful on what made that baby tick. I stayed busy down in my shop and never went out around Corinth.

By early March I had delivered the two customers' midgets and my new car was ready to go as well. I had barely finished it up in time to head out to that big midget race up in Nashville. I had already made a deal to sell the car to a local racer in Corinth after the race. I hated to sell that baby because I had built very special speed secrets into it and didn't want anyone to figure them out. But I couldn't pass up the money.

In Nashville I led for about fifty laps before the car began to run hot and in order to keep the engine from blowing, I had to back off. By the end of the 100-lap event I had fallen back to third. But it garnered a cool trophy and some cash; all in all it was a fairly good weekend.

Now, it was time to go big time sprint car racing . . . the season would start in three weeks over in Little Rock, Arkansas.

I was pumped . . . and a bit nervous. My first time to drive one of those man-eaters was going to be in a race. Wrecking or going slow was not an option.

Plus, I had been taking some serious heat from one of Steve's smart-ass drinking buds and a former driver, about not being able to handle the pressure of sprint car racing. According to Cid, I was too damn small and of course he had heard the rumors about my gender deal and was using that as political wedge to have Steve fire me and hire him. The irony was this: last time I had competed against Cid at a little ole midget race down in Batesville, Mississippi, I lapped him twice in a fifty-lap race, and there was nothing wrong with his car.

But to hear it from him, especially after he had consumed a couple of six packs of cold Budweiser, you would have thought he was Mario Andretti.

The disrespect for my talents confounded my dad, and he analyzed the situation.

"This bunch of hard ankles," he said, "they're just jealous."

Dad was right, but there was a bit more to it than jealousy. I wasn't, nor had I ever been a good ole boy and they couldn't stand someone who was smart, talented and cosmopolitan, let alone being rumored to be a silly little fag, beating their redneck butts. I had raced with some hot girl drivers like Teresa Gammons, Cathy Hartman and several others throughout my karting and midget days, and anytime those girls had any success, the hard core macho boys tried to demean their accomplishments. It was clearly a macho male thing.

So far I still had Steve's respect. In fact, Steve soon realized that Cid was just trying to make trouble and told him to hit the road.

By the first of April, Steve and I were ready to go racing. But it had been raining all spring so it was the first of May before I ever got to race that damn rocket ship.

In fact the night before the first race at Little Rock, Arkansas, I had never even cranked that baby let alone drove it. So that Friday at midnight, we hauled the car over to a mall parking lot and fired that puppy up. I cruised around the parking lot just getting used to the gas pedal and all the instruments and hoping the cops did not show up and take us to jail. To be honest, the sound of that big 750 horse-powered V8 took me back just a bit, but after about five minutes of driving, I was chomping at the bit to get over to Little Rock and check this baby out in some real race conditions.

But I knew I had to take it easy and learn how to do this. We could not afford for me to go out there and drive like a mad person and wreck the car. In fact, we were barely able to buy the fuel. So I had to be smart and finish the race and learn something.

The next night, in Little Rock, I was nervous as a cat on a hot tin roof. But by the end of the night I was standing on the gas and actually ended up finishing in the top ten. It was good enough to impress a few folks who had never heard of my skinny little ass, and we damn sure impressed the hell out of ourselves. After collecting our $300 prize money, we headed back to Memphis to party at the Nite Kap Bar and Pizza joint, which was one of our sponsors. Actually the bar didn't sponsor anything but our beer and pizza, but Steve made up for my lack of alcoholic consumption and then some, so I guess the sponsorship deal was worth it.

Over the next month we worked our way into the top five every night, both in Little Rock and over in West Memphis at the famed River Side Speedway located right on the banks of the Mississippi River. By the Fourth of July weekend we were pretty fast. With each week I had learned how to set the car up better. The next weekend in West Memphis, I set my very first fast qualifying time in a sprint car and went on to run third in the main event, which was our best finish to date.

Unfortunately, my dad had not been to many of my races that year. He was busy kicking everybody's butts through the Mid South with his new midget racer I had built him. I had missed having him and my mom at the track supporting me, especially since I was now driving in more dangerous races. But the weekend before Dad had flipped that baby and broke his hand. So he and mom came to West Memphis along with most of my hometown posse to help me that weekend. Dad was beside himself on how good we were doing, which really pumped me up.

It was good to have my family around again. This sprint car deal was not the same friendly setting that the midgets or karting had been. These competitors were more serious and political. I had already run into the cliquey politics there in Memphis, especially since we were beginning to run better, and it made me realize I was not in Kansas anymore. This bunch of good ole boys had known one another for years, half of them had grown up together as their dads and granddads had raced sprint cars against one another for several generations before us. I was an outsider coming into their little mud garden of Eden, beginning to beat them, plus a salacious rumor was following me around that hurt my chances of finding sprint car industry sponsorship anywhere in the mid South.

But at the moment I didn't give a crap. The important thing was to get better and better, and win my first main event in a sprint car.

That next night we hauled ourselves down to Talladega, Alabama to run a Sunday-night show at the dirt track located just across the street from the Super Speedway. Steve and my entire posse from Corinth, which included mom and dad and ten other hard ankles including ole Irv, pulled into Talladega ready to take the win.

I ended up qualifying second fastest and with absolute focus and a prayer I was running in that same position fifteen laps into the forty-lap main event when we had a caution flag for a car that spun around down in the first corner. As the track officials got the wrecked car off the track, we ran a few laps under caution.

Then, when the flagman waved the green flag to restart the race, all hell broke loose. There was a big chain reaction of a wreck that virtually caused the entire thirty cars to crash. I was run over from the back and eventually came to rest on my right side. The wreck had not been that bad, so I figured that they could just ease me back over and I would be good to go. As I sat there looking sideways down the track, my dad was coming at a trot with that broken wrist and white cast swinging back and forth, and he looked pretty pissed off. Behind him were all my posse boys and they were beginning to run at a pretty fair clip.

"Hey, that's cool," I thought, "they're coming to get me back on four wheels."

But when my dad got to my car, he went right on past without stopping. He gave me a thumbs up, which totally confused me. Then about ten seconds later all my buds went rushing by and now they were in a full sprint. I knew right then that my dad was up to something . . . he had a temper and had been in the Vodka all afternoon. I was thinking, oh shit, this was not a good sign! I was trying to look back over my shoulder but the way I was strapped in, I could not see a darn thing.

In the meantime a couple of race officials finally got to me, asked me if I was all right and got me back on four wheels.

Then like a scene out some Three Stooges movie, my posse came back by my car in a frantic trot. They had my dad up under his arms and they were taking him back toward our pit area.

Finally ole Irv came over to my car with a big grin on his face. He said, "Little Hayes, your daddy just about shot that guy that ran over you and caused this big ass wreck. He had his gun stuck right up under that guy's helmet and he was giving him a real talking to about running over your little ass. If we hadn't gotten there when we did, they would have taken his ass to jail . . . you would have been proud of him!"

That was my dad…when he got pissed off he was a damn bear to handle. He only weighed about 175 pounds but it had taken the entire posse to get his out-of-control ass back to the race hauler and take his gun away and lock him in the cab of the truck. They told him not to get out until we left the track.

Back on the track we finally restarted the race. I ended up finishing second to Mike Ward, who was rapidly turning out to be my biggest competitor throughout the Mid South. It was a hell of a night to say the least . . . we collected $1,000.00 for the night's winnings, let Dad out of the truck and headed back to Mississippi feeling thankful that he didn't have to go to jail. That guy who ran over me in the race, I bet he had nightmares for months about having my dad's gun stuck up his nose.

Here is dad with the cast on his arm, and Steve's brother John about an hour before his infamous Talladega moment when he pulled out his pistol and made his point to not run over me on the track. Go Dad Go!

Two weeks later, I won my first main event in a sprint car. Of course, Steve wanted to celebrate his ass off at the Night Kap Lounge where he drank beer and we ate pizza until the darn sun came up that next morning.

That next week we were still feeling the high from our first win. If we continued to progress, we could end up dominating this racing deal in the Memphis area. My driving ability and my understanding for what made these sprint cars tick was beginning to click.

Then all hell broke loose—we still had some dues to pay. The very next week end, one lap into a sure-fire new track record on the super fast West Memphis Riverside Speedway, I blew our 365 cubic engine up during qualifying and crashed big time in my own oil, almost flipping into the parking lot. It tore the hell out of the car but, but I did not get even a scratch.

We were a low budget group and I figured that wreck and blown engine would surely put us out of business. These engines cost upwards of 10 grand just for the basics. But somehow Steve managed to scrape up some extra cash from somewhere, and I wasn't asking any questions. He bought us a "new to us", but partially used, 406 cubic inch engine from Memphis Sprint car legend Big Bobby Davis. After about 80 hours of work, we were right back at it the very next weekend.

However, this time we had as much horsepower as the top guns. I could tell the difference in the power between the first engine and this new one in less than three seconds. Immediately I grabbed fast time for the second time that year and won two more races before the end of September.

However, by this time, most of that bunch of cowboys I was racing with had gotten wind of my gender issue. So they and their crew members were constantly teasing and harassing me. They hated it that I had become one of the people to beat.

One Saturday night in September, Terry Grey, one of my staunchest competitors, came and jumped all over my tail after he and I had a hell of a race, which he won. Terry was trying to break into the World of Outlaws championship series in sprint cars, and and he was the brother-in -aw of World of Outlaws National Champion Sammy Swindell. Now Terry accused me of running over him on a restart (which never happened) and he got in my face, cursing me for everything I was worth. I tried to tell him that I never got within two feet of his left rear tire. Instead, it had been Crazy Racing's Ricky Stinnhouse, whom I had passed on the next lap to finish second behind him. But he didn't want to hear it – he just wanted to jump my ass. It's a good thing my dad wasn't there that night, or he would have turned the shouting match into something bigger.

You know, I actually liked Terry Gray. He was just trying to make it in this crazy sport like everyone else. He was living in the shadow of his famous brother in law and just about as under-financed as we were. But he was out of line that night. If I had wanted to, I could have wrecked him any time I wanted to during the last laps.

Some of those guys I had to race with just didn't have any class. But there was no way in hell I was going to let them run me off. I'd have to grow some thicker skin.

So I make a decision on that night. No more being Mr. Nice Clean Racer. If they were going to accuse me of being a dirty driver, then I'd be one. Fact was, racing sprint cars out here in the heart land was like staring eye ball to eye ball with a pissed off rattle snake. At some point the rattle snake is going to strike you right between the eyes. If you were going to compete with these bunch of good ole boys in these crazy ass killing machines, you better have your game on and be willing to strike them back or strike them before they struck you. It was not if they would strike you, it was just a matter of when. Both on the race track competing for a win, or away from the track competing for a sponsor these sob's played for keeps and since I was an outsider and had this little ole gender rumor following me around, they were striking at me almost on a constant basis.

However, I wasn't all alone there at the track when someone wanted to smack me around. A few guys in the pits were looking after me, especially Shan Tillman, who my uncle Herman had specifically ordered to take care of me. Shan was a dead ringer for Elvis, had a switchblade knife and every one knew it. Most of the time he had a calm and easy personality, but if you got him riled up and he got that wild look in his eyes, look out.

Taking my first win in a Sprint car in West Memphis, Arkansas

Time to make a change

It was close to the end of the 1984 season. Much as I loved Steve and appreciated everything he did for me, he and his drinking were getting on my nerves.

For the last eight or nine years, I had already put up with my dad's drinking and the drama had worn me out. Unlike my dad, who could be mean and belligerent when he drank, Steve was just a pain in the ass. He wanted to stay out all night, and he always wanted to drive the race hauler when he was drinking. I had all the respect in the world for him, for his terrible sacrifice in Vietnam that had left him in a wheelchair for the rest of his life. But one alcoholic in my life was more than enough.

I knew that if I left Steve for another team, he and I could still be friends. Whereas if I continued to stay and drive his race car, I would end up resenting him and the friendship would most likely come to an end. I would rather have him as a friend. Plus, if I was going to make it, I needed to advance to a better financed team.

There wasn't any one in the Mid south who owned sprint cars that would hire me now. However, I had met a couple of guys, Leon Dezus and Ditto Basso (if you can believe those names) up in Centralia, Illinois when we traveled up there to race in August and we had developed a pretty good relationship. They ran an upstart racer supply company and seemed eager to help me land a ride with someone up in Mid West, where USAC (United States Auto Club) ran most of their races. If I could get hooked up in that series I could probably write my own ticket.

So I was calling those guys every week, schmoozing them to the hilt. The strategy was starting to work.

In the meantime, my dad had gone off the deep end with a two-week drinking marathon, and we finally got him into rehab. I was elated that he finally realized he had to stop drinking . . . but the entire time he was in the clinic I missed having him around to use as a sounding board for what I should do about Steve. I craved to be feminine with every breath I took, but I also craved to make my professional racing career happen, so the feminine needs were still getting put on the back burner.

But it was taking a toll. I couldn't eat and hid the emotions, especially for my mom's sake. She was trying to hold the household and the business together until Dad got out of rehab.

Appointment with my old doctor

Just a year or so back, I thought I would never have the opportunity to race cars professionally against the best drivers in America. My karting days had held grand ideas and goals for my racing career . . . Indy and NASCAR were on my mind, and I thought I could be racing in the Indy 500 by the time I was 25. Now I had other obstacles to overcome, other issues that had manifested themselves into almost insurmountable odds of ever attaining my goals. More than ever I needed my psychologist to help me figure out all this craziness in my head.

While I didn't want to walk away from this sprint car opportunity just yet, the gender deal was going to screw everything up. No matter how fast I could drive, I was not going to outrun it!

One of the new obstacles was, I needed to get my physical endurance up if I was going to excel in this new sport.

I was small and fragile, and those sprint cars were a handful to drive, especially on rough and ultra-fast race tracks. I really got physically tired driving those things. No matter how much I worked out, I just couldn't get my strength up to match those guys I was racing with. At the end of a 40-lap race I was virtually falling out of the car from being so tired. I decided to ask my doctor if there was anything I could do or take that would help. In a medical journal that my friend Victor had, I had read about male hormones creating more bulk and endurance. I was wondering if that would help me . . . not only with staying strong but overcoming my feminine desires.

My doctor and I had known each another for a few years now, and he was adamant on my staying in consistent counseling with him on a consistent basis. In my first session with him in over a year, he jumped on me about not taking care of my gender situation. He knew I was a walking time bomb . . . and he also knew how much I wanted to drive racecars for a living. There was always the pull, the tug of war over my soul. Those two things were hell bent on killing one another inside of me, at any cost to me and my family!

So, for the next few months, I made weekly visits to see him in hopes of calming myself down. Just as we were making some progress on finding a balance between my gender needs and my pro racing career, there was a defining and dramatic moment there in his office.

"I think," he said, "we should do a genetic test."

"A what?" I said.

"A genetic test," he said, "to see if there is something to this gender situation other than you just feeling that you are a girl."

He explained further. Clearly I was not a normal male. My body was formed and shaped like a girl's in almost every possible way, except for the reproductive biology. He had some theories that something else was up with me . . . that I probably had some female genetics going on. So he decided to test me just to make sure.

"Are you willing to be tested?" he asked.

The question both eased my nerves and took them to a heightened level. There were a lot of what if's to answer. What if I did have female genetics? What in the hell difference would it make anyway? Most likely people would never accept the findings. What if my genetics came back male? That would just add fuel to the fire that I was nuts for wanting to be a girl. It was a lose, lose situation. I was already too far into life for my family and other people to be comfortable with anything less than me being a male racecar driver.

Actually, I was afraid to find out, for fear that new questions would arise – questions that I couldn't even imagine. After all, genetics were only a base line to begin with. Even the United States government could not determine your sex on the basis of one's genetics – they were just too broad and diverse. Genetics was a human curve ball. I knew there were full-fledged drop-dead-gorgeous ultra-feminine fashion models working all over the world that were biological females but had male DNA or a little of both. There were hundreds of confused genetic codes out there that had taken the world's most brilliant minds many years to understand. For sure the simple- minded folk in Mississippi were not going to get it. So I was screwed no matter what the results produced!

"Yeah, sure, I'll take the test," I said reluctantly.

He took the swab from the inside of my mouth with a cutip.

It took over a month for the results to come back from the lab. To say I was a nervous wreck would be the understatement of the century.

"You're an XXY," he said.

My mind went blank for a minute. "XXY?" I said. "What does that mean?"

"It means you're different."

"Damn! What does that mean?"

He explained about the effects of having three sex chromosomes instead of the usual two, and the fact that they gave me characteristics of both genders, with the female characteristics predominating. That explained why my body was shaped like it was and why I virtually had no hair on my body. It also meant that I was probably sterile, and could not father a child.

My heart was sinking. "Are you sure?"

"Yes."

Now my mind was racing out of control. "No one will get it. I want to keep this a secret for a while."

"Of course," he said. "That's your right."

"I have problems with strength training. I can't get my muscle mass to bulk up. No matter what I do, I get really tired in the race car. Do you think my genetics have anything to do with this?

"Yes, I do," he said.

"Is there anything you can give me to help me in strength training?"

"Testosterone . . . steroids. They will help you bulk up. They're safe. They'll give you the endurance you need to drive those race cars."

The XXY test result was a complete surprise . . . not the answer I had been looking for. In fact it made me feel flawed and less than a human being, like I was damaged goods. Of course it did shed light on my physical appearance and feminine desires—at least I thought it did. More than the test though, I also knew I had more feminine biological issues going on than my doctor knew and I was willing to talk about to anyone. However, I was not ready to face that right now. In fact the results made me even more determined than ever to continue my racing career. If I didn't make a total commitment to the sport, I might miss out on the opportunity to get to Indy or Daytona.

So I ran from those test results as fast I could.

Looking back, it was a major case of denial. My doctor should have caught it and locked me away in a room until I came to my senses. But he was new to this situation as well and he was willing to give anything a try in order to help me get it together. So he made a few phone calls to make sure this was safe to do.

Within the week I had gotten my first shot of testosterone. Within a month I was beginning to have more energy. My muscle tone was pumping up, and my skimpy beard was beginning to take on a much coarser feel. I was even convinced that my feminine desires were subsiding. Hopefully, just hopefully, this little scientific experiment was going to work.

Hell, I even had a new girl friend, Kathy, in my life. Dad was out of rehab and back to being his old self. My girl friend and I were living together. Of course, Mom and Dad loved her.

Meanwhile I was on the search for a new race team that could take me to the top of the sprint car world. I knew I had to get into good racing equipment, with a decent budget to run the race car, if I was going to have any chance to escape the Mid South and make it to the big time. In the end though, looking back, this was all false hope . . . a dangerous attempt to make everyone love me, and to convince myself that I was not a physically and emotionally flawed human being.

That test had screwed with my head, and my heart, who knew what the future held now.

CHAPTER 9

Meet Blackie Fortune –
Go Racing

"Who in the hell is out there that can push my driving career to the next level?"

That was the question that roared through my mind every day. Plus, I had to ask myself, did I really want to do this, did I really want to fuss and fight with this sprint car racing bunch. Was it really worth the drama – only time, commitment and more rattle snake wrestling would tell.

Back in the summer, I had met these two Illinois guys and was wearing their phone out politicking them, trying to get them to sponsor me. Leon Dezus seemed to be the money man behind their business but his business partner Ditto Basso was the marketing brains, and he and I had become pretty good friends. Ditto was a hoot – a former used-car salesman who knew every trick in the book to make a deal work. He was good- looking, had a silver tongue that could talk you out of your last dime, and he liked me. I had sent him my racing resume and he was helping me work a who-to-call-in-the-sport list—car owners, sponsors and whatever else he and I could think of to get me in a good ride for the 85 season.

There was this big annual full midget race up in Fort Wayne, Indiana around the first of the year that he told me I need to attend. According to Ditto, every big shot in sprint car, midget and Indy car racing would be at that race and I needed to meet those people. So I packed up my van with a few clothes, 15 driving resumes, and my driving gear just in case. I was damn determined that I was going up to Fort Wayne and land me a job with someone driving their race cars for the next season.

One thing going for me was this: I had not only a good driving record, but also the mechanical and engineering side of the sport running deep through my veins. And with the hormone shots I was pumping up, and not looking so wimpy.

Ditto had made a list of high rollers to meet; he even described them to me so I could pick them out in the crowd.

"And no matter what, you have to meet Blackie Fortune. He's the man in USAC Sprint and champ car racing in the Midwest. He's a big time coal miner, and he's got enough money to buy the state of Indiana."

In fact, Ditto added, Blackie had parted company with Rickie Hood, one of his drivers, over the winter. Now he was looking for the next hot shoe. Blackie was also the team owner who put NASCAR'S newest hot shoe, Kenny Schrader, on the map. Filling Ricky Hood's and Kenny Schrader's shoes was going to be a tall order because they both had won the USAC National Sprint car championships for Blackie. But Ricky had gotten hurt while driving for someone else out in Phoenix in early winter. It had pissed Blackie off and he had actually fired Ricky while he was in the hospital with two badly broken legs. I thought that was pretty damn ruthless and cruel but, in auto racing, that was how it goes sometimes.

"When you get to Fort Wayne," Ditto told me, "you gotta get a room at the Holiday Inn closest to the indoor arena where the races are going to be held. That's race headquarters for all the racers and team owners. They will all hold up there in the

Holiday Inn lounge the night before the race. Most of the people on your list will be there, including ole Blackie Fortune."

So I headed up to Fort Wayne with a van full of hopes and just enough cash to get me up there and back.

Holiday Inn . . . race headquarters!

As soon as I checked into the Holiday Inn, I put on my best jeans and starched white dress shirt and I headed to the lounge to get in the action. But the bar was almost empty. Had Ditto missed this call?

Nonetheless, always keeping a positive spirit in the midst of a seemingly bad situation, I moseyed on over to the bar, ordered a beer and casually engaged the bartender in conversation.

"Is this where all the midget racers are gonna be hanging out later tonight?" I asked him.

"It's usually packed by now," he said, looking around as he wiped the bar. "But the word is out…all the racers are staying at a different motel this year. But I'm kinda shocked that there's no one here."

By now, I was getting nervous. Then three men entered the bar and took a seat in a booth next to the dance floor. I knew they were racers by their brightly colored ski jackets with Hoosier Tires embroidered on the chest and back. That was all the opening I needed. I walked there, took a seat in the booth directly across from them, which had to look really weird with one person sitting in that booth but what the hell. So I sat there looking like a goober, peeling the label off of the bottle, glancing around the room as if I was looking for someone.

After about a minute or so one of the men leaned over.

"You here for the races?" he asked.

"Yeah. I'm from the Memphis area," I said.

One of the other guys, the bald-headed one sitting on the far side of the booth asked me, "Want to join us for a few drinks?"

Right away I slid over to their booth. "I'm J.T. Hayes," I said.

One by one they introduced themselves. The man next to me told me his name was Rick, the man right across from me introduced himself as Don Waters and then the older guy, the overweight bald headed guy, reached out his hand to shake mine and said, "I'm Blackie Fortune. One of my drivers is from Memphis, Ricky Hood. Ever heard of him?"

That's when I knew I had died and gone to heaven. I was about to pea in my pants. However, I kept it cool and didn't show my cards.

"Yeah, I know Ricky," I said casually. " I know his dad Hooker better. In fact Hooker, who is a real sprint-car legend and one of my heroes, has really helped me get my racing in high gear with a lot of good tips about car set-ups. Plus, he has caught my back a few times when it got rowdy after a race or two."

Blackie laughed out loud because he knew exactly what I was talking about.

That night we all went bar hopping around Fort Wayne. When we got back to the Holiday Inn around midnight, he told me to meet them in the motel restaurant for breakfast, and then I could follow them out to the arena for the races.

That night, as I turned in for bed, I said a prayer, thanking my guardian angel for looking after me.

The next morning we all gathered for breakfast and then headed over to the arena. When we got pit passes, Blackie paid for mine and we went inside to mingle.

I was in awe. All my USAC heroes were there—Rich Vogler, Johnnie Parsons, Gary Betenhausen and one of my all-time heroes, now retired from racing and director of USAC competition, Roger McCluskey. Blackie introduced me to each and every one of them. They all asked me if I was Blackies new hot shoe which really shocked me.

"I just met him last night," I said. "And I'm a hot shoe, but not Blackie's just yet."

They all laughed. Rich Vogler leaned over and told me to hang in there with ole Blackie. "If he likes you, he will take care are of you . . . hang in there."

I could not believe my ears.

For the rest of the day, we all palled around the pits, then watched the races from up in the stands. I actually sat beside Donnie Waters, who I knew was the mechanical brains behind Blackie's racing success. Sitting with him gave me a chance to pick his national-championship-winning brain as much as possible. It was a damn honor to get to know him, he was a very cool person.

After the races were over, which Rich Vogler won in a resounding victory, we all went to the parking lot to head on back to our homes. Mine in Corinth, Mississippi and theirs in Booneville, Indiana. I grabbed a few of my résumé's and gave them to Blackie.

"If you know of anyone looking for a new hot shoe, please put in a good word for me." I added that I was friends with Floyd Bailey, the head guy at Gambler Chassis Company down in Nashville, that he could call him for a reference if he wished to check me out. Ironically, Gambler was one of Blackie's biggest sponsors so that little reference wasn't gonna hurt. I knew Floyd would put in a good word for me.

It was a long shot that Blackie would call. But what the hell, my whole life had been a long shot.

Tell Floyd Bailey about Blackie

I left Fort Wayne driving like a bat out of hell. It was urgent to get down to Nashville and check in with Floyd Bailey when he got to work. I drove all night, only stopping to get gas and hit the restroom. And I prayed the entire trip. This chance meeting with the big guy in Midwest sprint car racing was no accident. This had been destiny at its finest. I did not want to screw it up, and was more determined than ever to put the gender drama behind me. But something was still eating at me. Taking those testosterone shots seemed to be helping, but in my gut, it all seemed wrong somehow to be taking them, no matter the justification.

About 5:30 that Monday morning, I parked my van in the Gambler Shop parking lot and caught a few winks before Floyd got to work at 7:00. I caught him as he was getting all his guys going on building new Gambler sprint cars.

"Would you be willing to put in a good word for me if Blackie happens to call you?" I asked him.

"You bet," he said. "I'll catch your back. Me and your dad have been friends for a long time."

I thanked him, then high-tailed it back to Corinth, another four hours away. I had to be at work that night to help my dad finish up a big welding job. My new girl friend Cathy would be waiting too!

Terry, you got a phone call

Sometimes destiny does find you. When I walked into my parents' house, a note was waiting on the kitchen table. I slowly picked it up, thinking it might be about my dad being pissed at me over work. But when I read the message, I could hardly believe my eyes.

It read, "Terry, you got a phone call this morning from some guy named Blackie. He said he met you up in Indiana and he wants you to call him!"

Holy crap.

Right away I called Mr. Fortune up. For sure, he wanted me to come up there and go to work for him . . . he had a plan that he thought would work out for both of us . . . he wanted me to come up there that coming weekend, and go to the indoor midget races at the Hoosier dome in Indy. We could get to know one another better, and talk over our game plan for the upcoming season.

"Blackie, thanks so much for the opportunity," I said. "I won't let you down."

Then I called up Ditto un in Illinois and gave him the good news. He congratulated me and told to go break a leg, if I had to, to get it done!

That next weekend Blackie, his son Rick and me headed up to Indy for the indoor races in the Hoosier Dome.

As we drove, Blackie gave me the lowdown on his plan for me within their racing team. It was the perfect opportunity to get me in the seat of big time sprint car racing. He wanted me to work on all the race cars during the week, learn the system within their team and to start driving their sprint car by spring.

I was beside myself with excitement. My dad and all of his best buds—Dexter Bumbus and Hobert Patterson, who were walking historians for sprint and the bigger dirt champ car racing in the Midwest—were going to be really proud of me. They would live their dreams of racing in these series through me. This was the chance we had always wanted!

Once in Indy, we checked in at the Speedway Motel on the property of the Indianapolis Motor Speedway. Then we hooked up with their old friend and part-time crew member Wes, and their newly hired champ car driver, George Snider, the Indy 500 legend and best friend of A. J. Foyt, Blackie had hired George to drive their champ car for the '85 season after he had fired Ricky Hoods. George was racing the next night for some other team, but tonight, we were all going out partying.

I knew from my sense of motorsports history that George Snider and A.J. Foyt were notorious legends not only for their driving, but also for their partying and monkeying around. This night could turn out to be something I would talk about for years.

Wes, Rick, Blackie and I piled into the car with Wes driving. Then Wes drove on around to George's room, blew the horn and George came running out complaining about how damn cold it was-- it was getting down in the teens and it looked as if it was going to snow. He made me get out of the front seat so he could sit next to Wes, and we took off to the first watering hole to get some action going.

It did not take one minute before the shenanigans started. At the first red light, George slipped his left foot over on Wes's right foot and jammed down on the gas pedal. We went screaming through that red light, the gas pedal flat down on the floorboard, Wes cussing and raising hell at George who was laughing his ass off and me, holding on for dear life and laughing my ass off too. In the back seat, Blackie and Rick were yelling, "Go George go!" All while Wes was trying not to ram into the twenty or so cars in front of us. As we neared the bar, Wes slammed on the brakes with the tires squealing like a baby pig being chased by the big bad wolf, and the engine was screaming like crazy. Our car slid to a stop neatly right in front of the door.

George was laughing so hard he could hardly breathe. My eyes were as big as saucers. I was living in the fast lane and loving it!

That night when we left the bar, Blackie made George get in the back seat.

Speed weeks in Florida

Back in Indiana at Blackie's race shop that next week, we all got busy getting the dirt champ car and sprint car ready for the upcoming Florida speed weeks. I worked on the sprint car, Rick worked on the champ car and I froze my skinny white ass off every day. It was cold as hell up there, it snowed virtually every day but sacrifices had to be made.

Blackie was letting me sleep in the guest bedroom until I could get my own place. His lovely wife kept us fed, and at first everything seemed to be going according to plan.

But little by little, over the next two weeks, Blackie became more and more hard to get along with. A few times I asked Wes if I had said or done anything to piss Blackie off. Wes told me that it wasn't me, that Blackie was like that. He and his son Rick had huge fights all the time, and I should just hang in there.

"Once racing season begins," Wes added, "most likely things will even out."

However, in the back of my mind I was wondering if those Memphis assholes were badmouthing me to Blackie. After all, every one of those guys I raced against back in Memphis were fully aware of my position and opportunity with Blackie. Racing is a small world; it would only be a matter of time before Blackie and his entire team heard the rumors about me. I could only hope that the rumors would seem too outrageous to believe. Hopefully Blackie would pass them off as malicious politics.

In the meantime, I had been pondering what to do about my testosterone shots. My doctor was back in Memphis and it would probably be risky to open myself up to another doctor in Indiana. In addition, I was not so happy about how those hormones were making me look more masculine. I was coming to realize that a feminine appearance was what I identified with. About two weeks into Indiana, I woke up one Tuesday morning and looked at myself in the mirror and made the decision that the male hormones were a stupid idea. No matter that I probably needed them to help me in my racing, I hated what they were doing to my body. I would have to find a better way to get my stamina up. Maybe nutrition and a more intensive physical training program would do the job.

That morning, standing in front of that mirror, looking at the short hair and the mustache beginning to really grow,

I realized that was not who I was. This was a turning point for me. That was the first time in my life I actually embraced my gender situation and its biological implications. Oh, I wasn't quite ready to *totally* embrace it and forget about the racing. But I would never again talk myself into doing something stupid just to make sure everyone approved of me as a human being.

That Sunday morning, before we were to leave the next day for Florida, we were all out in the race shop finishing up on the race car and loading the race haulers. Around lunch time Blackie showed up and we could tell that he was more temperamental than usual. Everyone was walking on eggs, trying not to piss him off.

Around two p.m. we were pretty much finished but Blackie wanted one more race tire loaded into the hauler. He and his son Rick were arguing over whether they needed to take it or not. I was just standing wondering who was going to blink first.

After about ten minutes of bickering, Blackie yelled over at me to load that damn tire.

Without hesitation, trying to lighten the mood, I hollered back, "Yes sir, Mr. Benny, I mean Blackie." Then I put the tire on the trailer.

To my amazement, Blackie stared at me and said, "You're fired, you little piss head. That's it with you, you're fired. Get your stuff and get the hell out of here. I'll have your pay ready by the time you get your truck loaded."

Then he turned and walked off to the house.

Shocked, Wes and Rick and I just stood there with our mouths open.

"J. T.... damn ...I'm sorry for that," Wes said. "Are you all right? Do you want me to talk to him to see what set him off."

"I can fight my own battles," I told him, trying to look calm. "I'll just get my things together and get the hell out."

Rick chimed in. "Damn, I wish he had not done that. Where are you going to go? Do you have any place to go?"

"I can probably drive back over to Illinois and catch a place with my friend Ditto. I'll be all right."

Methodically I gathered my tool boxes and suitcases, and Wes and Rick help me load my truck. As I got the three hundred bucks that Blackie had left on the kitchen table, I was fuming with anger and ready to burst into tears. I had worked my ass off for him, minded my P's and Q's and tried to be the model employee! His argument with Rick had provoked his already pissy attitude and when I came back with that cute Mr. Benny remark, he went off the deep end. But the remark was probably not the real reason he fired me. Most likely he had begun to hear the rumors and was looking for any excuse to get rid of me.

I told Rick and Wes I would catch them on the rebound and left.

At the time, the only connection I had in that area was Ricky Hood. No way was I going to go back to Corinth or Memphis and eat crow. So I drove straight over to Evansville, twenty miles west, and called Ricky up. He was back at his apartment, recuperating from his broken legs.

"Blackie just fired me," I told him. "Could I catch your couch for the night?"

"Join the club, J.T. At least he didn't fire you while your ass was in the hospital. Screw him! Get on over here. You can stay as long as you need to regroup."

Over the next two days, Ricky Hood and I gossiped about Blackie, and I got on the phone trying to put together a new deal. Ricky gave me a few car owners' phone numbers, but everyone was already set for the season with a driver. Ditto was trying to get me to come over to Centralia, hang out with him and Leon, and then head down to Daytona for Speed Weeks. They wanted to get a dealership going with Gambler and knew I had a connection with Gambler through Floyd Bailey. Ditto assured me that if he and Leon could get a deal with Gambler, they would help me put my own sprint car deal together.

By Thursday, Leon, Ditto and myself were headed down to Daytona, in the middle of a snowstorm.

Make a deal . . . get back and get going!

When we got to Daytona, the three of us started networking like crazy.

Ditto was a master of disaster, he had everyone eating out his hand. By the end of the week, he and Leon had a dealership deal with Gambler, and it looked as if I was going to put my sprint car deal together. This was the best I could hope for— an opportunity to control my own destiny. In addition, I had made friends with Gambler's west coast representative, Wayne Bennett, and he was willing to help me get on track and into the winners' circle. Now I just needed to get back to Illinois with Leon and Ditto and work out the details.

The season was already kicking into gear, and I needed to be racing.

Three weeks later I was back in Corinth, and Dad and I were busy putting our own team together.

I was still new to this sprint car game but learning fast that politics, money, luck and perseverance would be the mission statement from now on. Talent was a given, but now we had to put the rest of the package together.

Through Wayne Bennett, Gambler Chassis Company's West Coast division, I worked out a deal with Leon and Ditto to sell Gambler parts in the Mid South Region, and use my own team with their financial support to promote the Gambler franchise. I would run the car for the season, throughout the Mid South circuit, then we would sell the race car and repeat the same process the next season. I made a deal with my ex car owner Steve Clark to buy the engine out of the car I had driven for him and I was working 24-hour days putting all of this new opportunity into play.

At times I wondered if I had bitten off more than I could chew. Even though Dad and I were partners in the race team, I was doing all the work. Plus, to make some extra cash for the team, I was building and selling some of the big wings that are the distinguishing feature in sprint-car design.

Basically, these wings are reversed airplane wings that generate down force instead of lift. They also have boards on each side of the center section that creates side force when you sling the car into a turn at 130 miles per hour. These wings not only make the cars run faster, they made a crash safer by keeping the race car from just flipping wildly like an out-of-control football. The wing's aerodynamics slow down the flipping car and cushions the impact with the ground.

Building these wings took a lot of time, so I was working seven days a week. However, they gave me a big bonus for my strength training. These babies have hundreds of pop rivets in them. Instead of using a pneumatic pop rivet gun, I used an old-style hand-held rivet gun that took a lot of physical strength to operate. By June, my forearms were hard as rocks and ready to handle the rigors of driving a sprint car for 40 laps. Or so I thought.

Team owner Bobby Sparks down in Olive Branch agreed to trade me a trailer for hauling the team's own sprint car. Finally I rolled out an old 1977 four-door Chevy pickup I had gotten in another trade, and put a new coat of white paint on her. By the time the truck was shod with a new set of Michelin radials, ready to hitch to the trailer, we were ready to go.

While all this frenzy of work was going on, my gender issue was walking right beside me every day, tugging on my heart strings. So was my new girl friend.

Kathy was a cutie, at 5'4" weighing barely 100 pounds. She had a killer body and looked like Mary Lou Metziner, the singer on "The Lawrence Welk Show." Her shoulder length light-brown hair was thick and full and it always looked great. She had big hazel eyes that could burn a hole in your heart at times when she was putting on her feminine mystique trying to get me to see her point of view. She was a little naive about life and how hard-ass people could be but she had crammed in some hard times in her own life with a bad divorce and a mean dad. Cathy worked hard at her job down at the telephone factory. She was being a real trouper concerning this racing stuff, though she really didn't understand why we were all so crazy about it.

Kathy was devoted to me and had been ever since high school. However, I didn't feel the same about her. I don't know why I was trying to make the relationship work, except that she really loved me and having a girlfriend eased the political and social climate around Corinth and in the racing community. My mom and dad loved that girl. Our relationship would make them happy and keep them thinking that I had beaten the gender issue.

In reality, the gender issue was still right there, under the surface of my new-found machismo, waiting to rear its head at any second. I was just trying to buy some time and have a few good years in the sport before I finally decided to have the realignment surgery. When I did, all hell would break loose.

June 14th . . . behind schedule but ready to go!

I loved Riverside Speedway there in West Memphis, only a mile from the banks of the mighty Mississippi River and two miles from downtown Memphis. That racetrack was old as hell—it had been going strong since back in the early '50s. Top sprint-car heroes like Hooker Hood, Don Curbo, Ted Fink and Sam Swindell (who was the father of current hot shoes Sammy and Jeff Swindell) had all raced there. Of course Hooker Hood, one of my childhood heroes and probably the coolest cat to ever race in West Memphis, was my friend Ricky Hood's dad. Hooker had actually taken a liking to me, so if anything major came up, he would catch my back. When it came to a good skirmish, you didn't want to take ole Hook on, because he was going to come out on top 99% of the time.

I loved everything about that old ditch of a race track. The black gumbo dirt that created the ultra-fast track surface. The smell of barbecue and steaming boiled corn swimming with hot butter swirling into the hot Arkansas air. The food vendors below the main grandstands yelling out, "Hot pit Bar B Q, H o t Pit Bar B Q, get your Hot Pit Bar B Q right here, enjoy the races with you Hot Pit Bar B Q." The hunger-generating smells from those barbecue sandwiches flowing up into the grand-stands, blending perfectly with the scream of 130 mph sprint cars rounding that killer race track as the track announcer yelled into the microphone that ole so and so just sat a new one-lap track record.

To me this was a magical place. Every time I pulled in there to race, I knew it was something very special. If you won on any given Saturday night, you not only had escaped serious injury or even death, you had done something only the best of the best sprint-car drivers in the world had done. There was a rumor that this mystical old racing arena was built on top of Indian burial grounds, that every night after the races were over and the lights turned off, you could see the ghosts of the tribes dancing around their camp fires and conjuring up the spirits. Hell, I believed it… in fact, one night the year before; I actually thought I saw a medicine man standing by my car blessing that puppy before the feature event.

Now, it was the second weekend in June, and we were ready to go.

There I sat, strapped into my new blue-and-yellow throt-tle rocket, waiting on the push truck to run my first laps. My mind was working on overtime, wondering if I had prepared the car properly. That's when I thought about that old Indian medicine man I had seen. Whether he was a ghost or a spirit guide, I didn't care – I just wanted him to bless me and this new baby with all the positive spirit he could muster.

That night I turned the second fastest qualifying time and finished third in the main event. Mom, Dad and I were elated over how well everything had gone. We were lightning fast, nothing broke on the car and I knew that with just a few adjustments we were going to win a bunch of races.

Some of my old buds, who had helped me in the pits when I drove for Steve Clark, had shown up that weekend to help me crew the car. Of course my bodyguard Shan Tillman was there, along with Curt Curtner. A new guy by the name of Bob Lamb who had just moved up from Texas to work for Federal Express came over and introduced himself and had asked if he could help. Bob was a former racer himself, and turned out to be a pretty good sprint car mechanic. Of course my uncle Herman was right there encouraging me too. So we had a pretty good posse going—if any one of those kamikaze race drivers wanted to start a fight, we could hold our own. Especially Shan who always had that big ole knife stuck down in his pocket.

Over the next few months we got our game going. I sat fast time virtually every Friday night up at Milan, Tennessee and on Saturday night there in West Memphis. We won four or five times and were always in the top three. I was thinking about taking my race team up to the Midwest after Labor Day to run for a few weeks. In the meantime, right there in West Memphis, I finished in the money in the United States Auto Club-USAC event ...even after crashing and getting upside down on the start of the race. They turned me back over, and I restarted at the back of the pack and charged up through the field and had a hard battle with USAC National Champion and Indy 500 veteran Sheldon Kinser to finish third.

After the race, we almost got in a big fight when I flipped off Bud Ward for holding me up when I went to lap him toward the end of the race. He and his posse of about 25 of the biggest rednecks this side of the Mississippi came down to my pits to whip my skinny ass. Thank God, I kept my mouth shut and let Shan do all the talking. I wasn't going to apologize because he had definitely blocked me, but I was thinking I might have to at one point. (I'll take that glass of Merlot and my smoked salmon now, please.)

Three weeks later up in Milan, Tennessee, still feeling the high from that USAC event, I was leading the feature with only three laps to go when I connected with a lap car and did an end over end 50 yard crash. For a minute there, I thought it had totaled the car and damn near totaled me.

This was a coming-back-to-reality-Jesus meeting on just how cruel sprint car racing can be. I never will forget the look on my dad's face when he got up to me and the wrecked race car. I had actually gotten myself out of the car and was sitting on the track behind the car unbuckling my helmet. The way the race car was laying on its side, Dad couldn't see me, so he thought I was still trapped inside the smoking and crumpled-up wreck. He was white as a sheet when he finally saw me sitting there on the ground.

So there we were, with parts and pieces of that beautiful blue and yellow race car scattered all over the red Tennessee dirt. We gathered up the mess, threw it on the trailer and high tailed back to Corinth.

There we worked all night making repairs. Dad stayed out there in the shop helping me and little Curt till daylight before he went into the house to get some rest. Mom kept the coffee and pimiento sandwiches coming and my fat-ass beagle Slick hung in there with us all darn night. Actually we believe that Slick, who was notorious for sneaking and getting your sandwich when you were not looking, had eaten most of those pimiento sandwiches. Curt and I never slept, and by 5:30 that Saturday afternoon we were pulling back into the pit gate at Riverside Speedway with that car looking brand new.

That night I sat fast time again and finished second in the feature with no brakes on the car. Who needs brakes any way, they just slow you down. Okay, I was damn lucky I did not crash because of not having brakes, in fact I scared the hell out of myself when I darn near ran over the top of Mike Brewer, the brother of Lee Brewer whom I had had my big crash with the night before in Milan. When I came up to lap Mike, he moved over on me, almost running me into the third-turn wall. I was going 40 miles per hour faster than he was, and only by the grace of God did I miss crashing into him at 130 miles per hour.

That got my attention and I decided to take it easy for the remaining ten laps—I could not afford to wreck two nights in a row. I was making our living this way, and we had to finish races in order to make money.

The next night we raced down in Tupelo, Mississippi where I sat a new track record and won the feature.

That Monday, Curt and I took the day off and caught up on our sleep then I went to the doctor because I thought I broken some ribs in the wreck that past Friday night. Plus, I was losing the feeling in my left arm, which had actually fallen asleep on Sunday night during the main event. I just figured I had a pinched nerve or something, and so did my local physician. He taped up my ribs and sent me on my way.

Amid all the wins and excitement, my gender issue was eating me up inside, so the day after that, I called my psychologist and had an emergency session with him. I just needed to vent my frustrations—caught in between two opposing life paths once again. If I did not nourish my feminine side from time to time in the midst of all of this violence and machismo my life entailed, I would melt down.

Adding to my stress level, my girlfriend Cathy and I broken up. She could not handle the racing, it was just too damn hard on our relationship. To be honest, I was not committed to her the way she was to me and she just got tired of it. She knew about my gender issue but she had loved me anyway and had just pushed the rumors to the side. But the night before my big wreck in Milan, we had decided to each go our own way. It was the best thing for both of us. She needed to find a nice guy and marry him and have a nice life. Having a girl friend, or even a wife, was just not in the cards for me. Anyway I was sexually attracted to men—not as a man being with another man, but me as a woman being with a man. It was something I had dreamed about for most of my life.

Another reason I felt like venting was that I suspected that some of my racing competitors were ratcheting up the gender rumors. My racing deal with Gambler had all them pissed off. I had a damn good sponsorship deal and was beating them every weekend, and they couldn't stand it. So, by Labor Day I was in a battle for my racing career with a group of guys in the Mid South who were hell bent on running me out of town so they could get my deals.

Dad shared my suspicions. He made a few calls and narrowed it down to three guys who were spreading the rumors. Dad called up one of his old biker boys in Memphis from back in the day, and asked him to catch my back, that we might need him to kick some people's asses. Ole Charlie drove down to Corinth and had a powwow with me and Dad, and told us that he and the gang would make a visit to whomever we wanted. The next weekend, Charlie and five of his biker boys came over to the races in West Memphis and hung out with us at the pits, just letting everyone know I had some friends in the house.

Even thought breaking up with Kathy was stressful, it was a relief. Even though my gender and sexuality was pretty evident to most everyone, women were always chasing me around. In fact, just there at West Memphis several hot chicks were after me. Even a car owner's wife was doing everything she could to have an affair with me. It was tempting – she was drop dead gorgeous. If I had been a horn-toad ass-hole male prick I would have gone for all of those opportunities in the blink of an eye. But I just minded my own business. Plus, if that car owner had found out about me and his wife (even though he was constantly cheating on her), he would kick my skinny white ass all over Memphis.

Looking back on it now, if I had pursued any of those women especially the married ones, that bunch of Memphis hard legs would have patted me on the back and told me I was a stud.

A new track record

West Memphis Speedway was having a big two-day Labor Day weekend event. Racers from all over the Mid South and the Midwest were rolling in there to see who would be the big dog standing in victory lane when the weekend was over.

Only a week before, Lee Brewer had set a new one-lap track record during qualifying there in West Memphis and it pissed me off. I owned fast qualifying there, so I was determined to not let his record stand.

Setting a new track record is virtually impossible in motorsports. Conditions have to be almost perfect to pull it off. The track surface has to be fast and smooth. You have to have your race car working perfectly and you have to drive it perfectly. Everything has to come together. But on this Labor Day weekend it looked like Lady Luck was on my side because the race track was lighting fast. The surface was smooth and tacky, just perfect to turn some very fast laps.

As each driver went out for their qualifying run, everyone was turning in good times. But even Lee missed his new record by a few tenths of a second. My confidence was up—I had made a few changes to my engine for some extra horsepower, so I might have a chance.

When it came time to take my run, I just stood on the gas like a crazy person and drove that 800 horse-powered sprint car for all it was worth. I was on a mission; I wanted that track record as much as anything in my life. My lap was run virtually wide open around that high-banked oval track. As I drove under the checkered flag, I could hear – even inside my helmet – that the crowd was starting to roar like crazy over the screaming sound of my engine. Something was up.

I quickly glanced up at the scoreboard just above the first-turn wall, where the qualifying times were posted immediately. To my astonishment, I saw the numbers 12.51 for my time. Hell fire, I had just beaten Lee Brewer's record by three tenths of a second. I was the fastest driver in the 30-year history of Riverside Speedway.

Back in the pits all of my crew was about to go crazy from the accomplishment. This was a big deal for them as well. Any time we as a team could do it, we loved making those hard ankles eat their words about me being a fag or a sissy. The facts were, I was brave as hell behind the wheel and I was kicking those guys' asses almost every weekend. That new track record would be a feather in our caps… for a little while, anyway, before it was shuffled aside in favor of new gossip about my life.

The cards are stacked

That night in the 40-lap feature event, I took off from the pole position and drove away from the field. After ten laps I had more than a straightaway lead on the second place car, which was driven by Mike Ward, my arch rival. If nothing happened I could possibly lap the field by the end of the feature.

But, as soon as I got that far out front, the flag man threw the yellow flag and slowed all of us down. I assumed that a car had wrecked or spun out, thus bringing out the caution flag. However, as I slowed down and the rest of the field caught to me, I didn't see any wrecks on the track. Right away I thought something was odd, but there had to be a reason for the caution.

When I drove by my pits, my crew member Bob Lamb was standing out next to the track with a look of confusion on his face. He shrugged his shoulders at me as to say he didn't know why the caution had come out either.

After we cruised around for five or six laps, the flag man waved the green flag to restart the race. I took off again like a bat out of hell. Just like before, I drove away from the other cars... and just like before, the yellow flag came out again. This time I was pissed off. Were the officials trying to manipulate this race?

After three or four more cautions, I was sure that someone was trying to get to me. Mike Ward was Riverside Speedway's beloved driver – the officials were trying to set things up so he could pass me to take the win. His car was fast on a dry slick race track, and my car was fast on a more wet and tacky surface, and everyone knew it. As the track began to dry out from all those race cars running at slow speeds and their engines exhaust blowing on to the track surface, slowly sapping the moisture and thus the speed from the surface, Mike Ward was beginning to keep up with me

By about the 37th lap, he was right up on my tail. Just as I had suspected, he kamikazed the first corner, hit my rear bumper and knocked me out of the way. Passing me, he went on to take the win. I finished second.

When I pulled into my pits, steam was blowing out of my ears. My team wore dark faces of disappointment and anger. We knew that we had just gotten screwed and there was not a damn thing we could do about it. Worse – over the past several months, I had had several chances to take Mike out like that, but I had chosen to not wreck him for a win. That was a wake-up call for me. From this point on, if he and I were racing close, I would wreck him if I had to.

I had never driven dirty, but you have to fight fire with fire. Ole Charlie, my dad's back-in-the-day biker buddy, might just have to hang out with me for the rest of the season.

Me and Mike . . . more to the story!

Mike Ward and I had never been total enemies. In fact, over the past two years, he had sometimes helped me out with advice. One time he loaned me and Steve a power-steering unit when ours broke. He was a good driver, tough as nails on the track and always had his race car perfectly prepared. I had never looked at him as a rival… heck, I was just trying to learn everything I could about sprint cars as fast as I could.

But now Mike and I were having these hard-fought races almost every weekend.

Two weeks after Labor Day, we were at it again. This time I passed Mike to take the lead. But as I headed for the win, my engine blew up in a big plume of smoke, causing me to fall out of the race.

In the meantime, my mom was sitting up in the grand-stands with her best friend Christine. Along with my third cousin Peggy who was my biggest fan there at Riverside, Mom and Christine always sat in the same seats just in front of the third corner on the back straightaway, about halfway up in the stands. On that fateful night there was this hardcore six-foot-tall bearded redneck wearing a Mike Ward T shirt and dirty Budweiser hat who was sitting two rows down, right in front of my mom and her girl posse.

When my engine blew, this redneck jumped up and yelled out, "Take that, you little son of a bitch, you will not win tonight! Go on back to Mississippi where you and all the other fags live!"

That's when my mom stood up. She swung her fist with the full can of Coke she had just bought, and decked this red-neck right in the back of his head. Coke spewed over everyone in the next five rows.

My mom yelled back at this guy: "That's my baby you're bad mouthing! JT is my baby and he can beat Mike Ward any time anywhere! Don't you be bad mouthing my baby!"

Well, the whole place went quiet. Everyone in the grand stands was looking on in shock that this five-foot-tall 95- pound woman had just about knocked out a big ole red-neck, and thinking that he was going to beat the hell out of her. But the redneck just stood there staring at her, dazed from the pop on his skull and confused that this little bitty woman had the gall to deck him like that. Then, as if heaven's angels had swept in to protect my mom, the redneck apologized to Mom, and turned around and sat down again as if nothing had happened.

At the time, I didn't know about this incident. Later, as the crew and I were loading the race hauler, Big Bobby Davis (whose son Bobby Davis Jr was out tearing up the World of Outlaws Sprint Car Tour) came down to my pits and told me I might need to go up there and see about my mom. He was laughing his ass off as he told me the story. Five minutes later, a big bearded redneck came by my pits and gave me a dirty look, and Big Bobby told me that was the guy my mom had decked.

That next week, I was in Memphis at Danny's Engine Service working on my engine. To my amazement, in walked that redneck. Right away he noticed that I was in the back of the shop and made a beeline right over to me. I was thinking, "Oh shit, I'm going to get my ass kicked by this guy and then my mom is *really* going to kill him."

But to my astonishment, he had a big grin on his face by the time he got over to me, and stuck his hand out. Hesitantly I shook his hand.

"Hey, I just got to tell ya," he said, "your mom is tough as nails. She hit me right in the back of the head with that Coke can. I have to admit, I was out of line. I was drinkin' and I should have never yelled out like that about you. Hell, man, you're a great racer. Anyone who can drive like you deserves respect. I have to tell ya, I'm still a Mike Ward fan. He is my guy. But now I'm your fan too."

Shocked and relieved, I went to my truck and got a Gambler T-shirt and gave it to him.

"I totally understand about your loyalty to Mike," I said, "and I honor you for it."

"Thanks," he said, flushing a little.

When he left the engine shop and went on his way, I stood there pondering. There was a virtual guarantee that he had heard the rumors about me. Now that he had actually met me, what was he thinking? One thing was for sure, though. Most of the time, race fans will give you the respect you deserve for being a committed and good race driver – for putting your life on the line to entertain them.

CHAPTER 10

Mom and Christine Pit Crew and Marriage

Mom's best friend Christine lived right next door to us. Christine was like my aunt—I had known her for over ten years. Every Saturday night, she and my mom always went to the races in West Memphis with me. They lived for it and I was glad to have them there.

Dad was busy racing his midget on many Saturday nights. Even though he always went with me on Fridays, he wanted to race his midget on Saturdays and who could blame him. He was still a kick-ass race driver in his own right and I wanted him to get out there any chance he could.

So on most Saturday nights, it was just Mom and Christine and I heading out to West Memphis.

They had a ritual that they always followed. First they both came down to the race shop to help me load the race car onto the trailer. Mom and Christine were very tiny women, and I wasn't all that big myself. So God had to be laughing his tail off while the three of us tried to load that sprint car. Even though it weighed around 1400 pounds, it didn't have a starter so you had to push that baby up onto the trailer by hand. You should have seen us out there, Christine and I pushing like crazy while Mom steered the car. Finally I soon got smart and put an electric winch on the trailer, so I could load the car myself.

Once we got to the race track, my good buddy Shan would pitch Mom and Christine the keys of his pristine '77 Blue Ford LTD with a white vinyl top and white leather interior. Mom and Christine would hightail it over to Panchos Mexican Restaurant about a mile down from the race track and they would feast on some of the best Mexican food you had ever eaten before the races started. My good friend Shan (who just recently passed away) gets a good shout out for doing that because that Ford LTD was his pride and joy and he never let anyone else drive it but Mom and Christine.

October . . . up to the Midwest

As fall came on, I itched to go back to the Midwest. I was fast in the Memphis area but could I make the grade in Indiana? Gambler Chassis had run an advertising piece in *Sport Speed News* about me setting that new track record and were encouraging me to try. So the last week of September, Curt and I took off for Bloomington, Indiana for a Friday-night show. But we would have to win some cash real quick. That engine problem from a few weeks back had put us in the hole. All we had was a couple of 55-gallon barrels of racing fuel, enough new tires for a few nights of racing.

There in Bloomington I turned in the third fastest qualifying time but then in the heat race a rocker arm broke in the engine and we missed the feature. We only made a hundred dollars. So we decided to go on over to Putmanville to race on Saturday.

"If we don't win some good cash over there," I told Curt, "you're gonna have to sell your body to science for money to get back home."

It was one in the morning when we got to Putmanville. After sleeping a few hours in the truck at a local car wash, we got busy working on the race car. I had to recheck the engine and Curt got busy checking everything else. The race there in Putmanville was a USAC non-wing show so we had to take the top and front wings off the car, and change all of the torsion bars and shocks to accommodate the differences in how a non-wing race car should handle out on the track. Some sprint-car series go non-wing, which is even more dangerous and kamikaze than the regular variety, because a wingless sprint car runs with less down force, so it's way less stable, especially on the turns. When you wreck in a non-wing race, you don't just kinda wreck – especially if you land upside down. But I was ready to take the risk.

By five p.m. we had everything ready and made our way on over to the race track. As we unloaded, I happened to see Blackie Fortune. He stopped by and chatted with me, like nothing had happened, and offered to let me use his race shop if I ever needed to. It seemed like he felt guilty for having fired me.

That night I qualified eighth out of fifty cars and went into the feature event with a good starting spot. Then my brakes failed. I crashed into the car running in front of me and took both of us out of the race.

Afterwards, that driver came over to my pits to kick my tail and I tried to smooth-talk him. Then my bud Rick Hood came up to where that guy and I were arguing and became the peacemaker, and everything was all right. Except, of course, we hadn't made any money. As we loaded everything up, Curt and I were thinking we might have to head back to Mississippi and regroup.

Then I looked over at Curt and said, "What do ya think?"

"What do you mean, whaddya think?" he asked.

"I mean… I got a hundred bucks left. That's enough cash to fill the truck up, grab some burgers and get back home on. Or we head on over to Springfield, Missouri and race on Sunday night. Do we head back with our tails between our legs? Or do we take one last shot? We're fast, we just need some luck."

Curt just looked back at me and grinned. He said, "Hell fire, JT, let's go racing!"

When we got to Springfield, we did a repeat of the day before. After we slept a few hours in the truck at a car wash, we fixed the brakes, put the wings back on the car, changed back the torsion bars and shocks, and headed to the race track. We had $10.00 left and I sent Curt to the concession stand to spend it on hot dogs for our supper. If we did not win some cash, we would have to do more than sell our bodies to science to get home.

In qualifying I sat fast time and the race car ran perfect. But we were not counting our chickens yet because the fast qualifier had to start sixth – this track had a rule that had the first six qualifiers reversed order for the start of the main event. That rule always made for a more exciting race for the fans but it was rough on the drivers trying to pass for the win. These Springfield guys were fast too and they did not intend for some Southern hot shoe to take their cash back to Mississippi.

But the racing Gods were smiling down on us. When the 40-lap main event started, I took off from my sixth starting spot and drove like a madman. Lap after lap I passed one more of the five drivers ahead of me, and on lap 35 I took the lead and went on for the win. Thank God!

After we collected our $3,000, we grabbed a sack of burgers from a local Burger King, got a motel and crashed from total exhaustion. Ain't life good!

The next day, Curt and I caught some breakfast at the local Denny's and assessed our situation. Next weekend there were a few more races over in Lawrenceburg, Indiana, that paid some pretty good cash. But the car needed a few repairs. My next call was to Blackie Fortune to see if he was serious about letting me use his race shop any time. "Sure, come on over," Blackie said.

Late that afternoon Curt and I pulled into Blackie's shop and began making repairs. Ricky Hood was now back driving for him, and came by to check in on us. By 8:00 p.m. we had found us a cheap little motel about two miles from Blackie's shop and were settling in for the week.

That next weekend, we did pretty good considering we were probably the least funded team there. The first night, I qualified fifth and finished fifth in the main event. The second night I qualified third but ended up finishing sixth after my left front tire went flat. But even after we bought new tires and fuel, we actually cleared a few thousand dollars for the weekend.

More importantly, I was learning valuable lessons about sprint car racing — especially how to fine-tune the car for dirt race tracks. And there were some better tires available if you knew what to ask for. Blackie and his son Rick gave me the secret handshake on some good info, so I finally understood why Mike Ward was so fast after the race track dried out in Memphis that time.

Now, it was time to get back to Memphis and regroup.

Go west, young man

The second week of October, racing season was winding down in the Midwest… but not in the Mid South or the west coast. In two weeks, West Memphis had a big fifty lapper coming up. But before that, Blackie and Ricky Hood were heading out to Phoenix for a World of Outlaws race the very next weekend.

When I told Ricky that I would love to go out there to just watch and pick up some more tricks of the trade, he asked me if I wanted to ride out with him and his girlfriend Robin in his new motor home. They could use the company and the help with driving.

That trip with Ricky and his beautiful girl friend Robin was pure pleasure. No, I'm not making this up, her name really is Robin. In Phoenix I helped Blackie crew the car for Ricky and made a professional connection with Ken Jenkins, who was now ramrodding Stanton Racing, soon to become Challenge Racing. Phoenix had been the headquarters for Stanton for years but since selling out to Harold Anette and being headed up by Ken Jenkins, they were in the process of moving the company to Des Moines, Iowa. Ken was a sprint car icon and the original brains behind Gambler Chassis, my sponsor. But Ken and Gambler had split up last year and, the split was not a friendly one.

I already knew there might be a storm brewing between me and Gambler as well, because of all the rumors about me, and because Gambler East and Gambler West were feuding. So I talked to Ken, hoping for advice on what to do if things turned ugly. Ken turned out to be a pretty good friend, and hooked me up with a lawyer in Nashville who was representing him. I could call this lawyer if everything blew up in my face.

Memphis, the fifty lapper

After I flew back to Memphis, Curt and I drove down to Corinth, picked up the race car, drove back over to Memphis and my friend Tommy Roland's house and race shop so we could be there in Memphis as we prepared the race car for the big 50-lap end of season race there at Riverside Speedway. I needed to do a few checks on my engine so I wanted to be close to Danny's Engine Service if my checks turned out be more serious that I thought. Being there in Memphis would save me time on preparing the car for the race. Luckily for us, every thing check out just fine and by Saturday afternoon me Curt and Tommy had that blue and yellow number 5 ready to go. I felt very confident about the race, I knew that if nothing went wrong, I could win that baby going away. My new tricks of the trade I had learned up in the mid west and through Blackie Fortune had begun to pay off in new found speed and reliability, so even though Bobby Davis Jr. and Terri Gray were in town, hot off the World of Outlaws tour I still knew I had something for them.

When we got to the track that Saturday night there was a sense of anticipation in the air. It had been a long hard fought racing season for all the race teams and every one really needed a winter break to regroup and recharge their batteries, both physically and psychically. The weather was cool and crisp instead of hot and humid and all the teams had their engines running, warming them up and checking their fuel mixtures.

By 6:00 PM, the sun had all ready set and the lights surrounding the speedway were on full glair, and the grand stands were packed. I had my entire posse with me on this Saturday night, my pit area was full of all of my buds. Even ole Dexter and Larry Killough from back home were out there wiping the car down, getting all the dust and mud from hot laps removed from every crook and cranny on the car. of course, dad was right in there supervising the whole darn thing.

By it came time to qualify, we were ready to go only on this night, the track was wet and heavy so there would no chance to set another track record, we have to just do the best we could.

When qualifying was over, I had set fast time once again and Eddie Gallagher had set second fastest time. Eddie was a good guy and would race you clean so I knew I would have no trouble from him on the start of the race. He would not wreck me like some of those other idiots like Ricky Sinhouse or Lee Brewer. Those two guys were kamikaze pilots and would wreck your butt for no reason at all. I hated racing with those guys. All the heat races went off with out a hitch, no one had a crash, even Rick Sinhouse and Lee Brewer managed to get through the heat races with out wrecking them selves or some one else. Our car was fast, I was confident and we were ready to run the main event, the fifty lap end of season championship race at exactly 10:00 PM. WE HAD A FULL FIELD OF SOME OF THE FASTES SPRINT CARS IN America in the line up that night including Bobby Davis Jr. who would be starting in the third row and Terri Gray who would be starting father back in the field.

Line em up . . . it's time to race!

I was very calm about the main event, I was in my element, my car was fast, my confidence was very good and the track surface had turned out to be just perfect. These sprint cars were going to be rocket ships during the fifty lapper. The pit steward came by right at 10:00 sharp, told us to get in our cars and fire them up. I slowly grabbed my helmet and racing gloves out of the trailer, walked over to my car and climbed in to that baby. She fit me like a glove, like she was an extension of my body and I could not think of a better place to be on a cool and crisp Saturday night only two miles from down town Memphis, Tennessee. I put my helmet and gloves on, fastened my seat belts, Curt reached down to the lap belts and pulled them even harder almost squeezing the breath out of me. I casually looked over to my left and gave my posse who was all standing only three feet from the car a big but very cool thumbs up and I was on my way out to the track.

I quickly took my place right in the front of the pack right next to fast Eddie Gallagher never looking at him and we made three more slow pace laps as all the cars took their proper position in the starting field all while I tried to position my self in just the right place on the track in order to get the jump on Eddie at the start. I slowly began to ease him more to the out side so my tires would have perfect traction when the green flag waved to start the race and stood on the gas. Then, on the fourth time around to the front stretch the cars were all perfectly lined up, I had my eyes focused like laser beams on the flagman knowing I had to be on my game for the start if I wanted to beat Eddie to the first corner.

Then, as we came off the fourth turn the flagmen trying to be coy, quickly waved the green flag and the race from hell was on.

Eddie and I both stood on the gas and as those 800 hundred horse powered engines came to life we took off like we had been shot out of a cannon. I immediately managed to get out in front of Eddie before we got to the first turn and I was long gone. My car was the fastest it had ever been and I was hitting my marks in the corners perfectly. I began to click off lap after lap in a blinding blur that even had me impressed at how fast I was going and by lap five, I was all ready lapping cars at the back of the field and I had a full half of a straightaway lead on Eddie. But I knew I could not take a chance by slowing down, I had to keep on standing on the gas because Eddie was no slouch and the heavy lap traffic I was in would slow my pace down allowing Eddie and of course Bobby Davis Jr. to catch up. I never looked back, I just kept my head down driving my ass off up top and passing the lap cars on the outside.

By lap 30, I still had a half straightaway lead and had just put my arch rival Mike Ward a lap down. By lap 44, I had lapped up to the fourth place car and was coming around to lap Terry Gray who was having some trouble with his car for the second time. I just needed to run six more clean laps and keep Bobby Davis Jr. who was now running in second place about forty yards back behind me. I could see that once I got by Terry Gray I had a clean race track for at least half a lap which would really allow me to stretch it back out and take the victory.

But when I came up to pass Terry on the inside coming up off of the second corner, his steering locked up and he crashed into me causing me to spin into the infield. I stood on the gas as soon as I got control of the car, did a quick 360 and took back out on the track to try and salvage my running position in the front of the pack. But I soon realized that something was wrong with my car because I could barely keep it under control, by the time I got back around to my pit area. I knew I had a flat right rear tire and I had to stop and get it changed. My crew changed the tire as quickly as possible and got back into the race but it was too late to take the win.

Bobby Davis Jr. took the victory and I ended up finishing fourth. It was very disappointing to lose that race, but what are you going to do, shit happens and in sprint car racing it happens a lot and very dramatically.

Back in the pits every fan in the place came down to get an autograph and to give me pat on the back for being so fast. Even ole Mike Ward came by to shake my hand which totally blew me away. One of his crew members told me that I was turning mid 11.50's lap times out on the track during the race which was a full second under my track record. He was completely impressed on how I had come into my own as one of the best sprint car drivers in America. Even Eddie Gallagher's car owner Bobby Sparks told his crew that night that I was the best race driver he had ever seen. That was saying something considering one of his drivers had been Sammy Swindell, a World of Outlaws national champion.

To put some icing for the good run I had, National Speed Sport news, the # one racing newspaper in America put me on the front Page the next week along with Darrell Waltrip and Bill Elliott. That run had put me on the map and I fully intended to take advantage of it if at all possible.

That was the positive, the negative was that my Gambler deal was falling apart and my finances were really low because of all of my racing expenses. I had made good money all year long, but when you're basically financing your own deal, it takes everything you win and then some to keep the team running. I knew full well I had to make some changes for the next season. I need a bigger sponsor and I wanted to get out on the World of Outlaws tour. I wanted to give that a try for at least one season and then give NASCAR a shot. My good friend Lake Speed had made the NASCAR leap and was having some success with those bunches of good ole boys. I knew if I ask, he would help me make it in that series as well.

One thing was for sure though, I did not have a lot of time on my hands, I had all ready decided back in the summer that within six years, I was going to have sex realignment surgery.

I just wanted to give this pro racing opportunity a real chance, I owed it to myself and to my parents. I did not want to waste my talent, God had given it to me just as he had given me this gender situation.

About two weeks after the final race of the season I was experiencing some major pain in my neck and my left arm was still had moments when I lost all feeling in it. So I figured I needed to go see a doctor just to be safe. When Dr. Welch got my x-rays back, he looked at me in a bit of bewilderment and asks me when was the first time I had broken my neck. I looked back at him and said, "What do you mean, I never broke my neck." He then showed me the x – rays and there it was as plain a day, not only was there scar tissue showing an old crack in my neck but a more recent one that had begun to heal. He looked at me and said, "You're real damn lucky, I don't want you racing anything for the next six months, I mean it." He gave me a neck brace, I reluctantly put it on and left the office. When I got in my truck, it took that damn thing and threw it in the back seat, I never put it on again.

November 1985
I had been kicking butt and taking names all season long . . .

Putting my own sprint car team together had been the best thing I had ever done for my career. But it had not come without a very high cost both financially and politically and I was glad to get the year over with so I could move on with my racing goals and away from the ass holes in Memphis. I had gotten caught up in a political quagmire between one of my sponsors and the company who built their racing parts . . . they had severed their ties in a bitter dispute and I had lost my sponsor - consignment deal.

Adding to the animosity between these two companies and me losing my deal was, my toughest competitors, which were a bunch of sure fire rednecks from Memphis area were adding fuel to the fire by telling both of these sponsors I was a fag and every other rumor they could think up to back stab me out of my deals. These bunch of rednecks had been jealous of my sponsorship deals from day one plus, I had been kicking their butts all season long even landing on the cover of the Nations biggest racing news paper, National Speed Sport News, so they were going after me any way they could.

I knew the fire was getting hot around September but I had no idea it had grown into a full-blown bombing raid on my career. By that October, I had enough of the back-stabbing had gotten a lawyer up in Nashville. He and I were on target to sue somebody, we just didn't know just who. He had learned that these guys who were badmouthing me all lived in the biggest glass houses of all. He had them dead on for selling and taking drugs, some to finance their racing. Most of them were having affairs with other men's wives and girlfriends.

"If you want to," he told me, "we can get every one of them for slander, including one of your sponsors."

At the time, I decided that suing them would cause some real animosity towards me in the sport. If I wanted to continue my racing career, I probably needed to let it go. Looking back, however, I realized that I should have turned my lawyer loose on them, because they really damaged my career.

However, one guy there in Memphis, Wayne, was still wanting to help me out with a full-blown sponsorship deal. We were out on the town getting to know one another and working out the details. Basically he was wining and dining me and I was schmoozing him and we were having a whole lot of fun — or at least he was — and I was acting the cool part.

One Saturday night around the first week of November, he and I and a friend of mine, Bob, who worked on my crew that season were standing in line to get into a local disco. Now, I really didn't want to be there chasing women with those guys but I had to play the game of being a macho horn toad because the rumors about me were red-hot by now and I was doing everything I could to squelch them. At the moment that meant chasing chicks at the dance clubs there in the River City. We had been standing in line for just a few minutes when Wayne took off to the head of the line to talk our way in without having to stand outside in the cold like the rest of the mere mortals. We were sprint car people, baby, and we didn't wait for anyone.

While Wayne was greasing the palm of the doorman, three good-looking girls walked up, a blond and two brunettes, and joined us in the line. Of course my crew guy, who thought he was Mr. Stud Muffin, started hitting on them and the girls seemed to like him acting like an idiot. So when Wayne came back, he realized the golden opportunity that lay before us, and we all went inside like we had known one another all of our lives.

Quickly we found a table and the blonde sat right beside Wayne and directly across from me. Long story short, we all had a great time dancing and drinking our tails off, and ole Wayne decided that we should do it again the next night. Damn I thought, I was going to have to be with the brunette who had been kissing me like crazy for the past two hours. The kissing was fine but I really didn't want to carry on this act every damn night.

Well, we re-played that scene five nights in a row and I was tired of it big time. Wayne had a cabin he was renting up at a resort area just outside of Memphis and I had been staying there with him off and on ever since he and I decided to get our racing deal going. Now the blonde beauty, Pam, was also staying up there for a few days while she looked for a new apartment.

She was working at a local department store, going to art college and serving in the Marine reserves . . . and she made me real nervous. Since the night we had met, she flirted with me at every turn . . . When we would be having dinner in a nice restaurant and she was sitting across from me, she would have her shoes off under the table and her foot firmly planted in my crotch! Damn I thought, this chick was bold and if ole Wayne found out what she was doing he would freak out. Plus, I wasn't interested at all but to tell you the truth, it was rather exciting and daring to have your team owner's date playing with your private parts.

Anyway, on Friday night, we were all going out to this hot country western dance club called Cowboys. Wayne and my date, Karen the brunette, both had to work late so Pam and I were just going to meet them at the club around ten o'clock that night after they got off work. Before we went out, Pam and I needed to take a quick shower before we went out and she insisted that I go first while she took care of a few phone calls. So I grabbed a couple of towels and hit the showers. After I finished bathing, I grabbed my two towels, dried off and suddenly realized that I had left my robe in the bedroom. At first I panicked because I had something to hide that I didn't want

Miss Pam to see. My little boobs had been growing like crazy because of the hormones I was taking for several years. Those little babies were pretty perky and I had been hiding then with tight tee shirts and duck tape . . . Now here I was with only two towels to wrap around my private parts. But what about my boobs? Quickly I draped the second towel around my neck and let it hang down over my breast. If I made a dash to my bedroom, she would never see my exposed breast.

But to my horror, she was standing right outside the bathroom door. She grabbed the towel from around my neck and wheeled it around like a lasso. Then, with a quirky grin on her face, she snapped me on the leg with it and started to laugh her head off. There I stood, my breasts talking to the heavens and she had her eyes directly focused on them like they were the finest thing she had ever seen. It scared the hell out me!

Quickly I tried to grab the towel back, but she lunged at me and gave me a huge bear hug, saying, "I knew it, I knew it . . . I always thought you were a girl! The first time I say you at the disco I thought that you just might be a girl dressed up like a guy . . . I thought you were probably a lesbian, but there is more to this than that, isn't it. I bet you want to be a girl . . . You don't have to worry about me because I'm a lesbian and I'm very attracted to you. I'm only putting up with this charade with Wayne because my girlfriend Karen who really has the hots for you wanted me to have one heterosexual experience just to prove to myself that I am really a lesbian. You are so cute and I want to be with you."

I could not believe what I was hearing. Then, just before I had a damn heart attack and died from the embarrassment, we just burst out laughing over how weird the situation really was. You couldn't make this crap up if you tried. The tabloids would read: *A Gender Identity (male) professional race car driver who actually looks like a real girl, and an undercover lesbian who is also an officer in the Marines Corps and looks like Marilyn Monroe and has the hots for the male race car driver who wants to be a woman, hook up in a cabin owned by her new boy friend who she really doesn't want to be with ... more on page six!*

Things could get out of hand if ole Wayne found out what was up with his new squeeze. After we calmed down from the shock of the moment and the uncontrollable laughter, we sat down and shared our life stories with one another. Then we began to kiss. Before we knew it, we were under the sheets. An hour later, we were still laying there talking about our lives and realizing that because we had so much in common, and so much to hide, we needed to be together. In fact, Wayne and Karen were perfect for one another and that's when the little light of infinite wisdom went on in our little stupid-ass heads.

"Let's swap dates," I said. It made perfect sense.

One problem though—we had to get Wayne and Karen to go for it too. Later that night, at the dance club, after Pam and I had slammed down a few beers to get our courage up, we calmly told Wayne and Karen about our little plan for all of us to swap dating partners. We were pretty slick about it, telling Wayne and Karen how perfect they were for each other. To our surprise they went for it. Both of them were horny as hell anyway.

From that night on, Pam and I couldn't get enough of one another. Clearly we were both girls and needed that feminine spirit in our lives, but more than the relationship possibilities, we understood each other's plight in life. Being with me made her look normal in the eyes of the Marines. For me, having a blonde bomb shell as a girl friend made those assholes I raced with in

Memphis have to eat their words about me. On paper it was the perfect situation. I would change my sex in three years, and then we would live as two lesbians happily ever after.

It was a real dumb idea, but it was the only one we had at the time!

In the mean time, Wayne and I continued to develop our racing program for the next season. But I sensed that something wasn't quite right. The funding for the team was slow in coming. If it didn't come, I would be in deep trouble. All the racing deals with other teams were all ready set so if this deal didn't pan out, there would not be anyone else to drive for.

The weekend after Thanksgiving, our whole gang was hanging out at the line-dancing club and we were pretty much getting out of hand A bunch of other Memphis racing assholes were also there, so I was acting pretty damn macho and flaunting my girlfriend in their faces. Pam was playing along with it big time. We were dancing our asses off and drinking tequila shots every chance we got. Since I wasn't a big drinker, by midnight I wasn't feeling any pain and got it on my mind that I was going to ask Miss Pam to marry my skinny white ass. I don't know where that notion came from because when all things were said and done, I like men, not women. But no, I had to get stupid and ask her to marry me just to prove to everyone else that they were wrong about me.

To my amazement, Pam said, "Yes, I will."

What was she thinking? . . . she had to be as nuts as I was to accept my proposal. One of my crew members, Bob, who was standing right beside us and heard everything, damn near passed out from the shock. Immediately he pulled me off to the side and tried to talk some sense into me. But I was hell bent on holding up my end of the deal.

It didn't matter that I had just met her a month earlier and didn't know anything about her other than that we liked to party, that she was good looking and a Marine. I was so elated to have someone I could share my secrets with, and starved for any kind of affection. The wedding was on…and my parents would be very happy!

The next day brought on clearer heads, but once Pam and I talked it over without the cloud of tequila we came to the same conclusion. We decided on January 1st, 1986 in Corinth, my hometown . . . It would be a New Years Day wedding—a grand affair—a big thumb of my nose to the people in Corinth. Of course, ole Wayne would be my best man and Miss Karen would be Pam's maid of honor.

Mom and Dad were happy and relieved that I was getting married. But, they thought I was rushing it a bit and I could tell that my mom wasn't that fond of Miss Pam. But they concluded that I was finally done with the gender issue once and for all.

The Wedding . . .

We all got through the month of December without backing out on our marriage plans. The race-team deal was faltering—we had yet to buy any new cars or parts because Wayne didn't have the cash yet. I was hoping that he would pull it out after the first of the year.

Meanwhile, the fateful day had come.

We had a full entourage of our friends and family coming in for the wedding . . . me, Wayne, Bob and little Curt were all staying with my parents, and Pam and Karen were staying with my grandmother next door. By lunch on New Year's day, we had gotten the rehearsal and a night of New Years Eve partying behind us. I was down in my race shop printing up a few signs to put along the road so the wedding guests could find their way out to the house.

Everyone else was up at my parents nursing hangovers and getting ready for the 6:00 p.m. wedding. I was busy working on those signs and just trying to not freak out when a car pulled into our driveway. It was my old friend Irv, the crazy guy who had been with us when I was injured in the Astro Dome. He grabbed hold me, slung me over his shoulder and started running around the shop laughing like hell. This big ole 6'2" country boy was always doing something like that, but you never really knew what he was going to do next . . . He was a big jokester and a lot of fun.

After he was finished ribbing me about getting married, my mom came down and asked him if he could take Pam down to the jeweler to have her ring re-sized.

About an hour later Irv and Pam came back, and he sent word to me that he had some unfinished business to tend to so he would see us at the wedding latter on. I took him at his word and never thought about it again. Pam looked a little aggravated, but I passed it off as her being nervous like I was.

Of course the wedding was fabulous and went off without a hitch. But our friend Irv never showed up.

Pam and I took off to Memphis, checked in at one of the better Holiday Inns and shacked up for a few days, just enjoying one another . . . We were running short on funds so we didn't feel the need to take off on a honeymoon. Once we got to racing and the cash flow expanded, we take a really good trip then.

Over the next few weeks we settled in to our new lives, and found a cool little apartment there in the midtown area. While Pam continued her Marine Corps career and attended art school, I continued to work on the racing deal. Now and then I traveled down to Corinth to make some extra cash by working at my dad's tool and die company.

But only a few weeks into the marriage, Pam began to pull back. She was cold and aloof, and every time I asked her what was going on, she would clam up. One night I got so mad at her coldness that I kicked over the ironing board as I stormed out of the house scaring the hell out her and out myself as well. I just hated the silent treatment, especially when I didn't think I deserved it. In the meantime the racing deal with Wayne had gone south and I was left looking for a ride in a very dry market.

That next weekend, when we were driving back to Memphis after a visit in Corinth, I had had enough of the pissy attitude.

"If you don't tell me what's up," I told her. "I'm going to make you walk the rest of the way home."

Nothing could have prepared me for what she finally said.

"Well, JT, I didn't want to tell you this, it's going to hurt your feelings, but you ask. You know when your friend Irv took me to go re-size my ring. Well, he told me some things about you that weren't very nice . . . In fact I thought what he said was hurtful, but it also started me to thinking that I made a terrible mistake by marrying you. He told me that you were no good . . . that you were nothing but a silly little fag, that your parents had always been embarrassed by you and that you were the biggest scandal this town had ever had . . . He told me that I had better run away from you as fast I could. I knew all about all the girl stuff, that's why I liked you. But the scandal thing and the fact that your racing deal is not working out is making me nervous. What are you going to do to earn a living? Plus I don't know if I really want to be married to you . . . I think it was a mistake. What Irv said about you was mean and you should do something about it . . . You should tell your dad, he needs to confront him."

My mouth was hanging open as I listened, but I kept driving.

I felt like I needed to defend myself but against what? I had been up front with her from the beginning about my life and my future. Of course she was nervous about the future. She was used to a sure thing, she had structure in her life because of her military career, so hooking up with a professional sprint car driver who had absolutely no job security had to be daunting.

I didn't have any answers for her at the time. The timing was all wrong, there was just too much pressure. Plus, I suspected that she was feeling the need to be with a girl, in fact I was feeling the heat from just the opposite end of the sexual spectrum. Whatever I told her to calm her nerves right now had to be short and sweet.

So I just told her, "You know me well enough to know I would do whatever I can to put food on the table, even if it means going to work for my dad full time to get us through the rough spots. But I don't intend to give up on my racing career. I'm too damn good at it and I'm just hitting my stride.

If she was thinking that she had made a mistake by marrying me . . . in reality I was thinking the same thing about her!

Two days later

The next day Pam was still cold and aloof. I deserved better than that from her and actually thought she was playing a head trip on me.

My dad had called me that Monday night and said that he needed me on Tuesday to help him out at the shop on a special welding job that no one could do but me. He would pay me a thousand bucks if I could get it done by Thursday. I would have to work two days straight but the money would be worth it.

I told Pam about the job, packed a few pairs of jeans and without a kiss or a hug I headed to Corinth.

That next night around 9:00, I called several times to check in with Pam but she never answered the phone. The following afternoon, after I finished up the job and got paid, I hightailed it back over to Memphis. Even though I was tired as hell, I had to see what was up with Pam. I had a few things to say and they were not going to be nice!

When I pulled up to our driveway her car was not there and the porch light wasn't on. Once I did get the door open and turned on the lights, I realized that the apartment was virtually empty and abandoned. There was a note laying on the kitchen table with a set of house keys on top of it.

A sinking feeling rushed over my body—I knew what the note was going to say.

"JT, I'm sorry but I can't do this. This was a mistake and its best if I leave before it goes any farther. Don't try to contact me. I'll have my attorney handle the divorce. If you try to fight me on this, I will show Wayne and the racing guys a picture I took of you in drag . . . Pam."

I had never felt so defeated in my life. There I sat alone in an empty apartment with tears rolling down my face, not because Pam had left but because I had tried so damn hard to make everyone happy and I had failed miserably once again at having a relationship. I didn't want to be with a woman. In my heart I was a woman and wanted to have a relationship with a man. But I had given up many of my dreams to be with Pam and to please my family and friends. I felt stupid and dirty about the marriage and, even worse, naive about letting Pam photograph me in drag one night before we were going out to a disco. At the time that photograph was just us acting silly, but now I realized that she was setting me up. What a bitch . . . What frikin' nerve she had—a lesbian in the Marine Corp married to someone who suffers from gender identity, and she was trying to threaten me with blackmail. Screw her! Ciao, baby!

No way would I fight her on the divorce but I did want to find her and smack her one time right in the mouth . . .give her a little dirt-track sprint-car racing attitude adjustment. But it was time to get on with my life. This had been a big lesson for me and it snapped me out of the fog of trying to please everyone else.

That night, I made the decision that I would focus on making it to the big time in motorsports, and develop a solid plan to change my sex within the next six years. I would need the time to get my career in gear and to save the cash for the surgery and to survive on afterwards.

CHAPTER 11

Next stop ... California Re Start

More Drama

It was the first week of April 1986, and I was talking to Deuce Terrell, a good friend and one of the best sprint-car crew chiefs in the world.

Deuce worked for Challenge Racing Enterprises in Des Moines, Iowa. They were arch rivals with Gambler Chassis, one of my sponsors the year before, so he was shopping my name around to teams that Challenge supported in hopes someone would put me in their driver's seat. He knew I had gotten the screws with the other company... and he knew I had what it takes to win on the national level. Since the break-up with Pam freed me to do damn well what I wanted, and there were no other opportunities in the Memphis area, I had hightailed up to Des Moines for Challenge's open house and the World Of Outlaws sprint-cars points event in Knoxville, Iowa, just a few miles from Challenge's manufacturing plant and offices.

"If you don't get your ass up here so I can introduce you to some potential team owners," Deuce had told me, "I'm gonna kick your butt."

After I hung out at the plant for a few days, feeling awe-struck by the company's high profile, Deuce introduced me to their west-coast distributors, Eddie and Sandy Chinin, who were based in San Jose. Eddie and Sandy were full blooded Hawaiians and obsessed with sprint cars. They had been on the mainland for a year or so, had sunk a ton of money into their Challenge distributorship and needed a hotshot driver for their house car. Challenge needed their west coast distributorship to be successful. So winning on the lucrative west-coast circuit was a must. Plus, their driver needed to work on the cars and have good chassis knowledge.

Even though the Chinins couldn't understand my Southern drawl and I couldn't understand their strong Hawaiian accent, we hit it off. Unlike so many of the drivers back then, I had put together a pretty cool resume and portfolio, and that impressed them. By the end of that week, they gave me a deal to try out in their car.

I drove to San Jose in two days flat . . . just in time to look over the car and head to the races at Hanford, California.

That first race started off with a bang—I qualified fourth fastest in a car I had never driven before. But during the main event, as I was running third, the left front brake locked up and caused me to hit the inside wall, knocking us out of the race. Luckily for me it wasn't my fault, and everyone was pleased with how I had driven. But the real test was next weekend: a big event at Baylands Raceway Park. Baylands and California Fair Grounds Speedway at Chico, where we would be racing right after the Baylands event, were the two most competitive tracks on the California circuit.

Meanwhile, the Chinins graciously had me stay in their home, and it was a learning experience for all of us. Communications were improving, because we were all racers and spoke the same lingo. But sometimes it was hilarious listening to them trying to figure out what in the hell I had just told them.

The funniest thing that happened was over food. The first night, Sandy cooked up this fantastic Hawaiian meal which included tons of rice, which I love. When I had finished the main course, I put one last scoop of rice on my plate and asked Eddie to pass the sugar. Without thinking he handed me the sugar bowl and I spread a good teaspoon of the white crystals over my rice like everybody did back home. The entire Chinin family were about to pass out from the shock. They had never seen such desecration of the holy mother of rice in their lives.

Of course I egged it on just a bit, trying to get them to taste it. They just held their noses.

Two other Hawaiians, Rodney and Larry, also connected with me right off. These two guys would turn out to be incredible allies throughout my time in California.

That first week at the Chinin race shop gave me the chance to check their car from front to rear. All drivers have their little tricks. Just getting the seat fitted to your body and positioned in the cockpit was critical to your safety, endurance and performance. I wanted the seat tilted back and to the left just a bit, and I didn't need for the steering wheel to be right up in my face. Also, because my broken ankle several years back, I needed to elevate my heel about an inch and a half in order to apply the gas pedal with ease and smoothness . . . which is imperative when running on dry and slick racing surfaces.

Most important, we cleaned every nut and bolt on that baby and had her shining like a new penny. I hate dirty race cars, and that one had been a dingy mess the week before. The way I see it, a clean well-prepared race car looks fast just sitting still. That gives you an edge on your competition – they know you have your shit together before you ever get on the track.

Baylands is a dirt track—3/8 of a mile, mildly banked—located right in the city limits of Freemont, California. It's pretty damn fast, especially during hot laps and qualifying, when the track has plenty of moisture and grip. By the time hot laps are over, it builds up a fairly decent wall of dirt around the outside of the turns, right next to the wall. So if you want to go really fast, you have to get up on the cushion of dirt and just stand on the gas. But you have to be careful, because if you run in there and hit that ledge of dirt sideways at 130 miles per hour, you're going to barrel-roll your race car into the next state.

My first night that track was fast and heavy with a big ole cushion around turns one and two. Those California hot shoes were banging that baby like crazy, and at least a couple of them had put their cars into the parking lot in piles of crumpled metal and fiber glass. So the air was loaded with anticipation and excitement.

For me, Baylands was similar to a track I had grown up racing on in Milan, Tennessee so my learning curve on the new track was relatively easy. After hot laps, I made a few minor adjustments to the tire pressure. Then, because I was going to run the cushion, I put a stiffer right rear shock on, and also lowered the car about a quarter of an inch. Hopefully those adjustments would make my run thorough the corners safer and faster. My job was depending on it.

The push car took me out to the pit road and I fired off on my qualifying run.

As I hauled that baby into turn one flat out, I had miscalculated my entrance by just a few inches. So I banged into the cushion going way too fast and my car began to bounce and bang into the track, and I was afraid we were about to tumble into the parking lot. But luckily, by the time I got to turn two, the car had settled down and I was on my way like a bullet down the back straightaway. On the next lap, I had a choice. Either enter the corner lower and slower. Or, if I wanted to have a shot at the fast time and the pole position, I had to drive in just as fast as before, but closer to the cushion to prevent me from banging into its ledge. The right choice was obvious: be fast and dangerous.

As I entered that turn next time, I hit the cushion perfectly, and never backed off the gas. When the lap was done, the crowd was on their feet cheering.

"The Tennessee Traveler," boomed the announcer, "has set fast time for the evening. JT Hayes is just 3/100ths of a second off of the track record set by the World of Outlaws two months ago."

Once I got back to the pits, my crew and the Chinins were cheering too. That was their first-ever fast time. Everyone was leaning into the car congratulating me.

Later that night during the 30-lap main event, I took off with a fairly good lead but then my car jumped out of gear. I couldn't get it back in gear and eventually coasted to a stop right in front of my crew. My heart sank. But my crew managed to get that baby back in gear, and I pulled back on the track again, dead last behind the 24-car car field again. There were only eighteen laps left. I stood on the gas and started picking cars off two at a time. I was on a mission! By lap 20 I was up to eighth place. By lap 29, with one lap to go, I had moved into sixth.

Then, on the last turn of the last lap, I made a daring pass to take fourth place. I had just driven the best race of my young sprint-car career against some of the best drivers in America.

When I pulled up to our trailer, my crew and team owners were going crazy. Not only had I given them their best finish ever, but I had done it with flair from the back of the field.

Needless to say, my ride with the Challenge Racing Enterprises house car was a done deal. My momma and daddy would be proud of me; I wished they had been there to enjoy the success.

The next week, I was at the race shop every day working on that car. The Chinins' son, Scotty, was fast becoming a good mechanic and he and I had hit it off. So we got organized and made sure that all our spare parts were in good working condition for the next weekend's racing, which would be a two-day show up in Chico – the Summer Nationals in sprint cars.

I had a good feeling about the coming weekend. Chico was a tacky dirt oval very much like my old home track in Memphis. Already the track announcers were calling me Gentleman JT Hayes, the Tennessee Traveler. My relationship with my psychologist back home was continuing through my diary and my hormone intake, and that thread of attention helped keep me calm. But no one knew anything about that but me.

Chico. . . Memorial Day weekend

The announcer's voice was echoing around the track.

"Ladies and Gentleman, JT Hayes, the Tennessee Traveler, just in from the east coast, is the fast qualifier for the evening . . . Look for this smooth-as-silk driver with a Southern drawl to pull off his first win on the tough California sprint car circuit here tonight. Line 'em up, boys!"

I liked that damn track. It was made for me. After I set fast time and got the pole position—my second in as many weeks—the car was ready for the 30-lap main event, and I knew my team was ready. That bunch of Hawaiians had taken a lot of crap off those arrogant California car owners ever since they came to the mainland, so I was proud to get some of the heat off their back.

Then the track announcer said, "Ladies and gentlemen, we are going to invert the field tonight."

What the hell? The fans had just voted for it. This was a tradition on the Golden Coast, to make races more exciting and less predictable. It was a night-by-night judgment call to invert the first six cars, or the first twelve, or the entire field. Tonight they decided to invert the entire field . . .which meant I would start last. Just my damn luck! Getting to the front with this crop of racecar drivers including Chuck Gurney, Tim Green, Brent Kading and David Bradway, as well as the baddest of the bad California hot shoes, Leland Mcspaden, was going to be a slugfest. Someone was going to get upside down. This wasn't tennis and a glass of merlot at the French Open, baby.

The track announcer shouted to get into our cars. The pit area was electric. But I was calm, almost lazy, which is how I get when I'm really focused. Eddie Chinin looked stressed out, but I just gave him a thumbs up, slid in and buckled up, and the push truck took me out to the track.

There, Scottie helped me slip the car in gear, making sure it would not slip out like the week before.

As I took my place at the back of the field, we made one more pace lap before the start. Over in the grand stands, as we headed down the back straightaway, the crowd were all on their feet roaring in anticipation of the start. Then, in a flash the green flag was waving. I stood on the gas and looked for the outside lane in hopes that the majority of the pack will dive for the bottom where the track had been fastest all night.

My intuition was right—before we made one lap I was up to 19th place. By lap 10, I had gotten up to eleventh. The track was tacky with tons of traction and everyone was fighting their asses off to keep from crashing but I had hit my car's set-up perfectly and I was a rocket ship. Then on lap 15, just as I worked up to seventh place, someone got upside down and the race officials red-flagged the race until they could get the wreck off the track.

During the red flag the Chinin crew came rushing over to see if I wanted to make any changes. I asked the crew to lower the front of the car ¼ of an inch and to add two pounds of air to my right rear tire, in hopes I could get the car to slide through the bumps a bit better. With 15 laps to go, getting past the remaining cars would be harder.

As we re-started, I fell into seventh place. Ole Chuck Gurney was running up there in second place—my job was cut out for me if I was going to catch him.

When the green flag re-dropped, I once again headed to the outside and realized that the changes we had made to the car were perfect. On the next turn, I moved up to fifth—then two more cars in the next five laps. Finally I got right up on Chuck Gurney's tail and took second when his car almost flipped coming off a turn. Now it was time to go after the leader, local hot shoe Dwight Forsberg, who was half a straightaway head. Scottie was standing beside the pit gate waving his hands like a windmill cheering me on. It inspired me. I wanted to win for the Chinins and I damn sure wanted to win it for myself.

With two laps to go, I came up behind the leader. As the white flag waved and we went screaming into the last lap,

I passed Forsberg going into turn one. Rocketing down the back straight, I charged through turns three and four and on toward the checkered flag.

I had done it! What a damn deal . . . from last to first. I was beside myself. The entire Chinin crew came running out on the track like madmen. I gave them a big thumbs up and headed toward victory lane.

Once there I killed the engine. The crew swarmed the car. The fans were going nuts. Managing to unbuckle and get out, I took my fire retardant driving gloves off and threw them up into the grand stands. They handed me the trophy.

The track announcer was pushing a microphone in my face and asking me, "How in the heck did you do that, JT Hayes? That was damn exciting. The fans got their money's worth tonight."

"I did it with the help of my Challenge Racing Enterprises crew and a little luck . . . and by driving my tail off," I said.

After we got the car back down to our pit area, the celebration continued. Fans lined up to get my autograph, and the chicks were being very friendly. Right away my crew started razzing me about already having groupies on the west coast. I was loving it.

Winning gets in your blood. Once you've won, you live for it. You can never get enough.

Later that evening, as we were having dinner at a local restaurant, two guys came over to join us and Eddie Chinin introduced them as new sponsors of our race team. These two guys had a good racing-engine business called Brand X, and they also brought us the Bud Light sponsorship. My impressive drive and win had convinced these guys to back our team, even though they had first wanted to land Chuck Gurney. It looked like my luck was turning for the better. However, on the ride back down to San Jose that night, my mind was on the old rumors from back in Memphis, and I wondered when they would finally catch up with me.

The next day I called my parents, and they were very proud of my win, and my pocket full of cash.

But, time waits on no one. The next week we worked 24-7 building a new car to run the remainder of the season . . . a new design that Challenge was promoting. I hated building new cars and not having enough test time to get the bugs out. We were going to be rushed to get her right before next weekend's big Summer Nationals there at Baylands. After that, we were due in Skagit, Washington for the West Coast's biggest race.

All the racing trade papers in America had my name in them for the big win in Chico. The Chinin team painted my name on the new car, which was very cool. But I didn't like the new braking system – it didn't seem strong enough to me.

Skagit misadventure

The Baylands race didn't go well. I finished fourth which I thought was good in a brand-new car. But I almost wrecked that baby at least ten times that night because the brakes were spongy and soft – they would not stop that car in a ten-acre field.

The next week we had hot discussions about changing the braking system but I was out-voted.

Tuesday morning, we headed north to Washington.

It was a 12-hour drive and suddenly I started feeling sick at my stomach. I crawled in the back of the sleeper and tried to sleep it off. But six hours into the trip, my stomach was cramping like crazy. Urinating was painful, and I was running a fever. When we stopped to gas up outside Seattle, I passed out in the bathroom, which scared hell out of the crew. Once we got to Skagit, I was so sick that the Chinins headed for the emergency room.

Skagit is a small rural community so I started stressing about the quality of their hospital. The Chinins were stressing out too . . . Their driver is sick and it is the biggest race on the west coast . . . damn! When we pulled up at the emergency room, I was feeling frightened and alone, three thousand miles from my home. What was I going to tell the doctor if he saw my breasts? I didn't have any hair on my arms, legs and chest, so with my clothes off, I did not look like a boy.

Inside the nurse handed me a hospital gown and told me to undress and to put the gown on, that the doctor would see me shortly. I hated to do that but followed her orders. Finally, the doctor came in and looked me over. Of course he spotted my little breasts but didn't say a word. When he had finished, he had the nurse take some of my blood and they both left the room. I lay back down on the table and tried to concentrate on not throwing up, but all I could think about was that the doctor might blurt the secret to my racing crew who were all waiting out in the lobby.

About twenty minutes of pure hell, the doc came back and told me that I had a bad urinary infection. He gave me a shot in my butt and some antibiotics.

I asked him what might have caused me to get that infection.

To my amazement, he said, "Well, some people are just born different . . . Like you. You take care of yourself out there in the race this weekend, and make sure you take care of your life."

Damn, what a guy . . . he knew I was in a fix with my body and my life.

By the next morning I was feeling better but wondering if I could drive that 100-lap killer of a race in my condition. For some reason the Chinins were being cold and distant. Their myopic behavior was confusing me. . . It wasn't my fault that I got sick but they were acting like I was killing their opportunity at this important race.

That night I qualified seventh out of 120 cars, and finished fifth . . . which was damn good considering that two days before I was sick, and had driven that 100 laps with virtually no brakes. When the race was over, other drivers and team owners were congratulating me for a good drive, but the Chinins were less than enthusiastic.

I thought they were being greedy. Up until three weeks ago they had never finished in the top ten in anything. Now it looked as if anything less than a win wasn't good enough. Ain't this racing stuff fun!

Get refocused . . . get healthy

Over the next week, as I slowly got my strength back, I knew I needed to get out of the Chinins' house before this deal fell apart. A few guys who hung out at the shop had an apartment in San Jose and told me I could catch the floor with them. But for now, the car had to be ready for a two-day show down in Hanford and Santa Maria, California. I wanted to change the braking system back to the one on the older car we had won in, but the Chinins said no.

Down in Hanford, I qualified fastest again. During the main event I had a 30-lap duel with Chuck Gurney and almost had him passed about two laps from the finish. But a lapped car cut me off. With the brakes so soft, I rammed into him going 130 miles per hour. The damn car almost went airborne but came down on all four wheels, so I stood on the gas and charged to second place.

Of course the Chinins blamed me for the second-place finish. That night on the trip over to Santa Maria, we didn't say a word to one another. Was something up? The Memphis rumors? Or were the Brand X boys lobbying the Chinins to put a California driver in the Bud Light car?

The next morning I tried to work on the brakes, but because of the way the master cylinder was mounted, they were not going to get any better. The Chinins told me I was being whiney.

"Look," I told them politely, "it isn't my fault that the factory made a mistake in how they mounted the master cylinder."

That did not go over well. Who was I to tell them what was wrong with the engineering? I was just a hick from Mississippi.

That night at the Santa Maria race, once again I had the fastest qualifying time. When the green flag waved and we hit the first corner, my brakes went straight to the floor and I careened off the outside wall and almost turned upside down. By the time I got the damn thing back under control, the entire 24-car pack had gotten past me. But I took off after the pack with red in my eyes, and managed to take third place.

By the time I pulled back into our pit spot, I was mad as hell. We had missed winning three events because I couldn't stop the damn car, not to mention putting my life on the line for the glory of the company product.

Getting out of the car, I told Eddie Chinin, "You can take those brakes and stick them where the sun don't shine."

Slamming my helmet into my helmet bag, I told them I would catch a ride back up to San Jose with my buddies. On Monday we would talk about our future.

I had decided to look for another ride.

Enough was enough!

In San Jose, a guy by the name of O. J. Mc Kenny had invited me to stay at his house. His wife was out of town for a few weeks, and he said he could use the company. O. J. was a hotshot sign painter with a handlebar mustache who lettered most of the sprint cars out there in the bay area. He was cool, and liked me because I stood on the gas. All the racers in the bay area liked him, so his liking me put a feather in my cap!

He also thought the Chinins had acted like idiots.

In the meantime, I had met a fine gentleman and his lovely wife, Virgil and Annie Owens, who were more than willing to help. Virgil was probably the bay area's most respected and successful car owner and he knew everyone on a first name basis. That's who Chuck Gurney was driving for, and when I took the win from him up in Chico, Virgil was the first to come over and shake my hand. He was pissed off at the Chinins for the way they had treated me, so he was calling other car owners and putting in a good word for me.

And it worked. I landed the next best ride out there, with the Lovell Brothers, specifically Richard Lovell. The Lovell Brothers racing team was based out of Yuba City, California . . . about fifty miles east of Chico, which was a good two and half hour drive from San Jose and O. J's. house. Ironically the Lovell team was sponsored by the Coors Lite franchise in the bay area, rivals to the Bud Light deal. They were legendary on the west coast. I had lucked out big time!

Richard Lovell was a cool and fun-loving type, and his crew of hard legs were dedicated but happy go lucky. There was no pressure here like at the Chinin team. Oh, the Lovell Team wanted to win, but they had been doing this for years and knew that racing is a fickle deal—you can only do your best while you're having fun. I welcomed the opportunity!

My first race with those guys was at Chico on a Saturday night, and it was like a fairy tale. I took fast time, set a new track record and won the main event going away, all the while trying to nurse a weak oil pump.

The Lovell team were ecstatic, and other car owners were put on notice. Including the Chinins, whom we had outrun with their new hired gun, Craig Keel. Of course the Coors Light crew partied their asses off after the win and I had found a new lease on my racing career.

The next day, we changed the oil pump and went down to Baylands to get some of that action. That night, I qualified second fastest, and finished third in the main event, even after the Chinins' new hot shoe ran over me on a re- start and spun me into the infield.

After the race my Coors Crew wanted to go kick Keel's ass. But finally cooler heads prevailed and we just blew off some steam with a few cold ones.

*That's me driving the famous Lovell Brother #71 Sprinter.
On this night I set a new one lap track record and took
the main event win.*

Big Fish, Little Pond

For the next month or so, that was basically my schedule. In San Jose I would hang out at O. J's. from Monday through Wednesday, drive over to Virgil Owens' race shop and tool and die company, and hang out with his gang a few times a week. Then on Thursday I would head up to Yuba City, hang my hat at Richard Lovell's ranch house with its big pool, and work on

the Lovell Brothers' car Thursday and Friday. Then on weekends we would head out to one race or another on the California
circuit. At least once a weekend we continued to win.

While I was extremely happy driving for those guys, I was
also on the phone working on a seat in a dirt champ car back
in the Midwest that I really wanted to drive. Champ cars are a
bigger, more traditional type of non-wing sprint car from back
in the day.

My good buddy Deuce Terrell back at Challenge in Iowa,
as well as Bob East, who also worked for Challenge, were both
trying to hook me up with a good drive in one of those big ole
dirt cars that had made virtually every Indy 500 winner famous
before they had ever gotten to the Indy 500. Plus Bob East
wanted me to dump my sprint-car deal and start driving full
Midgets for some of his buddies in the Indiana area. Bob had
a strong sense of what the future held for those little midget
racers. ESPN had inked a deal to televise many of the midget
events, and a good drive could take you right to the Indy 500.

Bob told me, "Hey man, you need to look at a midget deal
here in the Midwest. You could be a very big fish in a small
pond. You could have anything you want if you come back
here and win like you're doing out on the west coast."

He was tempting me. I had always wanted to race an Indy
car as well as transition to NASCAR. But I also wanted to
change my sex just as badly as I wanted to race in the Indy 500.
There were only a few years left in my plan to pull off that Indy
and NASCAR dream. I had to get busy!

O. J. and I were getting along pretty good there in San
Jose, though I knew he wouldn't feel the same about me if he
knew my gender plan. He was a man's man – women were

second-class citizens to him, so a boy who wanted to be a girl would rank even lower on his totem pole. His house was a little Mecca for racers. There was always someone from the gear-head world hanging out at his house and paint shop. It was almost like being in our race shop at home. We grilled steaks and chicken, watched television and just hung out enjoying one another's old racing stories.

At night, after O. J. had retired to his bedroom, I would stay on in the TV room for twenty minutes or so writing in my diary and making notes on my feelings for the psychologist back in Memphis, with whom I had stayed in constant contact with since coming out to the West Coast. It helped me relive some of the pressure concerning my gender quandary. Before I went to sleep, I was always careful to put the diary away.

The weekend before my birthday, which was Monday, July 29th, I went on another road trip up to Yuba City. O. J. and my other buddies there in San Jose had made plans to celebrate my birthday, so on Sunday night I made a special drive back down to San Jose for the party.

When I pulled into O. J's. driveway at around seven thirty a.m., I was surprised to see him sitting out on the front porch smoking a cigarette. It was even more surprising to see all my bags and belongings laying around on the lawn.

When I got out of the van, I said, "Hey O. J., what's going on?"

He looked me dead in the eye and said, "You're going to have to leave. This is not going to work out here with you. You just need to put your things in your van and get on down the line."

The look in his eyes stunned me, almost frightened me. At one point in our conversation, he looked like he was going to hit me. So I just threw my things into the van, told him I appreciated his hospitality, and left.

There was no reason for his behavior that I could see. I had been the perfect houseguest, and we had planned to celebrate my birthday. His wife had just come home from her trip – did she not like me for some reason? Had the rumors finally gotten through to the California boys? Racing is a small world so it was just a matter of time before the Memphis mafia got the word out to the west coast. O. J. was not the kind of guy to handle this issue well.

By the time I got back to the expressway, I was having a panic attack, just driving aimlessly for about ten miles. I didn't want to drive back up to Yuba City but I also didn't want to stay in San Jose. My stomach was queasy and I was tired as hell from no sleep the night before. So, when I spotted a Motel 6 at the next exit, I got a room and tried to sleep off the nightmare.

When I awoke that afternoon around 1:00, I felt like I had been run over by a truck. Laying there in that motel bed it dawned on me that if O. J. had gotten a call from someone back in the Mid South who was spreading rumors, my racing career was in serious trouble. Finally I managed to get out of bed, took a quick shower and drove to a mall just a few miles away. There I walked around most of the afternoon trying to figure out what to do.

That night I got some Mexican take-out and crashed inside my motel room. Calling home to check in with my parents, I wished my mom happy birthday – hers was only one day before mine. I didn't want them to worry, so I didn't mention the drama I was in. At least I had a damn good team to drive for, and I was making some money. If push came to shove, I could always go back to my buddies Larry and Rodney and shack up in their apartment again. Right then, I just wanted to sleep.

That Monday, on my birthday, I slept late, then drove to San Francisco and toured the city for the first time in my life. There was a really good sea-food joint down at the Wharf, where all the locals ate. I treated myself to two dozen raw oysters along with several glasses of merlot and a few Irish coffees…all by myself!

Making a mistake

Over the next few weeks I continued to race the Lovells' car, and won a few more races. Between times, I shacked back up with my buds Larry and Rodney in San Jose. When I needed to be in Yuba City working on the race car, I hung out up at Richard Lovell's farm house, catching some sun by the pool and cruising up to Napa Valley a few times checking out a few of the wineries.

Bob East called me a week after my birthday and asked if I wanted to drive a champ car at Springfield in a few weeks. Of course I did. I also had a possible ride with Larry Howard, owner of the best midget car in the country, who wanted to run it at the Springfield track later that same day as the champ car race.

Thinking about the advice I'd gotten to come back to the Midwest, I quit the Lovell deal and drove back to Knoxville, Iowa to meet my parents at the Knoxville Nationals, where I'd had a chance of driving for another team out of Indiana. But that team totaled their car two days before the nationals. A driver named Brent Kading also had a champ-car ride in Springfield, so he and I called a local flight service there in

Knoxville and charted a twin-engine plane. The plan was to fly to Springfield to run the champ car race on Saturday afternoon. After that race, I'd have to decide whether to drive Howard's midget, or fly back to Knoxville that night with Brent.

That Saturday morning, Dad and I, and Brent and one of his best buds, got up at the crack of dawn and drove to the air strip. It was in the middle of nowhere surrounded by cornfields, which you couldn't see because the area was totally fogged in. It might be hours before the fog lifted—we wouldn't get to Springfield in time to qualify. Brent was a big old monster boy, over six foot and known for his bravery, but he looked a little backed off by the fog. We mulled around for a few minutes trying to figure out what to do.

Then the pilot, very much the professional aviator with his freshly pressed khakis and navy blue polo, said: "Hey, look, guys, the sky is clear and blue three thousand feet up. I fly out of here in this soup all the time. There is nothing we can smash into for two miles. If you want to get to Springfield in time, we have to leave right now."

We looked at one another and said, "Let's do it."

Throwing our racing gear in the cargo hold, we piled into the plane.

As the pilot lifted us off, he put that baby in a damn steep climb with a lot of G's pulling on us. I never will forget the look on Brent's face when he turned around and looked at Dad and me with a what-in-the-hell-have-we-done look. He was white as a sheet. I was feeling queasy too – Jesus and I were definitely having a talk. You could not see one thing out of the windshield. Then, just like the pilot told us, about three thousand feet up the sky turned crystal clear and heavenly blue. All our stress levels went down two hundred points.

I looked at Dad and told him, "I'm never doing that again."

He smirked back. "Me wish me had stayed at home."

We all burst out laughing. It was great to be with Dad again.

In Springfield, I had a good practice run with the champ car. But going into lap 15, the car broke down. And that's all, she wrote.

Meanwhile Larry Howard and I had been trying to work out a deal for me to run his midget that night. But I didn't have a way back to Knoxville except on the plane with Dad and Brent.

After I agonized over the choice, I finally said no to Howard and got on the plane. All the while, as we flew through the darkness, I was remembering what Bob East had told me about the big fish and the small pond. Somehow I knew I'd made a mistake! And I had. Years later, I'd watch Jeff Gordon rocket to the big time in NASCAR by being a big fish in that small pond . . . racing midgets on that same circuit in Indiana.

After the Knoxville races, I headed back to California for the World of Outlaws sprint car swing. A different team offered me a new ride, and I hoped it would prove to be as good as the Lovell ride.

But time would tell. Slowly, little by little, it was going bad for me on the California facing front. People began to stop speaking to me. I figured that the old Memphis rumors were finally catching up.

The California Outlaws swing was a real learning experience for me. If you didn't run every lap like it was the last, you would get your ass beat like a dog. My new team and I had started out pretty damn good. But then we had some bad luck—a wreck in Baylands, a flat in Hanford, a sixth in Santa Maria from my seventh-place starting position. Our next stop would be back in Chico, my favorite track. But the social climate was getting worse—even my new crew was giving me the cold shoulder.

However, one afternoon during the Outlaw swing, I got another call from Bob East back at the Challenge plant in Iowa.

"There's a really famous car owner by the name of Bob Consani," he said, "who is missing a driver and wants you to drive his car up in Calistoga next Sunday night."

It happened that I'd be free to race for someone else that night, so I made a beeline to Calistoga.

Consani was a legend out there on the west coast. A Santa Rosa millionaire, he had a connection to the Bill Vukovitch Indy 500 clan . . . His cars were rocket ships. He liked to win at any cost, and expected his drivers to do one thing only – stand on the gas. I had outrun his team back in the summer, and he knew full well I stood on the gas.

Calistoga was his home track, located right in the middle of Napa Valley and a beautiful golf course. The entire back straight was lined with big oak trees, which regularly caught flipping sprint cars and prevented them from careening out into the Napa hills. I loved that track, it was fast and dangerous. But it always beat the hell out of you with all the rocks mixed into its dirt surface. The first time I raced there, a rock damn near took my head off, knocking a big chunk out of my helmet and peppering my body like buckshot.

Consani and his bunch were as hard-nosed as you get, but they were also the funniest bunch of nuts I had ever been around. When I got there, he introduced me to Billy Vokovitch III, who was his kick-ass super modified hot shoe and destined to win the Indy 500 like his granddad had done on two occasions back in the early '50s. I was starving and so was Consani, so he loaded us up in his Lexus and took us to his favorite restaurant for breakfast which ended up being cheeseburgers. We all got to know one another with an array of insults and unadulterated humor, and then headed to the track.

There I got fitted in the car, warmed up and then hit the track for practice. When I stood on the gas, I realized that this car was an absolute rocket ship. I immediately ran the entire first lap without lifting off the gas. I knew I had me a real race car to drive on that night. When it was time to qualify, I took fast time and never lifted for the whole two-lap run.

When I pulled back into the pit area, Consani came up and looked me straight in the eye. "You're fucking crazy, you know that? You just drove around this killer dirt track at 130 miles per hour. You're fucking nuts."

Then, with a big grin on his face, he walked off. I had just impressed a guy that could not be impressed.

In the main event, I was winning when the damn car broke the rear-end gears and we fell out of the race. Mr. Consani paid me two grand for my services and the thrill of seeing me flat-foot his car. It was a hell of a night!

Back to San Jose and the silent treatment. Hell, this was California where everyone is supposedly welcome. Something had to be up and it must be serious.

At Chico, as we prepared the car, the crew never said more than two words to me. But I had one of the biggest races in America to run so I couldn't let it get to me.

That evening, in practice laps, the car ran perfect. As we waited for the main event, I was sitting on the right front tire, when I spotted a crew member from Virgil Owens' team who had not given me the cold shoulder yet. He was on their four-wheeler driving through the pits. Quickly I ran out and jumped out in front of him. He slammed on the brakes and slid right up to me where I grabbed the handlebars and looked him in the eye.

"What in the hell is going on with everyone giving me the cold shoulder?" I demanded. "You know what is going on."

He sheepishly hung his head, avoiding eye contact.

"O. J. read your diary," he said. "He told everyone that you're a fag, that you wear women's panties…that you want to be a girl. I'm sorry . . . You're a great racer and you don't deserve to be treated like this."

At that moment, my entire life flashed before me. Suddenly I remembered that, just before my birthday, I had fallen asleep in O. J.'s TV room while writing in my diary. The next morning I rushed off and forgot the diary there, with all my deepest, darkest secrets in it . . . and O. J. had found it.

I couldn't say a word—just walked back to my car and began putting on my driving gear. On the surface I was calm as a fighter pilot but the stresses of my whole life were gathering together, building, running through my body like a wildfire. Deep down, I felt like I had just been raped by everyone there at the track. I was exposed. My whole life was fodder. In a world of sports intimidation where you get the advantage on your competitor by being more dangerous and brave, more macho than they were, I had just lost my advantage. This was a defining moment in my life. From this point onward, my life would be different in the racing community, and I knew it. Never again would people see me as the JT Hayes who had gone last to first to win the Summer Nationals at Chico.

Yet right now I had to get in that car and race. Not in a thousand years could I let anyone there in Chico know I was about to burst into tears. It would be hardest thing I had done yet.

Just as they pushed me onto the track, my boiling emotions surged through my body, and in a moment of pure and raw physical emotion I threw up in my helmet. It felt like I was going to die of anxiety right there in the race car. I could barely catch my breath; I just wanted to die from the embarrassment and knowing full well that my machismo, my racing cache was permanently damaged beyond repair. My edge of staring the rattlesnake down somehow now seemed damaged if not gone forever. I was crushed down to the core of my soul and for a moment I actually thought about just driving back around to the pits and parking the car.

However, once the race started, like a true racer, years of discipline took over, and I managed to get hold of my emotions. By lap 5, I had moved up to tenth and it looked as if I might get a top five. But on the sixth lap, Leland McSpaden crashed with another car right in front of me. There was no place to go, so I t-boned them and ripped the right front wheel off the car.

And that was it.

Sitting there in the wrecked car, breathing the smell of my own vomit, I realized that I couldn't face or fight the rumor-mongers any more.

"Screw it," I thought. "I'm going home; I'm real damn tired of this crap."

Mississippi was the best place to regroup for the winter. I needed to have a few sit-downs with my good doctor to get my life back in check. Now, my racing future, just as thought I had my professional career on track seemed over, how in hell could I ever overcome what O. J. had done to me.

CHAPTER 12

Back Home – A Place of My Own

Praying for a Reason

Four days later, I was back in Corinth, Mississippi.

My dad sensed that I had come home with my tail between my legs but he didn't know why. He just knew I was not my usual jovial self. As I looked back over the past 16 months, I was suddenly amazed that I hadn't committed suicide or had a breakdown that put me in a mental ward for the rest of my life. Having the deepest, darkest secrets of my diary spread all over California was the absolute low point of my life.

So if I was trying to escape the rumor mill about my life, what in the hell was I doing back in Corinth?

Once I settled in, I was asking myself that question almost daily. However, it was good to be out of the racing pressure cooker and hanging out with my old Corinth friends. The irony about my Corinth friends was, though they were all clueless about my professional racing status, they had no idea what I had just been doing out on the west coast.

After about a week, I rented a place of my own—a little garage apartment in town—and moved in. My plan was to live as a female there, as much as I could behind those four walls.

I would also help my dad's business enough to keep my bills paid, and work towards having the gender realignment surgery as soon as possible. That meant getting back into counseling at least once a month.

By Thanksgiving, the assholes there in Corinth were off and running again with the rumor-mongering. They just wouldn't quit.

So every day, most of the day, I hide in my apartment. I was too well-known in the community to go out—most everyone knew what my SUV looked like. Just getting gas or stopping at a convenience store was risky because you never knew who you might run up on. Perfect strangers just saw a skinny good-looking girl filling her tank or buying a soda. However, when someone did recognize me, especially a good ole boy who knew my dad and me from the tool and die business or my racing, things sometimes got close to dicey. They aimed mean hard looks at me – or look of disgust and scornful laughter. They yelled things that hurt. My occasional run-ins with these men kept me scared, raw, defensive and suicidal.

Trying to deal with the stress and self-esteem issues, I reconnected with an old high school friend, Phil, who was now a Baptist minister and had always taken an interest in me. Phil didn't have a clue that all the rumors he'd heard were actually true, until I told him one day when we were drinking coffee at a local restaurant. I wasn't sure how he would react, and held my breath as I studied his expression. But, unlike the rest of those Bible thumpers in the area, he did get it and just encouraged me to pray about what I should do. He knew I could not live on the fence like I had been doing over the past few years.

"Be faithful in your prayers," Phil said.

"Yeah, right," I said in disbelief.

"No, I mean it," he said. "Keep asking for answers. They'll come."

Plus my mom was pissed off at me because, as she so gracefully put it, I was doing my "girl thing" there in Corinth. She was so afraid of what my neighbors were going to think if they happened to glimpse me as Terri that she was beside herself with fear and hatred for me.

One weeknight around 8 p.m., Mom showed up at my little apartment and started banging on the door like a madwoman, all the while yelling at the top of her voice. Obviously I was in a feminine moment inside, not wanting visitors, so I didn't answer the door.

"Terry, I know you're in there and I know what you're doing . . . you're embarrassing me and your dad . . . [bang, bang, bang] . . . you better answer this door right now . . . I mean right now, [bang, bang, bang] Terry! ANSWER THIS DOOR...I WISH I KNEW WHAT WAS GOING ON IN YOUR HEAD! I JUST WISH YOU HAD STAYED IN CALIFORNIA!"

Finally, to keep the neighbors from calling the cops, I let her in.

Of coarse Mom jumped all over me the minute she got in the door. That was my mom at her grandest, chewing me or someone else out for not doing exactly what she wanted me or them to do. That's why I always avoided her when the heat was on. There would only be more hurt feelings if I smarted off back to her.

The thing that always got me was that Mom never took the time to educate herself on my situation. After all, she had seen my doctors and talked to them over the years. She was fully aware that I was physically different from other people…fully knowing that my feelings about this issue were sensitive. But no, she never got it. And the Baptist Church, the one she had attended ever since her daddy had built it, was right in the middle of her refusal to get it. In my humble opinion, if we as a family had told a few of those church busybodies to stay out of our affairs, the situation would have been much better. But right now she and her church saw me as a bad person, not as someone who had been given a biological challenge to overcome.

That night, I managed to calm her down and get her to go home by assuring her that I would never leave the house dressed as a girl.

Of course I was lying through my teeth, but that was what it took to get her to stop yelling.

My "girl thing" not only had Corinth and the racing community in a tizzy…it had me in a tizzy as well. Even though I really wanted to have the realigement surgery, even though I was physically and emotionally a girl, the social implications and the family dynamics were damn complicated and daunting. What if I had the surgery and all my friends and all of my family rejected me afterwards? I had to be absolutely sure I could handle that pressure of finding myself utterly abandoned and alone.

Night of Prayer

The Monday night before Thanksgiving, around 11:00 pm, I was in my apartment reading the Bible diligently and praying about my conundrum, the way Brother Phil had wanted me to do. I was looking for a few lines in that book that would personally talk to my situation…something, anything that would grab me by my heart and tell me why I had to take this terrifying journey instead of some other path in life.

I knew I was lucky to be who I was. Compared to some other people, I had great parents. Even my dad's alcoholism was not as bad as it could have been. But even as I counted my blessings, I knew that since I had come home to Corinth, my suicidal feelings had gotten stronger, and on that night I felt them surging stronger still. But I really didn't want to kill myself. Deep in my heart, I wanted to live, to be a girl and experience all that being a girl had to offer. I wanted my friends and especially my family to accept me and love me for who I was. What was wrong with that? I had never hurt anything or anyone. What was the big deal about gender all about? What was my purpose on this Earth?

After about thirty minutes of reading and craving for some affirmation, I felt frustrated. No answers were coming. I was getting nowhere. Frustrated and desperate, I closed the Bible, turned off the light, and began to pray there in the dark and wrestle with my questions with absolute passion and commitment.

Was it OK to feel this way? Why did I look and feel so much like a girl? Was I sinning by pursuing this? If God wanted me to stop my transition and go back to being JT, that is what I would do and I would never pursue being a girl again in my life. I prayed about my racing and my natural ability to drive cars. Most importantly, I prayed that God would give me a sign… a passage or a word in the Bible that would allow me to move on with my life.

Then I fumbled for the bedside lamp and turned the light back on but I kept my eyes shut. Groping for the Bible, I opened it and put my right forefinger on that page. Then I opened my eyes to see what scripture my finger was pointing to. As my eyes adjusted to the light, I got the surprise of my life to read these words:

"You are neither male nor female, Jew nor Greek, you are one in the eyes of the Lord." Galatians 3/28

The entire room became spookily silent as I felt a powerful angelic presence spreading its wings there in the house. Beyond any shadow of doubt, my Maker had just given me the answer. He made me and loved me just as I was or as I wanted to be . . . I was a human being and it did not matter if I was a male or a female. My soul was what counted, not my physical presence. Now it was up to me to determine what I would do with that heavenly answer. No matter what I did never again would I question or doubt my decision to be a female.

But would my family and friends get the spirit like I had? No matter how much clarity I had about my femininity and what God felt about it, having our local society embrace it would be another thing. Mom and Dad were still going to fight me on this every chance they got.

For now it was important to continue my counseling, stay focused on my plan to have sexual realignment surgery within the next year, and hope it all would work out for the best.

So I turned off the lamp, pulled the covers up around my chin, thanked God for the sign and went to sleep. That was the first time in months that I had actually had a peaceful night's sleep.

Surprise From California

That spiritual connection with my Creator calmed my nerves enough that I was less suicidal and worried about my driving career. Behind closed doors, I kept on living as a woman as much as possible. When I could, I slipped over to Memphis to hang out with my friends in the GLBT community.

Meanwhile I stayed in touch with Bob East at Challenge Racing Enterprises in Iowa. I was toying with the idea of building myself a new midget. There would be no politics to be played in that community; in fact I had already made a full set of patterns. For sure, my dad would be willing to help.

Then out of the blue, Richard Lovell called from California. He wanted me to come out in March to drive his car during the World of Outlaws California swing. If we did well, he wanted to run his car for the entire season. Could I get there in five days so we could get the car in good order?

So Richard didn't give a crap about my private life? Maybe I should have known. After all, he had the picture of a drag queen taking a piss right above his office desk. The first time I saw it, I wondered if he was freaky enough to not care what people said about me. Maybe he just wanted to race and have fun doing it.

A huge snowstorm slowed me down as I was driving through New Mexico, but I finally got to Yuba City and we worked on the car.

During the series, however, we did not run that well. Richard had switched over to the 87 series Gambler and the front torsion bars were designed in too high a position. So we fought a loose race car the entire series…I was always having to fight to keep it from loosing traction and spinning out. But, at least we knew how to fix the problem once we had time to take a break. The regular season didn't start for another six weeks, so I headed back to Memphis to gather my clothes and clear up a few loose ends with my psychologist.

Two weeks later, I was in my race shop working on Dad's midget, getting him ready for a race in Nashville that coming weekend, when the phone rang. It was Richard Lovell. He had decided to not let me drive his car for the next season. Instead he was putting a good-looking hotshot California boy in the car. It had nothing to do with my driving ability, he assured me. It just had everything to do with his sponsor Coors liking the idea of a California driver better.

Of course I knew what the deal was. He was hearing the rumors. What was I going to do about it?

"Thanks for the friendship," I said. I'll catch you and your crew on the rebound sometime."

After I hung up, I continued to work on my Dad's car.

In the back of my mind though, I pretty much felt that my professional racing career was toast—at least the sprint car end of it.

For a month after Richard Lovell fired me, it actually felt like a weight had been lifted off my shoulders. His action had freed me up to be myself and not worry about racing. I did keep up on the national racing scene, especially the Indy 500 practice. But mostly I was just enjoying my femininity in the privacy of my apartment, sometimes in my race car office when no one else was around...or in Memphis. It was almost like I was healing my soul, recharging my emotional batteries – getting a little time off from the hard-core macho world where I had lived most of my life.

Now and then, my few buddies in Corinth filled me in on the ridiculous rumors that were going around town.

According to one rumor—when I went to the west coast that past summer and won all those races, well, the REAL reason I went to California was to get a super duper female hormone treatment that would make me a girl. What misinformed idiot had come up with that one? My hormone intake was tiny—a 1.25 premrin tablet daily and that was it. I was allergic other hormones. Plus I didn't need a super duper hormone treatment; because my body was already feminine, and had been since the day I was born.

But that hormone story was making for some colorful coffee-shop conversation in Corinth. The fact that I had been beating the best sprint car drivers in the country just didn't count with them.

"There's a catch"

Two weeks before Memorial Day, I was at my race shop catching up on some paperwork for my doctor and thinking about building that new midget when the phone rang. It was Bob East from Challenge Racing.

"Hey, JT, is that you?"

I was a bit shocked to be hearing from him. After Richard Lovell fired me, I had stopped calling Bob, figuring that he had heard the rumors too and was done with me.

"Hey, I've got you a racing deal if you're up for it," he said. "Consani wants you to drive his car Memorial Day weekend at Calistoga. It's a two-day deal and it pays a lot of money. You'll have to work on the car and get it ready to run . . . Consani likes the way you drive, you stood on the gas the last time you drove for him. There's a catch, though. He only wants to race the car that one weekend, and that's it. He's got his super modified deal going, so he doesn't want to run this car after Calistoga. You'll have to look for another ride after that. Are you up for it?"

Damn, I thought. What a turn of fate. There I sat in my office with makeup on, wearing a tight pair of girl jeans and a cute little top, making a deal to drive a 900-horsepowered sprint car.

"Yeah, I'll go do it . . . He's got to get me a place to stay, though. Hell, I like his old crusty ass!"

"OK, I'll call him and tell him. He's got that motel up there in Santa Rosa that he said you could stay at. Just remember what I told you the first time you drove for him . . . drive the wheels off the damn thing and you'll be okay!"

Just when you think you finished, you get a call and you're back in the game. The surgery could wait, right? At least that night of prayer had shown me that being feminine was all right. The time to cross that bridge would come in its own due time. For the moment I was ready to give racing another try.

Making a beeline to my apartment, I packed clothes into my blue and white S10 Blazer, took everything else over to my race shop and stored it. Then I told Mom, Dad and Granny, and headed out to California . . . just like that.

Inches from the edge . . . dodging rocks

Racing at Calistoga is a hoot. This half mile dirt oval is fast and dangerous as hell. The track is virtually flat with no banking in the corners to hold you into the track, so driving wide ass open around that baby at 150 miles per hour is not easy but I had proved I could do it last season when I had won the trophy dash and damn near won the main event driving for Consani. Plus the track surface had a bunch of rocks mixed in with the dirt so you were taking your life in your hands when one of those quarter size babies came hurtleing at you faster than a speeding bullet shot like a lazer from under another competitors rear tires. I had almost broken my arm the year before when one of those projectiles just about knocked my left arm off during one of my heat races. Racing in Calistoga was clearly looking at the rattle snake eye ball to eye ball, you could get bit up there at any second, but the thrill of racing there was definitely worth the risk.

Consani's cars were fast and I loved driving them. At times he was a real smart-ass to me but I didn't care . . . He didn't scare me in the least. Even though I had not driven in over two months, I qualified on the pole and ended up winning the first night.

Consani was beside himself with excitement, and so was I.

That night, on the way back over to his race shop in Santa Rosa, we were taking a short cut on a twisty two-lane road through the Napa hills and I was driving the race hauler. The truck was packed with five or six of Consani's hard legs that worked for him at his construction company, and their macho bullshit talk was something to listen to as I drove quietly, enjoying the incredible view down into the Napa Valley.

Suddenly all the lights on the truck went out. We were rumbling down that mountain road with no guard rails to prevent us from going off the edge and crashing hundreds of feet to our death. Right away I stood on the brakes, but it was so dark you couldn't even see your hand right in front of your face. During the chaos, I heard doors opening and grown men rushing to jump out of that hauler and make a run for it. Fortunately, I managed to stop that baby. Slamming her into park, I got out too, so I could assess the situation.

To my horror the race hauler's front tires were only inches from the edge of the drop. I was standing there all alone, while that bunch of hard asses were fifty yards down the road trying to get up off of the asphalt.

"Hey, you bunch of pussies," I yelled back at them. "You're not very loyal, leaving me in there to die!"

When they came dragging back up to the truck, several of them had a big case of asphalt rash. It had been a close call, caused by a blown fuse. We changed the fuse and headed on back to the race shop.

The next night, I had fast time again but ended up finishing fifth after the engine overheated. All in all, it was a good weekend and I had a pocket full of money. But my deal with Consani was over.

What next?

It would have been nice to stay on the west coast, but there was nobody to drive for. Outside of Consani's team, the social climate was still pretty chilly. So I headed for Santa Maria to hang out at the sprint car races for a day, before heading back to Memphis and continuing my feminine transition.

I hate pink

At the Santa Maria track I got my pit pass and headed into the infield to hang out and enjoy a night of racing as a spectator. As I was walking across the track, someone grabbed the back of my neck. It was a friend and fellow racer, Lee James.

"Hey, congratulations on your win up in Calistoga," he said. "What are you driving tonight?"

"Nothing," I said. "My deal with Consani was just for that weekend. I don't have anything lined up for the rest of the year."

"Would you like to drive tonight for a team here at the track? Their driver can't get here in time for the race. It's a decent car. Not as good as Consani's car, but it's pretty damn fast."

When Lee and I got to where the car was pitted, I realized to my horror that the damn thing was painted pink. A frikin' pink race car. That's all I needed. My enemies would have a field day with this.

Lee read my mind.

"I know what you're thinking," he said. "But it's a good car."

Finally I relented and got my driving gear from my car. To my surprise I finished third in the main event. When the racing Gods are with you, they're with you. Needless to say the team owner was elated to have a good finish and even more relieved that I didn't wreck their pink car.

After the race, I was in the infield waiting for the team owner to get back from the pay window with my earnings when a woman yelled my name.

"JT, JT . . . Hey JT, hey . . . It's Nancy, it's Nancy . . . Hey, it's Nancy!"

When she said her name, I knew exactly who she was—a good race friend and out-of-control fan that I had meet the year before. She was a hoot, and we had stayed in touch throughout the past winter. Her husband Don was there with her. He was a balding heavy-set guy who made his living building and running coin-operated laundries in the Bay Area.

I walked over and hugged her, and shook hands with him.

"I have to leave pretty soon," I said. "But we can talk and catch up for a few minutes."

"What are you going to drive for the rest of the season?" Nancy babbled. "Is Consani going to race anymore? Are you going to drive for him?"

"No," I said. "I'm heading back to Memphis tonight."

Don weighed in now.

"Whoa, not so fast," he said. "Don't be leaving the west coast so fast. Here's what you should do. Come back up to San Francisco with me and Nancy. Hang out with us until some driver gets fired. You know it's just a matter of time before that happens. Then stay out here and race for the year. You can stay with us for as long as you like. Just give it a try. You belong out here. I don't know if you realize it or not, but you have a lot of fans out here. So what do you think?"

It was too good an offer to refuse. Besides, I liked them, so I gave in.

The next day we rolled through San Francisco to their apartment. They lived right in the Marina district, four blocks from the bay, on the corner of Filbert and Fillmore where all the hot action and upscale shopping district was located. It was a beautiful neighborhood and I could not believe my good fortune. As soon as we unloaded our suitcases we headed off to the Fisherman's Wharf, to a local seafood house that only the locals knew about, and had a fantastic dinner.

I wouldn't mind living there for the rest of my life!

Bad News

Over the next few weeks, those two lovely people kept my name in the mix with car owners in the Bay Area. Then an offer came from Al Least, whose team was based in San Leandro near the San Francisco airport. A week after making the deal, I had the kinks worked out of his car and we were on the track kicking tail.

Everything in my life seemed to level out…for the moment, anyway. My mom and dad came out to see the west-coast sights and go to the races. My racing was going pretty well. I was enjoying my time in San Francisco.

After my folks went home, I found a cool bar and restaurant in the Marina district that catered to the bluegrass crowd, which made me feel a little bit closer to home. Now and then I got to missing my buds back home, especially my best bud Victor Dixon who was an excellent bluegrass picker and singer, and a consummate Casanova. Out of everyone in my home town Victor had stood by me no matter what, and he got it. He was a biology graduate from Ole Miss so he knew full well that my situation was clearly all about Mother Nature getting crazy. So hanging out at Paul's Saloon gave me a little piece of home without the rumors.

In September, the Least team and I had been getting ready to run the Outlaw swing in California, which started in a few days. We had high hopes for some good runs. I had worked an all-nighter and slept in, and was just about to head on down to Santa Maria at around noon, when the phone rang.

It was Mom. She beat around the bush for a few seconds, just asking how I was, but I could tell from her voice that something was wrong.

Then she said, "I've got some bad news. Are you alone? Or is Don or Nancy there with you?"

"I'm alone." My heart was sinking. "What's up?"

Was my dad all right? Was Granny ill?

"Terry," she said, "Victor was killed last night in a house fire. His wife Kathy is all right, but Victor didn't get out of the house in time. Your friend Flat Top wants to call you and talk to you about it . . . He is really upset and just wants to make sure you're all right."

It felt like my heart was being ripped out of my chest. I told Mom to have Flat Top give me an hour or so. When I hung up, grief swept over me. I wanted to be alone but at the same time I had never felt so alone in my life. The feeling was cold and chilling.

Only a few weeks ago, I had called Victor on his birthday, which happened to be the day after mine. He got his guitar out and sang happy birthday over the phone, then we laughed together at how silly it was to be doing that. He was a real piece of work, the most handsome man I had ever known, and the most aware and compassionate person on earth. What a loss . . . not just for me, but for anyone who had ever known him!

Feeling that I was about to have one of my panic attacks, I rushed out of the apartment and walked around the neighborhood. After about 45 minutes I ended up at the bay overlooking the Golden Gate Bridge, trying find a reason for Vic's sudden passing. When it was all said and done, Vic was not made for this world. In fact this encounter with Earth was surely not his first. Like me, he was an old soul . . . that's why he had loved me unconditionally and stood up for me with all of his might.

Flat Top and Nathan and I had been good friends with him for over ten years, and we would feel lost without his presence. But I was even more worried about his lovely wife Kathy. She was strong but so in love with him . . . she would need lots of support.

Finally I said a prayer for Victor and his cosmic journey, then headed back home to call Flat Top.

That night I had to drive Al Least's car against the best sprint drivers in the world. My team was depending on me. I didn't tell those guys about Victor because everyone needed to be in a positive frame of mind.

But we finished sixth with a terrible vibration in the drive train. Later I discovered that the drive shaft was bent.

The next week my parents flew back out for the remainder of the Outlaw swing and to look after me. They were worried about me and the loss I was still feeling.

The racing went fairly well, but I was moving towards a decision. My shot at sprint cars was over. Rides were coming my way, for sure. But I wasn't being sought out by the best teams any more, or the big rich car owners and sponsors. It was time to do something different. I was tired of sprint cars, and wanted to take a shot at NASCAR before the surgery.

My good friend from Mississippi and my karting days, Lake Speed, had already made it to the NASCAR Winston Cup series. I had called him up and he was willing to help me get my chance in North Carolina.

"If you really want to commit to this," he told me over the phone, "you have to move here to Charlotte."

Lake was right. If you want to act you have to go to Hollywood, if you want to race in NASCAR, you have to live in Charlotte.

Don and Nancy wanted to help too. They were friends with some Levis executives and the famous Granatelli family who were legends at the Indy 500. Plus they had some happy-hour friends from ABC Sports there in San Francisco. They wanted to be team owners. So we formed a partnership and started nurturing the Levi guys for a sponsorship. Nancy called Vince Granatelli and he agreed to help with technical support. We got busy putting marketing proposals together.

The ABC sportscaster scheduled an interview with me on a huge yacht belonging to civil rights lawyer Melvin Belli. When I got to the yacht that day, I was surprised to see some famous people hanging out on the boat. A marketing firm was doing a photo shoot with some pro athletes and models from the Bay Area, which included Olympic champion Greg Louganis. We cruised around the bay all day as they did their photo shoot and the reporter interviewed my skinny ass. I was playing with the big dogs.

Two weeks later the interview aired, and it gave us some positive ammunition to take to potential sponsors.

I knew I had to watch my step. But maybe this time I could outrun the rumors. One night at dinner, Nancy point- blank asked me if I had my life under control concerning the gender issue. Now that we were trying for corporate sponsorship, she was worried that the subject might come up. I calmly assured that I had everything under control. She had no idea that I was wearing women's underwear as I said it.

Three weeks later, I loaded my S10 Blazer and headed to North Carolina to start nurturing my NASCAR dream.

Fear and fearlessness

Like an idiot I was in drag for the entire 3000-mile drive east. It was important to have one last go at femininity before I got to Charlotte. Just like that, at the snap of a finger, I went from being JT Hayes to being Terri. For most of the trip, no one noticed me.

But there was one big scare while driving through New Mexico.

As I was nearing Albuquerque, it was getting dark so I turned the headlights on and thought I'd drive for a few more hours before packing it in for the night. Suddenly a state trooper came up behind me in the fast lane. Right away I felt a wave of panic. Though I was dressed as a chick, my truck registration and driver's license said I was a male. So I prayed that the trooper wouldn't give me a second look. At first he passed me by and went on up the road, so I thought I was out of danger.

But then he slowed down dramatically. As I passed him, he pulled in behind me and flipped on his blue flashing lights.

As I pulled over, my heart was about to stop. What in the hell had I done? I hadn't been speeding. What did he want from me? So I went into a frenzy of getting the lipstick and makeup off my face with a paper napkin that happened to be lying on my console. Plus I was frantically searching for my nail-polish remover, to get the bright red off my fingernails before that cop could get to my window. It was a damn Chinese fire drill to get myself looking like a boy in 30 seconds.

By the time the trooper strolled purposely, ominously, up to my window, I had managed to get the nail polish off my right hand but not the left. My girl's tee shirt and blue jeans were not that big of a problem, but my little boobies would be staring him right in the face. As I rolled down the window, the telltale smell of nail-polish remover floated around me.

"Your driver's license and registration, please," he said in that tone of voice that cops like to use.

I handed them out with my right hand, keeping the left hand hidden.

He took the documents back to his car and called them in. Then he came back up to my window and handed them back to me . . . along with a warning ticket for a burned-out head-light. As he did so, our eyes met, and I knew that he knew.

"You'll want to get that light fixed in Albuquerque," he said, "before you go any further down the interstate."

Feeling faint with relief, I said, "Thanks, officer. I'll get that headlight fixed right away."

"You do that," he said. "Take care."

When he drove on down the road, I sat there for a few minutes and when I was done shaking like a leaf, I laughed my ass off. It was a nervous reaction to what could have been a very unpleasant situation – much like the time I was hassled by the cops down in Columbus, Mississippi six years earlier. Lucky for me, this time I was in New Mexico, not the redneck small-town South.

So I drove to the next exit, found a motel and got some needed sleep.

The next morning at an auto parts store, I bought a head-light and installed it. Then I got back on the road... as Terri, not JT. But this time I did not have nail polish on, just in case I had another encounter with the highway patrol. Taking the risk was stupid, but I needed to do it! It was the old fear and fearlessness attitude that had driven me since childhood.

On April 30, 1988, my Blazer rolled into Charlotte.

After I checked in with Lake and his wife Rice, I looked for a place nearby to live. In a few days I found a really cool trailer park (if there is such a thing) right across the street from the Charlotte Motor Speedway, which is now known as Lowes Motor Speedway – considered to be NASCAR's most beauti-ful racing arena. Out of my den window, I could see across the street to that grand old race track and dream about winning there.

Over the next few months, I became a familiar face around the Winston Cup garage area at the track, and a mainstay at Lake's race shop. His team was running for the Winston Cup, now the Sprint Cup championship, and I started hanging out with his crew – and finally was helping them as much as I could.

It was a great opportunity to learn about stock cars and how these NASCAR boys do things. I had won about every-thing in Karting and Midgets there was to win, but NASCAR was a bigger deal. So I felt incredibly excited, hopeful and com-mitted. It would be a fresh start in the biggest of the big time in professional motorsports. Maybe, just maybe I could escape the harassment and hate that I had endured virtually every step of the way in spring cars.

I'd known Lake since 1972, when I was just a kid and we met while racing go-karts throughout the South East, and of course we were both from Mississippi. So Lake and I had a strong bond and a sense of native pride—we were bound and determined to hold our own among those Carolina boys. We had always been good friends, and now I felt like I was a real part of his family. He was even helping me meet all the right people—including team owners who were looking for the next hot shoe.

So I stayed very busy pitching my racing abilities to anyone in the NASCAR community who would listen to me.

First I finagled a meeting with Carolyn Rudd, president and CEO of Sports Management Group, who managed the Tide and Folgers Procter and Gamble race sponsorships for Rick Hendricks and his two star drivers, Darrell Waltrip and Tim Richmond. Carolyn liked me well enough to share some marketing tricks that put the big-time sponsorship deals in place. She also hooked me up with some passes to the Speedway Club, the exclusive five-star restaurant and country club there at the racetrack. The Speedway Club caters to the Fortune 500 set who are involved in the sport – they do their entertaining there. So it was way cool to get into those hallowed halls and rub elbows with NASCAR's biggest stars.

On the side, I had a meeting with famed car owner Dick Bahre who had brought Michael Waltrip into the sport. From San Francisco, Don and Nancy were bankrolling me, and nurturing the Levis sponsorship hot and heavy – they had the company pretty darn interested.

Several of the sport's most famous citizens were pulling for me, and I had their personal phone numbers, including former NASCAR Champion Ned Jarrett, who was now the number one TV guy for ESPN. My uncle Buddy, who was now the president and CEO of Parts Plus Auto Stores , was all pumped up about my prospects.

I was sure I fit the NASCAR bill for the next generation of drivers. After all, I would look good on TV – I was cute, had a down-home Mississippi charm, and was articulate and could think on my feet. I could drive a race car like crazy without wrecking. Most important, I understood marketing . . . and I could build cars as good or better than anyone. So I was everything that NASCAR was looking for. Plus I had a host of power players trying to help me out. Even my parents were rooting for me.

I couldn't lose, right?

But the lethal secret I carried kept the pressure on me. By September I was once again teetering on the verge of a nervous breakdown.

The right move

Lake and his wife Rice sensed that something was wrong and asked me several times if I was doing all right. I had lost weight, my hands were always shaking, and my face had stressed-out written all over it.

For weeks I debated whether to tell Lake and Rice about my situation but I didn't know if that would be wise. She and Lake were very religious and even though my case was about biology going crazy, you never know how extreme fundamentalist people are going to react. These wonderful people overflowed with love for everyone but this was not the Village in New York City or a night out on the town in LA—this was the deep South, this was hard-core macho stock car racing. Telling Lake and Rice was going to be as risky as driving a race car at

200 miles an hour with 43 other crazy idiots. But I was so desperate that I was willing to risk anything.

Again and again, the memory of that night of prayer came back to me – the guidance that I'd been given. Surely God had been leading me to Lake and Rice from day one.

So my strategy was this: tell Rice first. Over the summer, she and I had become buds. She had a great sense of humor and more importantly, a very soft heart. It was only natural for me to talk to her first, to pour my guts out about my quandary. I was sure she would not judge me. Before she and Lake got married, she had a nursing degree and had worked as a RN. With her medical background, she would get the biological and genetic aspects of this before Lake would, and give me a chance to make my case.

That fateful Wednesday morning in late September, I got my courage up and drove over to Lake's race shop. First I stuck my head in the office door, and said hi to Lake's secretary and then walked across the paved parking lot about fifty yards to their little two-bedroom wood house surrounded by half a dozen towering oak trees

Shaking like a leaf, I knocked on the back door.

"JT, hi," Rice said. "What are you up too? You're out here awfully early . . . come on in. Can I get you a cup of coffee?"

Standing there about to burst into tears, I blurted, "No . . . Rice, I need to talk to you. I'm on the verge of a nervous breakdown. I have some real problems that I need to talk to you about."

With a genuine look of concern on her face, she told me to go on into the den while she got me that cup of coffee. As I sat there, I was already tearing up, on the verge of losing it.

Sitting down by me, Rice gave me a kleenex to dry my tears.

"What on earth is bothering you? You look like you lost your best friend. Is everyone back home all right? Are your parents okay?"

I swallowed my tears and blew my nose.

"It's worse than that, Rice," I said. "It's me. My life is in a tailspin and I don't know what to do. I mean…I know what I *want* to do, but it's so complicated. I . . . "

Taking a deep breath, I plunged on. "I have a very unique situation with my gender. I've always felt as if I'm a girl. Even my genetics are all screwed up. If I don't figure it out, it's going to be the death of me."

Rice sat there for a few seconds, then said, "Yes, I know about these kinds of things. Not a lot, but enough to know that they're complicated. Do your parents know? Have you told them?"

That's when I told her my life story, from day one.

All the while she sat there listening, with her mouth hanging open. When I finished, she began to analyze the situation. That was what Rice always did—analyze things to no end.

First she asked a lot of questions. Did I want to go for the surgery? What about racing? Will your parents support you? Then she inspected my feminine hands and feet out, and my physical size which was small and petite. Lake was only 5'5" but he was definitely not petite – he was built up like a man with narrow hips and broader shoulders. My hips were broader than my shoulders, and my waist was narrow like a girl's. Rice now realized that I had masked this feature over the years, making sure people would not notice by wearing my pants down on my hips and choosing shirts that were baggy and oversized.

"Obviously you're not a normal boy," she said, surprised. "I never thought about it until now. I just took it for granted that you were a small guy. But now I see that you are very feminine physically. So obviously there is more to this than you just wanting to be a girl. Right now you're trying to be both a boy and a girl and it's killing you."

Rice was getting it. It was hard to believe.

"We need to talk to Lake about this," she said. "He has to know."

"Will he be okay with it? He won't think I'm just nuts?"

She shook her head. "Don't underestimate him. He's got a good heart, and he'll give it a lot of thought."

Rice told me to come back over for supper that night and we would talk to Lake. Before that, she would get him up to speed. She said a little prayer over me and told me she would see me around seven o'clock.

Back in my trailer house across from the speedway, I fell on the couch and bawled like a baby, feeling as if I was taking my last breath on Earth. Then, completely drained from the overload on my mind, I fell asleep there for the better part of the day.

Giving up something

That night at the Speed's home, supper was a bit tense to say the least. Afterwards Lake and Rice and I went into the den.

As we sipped some coffee, Lake began to discuss my situation. Rice had clued Lake to my physical anomalies, and my fears drained away as I saw how remarkably supportive and respectful he was being. After all, he knew I was giving up something here—letting one of my best male friends on this earth see into my heart, past my macho exterior, letting him know a secret that could either bring us closer and have him support me even more, or that could risk losing his friendship forever. After all, he was still a good ole boy from Mississippi.

Over the next hour, all three of us tried to look at all sides of the question…what I should do from this point forward.

"Lake, I just can't live like this any longer," I told him.

"You have to get off of the fence," he said. "You can't live trying to be two people. You need to get into counseling full time. You need a good Christian psychologist to help you. I didn't want to tell you this, but I did get a phone call a few weeks back from someone who told me about your situation. I'm not going to tell you who it was, but they said some things that disturbed me. But I just kind of let it pass, considering the macho climate in the racing community…the jealousy at your success. However, you need to go home and fix your life. Rice and I will be here for you no matter what. But don't tell anyone else. Other people won't understand. So be careful."

By this time all three of us were all tearing up. I was humbled by their love, understanding and soft-heartedness. It meant everything to me.

Then we all held hands. Lake said a prayer that I would find my way and my peace.

When I said amen, he looked at me and said, "There, it's done. God will look after you. Now go figure this out."

Afterwards I kept thinking about what Lake had said.... about not telling anyone else, or accidentally letting it get out in Charlotte. He knew that a story like this would be a death sentence in the NASCAR community. I learned that the person who called him from back in our neck of the woods had told him that his association with me could blow up in his face because I was a fag.

By Thanksgiving, I had taken his advice and was back in Corinth, getting my plan together.

Calling my team partners Don and Nancy in San Francisco, I told them simply that I needed to call a halt for a while to fix my life. Not long after, they flew to Charlotte for a big NAS-CAR race, and I knew I needed to be more honest and open with them about what the situation was. But I didn't feel comfortable with telling Nancy – she was so obsessed with the idea of macho race-car drivers and wanting me to fit into that mold.

But I did trust Don enough to have a heart-to-heart talk with him. Thank God, he did understand my personal quandary, and said he supported me.

But they were not 100 percent happy about my decision. After all, they had invested a lot of money in my career and now I was walking away. I really didn't blame them for being pissed off.

Next it was time to tell my parents. It wasn't going to be pretty. I waited to get through the holidays before starting World War Three with them, and I dreaded the coming confrontation with every ounce of my soul.

CHAPTER 13

Edge of Despair – Pivot Point #2

My folks were wishing I'd get my act together and find my place in life, and soon. I'd made a commitment to myself that I was going to do this, and not let the rejection and humiliation derail me. As Lake Speed had so adamantly told me back in November, I'd have to get off the fence. Living a double life was killing me and driving my parents crazy. So I had to buckle down, be strong and accept the consequences. I could not keep it hidden—they were going to find out any way.

Telling your parents bad news—especially when it concerns your gender, or your coming out as gay or lesbian—is gut wrenching enough. No matter who your parents are or what community you live in, there is a huge price to pay. However, being a professional race-car driver and living in a right-wing highly religious Southern community among macho rednecks complicates the truth-telling to a point that is almost impossible to fathom. No matter that you and your parents have been dealing with a biological fact for most of your life, it is still potentially devastating for everyone involved. For several years I had been faking my parents off, telling them I had put the girl stuff behind me and was focused on a NASCAR future. They had no idea that I had just lived through several of the most traumatic years of my life, and weathered another near-breakdown while up in Charlotte.

So, telling them that I was now making a U turn, intending to start living full time as Terri and to pursue sexual-realignment surgery, would be a shock.

So, as I'd done before, I tried to avoid an eye-to-eye confrontation with them. Instead I wrote them a laborious three-page letter explaining my intentions.

"I love you deeply," the letter emphasized, "and appreciate everything that you've done for me during my entire life, and I hope and wish for your support."

Putting it in an envelope, I left it on their kitchen table. Expecting the fireworks to start the minute they read it that night, I went over to Sally's house and hid out until the smoke cleared.

Sally was a new close friend there in Corinth, whom I had met back in November. We had developed a close bond – she knew my story, and was trying to help me get me through all the craziness. She was Corinth royalty; her dad owned the biggest bank in town (National Bank of Commerce) so she had a bit of that snooty attitude that went along with small Southern town society. But she was personable, friendly and a bit eccentric. Like me Sally walked to her own tune, and that was what drew us together.

I predicted to Sally and myself that Dad wouldn't say a word.

"He never does," I told her. "Most likely he will just sit on the couch watching TV and wondering where he went wrong with me. Probably he's going to give me more tough love by not speaking to me... not allowing me to come back to the house as long as I'm pursuing the Terri thing."

Of course, I was right about how my parents would react.

When she found me up at Granny's a few days later, my mom was pissed off as hell. She told me that there was no way

I could stay in Corinth and do this that she was not going to support me in this.

"Terri, you live here," she raged. "You're embarrassing us, and your daddy is really mad at you over this . . . he said that you're just throwing away your racing career." Her voice got louder and louder, till she was shouting. "He doesn't want to see you again till you change your mind and get some sense about this! You're breaking our hearts!"

Granny stepped in and told Mom she was getting out of control. So Mom just went silent, got her purse and went back down to her house without saying another word.

I never shed a tear; I was not going to let her see me cry. As far as my dad was concerned, he was still my hero but the time had come to deal with this, whatever the consequences. Thank God for Granny and Sally, without them, I would have nowhere to go.

So I just took a deep breath and wrote them another long letter – four pages this time—insisting on my intentions. I told them that I had given it my best shot, that being a boy was killing me, that they had known since I was three or four years old how much this was hurting me. Without a doubt, getting them to understand at this point in our lives was a long shot. But it was all I could do.

Most likely, this was a journey that I was going to have to take alone.

It was the second week of February 1989. I'd been staying with my grandmother, right next door to my Mom and Dad, and living full time as a girl since New Year's Day.

My dad was not speaking to me. In fact, we never saw each other—I was avoiding him at all costs. He was drinking more heavily than ever, and everyone in town blamed me for that.

There was no way I was going to try and reason with him while he was stone drunk.

The whole damn town was abuzz once again. No matter how hard one tries to keep a secret around a small Southern town, it just ain't going to happen—especially when it's about a race car driver wanting to have a sex change. I don't know how people found out but they did.

I hated doing this to my parents. It ripped my heart out— took my soul and slammed it to the ground. I just wished there could be a better solution, some easier way to get through the shock and confrontation we all felt every time I told them what I needed to do to fix my life.

Even Sally got caught up in the whirlwind of gossip and rumor around me, simply by just being my good friend.

One Friday night when she and I were riding around town, just getting out of the house for a while, Sally told me that a casual friend of ours, Ron, was telling most of our friends that he thought Sally and I were sleeping with each other. According to an "unnamed source," ole Ron had told most everyone he could that the thought of Sally and me having sex, with me dressed as a woman, just made him sick to his stomach. We laughed about it because the idea was so ridiculous. But Sally was shocked – as a high-society "nice girl," this was the first time in her life that she had been accused of doing something salacious and my situation suddenly got more personal for her.

Ron had been picking on me ever since junior high school. I had always hated his ass with a passion and wondered what his problem was, since I never bothered him or pushed this on him and actually really never associated with him at all. But like Dewayne, he had a burr up his ass about me and couldn't leave it alone.

Later that night, we stopped off at the home of our good friends Nathan and Debbie Adams, who were having a small gathering of friends. Ron was there with his girlfriend. He was as shocked to see us as we were to see him. Right away he made a beeline to the kitchen where Nathan was fixing sandwiches for the gang. Nathan actually worked for Ron at his building supply and hardware store in town.

So Ron now got up on his high horse and told Nathan, "Hayes has no business being here. No one wants him here . . . it's just too weird for everyone. So he needs to leave."

My good buddy Nathan calmly stood his ground, at the risk of his job, and said, "Well, Hayes is staying. This is my house. If you don't like it, *you* can leave, Ron."

Ron was bowled over that Nathan called him on the carpet. He and his girlfriend left. Score one for me . . . and Nathan.

Of course, the Baptist Church that I'd belonged to all my life was also buzzing like a hornet's nest. Even my unflappable granny was pissed off about some of the things that church members were saying about me.

One Sunday afternoon, Granny and I were sitting in the kitchen drinking a Coke and she told me that she had to confront one of my so-called friends at church that morning before Sunday-school class. This man, Bobby, and his wife Karen came over to her all dripping their concerns over my so-called "sinful life." Bobby and Karen just happened to work at Sally's dad's bank. They point-blank asked Granny if I was working as a prostitute. They said they'd "heard" that some of their friends had seen me at a roadside park near Tupelo soliciting sex from men who stopped there to use the rest room. They had also heard that I was selling drugs to support my "sinful lifestyle."

As I listened to these lies in disbelief, Granny went on. "Terri, for the life of me, I can't understand why people want to be like that...why they just can't mind their own business. Being here in Corinth is not going to work out for you. It's just very sad, We have to figure something else out."

Ironically, around 95% of my granny's and my mom's generation at the church did not treat me badly. Most of them had helped raise me. They loved me and just wanted me to be happy and safe. Their generation was the Billy Graham and the Norman Vincent Peale generation who believe in compassion and forgiveness and giving people the benefit of the doubt before the judgment card is played. No, it was my own generation that boiled over with the most toxic prejudice and bigotry toward me. My generation was the Jerry Falwell and Pat Robertson generation. They were hard-core right-wingers who wanted to rid the earth of everyone who did not look like them or think like them. In their feeble and manipulated minds, I was the Devil's girlfriend.

"Damn," I told Granny, "I'm going to call Bobby and Karen up and give them a piece of my mind.

"No, don't do that," Granny pleaded. "You'll be wasting your breath. It won't change their minds in any way."

Pretty soon I was desperate to find some release from the town's rejection, the church's judgment and my family's disgust. So on the weekends, I drove over to Memphis to hang out with friends, especially my good buddy Michael whom I've known since the early eighties. But it wasn't enough. By the first of March, I'd was finally losing control of my emotions and all I'd could do for a solid week was cry. All the progress I'd made in that night of prayer seemed to be gone, and I was thinking about killing myself again. Corinth's rejection of me was at a fever pitch. It had me locked in the house, afraid to even peep out the window—afraid that some neighbor or my old racing nemesis Dewayne would be standing outside laughing, or wanting to kill me.

Any chance of chasing my NASCAR dream again was for damn sure done and over now. It was like I had already killed a part of myself, the only self I had ever been able to find when the chips were down. Racing had been my safe haven from a world hell-bent on destroying me since I was a kid. My race shop and my race cars were places I could go to find solace and acceptance. Now I felt as if I had thrown it all away.

My new friend Sally was also trying hard to help. I loved her fearlessness in dealing with situations. She would charge right in. At the time she worked for the local Welfare Department handling abused kids. If she got a report that anyone was knocking their kids around, Sally would clean their clock and make sure the kids were safe. She also had a temper – if anybody in town crossed her about me, they were going to get an earful.

Sally was five or six years older than I was, but the age difference did not matter, we just liked one another. She was pretty, only about 5'1", a bit overweight but always decked out in a crisp and clean preppy style and eye-catching shoes—she loved shoes. She had blonde shoulder-length hair that parted on the left side and combed over her right eye. Another important costume detail was the cup or glass of tea in her hand. Her car, a Ford Taurus, was always junked inside with empty cups, packages and fast-food wrappers. This made me nuts—I had to have a clean car!

Sally knew that Lake had suggested I get Christian counseling, so she was dragging my old minister friend Brother Phil over to my house every day in hopes he could get through my suicidal fog. I had promised Lake that I'd have an open mind on this front, so I tried hard to listen to Phil.

Finally my mom and grandmother slowly woke up to the danger that I faced from myself, and realized that something had to be done before it was too late.

In desperation, Mom called Don and Nancy out in San Francisco and gave them the sad state of affairs in Terriville. She asked Don if there was some way he could come to Mississippi and try to fix this mess. Being the compassionate soul that he is, Don got the message. He'd seen the pain in my face months ago when I told him about my plans. He liked fixing things – fixing laundromats, fixing cars, and now he wanted to fix me.

So he agreed to catch a flight to Memphis to somehow keep me from being burned at the stake in my home town.

The Golden Coast

Only two weeks earlier I had been at death's door. But on the West Coast again, I found myself coming back to life. It was a miracle—a roof over my head and a job where they knew me as Terri, not JT.

For the first time I could really focus on my transition – perhaps save some money for the surgery.

Don had found the job for me at a local print shop, Marina Printing, in San Francisco, down on Lombard Street, only three blocks from their apartment. He had known a couple of lesbians from years back who ran the shop there in the neighborhood, and had asked them if they would be able to help me out. They agreed to at least meet me and see if there was anything I could actually do around their shop. Ironically, when I went in to meet the girls for the first time and introduced myself as Don's friend who was going through sex realignment, they almost passed out from amazement.

"We can't believe you're a boy!" they said. "You're . . . uh, you're such a *girl*."

They hired me on the spot.

Helping the girls do everything from manning the copy machines to doing graphic design work, I was practically running the damn place soon. The money wasn't much, but I didn't care. I was just glad to be working as a girl and away from Corinth!

Everything went along pretty well for a month or so.

I reconnected with my old friend Chris who lived over in North Beach, and shared a few meals with him and his girlfriend in the Marina district. We would gather up at Paul's Saloon, that favorite bluegrass place of mine on Chestnut Street. It kept us closer to our roots, but we also tore up a few rock 'n roll nightspots over in North Beach as well. I also enjoyed all the cool bookstores and coffee shops in the area. But most of the time, I just hung out at the apartment in the Marina district.

Some people might think that, because I was in San Francisco where anything goes, I was letting my sexual taste overflow into the streets. This was not the case at all. When it came to sex, I had always been very conservative, and made a decision to be celibate after my marriage to Pam broke up in 1986. I wanted to be sure that my gender issue was not about having sex with a man, but about my heart and soul as a woman. Call it my Southern Baptist upbringing; call it being scared to take the plunge in the sack with some guy; call it my analytical engineering and motorsports background, where one needs all the facts in order to make the best possible decision. Call it what you will. But the time for sex would come once I was sure I had my head on straight.

But for all the positives of San Francisco, things were not going well with Don and Nancy.

I could tell they were getting tired of me living there. At times, Nancy was pretty pissy with me and I had to watch my mouth when she would smart off about just anything. Who could blame her? I had taken away her dream of being a NAS-CAR team owner. Evidently Don still hadn't shared with her the hints that I had given him about my gender quandary.

Sure, I could have been more honest with both of them from the get-go. But that is never possible with gender issues, no matter who you are. You always live with hope that you can handle it, get through it, and most importantly get past it. Telling people that your gender is in question is almost never an option, especially with people like Nancy. Even though she was a good person and loved me, and had supported me as if I were her adopted child, she had a hard-core macho spot in her heart that my gender issue was not going to fit into.

So I would have to find my own place.

Living in San Francisco isn't cheap. I wasn't making a whole lot of money working at the print shop so I would need to find a second job to afford my own apartment. But what in the hell was I going to do? Wait tables? Get a job in a department store? Since 1983 I had been a professional race-car driver, and before that, my entire background was in the racing and the tool and die business. I had to get my thinking cap on or I'd be living on the street.

Then it dawned on me that maybe there might be some owner on the sprint-car circuit who would let me drive their car.

Last year, I had brokenheartedly given up the idea of sprint-car racing forever, because of my social status I was no longer able to race at the top. But now I had to look at sprint cars as a second job. Any amount of pay would do! No one in the racing community but Don and Nancy knew what I was up to out in California. The rumors from last year were surely still swirling around the race shops, but not all of those hard-ass macho team owners cared about my sexuality. Hell, team owners were always looking for a bad-ass driver to get them into victory lane. Maybe I could drive on the weekends as JT, and work at the print shop during the week as Terri. This would help me pick up some extra cash if I could pull it off. Who knew what making a few phone calls could work up?

I could make the double-life deal work for at least four or five months.

And I did truly have an itch of missing the driving—not the politics and the culture, just the racing itself.

Twists and Turns of my Life

It was the second week of April, Tuesday afternoon, when I got out my trusty phone book with all my old contacts.

Sitting at the lunch table in the back of the print shop, I was patting my foot and getting my courage up to call up some old racing friends. Burt and Marilee were dyed-in-the-wool fans I had met back in 1986 when I first came out to the West Coast. I didn't know much about them except that they seemed to be fairly successful in some sort of business. I liked them, and it had always seemed that they liked me too. They had always hung around my pit area when races ended. I had watched the finish of the 1986 Indy 500 race in the comfort of their motor home in Chico at the Chico Fair Grounds Speedway, where I had won my first California sprint-car race that same weekend. If they had heard the rumors about me, they might not care one way or the other.

If anyone knew who was hiring and who was firing in the sprint car world, it would be Burt and Marilee.

I'm always surprised at the twist and turns of my life, and it never stops amazing me just how crazy my life is. God must have said to himself or herself that this life is going to make one heck of a book and movie. Anyway, once I conjured up the courage, with my hands actually shaking, I dialed the number.

Marilee answered. "JT!" she exclaimed. "It's great to hear from you!"

It was like I'd never been away from the racing culture there in California. Right away we were catching up about old times.

After a few minutes of chit chatting, I casually told her that I was on the West Coast again and looking for a ride, and asked if she knew anyone looking to hire a hot shoe from Mississippi. All during this conversation, I was sitting there dressed as a girl, working and looking like Marlo Thomas, and trying to conjure back my JT voice, which had virtually disappeared.

To my complete amazement Marilee told me to hold on for a second.

Then her husband Burt got on the line. "JT, would you like to drive our car?"

I couldn't believe what I was hearing. "Well, yeah, I didn't know you have a car. What kind of car do you have?"

He told me that he and Marilee had just bought two new complete cars from Challenge Enterprises out in Iowa, and two new engines from Gerte in Indiana. That was probably as good as you could get in sprint-car racing at the time. I couldn't believe my good luck. Hell fire—this could be something good.

Then Burt said, "Hey man, how about you meeting us up in Chico this weekend for a two-day NARC sprint car event. We can put you right in the car up there and start kicking their asses."

Why not? I thought to myself. What did I have to lose?

Without blinking an eye I told them I would see them Friday afternoon in the pits. Just like that, the deal was made. When I hung the phone up I had to pinch myself.

Then I caught my feminine reflection in the Coke machine right off to my side. Reality came rushing back over me and I wondered just how on God's green earth I was going to pull this off. I didn't look like JT Hayes any more—or least the JT that Burt and Marilee had seen over the past several years. This would take some doing. But what the hell—where there is a will and a sprint car waiting, there is a sprint car driver looking for victory lane.

When I told Don and Nancy, they hated the idea. Don took me aside and said, "I think it's a mistake for you to go back to racing. You need to focus on your transition."

"Hell, maybe it is," I told him. "But I need the money."

Plus this might help calm my nerves—just a bit. Let's face it, I missed racing, and last time I checked, that race car didn't know if I was a girl or a boy. Don and Nancy needed to get over their idea of who I was and what I should be doing.

Re-entering the Culture

On Friday, at 1 p.m., I begged Linda, my boss, to let me off work early. She relented and gave me her blessings. Heck, she was pretty fired up about it, to tell the truth.

I left the print shop right at 1:01 p.m. and hightailed it up to Chico, driving the three hours as Terri. Once I got to the Chico city limits, it was JT time. Finding a Motel 6, I checked in, took a quick shower to take off the makeup, and put on my only pair of boy's blue jeans. With duct tape, I bound my newly growing breasts down, and slipped on an old tee shirt with Lake Speed's race car on the front.

As I looked in the steamy bathroom mirror, I was as nervous as I've ever been in my life, but on another level, I was as sure of myself as I'd ever been. It was that old fear and fearlessness thing again. This was what I did; it was virtually who I was. Racing had been my life since the day I was born. However, the person in the mirror made me frown. I didn't look good. I was extremely skinny, my hair was down on my shoulders and without makeup, I looked like a washed-out lesbian, which was not so bad In the right circumstances.

But considering the culture I was about to re-enter, that little detail was a big negative.

Once I got to the track and made my way to the car, I immediately recognized Burt and we shook hands.

Jumping right in the car, I adjusted the safety belts and made that big seat—which was designed for Burt's 6'2", 200-pound body – somehow fit my 115-pound skinny butt. Within thirty minutes we were ready to go, and I was looking to qualify, buzzing around that high-banked dirt track that has eaten more sprint-car drivers than anyone could count. Within five practice laps I was standing on the gas and right back in form.

Back in the pits we made a few quick changes to the shocks and tires. Even though it had been almost a year since I had raced a sprint car, I knew what I was doing. Then, amazingly, I went out and qualified fifth out of 60 drivers.

In the main event, we ended up breaking a drive line while running third.

But I was hooked, and so were Burt and Marilee. We made a deal for me to drive every weekend and they agreed to pay me 60% of the winnings. I would need to work on their car—the throttle was sticking and I had damn near wrecked. If Burt would let me change a few things, that car would be lightning fast.

So the weekend was a success. I loved being back in the seat and enjoyed seeing my old friends from several years back. But

I could tell that most of them were giving me curious looks. No, I didn't look quite the same. But what I looked like to them didn't matter. It was me who needed to pay rent and work towards sex reassignment surgery.

I had to stay focused.

The Juggling Act

On the way back to San Francisco the next day, I had time to reflect about racing again, and about my relationship with my parents, especially my Dad.

I missed them like crazy. I missed my grandmother so much my heart ached every time I thought about her. It was time to give her and my Mom a call on Monday when I got back to the print shop.

But more than that, I missed having my Dad with me. I had always felt more confident, more at ease, when he was with me at the track. It was a damn shame we were at odds, that this gender ordeal had driven a wedge between us, that society had such a negative attitude toward people like me when it was so obvious that I was a girl and not a boy. But it was what it was, and it was also a nightmare that someone who had understood my situation at one point, my difference and my inner pain, had now turned out to despise me the most.

I also suspected that Dad was feeling the heat of politics from his buddies. Especially Dewayne and that bunch of rednecks at the Honda shop where my Dad went almost every day to chew the fat. Dewayne and one of his motorcycle mechanics, Roger, had seen me in my Blazer back in Corinth at a fast-food drive-through, and I suspected that they were the ones who had spread the rumors all over town right after New Year's.

Dewayne just could not leave it alone and let me and my parents work our issues out between us. He just had to get in the middle.

All this thinking tore me up inside, and at one point on my trip back to the city, I found myself with tears rolling down my face. Of course, like any chick who is anal about her appearance, I had to find a restroom to fix my makeup. It made me feel like an idiot, but I just had to have that eyeliner on correctly.

At some point before summer's end, I would need to try and reconcile with my Dad.

That Monday, I got busy looking through all the newspapers for an apartment I could afford that was close to the print shop. I didn't want to drive thirty minutes every day and end up fighting for a parking spot every single morning. I'm from rural Mississippi and the thought of fighting for a parking spot did not sit well with me. Of course driving a race car at extreme speeds is very logical, right?

Anyway, that afternoon I wasn't having any luck, so I vented my frustration to a lady who was in the shop making some copies. She was a regular customer, and I just started grumbling to her about how hard it was to find a place in the Marina district.

Right out of the blue, she told me that she had a friend who had a flat for rent. It was just around the corner, two blocks away. I couldn't believe my luck. The $600-a-month rent was a lot of money but, it was just a three-minute walk to work, and with me earning extra cash this would be a breeze. Besides, the neighborhood was the coolest and I could live there forever and never get tired of it.

The lady made a reference call for me and the next day I rented the place.

By the end of the week I had moved in. I was missing furniture and cooking ware, but I did have a few of my granny's homemade quilts, a pillow from K Mart, my clothes, and a tiny portable TV that was so fuzzy you could barely see the picture, that I had borrowed from Don. To me it was perfect. Now I had to get my tail in gear and make money!

Over the next two weeks things seemed to be on track, no pun intended. Every week day I worked eight hours at the print shop. Linda, my boss, had given me a key. She had really come to depend on me and I liked the extra responsibility.

At night, before I walked back to my flat, I would either hang out at one of the Thai restaurants I loved in the neighborhood, or you could find me just around the corner at Paul's Saloon, where they served a mean hot dog and five-alarm chili. Paul made a smooth cup of coffee, and there was this big old fireplace in there that took the bite off of the cool San Francisco evenings when the bay would envelope the Marina district in a thick fog. I loved it because it made me feel as if I was back around all my buds in my neck of the woods. Not that bluegrass and cowboy music was my perfect cup of coffee, but it helped me get through the week.

At least once a week, I checked in with my mom and grandmother and Sally from the phone there at the print shop, just to keep in touch and let them know I was safe. I missed them immensely.

The irony of my being in SF was that no one ever thought I was anything except a woman. You would think that in a city known for its diversity that someone would have figured it out.

In fact, I would see others who were clearly going through the change and talk to them, and they would never have a clue that I was in the same situation. Actually, I felt very fortunate to be me; it definitely could have been much worse.

All in all, I was working my skinny ass off to keep it together and most of the time I seemed to be handling the craziness pretty well. But there were times when the whole mess would catch up to me. Right out of nowhere, tears would start rolling down my face and I would have to turn away from people on the street or rush to the ladies' room to regain my composure.

Once a week, usually on a Tuesday, I would take off my makeup, stuff my hair up under a baseball hat and drive down to the race shop in San Leandro to help Burt and the guys work on the car. I was slowly making the car faster and more reliable, and we were on a roll. Over the last two weeks, I had set fast time and finished second up in Petaluma and third over in Placerville. My racing chops were back in good form and it was only a matter of time before we would be standing in victory lane.

But it was a major juggling act and I had to watch myself. Just hiding my growing breasts was enough of a pain. But making sure that this bunch of good ole boys didn't pick up on my feminine mannerisms and the changes in my voice was very tricky. Note to self: "Make sure you remove all nail polish." It's always in the details, isn't it? Remember to be macho, Terri… uh JT. Sometimes I found myself being a wee bit too macho, which is considered to be a strong trait and badge of honor for any hotshot male race-car driver, and when I was more macho it seemed to keep the wolves away from the door.

Then something happened.

I had been down to the race shop getting the car ready for a big race down in Santa Maria. It was 1:00 in the morning and I was later than usual coming back over the Bay Bridge. I needed to get back to the city at a decent hour so I could get some rest and be at work by 7:30 the next morning. The radio was tuned to the local oldies station and I was gazing out over the bay enjoying the city lights when I noticed that my Blazer was beginning to power down a bit. When I glanced into my rear view mirror, there was a horrifying plume of smoke billowing from the back of the little baby-blue SUV.

I didn't want to be stranded on the Bay Bridge at one in the morning, so I slowed to almost a crawl and prayed like crazy that I could please make it back to my place. It seemed like days but by the grace of God, I finally made it. When I pulled into my parking spot and turned off the engine, the little Blazer spewed one last plume of steam out of its engine. It was as if she was saying, "Thank you, Terri, for not leaving me on the side of the road all by myself!" Luckily, there was a garage next to the print shop. I would be there when they opened. I needed my wheels! Meanwhile, I needed my sleep.

Next morning at 7:00 a.m. sharp, I was at the garage.

That was the first time I had ever encountered the demeaning attitude that men give women when it comes to cars. No matter what I did to show them I knew what I was talking about, they dismissed me as being a cute little white bimbo who didn't know a thing about cars. I didn't want them to know anything about my past history so I just sucked it up and told them to call me when they had the verdict. Later on that afternoon, they phoned to say that the truck had a blown head gasket and it would cost around $700.00 to fix.

I was pissed but knew they were correct on their assessment, so I told them to make the repairs. The manager said I could pick her up in four or five days.

I ended up riding down to the races with Marilee in her big black Mercedes like a rock star. When we pulled into the track and got out of that baby, the redneck jaws all dropped!

That weekend, things did go well. On Friday night I turned second quick time and finished third in the main event. On Saturday night I turned the fastest time in qualifying and finished second in the main event – even after having a flat and having to restart at the back of the twenty-five car field with only fifteen laps remaining. I drove like a bat out of hell trying to salvage a good finish. A couple of those throttle jockeys I had re-passed on my way back to the front were pissed off, claiming that I had bumped into them when I passed their sorry butts. Whatever! Stop your bitching and drive the car, boys!

Needless to say Burt, Marilee and my crew guys were pumped up about our success. However, the success was getting to my competitors. They were badmouthing me and stirring up those old rumors. I could see them staring at me. One of the guys from Brent Kading's crew even flipped me the bird.

Hell Brent was the baddest cat on the west coast sprint-car circuit and I knew he didn't give a shit what I did. He was a big boy and could take care of himself.

My main crew guy, Grumpy, a bonafide bulldog of a man and a damn fine race mechanic, vowed to keep me safe! He told me, "Hey man, I don't care what they say about you, screw those guys. You're a hell of a race-car driver and they can't stand it that you just rolled in here and kicked their asses. You drive it and we will fight 'em if I we have to."

That's all I needed to hear!

So racing was good, for the time being, and I got paid enough to catch up on my bills.

But that night, as the team and I drove back to San Francisco from down in Santa Maria, I felt uneasy and empty. I was beginning to miss my family and friends to the point that I was obsessing about it, especially about missing my dad. I needed to call home and tell him how good I was doing . . . he just might forgive me and talk to me. It's amazing how much of a hold he had on me. I hated feeling like that but I always wanted him to approve of what I was doing.

That next Thursday the Blazer was ready. The bill was $850.00. It was more than I intended to pay but I managed to beg, plead and girl-talk them down to $750.00. I paid them half in cash and the remaining half with a check. We made a couple of test laps around the block to make sure everything worked properly.

Then I went back to my apartment, changed into JT and took off to the race shop to work on the car. I was really excited to have my wheels back. I need to be mobile like I need blood running through my veins. Without my wheels, I feel closed in, and completely out of sorts. As I was pulling out of my parking spot, I decided to cruise over toward Knob Hill to a local coffee shop before I got on the road. So I quickly turned the rear-view mirror to my face, put on lipstick, fluffed my hair and Terri was back.

Then, about two blocks from the coffee shop, the engine shook violently and smoke billowed out of the tail pipe just like on the Bay Bridge. Then it just shut off completely. I knew the deathly sound of an engine puking its brains out. I'd blown up enough race-car engines to know that sound very well.

Quickly I got out and just managed to push it off the road far enough to be safe when I began to bawl like a baby.

The whole affair was too much to bear. Not twenty minutes before, I had paid that garage my last dime. Now here I sat, busted, broke down and alone, three thousand miles from my family and trying to jumble a lifestyle that would kill the strongest of the strong. What in the name of Jesus was I going to do now?

I sat there crying my eyes out for what seemed like an hour and it was beginning to get dark. Finally it was time to get a hold on myself. I couldn't afford a wrecker so I had to be creative. My friend, Chris lived not far from there—he would help me figure out what to do with my truck for the night. He had a new truck so we could possibly push or pull my Blazer to a safer place.

I walked to Chris's home. Lucky for me, he was there, and sympathized with my dilemma. So we hightailed it back over to where the Blazer was parked. He got behind my truck and gave me a push down the hill. As if the gates of Heaven had opened up to protect me, I coasted down to his apartment about four blocks away and gently pulled into a parking spot just across the street. At least the truck would be safe there for a little while.

Chris could tell that I didn't need any more negatives in my life at that moment. He said, "Look, let's go get a beer and a bite to eat, and talk about this."

I agreed. So we headed over to North Beach and got smashed.

Storm on the Horizon

That weekend, I told Burt and Marilee about my dire straits – except, of course, I didn't tell them that I had already been living as a girl. I just told them that I needed to cut my costs. If they were willing I would like to start racing a little more.

Marilee said, "Why don't you rent the room attached to the race shop? I will only charge you $250 a month and you will be right there to work on the car every day. You would save a lot of money and get your truck fixed sooner . . . and, we would love to race more."

The only thing wrong with that idea was that I would have give up my job at the print shop and, more importantly, stop being Terri. I didn't know if I could do that or not...or even if I should. If I did take Marilee's offer I would be giving up on everything I moved out there for. However, if I only pursued that option for the remainder of the summer and then returned to my transition that coming winter, then I might not totally screw everything up. After all, I could catch the BART train up to the city and be Terri at least once a week, and no one would be the wiser.

After struggling with my decision for three or four days, I realized that I didn't have any choice in the matter.

After my buddy Chris and I moved all my stuff to the race shop, I worked on the car every day and it was paying off with consistent good finishes at the track. I was totally focused on being the best damn driver I could be but I was feeling the pressure in a big, big way to be Terri. Plus the fact that my dad still hated me was just killing me.

I also felt stranded living at the shop without my truck. Fortunately a couple of the crew guys would come by and get me from time to time, especially my new-found friend Allan, and we would go get a bite to eat or hit a sports bar for some male bonding.

Allan was obsessed with being a sprint-car driver and pumped me for information every chance he got. Hell, I didn't mind though — he was a good-looking 20-year-old kid with nice manners and I liked him. He thought I was the best driver on the West Coast, which was good for my ego. He actually helped me get my truck out of the city by taking his old beat-up Jeep Wagoner to the city and pulling my Blazer down to the race shop. He and I were beginning to make the truck repairs ourselves.

But a storm was brewing on the horizon with team owner Burt.

He had turned into a real pain in the ass. Don't get me wrong, I was thankful to be driving his and Marilee's race car. But before I started working on that car, they were running in the rear of the pack, and everything on the car was only half taken care of. But I had made all types of changes, and made that team a winner. Now ole Burt was suddenly the expert engineer and sprint car mechanic. We were now frontrunners and winners, and he was telling everyone it was because he was so damn smart!

Anyway, I was getting pretty damn pissed at him, as was the rest of the crew.

We headed off to a big Father's Day weekend of racing up in Chico and we were all fired up about our chances to win. I was completely back in racing form. As a driver my mind was clear and focused on the sport. Of course my personal focus was a different matter altogether but at least my stamina was finally back.

After Chico, the biggest sprint-car race on the West Coast was coming up in two weeks in Skagit, Washington and it seemed as if we would peak just in time to win that big event.

So that Father's Day weekend, Grumpy and I had that baby ready to sing a song in victory lane. The first night I set fast time and won by a pretty good margin. We fully expected to kick their tails on Saturday night as well, and couldn't wait. All day Saturday, Grumpy and I made adjustments to the car out in the hot sun in the race-track parking lot. When qualifying came around that night, we just knew we had everyone covered.

In hot laps we were a rocket ship, the car was perfect and I was on my game. When qualifying rolled around, a few of those guys were turning some really fast runs, including my old arch rival Brent Kading. When it came time for his qualifying run he immediately set the tone for the night by setting the fastest time yet … right before my qualifying run.

The crowd went crazy when Brent turned in that lightning-fast lap—everyone was positive that no one could possibly beat his time. The rednecks had their Budweiser hats flying as he pulled of the track and into his pit spot right off the first corner. They were about to tear the grand stands down with excitement. You would have thought he was Dale Earnhardt Jr.

As I heard the track announcer tell the fans what Kading had just done, I casually looked over at Grumpy and he just smiled and gave me a thumbs up. Then, the race official slapped me on top of the helmet and told me to go out for my run. Just as the push truck was getting ready to push me onto the track, one of Kading's crew guys came strutting by my car and flipped me the finger.

From the corner of my eye, I could see that Grumpy wanted to kick his ass but I just laughed at Kading's guy. Hell, that was part of racing sprint cars. You have to take the heat— this ain't a tennis match and a glass of merlot at the French open, Sugar. However, the middle finger pointed in my direction made me more determined to beat their tails than ever. I had not been out-qualified there in Chico very many times and that track was perfectly suited for my driving style. I would not be denied!

As soon as I fired off, I stood on the gas and hauled that 900 horse-powered rocket around that race track with the drive of a madman/woman.

My first lap was two tenths faster than Brent's and my second lap was a tenth better than my first. On my cool-down lap I glanced up at the scoreboard and I knew I had made it fastest. Those rednecks in the grand stands were going even crazier than when Brent had qualified.

I was really feeling my oats so when I pulled off the track, I noticed that Brent's truck and race car was parked right in front of where I was headed through the pit area. His guys seemed demoralized and I thought that I should rub it in their faces just a wee bit. So I gassed it, spun the rear tires and drove straight through their pits slinging a cloud of dust all through the $100,000 trailer and onto their race car. There ain't nothing like a little feminine revenge on a bunch of macho boys.

Needless to say, the fists almost started a-flying. But fortunately cooler heads did prevail. There ain't nothing like a little rivalry to get the blood flowing on a hot Saturday night.

That night in the main race, I led most of the event but with about ten laps to go, the drive line broke, sending me to the pits and out of the race . . . damn. We were very disappointed but we had a good weekend anyway. So after meeting all the fans and signing a few autographs, we loaded up the trailer and headed back to San Leandro.

But there was tension in the air between Burt and me. Right before the start of the event, he and I had butted heads when he wanted to replace one of the high-tech racing shocks with one he had modified. There was no way I was going to put that piece of crap on the race car. We had a few words and I walked off with him calling me an arrogant little prick. I should have been more diplomatic but I was tired of his arrogance.

The whole way back to the race shop that night, Grumpy and I talked about how fast we had been and what we needed to do to be super-fast up in Skagit. He was smart and committed to the team and I truly liked him. More importantly I knew he was going to look after me no matter what!

But, as we talked about racing, I was feeling the crunch of Father's Day weekend creeping up on me, and missing Terri so much I was about to explode from the pressure. Racing full time was putting a roof over my head and some financial rewards. But I was beginning to realize all over again—just like before in Charlotte—that I needed more than racing in my life. My gender was being starved to death because I refused to be totally committed. Plus, this double-life situation was crazy.

Lake Speed was right. I couldn't live on the fence.

A Million Pieces

I had always wondered why my Maker was forcing me to choose between the two . . . or was He? I was working my mind and heart over time thinking about it. Maybe I just needed to be more honest with the people who loved me, instead of leading them to think I was doing all right, only to go off the deep end and re-spring my feminine intentions on them when they were unprepared to handle it.

We drove all through the night, and reached the race shop at 7:00 AM. worn out and glad to be back. Grumpy grabbed his bags and hightailed it to his home, and I stumbled off to my little room and collapsed into my tiny bed exhausted both emotionally and physically. Before my head hit the pillow, I was sound asleep!

At about 11:00 AM, I suddenly awoke staring straight up at the ceiling.

It was Father's Day and I dreaded getting out of bed. But I had only eaten a fish sandwich the day before, so my stomach was growling. I figured I would take a quick shower and walk over to the Western Sizzling only a few blocks away for a quick lunch, and then take the BART train up to the city to hang out with my friend Chris for the day. Whatever I did, I had to get out of that room.

By the time I got to the restaurant, it was 1:00 pm.

There was a short line of people waiting to eat, but what the heck, it was a Sunday and it was Father's Fay . . . people go out to eat. So I endured the crowd and after about twenty minutes I got a table and ordered my food—a small rib eye cooked medium rare with French fries and a Coke. I barely weighed 117 pounds with my clothes on, so the steak and fries would be good for me.

The place was packed and after a few minutes, the crowd began to close in on me. This was a family place and I was the only one in the entire restaurant sitting by myself. By the time the waiter brought my food, my hands were shaking, there were tears welling up in my eyes and I felt like everyone was staring at me. After I took a few bites of my steak, I thought I was going to throw it back up. One of my anxiety attacks was coming on, and I needed to get the heck out of there before I passed out on the floor.

Rushing over to the cashier, I paid my bill and virtually ran outside and sat down on a bench by the door, all the while trying to fight back the tears. The sun was glaring and brutal and I didn't have my sunglasses so I could barely see through the glare, but thank God, the air was clear and crisp and allowed me to catch my breath and to collect my thoughts.

Damn, I thought, what in the name of Holy Jesus is going on here . . . what am I going to do with myself?

If I couldn't talk to my dad within the next few minutes I was going to break into a million pieces. I needed to tell him I loved him and missed him so much that I could barely stand it...to tell him how good I was driving the race car, which would make him happy. Just maybe, just maybe he would forgive me.

Rushing back in the restaurant, asked the cashier to give me change for five one-dollar bills so I could use the pay phone outside. As I collected the change, I couldn't keep my hands from shaking, even dropping a few quarters on the ground. But I was slowly beginning to get my composure back, so I made my way out to the booth and began to put quarters in the phone. Confidently I dialed my parents' number.

It rang four or five times, when suddenly, my dad picked up the receiver. In the baritone voice I knew so well, he simply said, "Hello."

I quickly said, "Dad, it's JT . . . what's going on back there?"

The phone went dead.

"Hello, hello," I said, "is anyone there . . . Dad?"

At first I thought we had been cut off. So I quickly put in more quarters and redialed . . . ring after ring after ring with no answer.

Then just like before, my dad picked up and said, "Hello."

"Happy Father's Day," I said.

Just like before, the phone went dead. An eerie silence.

This time I realized that he had hung up on me.

I was beginning to feel the disabling anxiety flow over my body once more, and my hands were shaking like crazy. I had to give it one more try. He had never been that pissed at me before—at some point he would surely come to his senses and talk to me. He must be drinking…that would explain his actions. Hell, he was my dad, he loved me.

In desperation, I redialed one last time. This time, it only rang once before my mom picked up the receiver.

"Terri, is that you?" she said. "I'll call you tomorrow. I can't talk to you today. Your dad is drinking and he doesn't want to talk to you. He doesn't want you calling here either. I have to live with him, so I will call you tomorrow."

I began to feel light-headed and my knees buckled under me. I tried to hold onto the phone booth but lost my grip and fell onto the concrete sidewalk with a thud. By this time, I was crying uncontrollably and the crowd in the restaurant was noticing the drama just outside their windows. I was laying there flat on my back looking directly into the beating sun, bawling my eyes out. All the while the receiver dangled right above me with my mom screaming my name on the other end of the line.

This was a scene right out of a Hitchcock movie, except it was real and it was happening to me. I had gone over the edge. My body, my mind, and my heart could not take any more. All hopes that I could ever have my dad's respect and love again seemed to be gone, crushed. The rejection had pierced my soul like never before.

For what seemed like an eternity, I lay there staring straight up. A crowd of curious and horrified people gathered around me, wondering what in the hell was going on. I could barely see them through all the tears and the glaring sun. One lady was asking someone to call an ambulance. That shocked me into trying to get up. Some big guy grabbed me by the arm and helped me balance myself. If I didn't get back to my room fast, I would damn sure wake up in the psychiatric ward.

So I just took off, half running and half walking, leaving all of those freaked-out people standing there. I could have been on drugs for all they knew!

It took about fifteen minutes of bloody hell to make it back to my room and I was screaming out loud the whole way. "I can't take this anymore! God please help me get through this, please help me! Oh God I just can't take this anymore!"

By the time I got to the front gate of the shop, all I could think about was killing myself. Everyone hated me. I would never be able to restore my reputation in the racing community. I was a frickin' joke no matter what I did. I was the best damn racer to ever grace the entire state of Mississippi, but no one would embrace that fact ever again like they had before my reputation was smeared. If I killed myself, everyone would be happier, including me. Just get it over with.

For twelve solid hours, I sat there in that dark room running all of that craziness through my head, reliving my life with excruciating recall. I ached to my very core with fear of ever walking out the door of my tiny room again. One minute I wanted to kill myself, and in the next breath, I became defiant and yelled at the top of my voice, "Screw all of them!" Through it all, I clutched a knife I had retrieved from a tool box in the race shop. Every tick of the clock could have been my last.

I don't know how, except for God's grace, I survived the worst day of my life, and when you're dealing with this gender identity issue under the circumstances I had been in, that's saying a lot! Just like the cleansing of a heavy spring rain and the clean crisp smell of a new dawn, the morning light brought a new vision, a new direction. . . hope that I needed to give this life one more try.

I made the decision to go home to Corinth knowing all too well that it would be difficult to regroup once more. But I had to try and fix things with my dad and, to give that damn NASCAR dream one more try.

It would be extremely risky to say the least but I just felt that my angels were guiding me toward that decision. That was why I had survived that horrible night – to fix things with my parents, to see my granny once again, to get back to my trusty race shop and office I had abandoned trying to find my way in the world—to re focus and rekindle my dreams. That was my hope; that would be my goal, my connection to the now-broken bond between me and my father. I wanted my hero back in my life, I craved it and I was willing to make the sacrifices to make that happen. How and when that would happen, I didn't have a clue but, by God, I was going to do it even if I died trying.

I called my mom and told her the news.

"Mom, I'm coming home. I'm giving NASCAR another try . . ."

CHAPTER 14

Going Home – NASCAR?

It was July 1, 1989. Sally picked me up at the Memphis airport.

Two days before, when I had called her to tell her I was coming home, she asked me, "Who are you going to be—Terri or JT?"

Who knew with me? One always needed to ask.

She picked up JT and we drove right over to the race track in West Memphis. Before I left California, I had gotten on the phone and made a deal to drive a sprint car belonging to a guy, Ron Pack, based in Little Rock, Arkansas. I didn't know how long that would last because he was notorious for firing drivers at the drop of a hat. Past hot laps, there was no job security with Ron! But I needed the money.

Mom knew I was going to race at West Memphis and she had somehow coaxed my dad into coming over to the track. She told him JT would be there. That was the icebreaker. That night we actually ran very well and contended for the win, though I cut a right front tire down and didn't finish. But that was not important.

The moment Dad and I had first looked each other in the eye, I felt like I was back home in his heart. My mom was beside herself with joy.

But the moment was surreal, to say the least. As a family we would never talk about what had transpired over the past six months. My parents would never know what I had been through.

Over the next few weeks I resettled in Corinth at my parent's house, cleaned out my race shop and remodeled my trophy room and office. Although I hated being back in my home town, I truly enjoyed being at my race shop again with all my stuff. For the time being, the pressure of being 3000 miles away from my family was off my shoulders. However, I did feel that so far I had failed miserably to get my life together. The last year had been a train wreck and I was the engineer.

Right away I reconnected with Lake Speed and told him that I might want to try that NASCAR deal one more time. So he invited me to come down to Talladega at the end of July to talk about how to rekindle those opportunities. He was really concerned about me, but he had no idea what I had been through in California. There was no reason to tell him, and he was just glad that I was back to being JT. To Lake, it looked like I had finally decided which side of the fence to live on.

The other positive was that Sally and I finally connected as friends. We were together almost all of the time. She too was fired up that I was interested in NASCAR again, and that I had decided to be JT instead of Terri . . . at least for a while.

Of course my mom and dad were trying to do anything possible to keep me happy...or at least to keep me on any path that led away from Terriville.

My Blazer was still back in California, and so was my good friend and crew member Allen. So we sent him money to fix my truck, and he drove it across the country to Corinth. He wanted to go racing with me...to see what the planet looked like outside the Golden Coast. Why not? He was a good guy and I could use some loyal help while trying to keep Ron Pack from firing me. This could be tough—all those redneck race-car drivers would be bad-mouthing me and trying to get my job. I was going to enjoy beating their sorry asses!

But the deal with Ron Pack fell through before we ever got started. He just could not stand up to the rumors.

"I'm glad you're not driving for that s.o.b.," Dad told me. "You should just move on, and aim for NASCAR."

For a few weeks Allen hung out with us in Corinth and then we sent him back to California. He left us with a new sense of reality about the good ole boys in the South . . . it was as different as daylight and dark on how the cultures clashed between the Mid South and the West Coast. We were all racers in our hearts, but the California cats were more socially aware. Allen got to see the difference first hand!

By the first of August, my NASCAR plan was together enough to share with my dad. I would start by promoting my name to sponsors in Mississippi, then use the NASCAR PR machine to promote the economic resources within our state. As I talked it up around Corinth, people began to take notice. Some of the people who had smeared my name all over town were now patting me on the back and encouraging me to go for it. I was thankful for their help, but sometimes I wanted to smack them for being hypocrites! Oh, the power of racing and NASCAR in a small Southern town!

For the next month, Sally and I busted our butts trying to round up sponsors all around Mississippi.

Then in August we made a trip up to the NASCAR race in Richmond, Virginia to meet Mr. Junnie Donleavy. He was an established and well-respected team owner who had a reputation for helping up-and-coming drivers break into the sport. Lake had put in a good word for me. I gave Mr. Donleavy my driving resume and we had a deal. We targeted October and the Goodwrench 500 in Rockingham, North Carolina as my first race to run in stock cars. I had never driven a stock car in my life!

In fact, I would be starting out right at the top, in the chase for the national championship Winston Cup in NASCAR. It didn't get any better than that.

While we were discussing with Donleavy, the tragic news broke that NASCAR superstar driver Tim Richmond had died of AIDS. His passing had everyone gossiping and backbiting like crazy. Richmond's death sent cold chill bumps down my back, because of how he and NASCAR had battled bitterly about his disease over the past few years. If NASCAR got wind about the rumors concerning my life, they would most likely go after me as well. I knew for sure they did not want anyone like me coming within a thousand miles of their races.

Richmond's mom was on my mind as well. I had met her back in 1985 when I was in Daytona with Leon and Ditto. One morning we gave her a ride to the speedway from our motel where she was also staying. She and Tim were full of life then; his career was skyrocketing and his mom was running his fan club. She was a wonderful person. But now she was surely brokenhearted and devastated. It was very, very sad.

Meanwhile, with Donleavy wanting me to drive for him, the pressure was on to put our financing in place fast. I needed a gimmick to get sponsors and media behind the project, and decided it would be Corinth. Why not? This was my home town, and Corinth needed a shot in the arm—new jobs in the community. So the words CORINTH, MISSISSIPPI would be lettered on the side of the car, promoting our town to the world. Surely some company in the area would help me.

Sally took charge of developing a favorable relationship with the Corinth city council and the board of supervisors. She worked a miracle – they all, including the mayor himself, gave us endorsement letters. In Corinth these went a long way in validating the project to businesses and local citizens. Meanwhile I coaxed Mr. Donleavy into letting me have one of his cars to use for personal appearances at the local Wal-Mart, the local Ford dealership and a grocery-store chain in the area. That helped us raise about $3000.

But time was running short and we were still $22,000 short on the budget for testing and the race.

Even though Sally was committed to getting me out on the track, she was an unlikely player in this deal. Since she came from local high society, she had a snide attitude toward rednecks. So she had to bite her sharp tongue whenever we were promoting our cause to the local rednecks who loved motorsports. And she had a temper.

One day I ran into Sally's temper myself. Dan McLemore, one of my best friends, had met a good-looking chick at some car show in Tupelo and told me that we should hire her to help out at our PR gigs. She would get the macho males all worked up and help make me look a little more macho myself. I thought it was a brilliant idea.

The morning of the event, we all showed up at the Wal-Mart parking lot and set up our show car. By lunch the personal appearance was in full swing and the good-looking chick was a big hit with the rednecks. But Sally was missing in action. We all tried to call her but she didn't answer the phone.

"It's not like Sally to just not show up," I told Dan. "Something has to be going on."

Dan just smiled strangely and said we would talk about it later on that night.

After we had closed down at the Wal-Mart and put the car back in the race shop, I hightailed it over to Sally's to see if she was all right. When I got to her house I could see through the window that she was sitting in her den, and went inside to check on her. That was when I suddenly realized that she was not a happy camper.

"Is something wrong?" I asked her. "Are your mom and dad okay? Are you feeling ill? What's up? We really missed having you at the promotion this afternoon."

Sally looked me dead in the eye and said in a dramatic and sarcastic tone:

"Well, I wasn't coming down there and being seen with that white trash yawl had helping you. That girl is nothing but white trash. I was not going to have all my mom and dad's friends calling them and telling them that they saw me down there with her."

I was shocked. And the way she lit into me about that chick was hilarious, especially with her knowing that I had no interest in any female. So I burst out laughing and told her that she had to be kidding.

All hell broke loose. Sally got out of her chair and lunged at me with all her might. I barely dodged her wrath by a whisker and took off. As I vaulted out the door, she kicked me in the butt. I laughed even harder as I took off down the steps and raced to my Blazer. Flooring it down the driveway, I could not believe she had gone crazy like that.

So down the street a ways, I figured I needed to go back to see if I could smooth everything over. As I made a U turn back towards Sally's, a car was coming right at me with its lights blinking like crazy. It was Sally. She had her head stuck out the window and she was grinning. When she pulled up right beside me, we both just lost it and laughed so hard that tears were rolling down our faces. She apologized for kicking me in the ass and acting so snooty, and I apologized for laughing at her and not realizing how she felt.

I got her point and fired the good-looking chick.

Later I told Dan what happened. He said there was more to the story than just the trashy chick incident. Sally had told him that she had feelings for me.

"You need to find some way of dealing with her," he said, "because she is clearly in love with you."

I was shocked and confused that she would feel that way, considering she knew my desires in life.

Lucky for me, Sally and I never did have to talk about her personal feeling. To my surprise, she rekindled an old relationship she had back in collage and married the guy that next summer. You just never know what effects you have on people, no matter the circumstances.

My uncle Buddy, who was the president and CEO of Parts Plus, a national auto-parts chain, was being a bit sticky about supporting my NASCAR effort. But he did give us the supplies and paint we needed to paint the show car in the color and scheme I had designed to promote Corinth. Uncle Buddy was clearly concerned over the rumors, and who could blame him? But a little nepotism and a little return on my looking after his son, which I did one time when he got in trouble, would have been nice!

On the bright side, by the end of September, Mr. Donleavy had agreed to let me do a day of testing in Rockingham, to try and qualify for the Goodwrench 500. To do this I needed $5000 to buy racing tires and pay his crew for the day, but I was still short two grand. Even if I wound up not qualifying for the race, it was crucial to do that test, to showcase my talent to potential sponsors of his that might be watching.

Sally and I racked our brains trying to figure out where to find the money. The pressure was brutal.

Then, at the last second, Mom stepped in. Without my asking her for one dime, she wrote me a check for $5000. She was so proud that I wasn't being Terri, that I was focusing on my racing once again, that she gave me money she had saved by getting up at five a.m. and working in that telephone factory for 20 years. She had retired back in 1987 and this was part of her nest egg that she had kept from my dad. To say I was blown away by her gift was one of the understatements of the century. She deserves maids, jewels and anything she wants for helping me so much. I was humbled and more determined than ever to not let her down.

So Sally and I rushed over to the National Bank of Commerce, where her dad just happened to be the president. We turned that check into a cashier's check for Mr. Donleavy and roared off for Rockingham.

While JT had been getting his career together, Terri hadn't been doing so well.

The night before we left for Rockingham, Sally and I had decided to go get a bite to eat. As we were pulling out of her driveway, I abruptly stopped the Blazer and began to weep uncontrollably. Just like that, right out of nowhere. This was not the first time Sally had seen the emotion flood out of my soul. She had to be thinking that this was bad timing. Would I be able to handle the pressure in Rockingham?

Sally gently consoled me, never saying a word but simply holding my hand and stroking the back of my neck as I sat there sobbing. After a few minutes, I regained my composure and we went on our way.

Just the day before, my mom had told Sally that she thought I was doing much better—that I was beating "the girl thing."

Sally just looked at my mom with a blank stare and said, "Yeah, Terry is doing better," and left it at that.

When Sally told me what my mom said, she added, "She really doesn't get it, does she? I mean, they really don't get it, do they."

I just looked straight ahead and shook my head.

"No, it's easier for them to not get it," I responded. "It takes Mother Nature out of the equation. If they got it, they would have to deal with an outcome they clearly do not want."

In spite of Terri's tears, I had to stay focused. A lot of people were counting on me – especially those in Corinth who had braved the rumors and were helping me any way they could!

But plenty of people in Corinth were not helping. For example, a new car dealer had decided to host a fishing tournament with the proceeds going to sponsor my race team. But so many people jumped all over him for helping me that he actually confronted me about the rumors. Not wanting to lie, I had to sit down with him in his office and talk him through this deal as best I could. To my amazement, the car dealer actually got it and supported me even more than before.

One man who tried to blockade the fishing tournament was one of Dad's best friends, Larry Roberts. I had always considered Larry to be a surrogate brother. As a little kid I had slept in his lap a hundred times when we were all crammed into the car and heading home from a midget race in the late Sixties. He had practically grown up over at my dad's race shop and helped me since I started racing in the early Seventies. And he was the peacemaker between me and Dad when my story ran rampant through Corinth back in 1982. But now it was different.

When my dad found out that Larry had spouted off to Dan McLemore about the fishing tournament, he and I hightailed out to Larry's machine shop to see if we could smooth things over. But Larry dug his heels in, and that was that.

Dad was really pissed—he felt Larry owed him for years of support when Larry was trying to get his own racing deal started. Dad had treated him like a son. Larry had broke bread at our kitchen table more times than you could count over the years. Many times at two in the morning, my mom would cook up a skillet of eggs and bacon when the guys were done working on their race cars. Dad and Larry had been close for

25 years. But the rumors and gossip had gotten to Larry and he was done with me.

In the end, it didn't matter anyway, because the fishing tournament was canceled due to bad weather.

The NASCAR Test

Friday morning, 7:30 a.m., Rockingham Motor Speedway.

It was a bit cool and foggy. All of us—Sally, Mr. Donleavy, his crew and I—had lightweight jackets on. Five or six of the top NASCAR teams were there to run their own set of tests for the upcoming race in two weeks. Rusty Wallace, Richard and Kyle Petty, Alan Kulwiki and Davy Allison were driving for those teams.

But at 7:30 Allison had not shown up yet.

Then, out of nowhere with engines screaming like a dive bomber, a twin-engine Cessna came blasting out of the fog and did a daredevil barrel roll right over the Speedway, climbed straight up to the sky, made a sweeping turn circle and then landed at the airstrip behind the track, like it was normal!

"What in the hell was that all about?" Sally exclaimed.

The entire pit area was laughing their asses off. One of our crew guys explained, "Oh, that was Davy Allison. He's always doing that."

I thought to myself, Yeah, whatever . . . these racer boys are just a wee bit too brave sometimes, ya think! That kind of stuff was going to get one of them killed someday, probably sooner than later. Confidence and blind faith will either make you a hero, or make you a damn fool! In a short while, we were going to find out which one I was.

Not only had I never driven a Cup Car before – I hadn't even raced a sprint car on anything bigger than a half-mile oval. This speedway was a fast-as-hell high-banked one-mile oval, and a killer. I did have some pavement experience but not in this kind of race car. Stock cars weigh almost three times as much as a sprint car, and their tires are very skinny compared to sprint cars. I was going to be traveling at a high rate of speed in a heavy race car with hard and skinny tires. It was going to feel like driving on ice. One positive thing: I was a smooth driver and very good on dry slick tracks.

This was not going to be easy, and wrecking Mr. Donleavy's $100,000 race car was not an option. However, if I didn't stand on the gas, I would disappoint everybody, and that was not an option either!

"Get ready and get focused!" I told myself.

That old fear-and-fearlessness thing was showing up again; my blood was pumping, but I was pretty damn calm.

Mr. Donleavy was visibly uneasy. After all, he was letting some stranger throttle jockey buzz his expensive car around this killer track at over 170 miles per hour just inches from that concrete wall. What was he thinking?

So, to calm his nerves I got out a little present I'd brought him. It was one of those stress dolls to hold onto while I was out on the track. He immediately grabbed the doll and started rubbing the top of its head. That broke the ice and we all chuckled.

Then Mr. Donleavy looked me in the eye and said in his well-tuned Virginian accent, "JT, it's time to strap in and make a few laps."

This was what I'd been dreaming about for most of my life. This test could put me in the motorsports history books, or it could put me in the Rockingham hospital.

The first test session, only about ten or twelve laps, was aimed at shaking the car down and getting me used to it. I only ran a top speed of about 130 or so, and I could tell from the way the car felt that once I stood on the gas, it was going to be touchy.

But my confidence was building lap by lap.

After I brought the car back to the pits, the crew checked it over to make sure nothing had gone awry. Mr. Donleavy and I took a walk over to Richard Petty's race hauler and climbed up on top so we could watch the other cars making their test runs. While we stood there, I downloaded to him everything that I'd learned from my first turn at the wheel. He was satisfied at what I had shown him, and just told me to take my time, that we had all day to get up to speed. He was very gentle and fatherly and kept me feeling confident.

When we came back, the crew had already put on a new set of Goodyear Eagles. Rockingham's track surface is like sandpaper, and 40 laps there on one set of tires is like driving on regular tires with the cord showing.

In another minute, I was back on the track.

This time I pushed my overall speed by ten miles per hour within a few laps. I could feel the extra speed that I was carrying into the corners. Ten miles per hour may not seem like that much of a jump, but in a race car when you're already traveling at a pretty good clip, ten miles per hour is a big deal.

Throughout the morning, we repeated this process—running eight- to ten-lap segments, then coming in and downloading, and finally going back out to improve on the previous run. Mr. Donleavy's crew started out by just going through the motions for another new hot shoe, and they watched me progress lap by lap. By our lunch break, the crew was beginning to take notice. In fact, during the lunch break, Kyle Petty and his dad Richard had moseyed over to get the goods on the new Donleavy driver.

In fact, just before they shut the track down for lunch, I turned the fourth fastest lap of the day and did it with 40-lap-old tires! It was like driving on an ice-coated road at 170 miles per hour, and I almost spun that baby out. After that, I tried extra-hard to control my self-confidence. It wouldn't be smart to show off and slam Mr. Donleavy's car into the wall.

After lunch we picked up where we left off—run a few laps, pull in, think it over and repeat. Little by little, a tenth of a second at a time, I increased my speed.

By 4:30 we had pretty much done what we came there to do. I was going fast enough to qualify. In fact, I was already into the top 15 qualifying times of the best 43 NASCAR drivers in the world who had raced there back in March.

Mr. Donleavy and the crew were pumped up about my ability to drive in the Cup series. I had the talent to do this and the proof was right there on the stopwatch.

We were all feeling pretty damn good about the day's progress and had just started to put the car in the trailer when I made a comment to the crew chief and Mr. Donleavy.

"If I can kept the car from getting loose off of Turn Two," I said, "I feel I can whittle at least another tenth of a second off my time." Turn Two was the trickiest turn on the speedway.

"Hell yes, let's do it," Mr. Donleavy said. "That's what we like hearing from a driver."

So the crew made a sway-bar adjustment and I hit the track for one last hot five-lap run. The first time I ran that baby off of Turn Two, I could feel that we had made the car better and my confidence surged. The next three laps felt like the fastest I'd run all day, and I planned to pull in the very next lap. But on this last lap, when I began to exit off that notorious turn at 130 miles per hour, the damn car went straight ahead instead of turning smoothly off of the corner. The outside wall loomed ahead.

Shit! I immediately backed off the gas, eased down on the brakes and tried to turn the steering wheel to the left as quickly as I could. The wall was coming at me like a bomb. If we didn't turn within the next tenth of a second, they were going to be picking concrete out of my teeth, and this $100,000 race car was going to be flat as a pancake.

Then, just inches from slamming the wall head-on, that little darling took a sharp left hook and headed off the banking and down toward the inside wall. I quickly steered the wheels back to the right as hard as I could and slammed the brakes down as hard as my size 6 left foot could possibly do, and braced myself for a hell of a smack into the inside wall. This was not going to be nice!

Then the damn thing got some traction and spun back to the right, and we began a long smoke-billowing slide down the entire length of the back straightaway. Finally we came to a safe stop only inches away from the inside wall, one hundred yards from where I had started this high-speed slide . . . without a scratch.

Some people might think that I sat there and collected my thoughts and thanked the good Lord for looking after my butt. Instead, I reached down to the starter switch, fired that puppy up and hightailed back to the pits. What else was I going to do...cry? This was NASCAR racing, not a tea party!

When I pulled into the garage stall, Mr. Donleavy came rushing up to me with a big smile on his face and what I thought was relief that I had not destroyed his race car.

"JT," he said, "you're the luckiest person on earth. No one in NASCAR history who spun off of Turn Two has ever missed slamming that damn wall! Whew! That was close."

That's the way it goes sometimes. Some you win, some you lose, some get rained out. And sometimes you actually get lucky and don't hit the wall. Yeah, baby!

Within moments, there were several crew members from the Petty team hovering around my car, including Petty's renowned championship-winning crew chief Dale Inman. I had made that last run on tires with over 80 laps on them. We didn't have the budget to put on a new set of $1,500 Racing Eagles so we were just easing through the day to get me some seat time.

Dale Inman had kneeled down and was looking over my right front tire. Then he stood up and told Mr. Donleavy that the tire had a puncture right in the sidewall. That was why the car pushed up toward the wall – the tire was going flat. So the spin was not my fault whatsoever.

Dale patted me on the back and told me I had done a hell of job driving all day. He said, "You have a future here. Just stick with it . . . you will be fine. Rockingham I a tough sob, it's the toughest track on the circuit, you did a good job today."

I couldn't believe what I was hearing…praise from the likes of Dale Inman, the man who had made Richard Petty a regular fixture in victory lane throughout his entire seven-champion-ship-winning career!

So the test was a big success. Mr. Donleavy and his crew were very pleased. Sally was about to pee on herself! Most important, I knew in my bones that with the right situation, the right team and sponsor, I could do well in the NASCAR Winston Cup series. Anyway you cut it, my mom and dad were going to be proud of me.

We all shook hands. I told Mr. Donleavy I would call him the next day and we would get lined up on the next race only two weeks away.

I didn't have the first notion how I was going to come up with another $20,000. But now I had proof that I could drive one of those babies. This would go a long way in convincing some of the people and sponsors I had been negotiating with. In fact, Sally and I had a paying personal appearance at the local Ford dealer there in Corinth . . . it was already 5:30 p.m. and we had a 12- hour drive in front of us.

Sally pulled me by the arm and said, "JT, we have to get on the road."

You're damn right, Sally baby, I thought. The road to
NASCAR!

*Here I am down loading information to Mr. Donleavy after one
of my test runs at Rockingham*

CHAPTER 15

Dad Comes Through – Lets Race

Sally and I drove all night to get back to Corinth in time.

The Ford dealership was paying me a thousand bucks to show up and sign a few autographs and promote their new Thunderbirds, so we couldn't be late. I was so pumped up about the accomplishments that day that I drove Sally nuts, re-hashing every lap. We rolled into Corinth at daylight, completely worn out, and caught a few hours of sleep.

At 11:00 a.m. we were at the dealership and stood around in the hot sun meeting customers and signing autographs for the next five hours. To say I was exhausted would be an understatement.

Then we got busy raising another $19,000. For the next week we called every sponsor in America to see if they would sponsor us in the Rockingham Cup Race… to no avail. It was like trying to pull off a a magic trick because we didn't have enough time or money to pursue a sponsor in the right way that would get them on board. So we were sucking wind, and I had almost concluded that we probably were not going to race again.

Dad was up to speed on my adventures, and he probably thinking, "Damn, this could be all right." He must have realized that someone had step up to the plate in the next day or so.

Right out of the blue, a week before the cut-off time to enter the race, Dad came down to my office at our race shop and handed me a check for $20,000.

"Go on down to the bank and get Junnie a cashier's check," he said. His eyes twinkled in a way that I hadn't seen in years. "Let's go racing!"

My heart was racing at 200 miles per hour. We were going to race against Richard Petty and Dale Earnhardt, and Darrell Waltrip . . . damn! I gave him a big hug, thanked him at least a hundred times and called Sally to tell her the good news.

Then I called Mr. Donleavy.

Then, after all the stress of trying to find a sponsor, NASCAR called us up and wanted me and Mr. Donleavy to wait until the March race to get me on track. Rusty Wallace and Dale Earnhardt were in a heated battle for the Winston Cup Championship, and the past weekend in Phoenix, one of Mr. Donleavey's young drivers, Stan Barrett, had spun Rusty out. Rusty was bitching about rookie drivers screwing up his chance to win. NASCAR and Mr. Donleavy thought it would be better for us to wait till the spring when the Cup chase was over, and Rusty and Dale were not so pissy with one another. Believe me, I didn't want to be the one who crashed into Dale Earnhardt or Rusty Wallace in my first Winston Cup race. That would be murder for my career. So I agreed to wait until March.

We were all disappointed, but we sucked it up like troopers and got busy trying to find sponsorship for the entire 1990 season. It was going to be a long winter.

Over the next few months we worked hard at polishing up our marketing skills, and nurtured a relationship with several

Mississippi companies including Bryan Foods and America's Catch, a farm-raised catfish grower and distributor based in Mississippi. I thought we had a real opportunity to get Bryan Foods on board for at least three or four races so we were working them hard. Over the Christmas holidays, I made a few personal appearances in Memphis.

Then, in January, I got a call from Chris Econimaki, the dean of auto-racing journalism and executive editor for the *National Speed Sport News*, which is the Motorsports Bible. He wanted get the scoop on my NASCAR deal with Mr. Donleavy, and interviewed me over the phone.

In that distinctive nasal voice he is so famous for, Chris said: "Junnie Donleavy says you're going to be the next hot shoe in NASCAR. What do you have to say about that?"

I tried to blend honesty and humbleness in my answer.

"Well, that's a pretty darn cool thing to have such a great man say about me," I told Economaki. "I'm big-time flattered and hope I can live up to his phrases. As far as me being good goes, we will just have to wait on that verdict until I've run a few races."

That interview was a real feather in my cap. Everyone who knew one darn thing about auto racing knew about *Speed Sport News*. In a recent interview on the Speed Channel, Mario Andretti had said, "If Chris Economaki wrote about you in his weekly personal column in that newspaper, you were or you were going to be somebody." That column was the one everyone from Andretti to A.J. Foyt to the Formula One boys in Europe read religiously. I had already been on the front page a few times, through their coverage of sprint car racing, but this time I was going to be in Chris's personal column.

The next week, when Chris ran the piece, it was a real boost in our sponsorship search. All the motorsports sponsors read that column as well.

While all this racing flurry was going on, Terri was languishing on the sidelines. Every single day I was tempted to get myself all dolled up and head out to Memphis, just to have a day to myself. However, I fought off the feminine desires with every ounce of my soul. I knew who the heroes were in this deal. Without my mom and dad financing the project I would be sitting on the sidelines just wishing I could drive a Cup Car. There are always compromises!

In the back of my mind, though, I knew the day would come when the racing deal would not be enough to keep my femininity from overflowing once more.

All winter long Sally and I worked on putting sponsorship deals in place.

We had my uncle Buddy and Parts Plus leaning our way as well as some positive interest from Valvoline. They were probably just waiting to see what went down once we raced at Rockingham in early March. We did a few PR events around the Mid South, including a huge auto show at the convention center in Memphis.

But we felt ourselves working against more and more pressure and nerves right in our own group. The problem was Dad. Even though my dad had every reason to be happy right now, the pressure of looking for sponsorship was getting to him, and his drinking addiction was getting worse by the day. When he got totally drunk, I had to struggle to keep my mouth shut. As long as you did not piss him off, he was cool with whatever you wanted to do, but once he got pissed, all bets were off and he could turn ugly in a flash.

Alcoholism is devastating, and it had been in my life since I was fourteen years old. Day after day I had had to handle Dad with kid gloves, and it had taken a toll. Just the gender situation alone was devastating to any one, let alone to someone who had become the ultimate scandal of a small Southern town. Take professional motorsports where you can lose your life at any given second, and add an alcoholic parent into the mix, and it will make the situation 99% unbearable. Right now I was doing my part to keep everything going on all eight cylinders, and I felt that it was time for Dad and his closest friends to do their part as well.

One Sunday afternoon right after Christmas, Sally, Dan and I were polishing up the show car getting ready for an upcoming PR event the next week. Dad showed up at three in the afternoon and he was smashed. I felt sorry for him and pissed off at him, all in one pitiful emotion.

Dan got me off to the side and said quietly, "We have to do something about this."

"I know," I said, feeling very frustrated. "But how in the hell are we going to do it? If you piss him off, all hell breaks loose."

After thirty minutes or so, without our realizing it, Dad headed back to the house. Dan and I both freaked out when he realized that he was driving home as drunk as he was. But he had slipped out before we could get the keys away from him.

About fifteen minutes later, one of my dad's best friends came rolling in to check on our racing progress. This was Dexter Bumpbus, who had given my mom enough blood to fill the Mississippi River during her daunting and fragile pregnancy with me 25 years ago. He was my unofficial godfather.

I immediately jumped Dex about Dad's drinking. At first Dex really did not want to hear what I was saying.

"Dad won't listen to anyone else," I told him. "But he will listen to you. I know he is feeling the pressure too, but this drinking is killing him. You've got to help us out!"

Dex and Dad had been friends for 50 years, and Dad respected Dex more than anyone else on this earth. I knew he would be more receptive to listening to Dex over anyone else. If things did not change Dad might kill himself and someone else in a big accident, or just die from drinking too damn much.. Dexter was a proud man and did not like having me put him on the spot like that, but he got the message. So, the bottom line was, it was going to be Dex and most likely, asshole Dewayne would have to get involved too. Dewayne owed me at least one good deed while on this earth.

Over the next few weeks, I never knew if Dex and/or Dewayne actually talked to my dad.

But by the time March rolled around, and we loaded the car and the pimento sandwiches for the drive to Rockingham, Dad was back to being his old self.

The Cup Race

It was the evening of March 1, 1990.

Mom, Dad, Sally and I got back to our motel around 9:30 p.m. after getting a bite to eat at the local Shoney's, and we tried to get some rest. Along in my motel room, I tossed and turned. Tomorrow will be the biggest day in my racing life. I would be starting 36th in NASCAR's Goodwrench 500. This is like playing quarterback in the NFL, as the famed motorsports analyst Robin Miller likes to say. Finishing last, just getting in the race at any Cup race is like winning in any other racing series.

For many people in the sport, the Cup deal is hard to achieve on any level. For my family and me, it was damn amazing that we made it this far. Who would have thought that I'd be competing against Dale Earnhardt, when you consider how close I had come to leaving this planet only eight months back. The night before, driver Darrell Waltrip had come up to me at dinner and wished me good luck on my first NASCAR Winston Cup event. I wondered if anyone had given Darrell the same kind of thumbs up right before his first Cup race back in the early Seventies. Every driver has their first NASCAR Cup race. Everyone has to start at the bottom and work their way up in this tough ass racing series. I intended to do just that.

But I was a bit worried about my car. During the last test run that afternoon, I had felt a vibration and wondered if there might be something wrong with the transmission or the rear end. But the Donleavy Racing crew assured me that they would check her over carefully before the start on Sunday at 12:00 o'clock sharp. I trusted those guys and knew they would have that baby ready when the green flag fell for the start.

I finally fell asleep.

On race morning, we were all up bright and early and headed out to the track at around 8:00 a.m. so we could miss the traffic. I was pumped up and a wee bit cranky, and couldn't wait to get to the track.

But first we had to detour over to the track's campgrounds just across from the speedway and hang out with my aunt and uncle who had driven up on Saturday. Their motor home was parked just outside the speedway, so we popped inside for a few minutes. I had a small bite of breakfast and a few cups of coffee.

Then Dad and I walked over to the garage to see if we could help the crew do anything on the car. When we got there, my good buddy and mentor Lake Speed, who was not racing that weekend, had shown up to help. Mr. Donleavy had decided that Lake would serve as my spotter, ensuring a familiar voice over my helmet radio. Lake would help keep me focused and aware of anything happening on the track that I needed to know during the high-speed pressure-packed 500-mile endurance test.

So Lake and I got busy installing the microphone on my helmet and installing some extra padding on my head rest so my neck wouldn't get so tired from the extreme G forces that would almost sling my head off of my body about a thousand times for 500 miles.

Kenny Schrader, one of NASCAR's superstars, moseyed on over to where Lake and I was working. He had started his NASCAR career with Mr. Donleavy plus he and I had sprint-car connections and roots up in Indiana so he was interested in how I was feeling about it all. By this time Dad and Mom and my aunt and uncle had headed over to the grandstands to take their seats just off of Turn Four.

About thirty minutes later Sally showed up and helped me adjust some extra padding in my racing seat.

This was a very surreal experience for me. I had been in the garage area at many NASCAR races but never as a driver. It was cool to have crew members who had known me when I was helping Lake now coming up to wish me good luck. They knew just how big a deal this was. There would be some pretty big odds to overcome. I wasn't driving the best equipment out there, nor did we have the big-dollar budget. But this was a start. Today 40 of the best stock-car drivers in the world would take the green flag, and I'd be one of them! Nobody could take that away from me.

Standing there beside Lake and Kenny, just for a second I thought about all of those redneck s.o.b's who had bashed me for the last seven years. It must be damn hard for them to see me in the starting field here in Rockingham. They could all kiss my skinny ass! I had bound my growing breast down with duck tape—if I crashed during the race, the doctors were going to wonder why I had all that duck tape wrapped around my chest. How would I explain that? At least this time I'd had the good sense to leave my girl underwear back in Mississippi. The Astro Dome booboo was not going to be repeated.

An hour before the start, at the drivers' meeting, the NASCAR officials went over all of the race procedures. This was pretty routine but that's when it struck me all over again that I was sitting in some big company. When I looked over my right shoulder Dale Earnhardt and the King of NASCAR racing Richard Petty were sitting there, as well as Kyle Petty, Richards son who was on the pole for today's race. Right in front of me sat Alan Kulwiki and Davy Allison. For a moment, a few drops of salty water welled up in my eyes, but I kept my cool and acted like I was supposed to be there.

After the drivers' meeting, I hightailed it over to the trailer, and quickly changed into the red, white and blue fire-retardant driving uniform with Crossroads City emblazoned across the chest, that promoted my home town. As I finished tying the royal blue driving shoes, I looked over at my Donleavy team-mate for the weekend. This was Ernie Irvin, and he was staring a hole in me. Ernie was on his way up as a NASCAR super-star and future Daytona 500 winner, and he was a bit of a smart ass. I could tell he was trying to come back at me with something.

Driver introductions were about to start. So, just trying to make light conversation, I casually said to Ernie, "I've never been to driver introductions before. So I'll just follow you up to the podium."

Right in front of Sally, he said, "I have to go get a blow job first, so if you want to follow me, it's all right with me."

My cheeks flushed red as hell. He was disrespecting me but worse, he was disrespecting Sally. And I knew the reason why. Ernie was pissed off that I was driving Mr. Donlavey's second car because he wanted all of the attention for himself. I also suspected he had heard a rumor or two about me, so he was looking to take a jab at me. Screw him, I thought, he's nothing but a classless redneck.

"I think I'll pass on the offer," I jabbed back.

Driver introductions happened right in front of the start/finish line where there was a real circus of hotshot VIPs, beautiful babes and a hundred media guys standing around waiting. As I walked across the platform filled with NASCAR bigwigs, the track announcer blasted my name over the speedway's speaker system. I waved to the crowd and about a hundred fans out of 75,000 cheered.

Richard Petty patted me on the back. "Stay low and be careful," he said.

Then I quietly made my way over to the car about fifty yards away. Rows and rows of high-strung fans were reaching out to touch my uniform as Sally and I slithered through the crowd trying to reach the red white, and blue number 91 Ford Thunderbird. It had JT HAYES written right above the driver's door, which I found to be both exciting and bothersome.

My crew guys were making final checks. So Sally and I just sat down on the pit wall and waited on the crew to give me the OK sign to get in the car.

After about five minutes, a local minister said a prayer over the speedway, the National Anthem was played and 75,000 hyped up fans yelled at the top of their lungs.

Then Mr. Donleavy motioned for me to get in the race car and buckle up.

Pausing to glance up into the packed grandstands to grab the moment, I crawled inside the race car. Reaching over to my right, I picked up my helmet, grabbed the ear pieces for the radio . . . placed them in my ears, applied a piece of duck tape over the ear pieces and my ears to keep them from falling out during the battle, then slipped the helmet onto my head and finished buckling my seat belts. I was focused, and finding my zone . . . and determined not to do anything stupid like crash into Dale Earnhardt. But I was also going to drive my ass off.

It felt like my mom and dad were sitting right there with me. What a long time ago it was—my first kart race down in Columbus Mississippi 20 years ago. I could feel their spirits cheering me on. This was very personal for all of us . . . hopes and fears for the future were on the line more than anyone in that great sporting arena could ever know.

"Gentlemen, start your engines!"

I hit the start button and that baby fired right up...and just as quickly it shut off again. What the hell. The crew looked worried. I re-hit the start button and at first it seemed as if the engine wasn't going to fire back up. But then that baby cranked with a crackle and a boom. I made a quick check of the gauges to be sure the machine was operating properly. Everything looked good and I was ready to go.

Then the NASCAR official standing beside the car motioned for us to move out.

I gave Sally a big thumbs up and eased out on the clutch and began to roll down pit lane right behind Richard Petty. We all pulled out onto the one-mile high-banked asphalt oval in 20 two-by-two rows, and took a slow pace lap, then another, to get all the engine operating temps up to the right temperature.

Then the flagman gave us the one to go. Next time by him, we would get the green flag to start the 1990 Goodwrench 500.

I reached down and gave one more tug on my seat belts. Lake came in over my radio.

"Stay heads up," he said quietly. "Stay heads up."

"Ten four," I responded, and got ready for the start.

We rolled down the back straight and out of Turn Four, and then the flagman waved the green flag. The fans surged to their feet and made such a mighty roar that I could actually hear them over the sound of my engine. Chills raced over my body. The race was on.

"Green! Green! Green!" Lake yelled in my ear.

I stood on the gas, shifted up through the gears and hauled that baby off to the first corner. To my surprise I was able to keep up with the field pretty darn good. This was the first time I had been on the track with all the other cars at the same time and it was quite different than I thought it might be. These guys were driving their asses off and I realized I had better find a whole new level of focus. I was running 34th in a 40-car field, and no one was on cruise control, and we had 500 miles to go.

My goal was to try and keep up with Richard Petty to see if I could learn a thing or two about driving these babies. For a while the strategy was working for me. I was actually holding my own with only about two car lengths separating us.

After every lap, Lake called my lap times off and made sure to let me know what was going on in front and in back of me on the track. I made damn sure that I was checking my rear-view mirror, which was something I wasn't used to doing because in midgets and sprint cars there are no rear view mirrors! I didn't want to block or pull down on whoever was behind me and cause a big wreck, which had just happened to Butch Miller, a superstar from the ASA series.

Then, after about fifteen laps the car began to vibrate again, just like it had in practice the day before. When I entered the corners, the car felt like it was trying to spin out. So I started backing off earlier and earlier to keep from wrecking the darn thing. Finally the car was shuddering like crazy.

I keyed my radio and told Lake I wanted to talk to Mr. Donleavy.

"I think I might be having a flat or something," I said.

Mr. Donleavy radioed back.

"The car has started to smoke at the end of the straights," he said. "Maybe we'll bring you in, in a few laps, to check it out. Right now just stay out there and be careful."

I checked all my gauges but everything was normal, so I thought it had to be a tire.

Then Lake came over the radio in a stern voice and shouted that there was a crash in turn two.

"Stay low, stay low . . . car in the wall, car in the wall, caution, caution!" he yelled.

I checked my mirror to see who was on my tail, then backed out of the gas and slowed that baby down. Then, as I shifted down into third gear, the car completely jumped out of gear and almost spun out. I quickly tried to get it back in gear but it wouldn't catch. So there I was, coasting down the back straight frantically trying to find any gear that would work. Finally I got first gear to hook up and radioed back to my crew that I had transmission troubles and needed to come in.

By that time the car was smoking pretty good. My crew chief called me on the radio.

"NASCAR wants you to pull in," he said. "They think you might be dropping oil on the track."

That was a huge faux pas in the NASCAR rule book. Oil on the track causes big wrecks.

Damn, I thought. This was just getting to be comfortable and it was an absolute blast to be racing out there with all of those guys but… it was over. Twenty short laps and it was over.

I obeyed the order and left the track.

But by golly, I had just driven in the Goodwrench 500 against Dale Earnhardt.

It was disappointing as hell to be out of the race but I was pumped up about the incredible experience. I was hooked. I wanted to do this again and again and again! I didn't want this one race to be all I ever ran in the Winston Cup chase. I knew I had the talent to do this but I also knew I needed big dollar financing if I was to ever have a chance of being successful in the national championship series.

As we all crammed into our Ford van and headed back to Corinth, my feelings did a strange U turn and went almost melancholy as I reflected on my life. My 25 years had been challenging both physically and emotionally, yet they were also exciting and rewarding, thanks to the gifts I had been given. I had always felt fearful and fearless as one daunting emotion. Afraid of life and its challenges, all the while being fearless to challenge life head on. Fearful of the prejudice and the rejection I had endured most of my life over my gender issue, but defiant and confrontational over the exact same prejudice. Fearful to get out on the track two thousand miles from my home and compete with the best drivers in the world, but fearless to go anywhere in America and let it all hang out in order to win the race.

After today, no one could know where this NASCAR opportunity would take me. But wherever it would lead, there would always be one redeeming thought to hold on to through it all. I had pushed through the fear, the prejudice and the overwhelming financial odds to race against the best stock-car drivers in the world. On this day, by God, I had survived a lifetime of challenges that might have killed most people, and with the help of my mom and my dad, I was one of those best damn stock-car drivers in the world as well.

Besides, as my dad reminded me while we were driving home, Winston Cup national champions Dale Earnhardt, Darrell Waltrip and Bill Elliott had finished no better than I had done in their first NASCAR Cup race.

Two weeks after the race, I was in Memphis being Terri. I just had to have one day for myself, to let off the feminine tension! No one knew about it but me and Sally. But I had to be very careful!

What a hell of an eighteen months this had been. What was next? Could it get any more dramatic than this? Oh yeah, you could count on it!

At speed during the Goodwrench 500.

*That's me, Lake Speed and Derrick Cope chit chatting before the
start of the Goodwrench 500. Derrick had just won the Daytona
500 only two weeks before.*

CHAPTER 16

Big Wreck – Good by JT ... Hello Terri Pivot Point #3

If someone had told me a year earlier that they thought I would race in the Goodwrench 500 within the year, we would have told them they were crazy.

I had always been torn between defiance and determination to pursue my true gender identity, and to not lose the love of my family, especially my dad. Though I hate to admit it, that good ole dose of rejection my parents threw at me every time I pursued my femininity was continuing to work. Rejection and emotional blackmail were always the catalyst to get me back home to Corinth and into the driver's seat. My parents and I were all co-dependent on one another. Rejection was my weak spot, my Achilles heel and it seemed as if my folks knew my soul like they knew the back of their hand.

Now I'd tasted the big time, and it tasted good. If I wanted to continue my NASCAR quest, to please my friends and family and not follow my heart at least until I played the NASCAR card, I had to find someone to finance me. I could be as succ essful as anyone if I could put the money together for good equipment and enough testing to get a feel for those Cup cars. I needed laps and the only way to get them was with a lot of money. The rumors about me would surely follow me around, so I would have to lie like hell if the subject came up.

Was I buying into false hope that would ultimately leave me old and broken hearted because I didn't find the courage to be Terri until it was too late to enjoy all that my dreams anticipated?

The clock was ticking.

A Memphis Fling

It was the second week of April 1990. Ever since I had returned home from California nine months a go I had put my feminine needs in the closet and neglected my mental health. With the NASCAR race behind me, I felt an overwhelming desire to go to Memphis and be Terri for a few days, so that's what I did.

I called my old friend Cathy, widow of my best friend Victor Dixon, and asked if could hang out with her. She fully understood and told me that it was ladies' night at the Hilton.

"Bring a dress," she said.

No problem, I had plenty.

Hanging out with Cathy was always a hoot. Like her late husband she had always accepted me without question. In fact, over the past several years, she and I had tore up many a dance floor on ladies' night. I could pop a wig on my head, put on makeup and a dress, and be in the top five at any hot-chick contest. Looking back on that time in my life, I'm amazed at how I pulled it off. But I did. and 99% of the time, it was with Cathy.

After a few days of shedding stress, it was time to go home and refocus on racing.

I had been thinking about getting back in a sprint-car deal there in the Mid South to make some cash and keep my driving skills sharp. On the way back to Corinth, I stopped by the house of Tommy Roland, good friend and local sprint car team owner. According to the grapevine, he and his driver had parted company and he was looking to find a new hot shoe to pilot his blue and white racer. Tommy was notorious for ultra-neat and ultra-fast sprint cars. He and his wife Jan had never paid attention to the rumors – in fact, Jan had always been my a champion of mine, sticking up for me back in the mid 80's when the Memphis assholes were running my name through the mud.

When I pulled into the driveway Tommy, Jan and their 12-year-old son Jody were in the race shop working on the car. Tommy straightened up—a six foot Southern replica of Charles Bronson with tools in his hand.

The first thing he said to me was, "Do you want to drive my race car and kick all these assholes around here's asses?"

I couldn't believe my ears. "Hell, yeah," I said. "Let's do it."

This would give me the best of both worlds. I could race sprint cars around the Mid South and also pursue NASCAR efforts from my office in Corinth.

So, the very next weekend we got busy racing that blue and white rocket ship. I won our first race in a daring fashion by coming from the back of the pack and making the pass for the win on the next-to-last lap. It was a sweet win because the guy I passed was my old West Memphis rival, Mike Ward.

Over the next few months I raced sprint cars on the weekend and pursued sponsors for my NASCAR deal during the week.

By now it was May 1, 1990. My dad was all pumped up and helping me with the NASCAR effort. But his drinking had escalated once again, so I always had to be on my toes. Any little thing would piss him off.

Adding to the pressure, a rumor was floating around Corinth that I had taken my sponsor money from the NASCAR race in Rockingham and spent it on a sex change. Those redneck pinheads thought that since we didn't run the entire race, we had money left over. The fact was this: my mom and dad had kicked in 99% of the sponsorship money and we had paid Mr. Donleavy with a $25,000 cashiers check right before the race. We had raised about $500.00 dollars from outside contributions in the Corinth area. That money, plus the other $2500 I raised myself, went for our motel and traveling expenses.

These people had no idea how expensive a NASCAR deal was. They were just a bunch of jealous redneck small-timers who didn't want me to be successful. In Corinth, they were everybody's buddy so what they said had to be the truth. In fact, the fine folks who were kicking this rumor around town were drunks and wife beaters. So I don't know why I let them bother me, but I did. Dad and I talked about the rumors a couple of times and it pissed him off more than me. But we just had to let it slide and stay focused on our work. Dad stated when he heard the same rumor down at the coffee shop, "These people are nothing but a jealous rednecks who only wish they had your talent and desire . . . J. T. they don't have the brains to carry your helmet bag, let alone accomplish what you have in the sport. So, just let go. They're nothing but a bunch of idiots."

In fact one of my best buds, John Marsh, made a profound statement one night. He was a bonafide good ole boy from

Mississippi who drove the tour bus for the country music super-group "Brooks and Dunn" and had always hung in there for me. That night, John, Sally and I were driving back from a sprint-car race in Arkansas at two in the morning on Interstate 40.

"You know," John said to us, "you don't fit the stereotypical image those rednecks have in their minds about what a race-car driver should be or look like."

He went on to explain that because I was small, and wore cool clothes like those Indy car drivers, it gave everyone fuel for the rumor fire about my gender.

"If anyone else in that town had the same success as you did, he added, "they'd put up a statue to you on Courthouse Square."

That's me and the Roland gang after taking the win over in Little Rock, Arkansas.

Looking for sponsors heats up

Every week day, for twelve hours and sometimes more, I was busy dialing for dollars like I was some politician running for office. Sally and I were calling every person and every company I could think of, trying to round up the needed funds to run a few more Cup races before the year was out.

I had a friend, Kim Kimbrough, who had just taken the public relations and marketing position at Memphis Motorsports Park. She and Sally and I were getting real aggressive trying to chase down some sponsors. Kim was developing the marketing package for an upcoming NHRA drag race there at MMP and because of mutual media and sponsor contacts in the Motorsports world, she had developed a close tie with a group in New Orleans who were promoting the upcoming Off Shore Power Boat championship race on Lake Pontchartrain. With her smooth talking, Kim had talked the folks down in New Orleans in to getting us an introduction with Don Johnson and film star Kurt Russell in hopes that these guys could help me build my NASCAR program. A little star power couldn't hurt.

Don and Kurt were looking for engineering sponsorship for their power-boat team and I had an ace in the hole they wanted to get their hands on: a personal connection with Valvoline through their National Accounts Director Bob Campbell, as well as with the President and CEO at Parts Plus Auto stores, Buddy Tankersley. Bob and Buddy had made me a deal that if I could put some sort of marketing partnership together with Don or anyone who was high profile enough to get the media interested, they would be willing to help develop a sponsorship package with me on the NASCAR side, and in this case with DJ and the off shore power boats.

It was a hell of a deal…if we could get everyone on the same page.

Just as we booked our plane tickets to New Orleans, there was another lucky development. Another friend of mine, Dan McLemore, who was also helping me chase down sponsors, introduced me to a millionaire friend who was willing to help out. This guy didn't know crap about car racing but had once owned a big-time powerboat racing team, and ironically, he just happened to be friends with Don Johnson too. The guy's name was Joe Rupert, a real-estate tycoon from Memphis and a former owner of the famous, highbrow and controversial marina, Fort Apache, in Miami. At first I didn't know what to think of Joe, considering the checkered history of Fort Apache Marina, which had allegedly been used in an international marijuana smuggling operation back in the 1980s. But he was well-connected, rich as hell and he was willing to get involved and help me out.

Within a day Joe had called DJ up and sweetened the pie. By coincidence, Kim had made a deal for us to see DJ and through a totally un-related connection, we had another contact with the actor. It seemed as if some positive destiny was on my side for once. But I was holding my breath.

When Kim and I landed in New Orleans, we were running about thirty minutes behind schedule, so we quickly rented a car and sped to the Landmark Hotel to meet up with Don Johnson's PR people. Once there we met his race team's general manager, multi-time world champion boat racer Ritchie Powers, who also happened to serve as the vital throttle man on the million-dollar offshore powerboat that DJ drove and Kurt Russell navigated. The plan was to have some lunch, get to know one another and see if we all would feel comfortable putting our names on the deal. So we adjourned to a nearby four-star restaurant.

As we sat down, I let Joe take the lead. Once he gave DJ's people a quick overview of the project, we all ordered our salads and gumbo, and settled into discussing how we'd make DJ comfortable about supporting some shaggy-haired kid from Mississippi he had never heard about until four days ago.

Since Ritchie and I were racers, we hit it off right away, quickly got into the racing, and almost forgot to stay focused on the sponsorship deal. But by the time dessert and coffee came, we managed to cover what we'd need to do to get the Valvoline - Parts Plus deal signed. Ritchie seemed to be fired up about the opportunities. When he finished up the meal with a toast and good will for our relationship, I was beside myself. This was very cool stuff.

After the two-hour lunch, we eased back down to the Landmark Hotel where the lobby was filling up with rich and famous in the powerboat-racing world. Because it was so crowded, we stood outside in the valet area and continued to talk.

Then, out of nowhere, Kurt Russell and his PR person drove up in a black Mercedes, pitched the keys to the valet and joined us right beside the hotel steps. After the introductions, Kurt struck up a conversation with me about my NASCAR stuff. Come to find out he loved the sport.

"I look up to you guys who do that crazy stuff," he grinned.

Like he wasn't doing his own crazy stuff racing that power boat.

When I glanced over at Kim, I almost burst into laughter at the intense look on her face, which actually surprised me because Kim was no stranger to celebrities and had hobknobbed with the likes of actor and racing driver Paul Newman. But Kurt was young, and sexy, and drop dead gorgeous, and Kim was clearly attracted. To be truthful, I was checking him out too. But at the time, I would have never let anyone know that . . . I mean no one!

After about ten more minutes of race talk we made plans to attend a big blow-out party that night, then catch up around 11:00 the next morning and meet DJ and his business manager.

"I'll have your VIP credentials in order," Richie said, "and we'll share some lobster and beer later on tonight."

So we shook hands, and headed downtown to our hotel right off the French Quarter. What a damn day…it could not have gone any better.

Now, it was time for some raw oysters from the Acme Oyster Bar in the French Quarter. No matter that we had just eaten lunch.

That night, Kim and I got all jazzed up in our coolest clothes and cruised over to the banks of Lake Pontchartrain.

The big party was being thrown by business tycoon Al Copeland, the owner and founder of the Popeye Fried Chicken franchise and race host, for all the weekend's boat racers. We picked up our credentials at the VIP entrance and hit the party for a few hours enjoying some of Al Copeland's fried chicken and gawking at some of the richest people either one of us had ever seen. I had never seen so much money walking around in one place in my life. These boat racers definitely had big time outrageous cash flow.

About 10:00 p.m., we decided we didn't want to wear out our welcome so we packed it in early. I wasn't down there to party all night, I was down there to put a racing deal together.

The next morning we got back to the race pits by the lake. Ritchie met us at the pit gate and we strolled on down to where DJ's million-dollar powerboat was located. I had never realized just how damn big those babies were. But she was beautiful

"Sit down in the cockpit and see how she feels," Richie suggested.

"I'd love to sit down in that monster," I said.

What a damn honor… especially considering I was wearing my coolest Kenneth Cole saddle-tan suede cowboy boots I had bought in San Francisco, not the appropriate deck shoes.

After killing an hour there, we walked on down to the VIP area where DJ had his tour bus parked and went inside. The conversation started out light and almost comical, but soon we got down to business about how we could make this deal with Valvoline work for both of us. DJ's manager did most of the talking, and he was pretty direct at times.

I kept my cool. "If you need to know any more than what I've told you," I said, "you can talk to Bob Campbell at Valvoline – he'll bring you up to speed."

When the meeting was ending, DJ did finally speak up.

"If we get this all together," he said to me, "I'd love to drive one of those damn stock cars around Daytona."

"If we get this deal worked out," I responded recklessly, "we'll rent the track and you can drive around that speedway for a whole day."

After thank you's all around, Kim and I headed for the airport. I had to be in Little Rock, Arkansas that night to race the sprint car.

Was I chasing a pipe dream? Would this once-in-a-lifetime opportunity turn into yet another rumor, leaving me out of the business? On that flight to Little Rock, I was fighting like hell to keep the doubt from consuming my thoughts.

That next week back in Corinth, I was in my race shop getting ready for a big weekend of sprint-car racing in Texas and Arkansas when the phone rang up in the house. My mom yelled out the back door of the house.

"Pick up the phone! Don Johnson wants to talk to you!"

DJ and I updated for a minute. I gave him my contact's phone number up at Valvoline in Richmond, Kentucky, and he gave me his phone number out in Colorado.

"I'll give those guys a call next week," he said. "Let's catch up in a week or 10 days, and see where we stand."

When we hung up, my mom was standing right there beside of me with a big ole grin on her face. She had just talked to Don Johnson on her very own phone and she was about to pee in her pants . . . I thought it was cool as well, that he had the courtesy to call me personally instead of having one of his people make the call.

The racing Taliban

I'd never done anything that gives me the feeling of love-hate that sprint cars gave me. And I'm not the only one. Before the start of a sprint-car race, grown 200-pound bad-ass macho Neanderthals sometimes can be seen throwing up from a case of the nerves. These cars are crazy dangerous to drive. It is looking at a rattle snake eye ball to eye ball. The drivers are crazy competitive and will wreck you in a second. But it was the most exhilarating and frustrating thing I've ever done. Two time NASCAR Sprint Cup champion and all around racing bad boy Tony Stewart recently said on his weekly Sirius radio show that the hardest thing he ever had to learn to do was drive a winged sprint car. I'd had won over a hundred sprint car races over the years, I had beaten some of the best the sport had to offer, so in all reality, that made me a racing bad ass too. Yet, some people in the sport had tried to kill my career with rumor and gossip ever since I first came through the gates at West Memphis back in 1984.Clearly I should have sued their tails off ten times over, but I always just kept my mouth shut and kept on beating their tails on the track, which pissed them off more than anything else I could do to them. For me, every time I went through the gate of a sprint car race, it was like being in a rattle snake pit.

By now, since I had been back on the Mid South circuit, the racing Taliban was determined to get me at any cost. It didn't matter that I was a kick ass driver, my social status just would not let me have the credit I was due. There was this one driver who headed that effort. Racing Ricky was a good-looking stud muffin from Memphis who worked at one of the high-tech racing engine specialist company's there. In the beginning, he actually befriended me and helped me out with some engine technology. But as soon as I began to win and the rumors filtered through the West Memphis racing cult, he started harassing me.

Ricky was dangerous. He would run over your ass without blinking an eye. I had seen him crash so hard that I thought no one could have survived the impact but, he kept on coming back for more. When you raced with him you just had to know that and plan accordingly . . . If you gave him a chance to take you out he would. So I always took the attitude that I was going to be so much faster that he couldn't get to me. In fact, he had only out run me once—and on that night, he had run over my front wheel causing me to have a flat. I had to restart dead last with only twenty-five laps remaining. I drove my ass off and finally ran him down coming to the checkered flag. He beat me by only a car length.

He and his West Memphis buddies hated the fact that someone like me could be that successful. They couldn't beat me on the track so they made a decision to beat me behind the scenes by rumors. This year it was worse than ever.

Up till now I'd had a good season . . . won several main events and never finished out of the top three in over two months. We were a really low budget team so we were doing real damn good considering what we were competing against. But I was getting tired of the bullshit. Maybe it would be a good idea to quit this deal in a few weeks, to focus on my NASCAR opportunities.

On this weekend we were in Texarkana, Texas for a Friday night race, then a big show on Saturday night in Little Rock. Our team was pretty confident about pulling out at least one win. The purse was hefty, so I could put some good cash in my bank account.

After we had unloaded the race car and warmed the engine up, I needed to walk over to the pit stand to see when it would be my time for hot laps. So I called over to the Rolands' 12-year-old son Jody who thought I was a sprint car God, to see if he wanted to walk up to the stand with me to check out the schedule. As we were walking over there, we ran to my ole buddy Racing Ricky, and he just had to smart off at me.

"Hey there, cutie, how about a little blow job before we all get to racing . . . I need some relief so how about it, cutie."

I couldn't believe he had the gall to say that in front of a twelve-year-old kid.

But I just kept walking. I didn't want him to know he was getting under my skin. Besides, if I did say something back, we would be on the ground fighting like hell.

About ten minutes later, Jody sheepishly came over to me.

"Can we, uh, go behind the hauler? I want to tell you something," he said.

His face wore a look of hurt and disgust, and I figured it had to do with what Ricky had said. My intuition was right.

"JT, hey man, uh . . . Hey, you can't tell my dad what I'm going to tell you. You're not going to tell my dad, are you ?"

"No, I ain't going to tell your dad," I said.

He still hesitated, looking down.

"Come on, Jody, get on with it," I urged him. "It's almost time for hot laps."

"All right, well . . . Racing Ricky just asked me if you had been playing with my legs. He even asked me if you had given me a blowjob on the way over to the races." Jody finally looked in my eyes earnestly. "Fuck him, JT, he ain't nothing but an asshole . . . I know you're not like that, you would never do something like that . . . he's just jealous that he can't beat you. He's a redneck who wrecks all the time anyway."

To say I was livid at Racing Ricky is an understatement . . . and Jody knew it by the look on my own face. But I just looked down at the kid and said, "Don't worry about it. You're right about Racing Ricky."

The irony of Racing Ricky making criminal allegations about me was—he had been in more trouble with the law than anyone I knew. In fact he had done time there in Memphis at the penal farm for DUI violations.

However, at the moment I had to forget about Racing Ricky and strap myself into that 900 horse-powered 1200-pound rocket ship. It was not a time for adolescent redneck bullshit. My life depended on it.

In the race, I got off to a good start and by lap eight I was challenging for second place. But as I made my move to take first place position, my right rear tire blew out and the car nearly flipped. Luckily I kept control and nursed her back to the pit lane where Tommy and Jody made a lightning-fast tire change.

By the time I got back on the track, 22 laps remained and I was running in 23rd place, dead last. If I was going to rescue any kind of good finish in this event, I had to take some chances. When the flagman restarted the race, I stood on the gas and picked off the cars off one by one. By the time the checkered flag dropped, I had worked my way up to fifth place. If that tire hadn't blown, I could have won.

But, as my dad always said, "That's what those if's are for."

Anyway, we salvaged a pretty good payday and headed for Little Rock. I liked that track and, my mom and dad were coming over so, I would have some moral support.

Also the Racing Ricky and Jody Roland situation had to be addressed at some point. I didn't want to go behind Jody's back and tell his dad but Racing Ricky could not be allowed to get away with that kind of behavior around a minor. Jody's dad would probably beat Ricky to a pulp once he found out. But I wanted to wait, and not have an altercation while we were out racing.

A Feeling of Doom

The next morning, we all got up around 8:00, had some breakfast and got busy cleaning the car and going over every nut and bolt. It was hot as hell there in Little Rock and Tommy and Jodie were sweating like pigs out there in the hot sun. But we all hung in there, got all our jobs done and by 3:00 that afternoon we were back at the motel showering.

By 4:30 p.m. my team was pulling into the track, along with 50 other tight-wired sprint car drivers hell bent on redeeming their machismo from the night before.

It was going to be one hell of a night in Little Rock.

By the time we had gotten the car unloaded out of the hauler, my parents had arrived, and Dad was busy bullshitting with Jody. Mom was hanging out with Jan who like my mom was a real fireball, and damn good looking, a dead ringer for movie star Jill St John. I also knew that her husband Tommy, my car owner, had been stepping out on her for years . . . I hated the fact I didn't have the courage to tell her. She deserved better. But what are you going to do?

The track was heavy and very fast. Every time you passed, you were taking a big risk. By the time practice and qualifying were over, five guys had flipped and crashed their cars big time. There was a sense of gloom and doom in the air. That little fact had not passed me or my dad.

So when it came time to strap in for the main event, I felt uneasy and pulled my safety belts tighter than usual. These guys were driving way over their heads tonight. If that continued, someone was going to pay.

Just before the push truck got behind me, my dad patted me on the back and leaned into the car.

"Just watch your step," he said quietly. "They're out of control tonight, so you be careful. You don't have anything to prove. You've won here several times. So just drive smart. You're starting fifth, so if you take your time you can win this deal."

I nodded my head yes, and shook his hand. In the next second, the push truck took me out to the track.

It took three tries to start that race. The guys in front of me smacked one another around and bottled up the field, so once we did get the green flag. I found myself caught in the traffic jam, causing me to fall back to tenth place right off the bat.

But by lap 10 I had worked my way back up to fourth place and was having a hell of a battle with the new Memphis hot shoe Greg Hotnet. On lap eleven, he gave me a slight opening…and I took it, slightly bumping his left rear wheel as I went by. Now I had my sights set on second place about five car lengths up ahead. The first-place guy, Gary Wright from Texas, had really checked out on all of us.

Then, as I exited turn four to head down the front straightaway, with my foot on the gas, I felt a big thump and bump on my left side. Hotnet's car had connected with mine, solidly and deliberately.

This is the moment that changed my life, ten seconds later the car was totaled and I was lucky to be alive.

Before I had time to think about correcting the spin, I was upside down and flipping violently down the entire length of the front straightaway . . . end over end, side over side. All the while the damn car was hitting the ground so hard my eyeballs almost popped out of my head. This wasn't my first flip so I knew the drill. Keeping a death grip on the steering wheel, I managed to tuck my head down as far as I could.

Everything is in slow motion in a crash like this. I could hear every thump and thud, as well as the engine screaming out of control. The first flip had caused the gas pedal to stick wide open as well as snapping the drive shaft in two, so the sound of that engine screaming at 12,000 rpm's was daunting, and spooky. After what seemed like minutes of unbelievable heart-pounding slams and screeching sounds, that out-of-control machine came to a pounding stop about 75 yards from where it started this madness. My rocket ship was now a heap of smoldering metal and fiberglass – and I was inside it.

Just for a second I didn't hear a sound, but my vision was as clear as a bell. I was laying on my left side staring right at the wall right in front of the grand stands where my mom and dad were sitting. Then in a flash, the unbelievable screaming of the engine penetrated my brain. It had a death sound to it, like what you hear when an airplane is dive-bombing straight down at 600 miles per hour, about to crash into the ground. Luckily, I still had enough sense to realize what it was, and reached up to hit the kill switch.

Suddenly everything got deathly quiet again. At that point you know that some other out-of control-racer might slam into you at 120 miles per hour. If the first wreck doesn't kill you, the second one might.

But, after a few more seconds, nothing happened. I was feeling relieved that I dodged a big bullet there in that Arkansas dirt. No blood was splattered anywhere and I wasn't hurting anywhere, so I thought I just might go ahead and exit that little machine. Then head on back down to our pit area, grab a soda and a lawn chair and let everyone else deal with that broken heap of steel. My day at the office was over.

Then I realized that I was trapped, and couldn't get out.

Suddenly a crowd of track personnel were rushing up the track toward my wrecked car.

"Don't light a cigarette!" one guy yelled. "The fuel tank is ruptured!"

Not only was exotic racing fuel flowing all over the track . . . it was flowing all over me. It had soaked my driving uniform. Every driver hates fire – it's our worst nightmare to be trapped in a burning race car. This was a little old dirt track in Arkansas where fire equipment virtually didn't exist. I had to get out of that H-bomb, and fast. Whoever was in charge of getting me out of that mangled mess had better have a cool head.

So I took a big breath, calmed myself, and just sat there as the emergency crew spent several endless, haunting minutes trying to pry me out of the car.

Dad's and Mom's and Tommy's voices came at me from behind, strangely mingled. "It's going to be all right…" "The crew has everything under control…" "They'll have you out in a minute…"

"I know…I'm okay," I responded with a strange calm.

Were they telling me the truth? Spilled fuel was all around us, reeking in our nostrils. One spark and I'd be a toasted marshmallow.

Finally they got my skinny tail out of that wreck. I was a bit dizzy so asked the paramedic to let me stand there for a few seconds and gather my wits.

Suddenly the fans began to applaud like hell. Their yells cascaded down over me from the grandstands. "You go JT... you're the man, you'll be back . . . kick their ass next week!"

The cheers were because I'd shown bravery...and more than that, because I had just given them the big thrill of the weekend. Fans like the racing but they just love a good wreck...it gets their blood pumping and the Budweiser cans popping. I had done them proud.

So I took my helmet off, handed it to my mom and gave the fans a big ole thumbs up. Then we casually headed back down to our pits. There was nothing else to do. My ribs and neck were starting to hurt.

To make things worse, just as we got to our pits, I looked over toward the exit gate and saw Tommy and my dad. They had Greg Hotnett and his dad cornered and were chewing their asses out because Greg had run over me and caused the crash. They weren't fighting but it was getting real close. Just another summer night and another sprint car race in Little Rock. Just a normal deal.

Walking over to them, I said, "Hey...cool down, everybody. This is between Greg and me."

Greg and I faced each other.

"I know you were probably pissed me for bumping you the lap before the wreck," I growled at him. "But taking me out was not cool. Hell, I could have taken you out three or four times in this race but I didn't. You need to think about that the next time you're pondering the idea of slamming anyone again. What goes around comes around. But it ain't worth fighting about. Let's just pack up our stuff and get on down the road!"

Greg looked at me square in the eye. "I didn't mean to crash you like that. I just got too aggressive trying to bump you back."

He shook my hand. That was all the apology I was going to get.

To be honest, I didn't expect an apology. Racing ain't playing with your rubber ducky in the bathtub. It ain't a smooth cup of Joe sitting in a coffee shop up in Seattle discussing how we can save the trees. It's a war zone in the middle of the South on a hot summer night. It's a bunch of alpha males who eat red meat, liberal college professors and Democrats for supper and wash it down with a shot of Jack Daniels and a belch at the end. If you can't stand the heat, you have no business in this sport.

Oh well, you will have this kind of stupidity in motorsports . . . and very often too!

We finally got the totaled racecar back in the hauler. Instead of riding with the Rolands, I jumped in my mom and dad's van and took the wheel. I needed to do something with my pent-up anger. Plus Dad couldn't see that well at night now, so it was just the right thing to do.

We headed back to Memphis. At 12:00 midnight, we hit I-40. By then I had drank two cups of coffee and run that race over and over a hundred times in my head, trying to figure out if there was anything I could have done to prevent the wreck.

In reality, there was nothing I could have done. I just got ran over by a young and overly energetic driver and that was it.

However, one more thing was definitely making my mind go round and round. The fuel tank could have gone up in a ball of fire leaving me to roast in that baby. I had crashed race cars many times. It isn't _if you're_ going to wreck, it's _when_ you're going to. Crashing had never frightened me. Oh, I'm not stupid enough to say that wrecking didn't get my attention. But the violence of a wreck never got to me to the point that I was afraid to race again. In fact, I was always chomping at the bit to rebuild the car and get back on the track.

But this crash was different and I fully understood what it meant to my life. This could have been the big one. If that screaming engine had blown up and scattered fire and hot engine parts all over the track as I lay trapped upside down inside the war, I would not be sitting here in the quiet dark, with the quiet glow of the dashboard before me, and my mom and dad dozing as we headed home.

I was on my way to NASCAR racing full time within the year, yet my private life was crashing down around me. My gender situation had me trapped inside a lifetime of hurt and pain that would never subside. I was a woman with all my heart and soul, yet I lived in a world of extreme machismo. I was physically small and fragile, and lucky to have survived this wreck with only some busted ribs and a sore neck. I was in the prime of my life…but my life was passing me by faster than an out-of-control race car. I had given the boy thing my best shot and I hated it. It left me cold inside. But the girl thing created so much controversy that I could barely stand it.

Not religion, not my family, not racing, not even the fear of rejection had ripped the desire to be a woman out of my heart.

What was wrong with being a girl, anyway? Was it that terrible? Was being a woman less than being a real person? Was being male that much more important?

Clearly, I could not go on like this. The crash had given me the wake-up call of my life. If I had died tonight, I would have never had the chance to be who I really was. The next time I might not be so lucky. So if I ever wanted the chance to live in peace and harmony as a female, I had better get on with it.

It was time for a new plan—one to move me into womanhood that would not wreck my life like all the times before. Making that decision and following it through would be the most difficult thing I would ever do in my life. Once I announced to the world that I was going to have the sex realignment surgery, there would be no more chances for the NASCAR dream to come true. My folks were going to go nuts, so I would have to be strong enough to stand the heat.

I was done with sprint cars for good. When I got home, I would build myself a new and innovative midget racer that had been on my mind for a few months. I would own the car, so I wouldn't need to kiss anyone's ass to get a ride and no one could politic me to other car owners and get me fired. I would race that baby against people who were less mean spirited. This deal would allow me to move into my femininity without the scrutiny of a bunch of macho rednecks.

This plan would start tomorrow.

As the lights of Memphis came into view I glanced over to the passenger seat where my mom was sound asleep. A cold chill ran over my body. The battle for my life had really just begun, but no one in the van knew this but me. It would be a while longer before they would know that this night had changed my life forever.

Two days later, me and dad were hanging out with Lake Speed and Darrel Waltrip down in Daytona . . . go figure.

CHAPTER 17

NASCAR or Terri – Drama in a Small Town

That winter, the financial part of my plan got up to speed. Working like a demon, late nights in my race shop, I designed and built a cutting-edge midget racer. The idea for it had been kicking around in my brain on for over a year now. It would win me money at races. The money would pile up in a private bank account so I could pay for my gender re-alignment surgery when the time came. Worst case scenario, if the medical bills were bigger than anticipated, I could sell the racer.

By spring, I was kicking everybody's butts with that racer. It looked sharp as heck, with some speed secrets built into it. Four or five hard ankles were already wanting to buy it. Sitting in my shop was a duplicate model, in parts. I figured I could get $10,000 apiece for them.

Keeping the racing dream alive in spite of my gender future, before I had the surgery, I was still hoping against hope to develop those opportunities in NASCAR.

The deal with Valvoline and Don Johnson was looking pretty damn good. By the start of 1992, I could be driving full time in NASCAR's Busch series and doing a limited schedule in the Winston / Sprint Cup Series. It looked like Bob Campbell at Valvoline was setting me up to be their next young gun. Bob also wanted someone to help me get ready for the big time, both from the driving standpoint and a marketing perspective. So he hooked me up with TNN's Pat Patterson who was one of the newest players in the motorsports world. Pat had a cool motorsports show on The Nashville Network (now Spike). My first meeting with Pat went well…but I worried about his friendships with some of my competitors throughout the sprint-car community. It was only a matter of time before the rumors might reach Patterson's political circle.

Meanwhile, I hooked up with Bobby Waltrip, who was running his brother Darrell Waltrip's cup team and he and I started laying the ground work for me to do a few races in one of Darrell's Busch cars. I had some sponsor money from my dad's tool and die business and we were very close to putting something together.

But, as I had feared, the rumors were slowly creeping into the NASCAR community. Should I drag all the people who were supporting me into the media nightmare that was sure to break once I hit the circuit full time?

In early November, I made a trip up to Charlotte to work on my deal with the Waltrip Busch team. But on the way there, just outside of Atlanta, I found myself pulling over to the side of the road on I-85 and falling to pieces weeping. I had given it my best shot—in the end Mother Nature would win out, as well as she should. My time to be me had finally arrived.

Two days later, I was putting together a multi-stage plan.

I had already done some research, and knew how much money I'd need. And I wanted to ease into it step at a time. First would come the breast implants – I wanted to enlarge my 34A breasts a little. That would be around $3500. A little later on, the urology surgery would cost me ten grand. The hormones and some minor electrolysis on my chin area had taken care of the hair on my face. I did not need any facial surgery because I already had a feminine face. The most important part of this equation was the urology surgery; everything else would be window dressing.

In addition to the physical changes, I still had to pay my psychologist $100.00 a visit. All told, I would need at least fifteen grand to get me into my next life, including some cash flow to re-start my life.

So I called a Memphis plastic surgeon who had been recommended to me by a very close friend in Corinth, and scheduled an appointment to discuss breast implants. After that, I would go west for the gender re-alignment surgery. From one of my Memphis girlfriends, I had heard about a surgeon, Dr Bieber, who had a practice in Trinidad, Colorado. My psychologist, Dr Battles, knew about Dr. Bieber and said he was the absolute best specialist in this type of surgery. In the end, it just felt right!

Calling my contacts in Charlotte, I told everyone that all my deals had fallen through and I had to regroup. However, I told my mom and dad that my NASCAR deals were on go and I would be moving back to Charlotte to get everything organized.

Of course, I was lying my ass off—what I had planned was to start my transition at the end of February.

Adding to the pressure, only days before, dad had told me to keep on plugging away at the NASCAR deal, that my uncle Buddy just might come around after all and help put some financing in place.

Here I am driving my tricked out blue and white midget at the Nationals up in Indiana. I won over seventy five races in that little car.

On February 20th, Saturday, I raced my midget in Memphis. The next day, I quietly checked into the hospital and got breast implants. My friend Cathy checked me out of the hospital. Two days after my race in Memphis, I was a 34C. Adding to the irony in that, my plastic surgeon had no idea about my current situation; he only thought I was girl who wanted her breast enlarged. Kathy and I just thought that was nuts that my doctor and his entire team had no clue who they were working on.

Back in Corinth a helpful doctor who was keeping my story quite had provided me with the medical letter that I'd need to change my legal ID. My old friend Sally had connected me with this doctor, who was compassionate and understanding. With his letter in hand, I was able to go before a judge and get my Social Security ID changed, then my birth certificate and driver's license. The documents no longer said, James Terrell

Hayes, male…but Terri Lee Hayes, female. It was a relief to have the accurate ID – with all the driving we did to races, I had started to worry about being pulled over by a state trooper who might notice the discrepancy between my driver's license gender and my brand-new breasts.

Drag queen nights

It was March 1992. A few days after my breast surgery, I woke up one morning and almost had a heart attack over the situation I'd put myself in. How in the hell am I going to tell my parents what I've just done? And what was I doing to do next?

There was a little time to figure this out because my parents and virtually all of my friends thought I was up in North Carolina working for Lake Speed and trying to find NASCAR sponsors. If I was not careful, this little scheme could cause lots of family trouble for me. But at least I had the plan in motion!

In a couple of weeks, with my breast surgery healing, I decided to move to Memphis to reconnect with my old friend Michael and restart my life . . . as Terri, not JT. I already had a few dollars saved up but not enough for more than a month or so. I had no idea what I was going to do to make a living away from motor sports. The idea of telling my parents what I just done was eating me up inside.

Michael was a lunatic with a heart of gold. Reconnecting with him was easy. Right away he hooked me up with a 300-pound drag queen friend of his, Kirby Kincaid. She offered to rent me part of her apartment. In a few days I was settled there, and looking for a job – any job.

Over the next few months I got really connected with my femininity … my voice, my mannerisms. It was amazing that it came so easily. Meanwhile I managed to find some work at a demo company that promoted new food products there in Memphis. It wasn't the kind of cash I had been used to as a professional racecar driver, but at least I was eating and putting gas in my car.

But by then, someone from Corinth had glimpsed me there in Memphis, and they went and told my parents. So the little charade about me being up in North Carolina came to an end. My parents now knew what I was up to. They weren't happy about it, but surprisingly, they weren't pitching a fit either. In fact, Mom was on me to move back home so she and Dad could look after me during the adjustment period. I appreciated their support but wasn't so sure I wanted to move back to Corinth. But my mom and my grandmother kept working on me.

Meanwhile, in Memphis, things were not going so well with Miss Kirby either. She had a cocaine problem and she was also dealing. I hated the drug scene and knew it was only a matter of time before the cops would show up.

By that time, my dad's best bud Dewayne, my old arch-enemy, had my Memphis phone number, which he had gotten from my mom. Dewayne who by now had found religion and wanting to help too was trying to talk me into moving back home. I couldn't believe he was actually being nice to me. Several times he got me crying like a baby with his genuine concern over the family dynamics this ordeal had caused. My parents would look after me and I could probably continue to race my midget racer (which I was already missing) while I completed my transition.

I agonized over the decision, knowing I needed to get out of Kirby's but I was not ready to leave Memphis.

Then, as if by divine intervention, one Wednesday night around 9:00, the third week of June, I came home from work tired and hungry and found Kirby and several of her bar buddies gathered around a big mound of cocaine on the dining room table. The girls were doing lines and having a big ole time before heading off to the Wednesday-night drag show at the bar. The door was not even locked when I walked in.

"Hey there, girl," Kirby yelled, "are you going out to party with us tonight? There's free draft beer and the place is going to be packed."

"No, I don't think so, Kirby," I said as smoothly as I could. "I'm beat and I've got to work tomorrow. You girls go have fun, I'm going to bed."

In reality, I was so afraid and pissed off that I wanted to beat the hell out of them, but I knew better than to say anything since they were all stoned out of their heads. So I just joked with them and headed to the shower. This was the sign from Heaven to get out of there. Otherwise the headlines would read, "EX NASCAR DRIVER GOING THROUGH SEX CHANGE GETS BUSTED FOR COCAINE WITH ALL HER DRAG QUEEN FRIENDS."

When they headed off to the bar at around 10 p.m. I packed my belongings and hit the highway to Corinth.

All the times before, when I had moved back home, I had always felt defeated. This time I didn't feel that way! The thoughts of my bed at my mom's and the security of my office and race shop had a warm glow.

Three days later, after my parents and friends had the shock of seeing me as Terri for the first time, I was trying to figure out how to earn a living in Corinth. Tool-and-die-making and welding had always been my fall-back jobs but I didn't want to do that stuff anymore. Besides, who would give me a job in those industries with me looking like a chick?

In an amazing twist of fate, my dad seemed to be relieved I was back home instead of laying in a ditch somewhere.

One day, Dad actually told me, "Look…if and when you finally decide that you're going to have the surgery, and you haven't sold the two midgets yet, I'll loan you the money to tide you over."

That commitment by my Dad amazed me and cheered me up like you can't imagine.

Like clockwork, within a few days I was back working on my race car like I had never been away. It had been four months since my breast surgery. Probably I should have worried about crashing and bursting one of those babies. Instead I just bought myself a Nike sports bra and got ready to go back racing…as Terri. The dirt-track racers throughout the Mid South would give me holy hell. But the way I saw it was this: if they could outrun me, they could say anything they wanted to. Once a racer, always a racer!

By now, I was seeing a new counselor, Dr Battles. "Gender dysphoria" was what he specialized in. He had no idea I'd been a boy, and freaked out when I told him. It was the first time in 25 years that he hadn't been able to identify a new gender dysphoria patient. I totally got him!

After a few sessions, Dr. Battles told me, "I'm absolutely certain that you're perfectly suited for the surgery. But I still want you to put in a year before I sign off on the surgery. You'll want to be 100 percent sure that you want to take this step."

A year! My heart sank. If I was going to live in Corinth while I put in that year, I had to be ready for what the town offered socially. There was no doubt that this was going to be a very temperamental relationship.

Little stories around town

I had never been a recluse. I loved to get out in the world. So I just made up my mind that I would walk proudly with my head up anywhere I went in Corinth. After all, the local newspaper had covered my racing career since 1972 when I was just a kid. At one time, I had been one of the towns up and coming VIP's. There was nowhere to hide. If I went out to a restaurant or shopping center, someone was going to recognize me.

The first week I was back, my granny and I were driving around town when we needed to stop for gas. Out on highway 72, I pulled into a local gas station and convenience store, and went inside to pay for our gas. Several men were standing in the back at the soda cooler, checking me out with their eyes. For a moment, I was a just a cute girl to them. Among them was a good-looking guy, Jamie Ray, who had gone to high school with me. I wasn't sure Jamie would recognize me, so I quickly paid for the gas.

But, just as I feared, Jamie Ray started yelling, "Hey, guys, that's JT Hayes!"

So there I stood, out at the pumps putting gas into my SUV, not able to escape the gawking and catcalls. I was steaming mad and wanted to smack him… but I was also afraid of what they might do next. In a small town in Mississippi, things can turn ugly in a hurry. As soon as I finished, I drove off while Jamie Ray and his buds stood yelling obscenities after me.

Sensing something, Granny asked me, "Is everything all right?"

I just looked straight ahead and into traffic and said, "Yep, it couldn't be better."

But I knew I could never go back into that store again. This little story was going to run through this community like wildfire.

For two weeks after that, I felt fearful about just leaving the house. But finally I ventured out to shop at a women's boutique in town. While I was checking out the fashions, an old girl friend, Angie, recognized me. She came over and actually commended me for my decision to go through the surgery. I was shocked and surprised.

"Do you want to go out some night and catch up on our lives?" she smiled.

For the next few months I re-connected with Angie and a few of her friends. It was wonderful for my self-esteem. I had never felt at home at the gay bars, not that I was doing that any way so hanging out with the straight girls was right down my ally. At first Angie seemed genuinely interested in my being happy and included me in everything she and her family did. Her husband Ben was a gentle giant who liked me and never saw me as anything but Terri. But all was not well in their family. Angie had ended three previous marriages through her infidelity, and now she was at it again. I finally figured out that she was using her evening outings with me as a cover for her midnight rendezvous with her boyfriend. It made me feel uncomfortable, and I told her so.

Well, Angie didn't like hearing this, and turned on me. When her parents found out that she was cheating on Ben, she justified her cheating by saying that she suspected Ben and I were having an affair. Of course this was a lie, but the story got around town, and planted a seed of doubt about my "moral integrity." Since I was already considered a bad person anyway, Angie was off the hook.

That little story became one of many swirling around Corinth. I just wrote it off to being taken advantage of by a backstabbing bitch.

Over the next month or so, I was enjoying my newfound womanness.

Granny and I spent a lot of time together. At least once a week, I took her fishing. Every day around 3 in the afternoon, we would grab a Coke or coffee and ride around on the county roads for an hour or so. The family had taken Granny's drivers license and car away from her because she had become a lethal weapon behind the wheel. So it was good for her to get out of the house, and it was good for me to bond with my best friend. Granny had always gotten it with me, and she got it now. She had a healing effect on me and my parents, always telling my mom, "Now Kate, you know Terri is different. You've know this all of her life. So you need to deal with this and get on with it."

When I told Granny what my ex friend Angie did to me, she cried.

"You just need to put it behind you," she said. "Some people are just mean and hurtful. God will look after you."

The midget Nationals

It was July 1992. My nerves were getting a little frayed, but at least my race cars were keeping me busy and sane. I spent most of my time in the race shop and my cool office behind our house. I was safe there…or so I thought.

The national championship midget races were coming up in Illinois, and Dad and I thought I had a good run at them. My heart wasn't quite in it like before, but I was still fired up about going. Dewayne and my dad's other racing buddies were going with us. I wanted to compete on a national level against the best in the country no matter if I was a male or a female.

However, a week before the races, Dewayne started hinting around, saying things like, "Do you really want to go?" "What are you going to do about your hair at the races?"

He was fishing to see if I was going as Terri or as JT. I didn't think much about it, because I had been going to the races for the past few months as Terri. I never pushed the envelope as a girl thing—always wore a loose fitting shirt and blue jeans and tied my hair in a ponytail with a baseball cap stuck on top. However, I did not look like a boy, not even without makeup.

Three days before the Nationals, around noon, I was out in the race shop. It was hot as hell, and I was just about to go in the house for a soda when Dewayne came charging into the driveway, as he sometimes did on his lunch break to see how I was doing on the race car. Today, however, he had a different reason for his visit.

"Terri," he said, "Dexter and I have decided that you can't go to the Nationals as a girl. We've talked it over and there ain't no way you're going with all of us . . . It's too embarrassing. So I just wanted to let you know that you ain't going! You're not doing that to your dad . . . and for damn sure you're not doing that to me."

I couldn't believe my ears. The anger I felt was not the kind where you lose your cool and start a fight. Instead I began to tremble and knew that if I didn't get away from him I was going to do something I would regret forever.

So I casually laid down the shop towel that I was cleaning my hands with, and turned my back on him without a word. Leaving the shop, I walked up to the house and locked the door behind me. Inside, as I sat down on the couch, tears were rolling down my face like crazy.

The hurt went especially deep because Dexter was part of the scheme. Hell, Dexter's blood was flowing through my veins. He was my godfather, my favorite uncle every day of my life. But he had never dealt with my gender issue so it wasn't surprising that he had teamed up with Dewayne. To them, I was a sick puppy. Dewayne's compassion that he had been dishing out over the past several months had turned out to be nothing but a set-up, to try and do an intervention. For an hour or so, I just sat there flipping the television channels, crying and pissed off at the same time. One thing was for sure . . . this was a test of my will to stick to my plan.

Then, as my guardian Angels always do, they showed up. Over the sound of the television I heard Granny beating on the back door. When she got inside she could tell that I had been crying. She also knew that Dewayne had been here.

"What did he do to you?" Granny roared. "I'm tired of him running over you and stirring up trouble."

I told her what Dewayne and Dexter had said.

"I'll be all right," I told her. "He is just being Dewayne. So forget about it." After all, Dexter and Dewayne didn't have any say in whether I went to the Nationals. My dad and I owned the race car, not Dexter and Dewayne!

Well, me telling granny to forget about it was like telling a python snake not to bite someone between the eyes. She went straight to the phone and called Dewayne up at the Honda dealership and reamed his ass out to kingdom Kong and back. She rubbed Dewayne's nose in the fact that my dad had financed the entire racing operation not him, plus the racecar he was driving belonged to my dad too.

Then she called my dad and gave him hell over the whole damn affair.

"If you don't straighten out that Dewayne," she said, "I'm going to put a curse on your head."

My dad took this real seriously. He had lived with her for almost 40 years and an unhappy mother-in-law who lived right next door was not a pleasant prospect. Needless to say, he took care of it.

We all went to the Nationals and I went as Terri. If Dexter and Dewayne wanted to have a racecar to drive, they didn't have any choice. In the end though, I was just miserable being there with them. At the race, my engine blew up and I finished almost dead last. The entire damn thing was just a bust. Go figure.

Over the next few months, I lost some focus on racing. It was important to find more ways of making a living, so I wasn't dependent on my folks and could save towards the surgery.

Ever since I worked for Reid Brothers in high school, I had loved the apparel business and dreamed of having my own clothing store at some point. My friend Dan McLemore, Dewayne's brother, had a little wholesale apparel business going with his wife Becky. So Dad and I hooked up with Dan and Becky and we were now in the business of matching boxers and T-shirts, which was quite the craze on college campuses. Over the next few months, Becky and I traveled all around the Mid South selling our matching sets at wholesale apparel markets. But by Christmas, I wasn't getting along with Becky, so we started our own apparel concept. With the NASCAR deal getting bigger each day, we could sell sets with driver logos all over them. I was brain-storming to come up with the right concept.

That winter of 1992, as we raced the midgets in the Memphis arena, I got my mojo back. Some trick engine pieces and a cool shock package had my little car hooked up. Into the summer of 1993, I never ran worse than third. I finished third at the National Divisional, won everywhere else and without a gear breaking at the Nationals, would have finished second.

On the home front, things in Corinth had settled down a bit but I still had to watch my step. In Memphis where I socialized quite often, no one had any clue of my past as a male. When my girlfriend Kathy and I hit Beal Street, everyone from waiters to guys I danced with saw me as a 5' 6" 117-pound girl.

Even at the races in Illinois or up in Kentucky, for all the pressure Dewayne and Dexter had put on my dad about my appearance, no one ever thought I was anything but a girl racer.

In fact, at the divisional championships up in Kentucky, as we were going through registration before the race, one of the officials looked at me as Dewayne stood there sweating bullets that someone was going to think I was funny-looking. Naturally I had registered as Terri Hayes.

"Hey girl," the official said, "you're not the only girl racer tonight. Who's better, you or the other girl racer?"

"Why me, of course," I shot back.

The official laughed and said, "Well, I hope you kick everybody's butt tonight." In the meantime, ole Dewayne was about to blow a gasket and fled back to our trailer as fast as he could.

That night, I finished third. When I came off the track to go to tech inspection, here came Dewayne who had failed to qualify for the event out of hiding. He slapped a Lake Hill Motors sticker on the side of my car so it would look like he was helping out. That pissed me off and I ripped the decal right off.

"I don't need your help," I barked at him. "I can handle the tech inspection by myself."

The next day Mom, Dad and I along with John Marsh and his family headed out to Nashville to spend the day at Opryland. Dewayne and his wife and kids declined our invitation to join us for the day. But John Marsh, who was one of the most macho men I knew, supported me in every way. His two small boys traveled with us and thought I was hot buttered popcorn because of my driving skill. In fact, that same weekend I had won a divisional championship in Nashville and the two boys got into a huge argument over which of them was going to get one of the trophies I had won. John had to step in and separate those two little whipper snappers before they killed one another. It had almost turned into the WWF right there in the back of the SUV. It was pretty darn funny.

You just never knew what you were going to get from people. Religion, politics and social prejudice lit a white-hot fire under gender questions.

Fred, grow some hair on your chest

That summer of 1993, Dad and I took a local racer under our wings.

Fred was a mechanical engineer from Baldwin, Mississippi who was employed at the NASA plant up the road. He was a true blue Southern redneck who had done a little dirt track stock-car racing, but wasn't successful, so now he was trying midgets. He was at our race shop constantly, trying to learn more, and to tell you the truth I liked him. He had a good sense of humor and seemed to take a liking to me, with an interest in knowing more about my gender issue. So I told him and his lovely wife a little of my life story, and he seemed very respectful.

By the first of August we had Fred running pretty good.

I had also been doing some engine modifications for another guy. Anthony was a construction-company owner from Ripley, Mississippi and I had a special place in my heart for him and his family, because they were good people and always went out of their way to help me any way they could. I never charged Anthony a penny for the engine work I did for him and out of respect, he was always eager to buy dinner or put gas in our race hauler.

But Fred was getting so he felt like we owed him something.

"Feels like ole Fred is getting the better of us," my dad said.

Then one hot Tuesday afternoon, around the first of August, Anthony, showed up at my race shop. After beating around the bush, he said:

"Terri, uh . . . I don't how to say this because I don't want you to think I'm making trouble. But Fred is bad mouthing you behind your back. You and your dad have been good to him when no one else would give him the time of day. Now, he's talking trash about you every chance he gets. I just felt you should know."

When Anthony got done talking, I felt like taking a blowtorch to ole Fred's race parts laying in the corner of my shop. Instead, I kept my cool and thanked Anthony.

That afternoon, when my dad got home from work, I told him. Dad wanted to drive down to Baldwin right then and kick Fred's tail. However, we decided that we would handle it differently.

Two weeks later we were at a big race at the Baldwin Speedway about 30 miles from Corinth. This was a big fast stock-car track with a hard packed dirt surface – if you crashed here, it could be curtains. I ended up being fastest in qualifying and to my surprise ole Fred was second on the speed charts, so he and I—little sissy Terri as he had called me to his redneck buddies—would be starting side by side for the start of the feature event.

NASCAR or Terri - Drama in a Small Town

Fred was not completely stupid—he knew that I was probably going to beat his ass. So, like politicians do when they need to cover their ass, he swallowed his pride and came to find me at our race hauler.

"Hey, I got these sponsors on the hook," he said. "If I can win tonight they said they would sponsor my car for the next season. You win all the time and it wouldn't be a big deal to you if someone else won tonight. Can you help me out?"

I just stood there with my hair in a ponytail and a bit of lipstick on my lips and smiled back at ole Fred and said, "No problem, man, I would be glad to help you out. Just take off at the drop of the green flag and I will jump in behind you and we will make a cool race out of it for the fans."

"Thanks, Terri," Fred said, and left grinning like a bear.

Ten seconds later, my dad came walking up to see what ole Fred had wanted. I told him.

My dad looked disgusted. "Well, what are you going to do?"

"I'm going to give Fred a driving lesson," I said.

My dad just smiled slyly and took a seat in his lawn chair right outside the ramp to watch the race.

During the feature event, with 26 other high-strung racers, I lapped the field including ole Fred in twenty laps and won the event going away. The fans went wild. Afterwards, in a fit of humiliation and disgust, Fred loaded his racer onto his trailer with his redneck tail between his legs and silently left the track.

Anthony came by my hauler, shook my hand, and grinned, "Old Fred got a lesson in life tonight. You've just been taking it easy on all of us haven't you?"

I just grinned back. Yeah, Fred ole buddy, who's wearing the pants now? You just got your ass beat by a sissy.

As it turned out, though, Fred wasn't the only one in Corinth and around the racing community who was double-dipping me.

Granny goes frail

It was almost Thanksgiving 1993. That Sunday, as usual, our family had the late breakfast after church. We had been doing it for twenty years, if we weren't on the road racing. Mom rushed home from church, fired up the stove and by 1:00 p.m., we gathered around the dining table knocking down some scrambled cheese and eggs, country sausage and homemade biscuits.

Right after breakfast, Granny was impatient to get back to her house next door. That weekend, a cold front had blown in and it was freezing outside. Mom didn't want Granny catching a cold out there, so she told her to wait till she'd finished the dishes and she would take her home in the car. At 82 years young, Granny was slipping a little—a heart condition and diabetes. But she got around pretty good, and she was still a pistol when her patience ran thin.

Around 2:00, while my mom was still cleaning up, Granny slipped out the back door towards her house twenty yards away.

When Mom realized she was gone, she ran out to see if Granny had gotten home okay. To her horror, she found Granny laying out by the road in horrible pain

Mom screamed for my dad to come, and they called an ambulance. Granny was in and out of consciousness and it looked like she might not make it. When they got her to the hospital, the doctors discovered that Granny had broken her hip and her heart was not holding up very well. But by the next day she had stabilized, so they operated and set her hip.

Granny had always been tough as nails. But over the next week it became clear that her recovery was going to be long and hard. Two weeks later, Granny's doctor told my mom that she needed to put Granny in the nursing home right across from the hospital so she could get the proper medical care.

My mom took it hard. She and Granny had been attached at the hip all her life. Now that fateful day had come, that every adult child dreads. Mom toiled over the decision for a week and so did I. I couldn't stand thinking about Granny not being in her home on Confederate Street where she had lived for over 60 years. Her entire life had been put into that house and the church across the street. At the end of that week, Mom relented and allowed Granny's doctor to place her in the nursing home. The woman who had been the bedrock of our family, and my greatest champion, would not be coming back home.

Over the next few months, Mom, Dad and I made daily treks to the nursing home. It was hard seeing Granny in there, small and frail and shrinking by the day. Of course, her other ailments took over, especially her diabetes. When she developed a bedsore on her right calf, we all held our breath. Then the bedsore would not heal and the doctors had to remove her lower right leg. It broke my heart. My vision of Granny had always been this little firecracker of a woman doing damn well whatever she wanted to do—out in her yard keeping the flowers in bloom, or in her vegetable garden harvesting the best tomatoes and butter beans you have ever tasted. Knowing that she would never run up and down the bank trying to hook Old Buster, the biggest catfish in the Tennessee River, tore the heart out of me.

My mom was just as devastated and took Granny's losing her leg very hard. Nevertheless, just like most families in America who struggle through similar circumstances, we hung in there as a family, prayed about it and did the best we could.

Approved for surgery

Nothing in my personal life is ever easy for me. That's why I always hold on to my racing so closely. Racing has been the only thing I could always depend on to get me through the day. Everything else in my life is just crazy and fickle. No matter what I attempt, there is always some sort of a monkey wrench thrown into the wheels and I come crashing to a stop.

The first week of December, when I got the OK from Doctor Battles, to have surgery the first week of December, I was beside myself with relief and joy. Now I had the official documents in my hand that would send me to Colorado for surgery that coming March. All I needed to do was get the money situation taken care of.

One year and nine months earlier Dad and I had made the deal that if I stood the test of time and got the OK from my doctor, we would sell my race cars and use that money for my surgery. That bad-ass little car I had built with my own hands and won over a hundred races in over the past two and half years was worth some real cash. Moreover, I had been building a new up-dated version of that little racer; it was 90% finished, and we were going to put that car up for sale as well, making the pot even sweeter.

Using those two beloved machines to pay for my surgery was a daunting commitment – it would not only be the end of my racing career but the loss of my safe zone as well. . . the place I went to escape life's troubles. But I had to stick to that decision, and I was sure my dad would as well!

So, I gave my dad the good news.

"I need the cash in the next few weeks," I said, "so I can book my surgery date. If you'd loan me the money now, we'll put the car up for sale and once it's sold, I'll pay you right back."

I knew Dad had the cash in the bank – he had just sold his successful tool and die business, so he and my mom were doing just fine economically.

To my complete surprise, Dad reneged on our deal.

Through a haze of shock, I heard his voice telling me that he was surprised the doctor had given me the green light for surgery. He just never thought I would actually go through with the whole deal. He thought I would grow tired of the entire mess and go back to racing sprint cars like all the times before.

"I'm not going to have any part of it," he said.

We had some hard words that I cannot remember. I got in my Mazda Miata and sped off in a tearful rage.

As I drove, my mind was going 200 miles per hour. There I was, half male and half female and living in a shit hole of prejudice and hate in Corinth and now, at that moment I felt as if I had no way of escaping. At that moment, all I could think about was killing myself. I would make damn sure that all my friends and all of my family suffered from knowing that they were responsible, that they were the ones who had killed me. Most of all I wanted my dad to suffer for teasing me with hope, and then ripping the life from me at just the last moment.

For what seemed like hours I just rode around Corinth and along the back roads in the county trying to make sense of the situation I was in. Sometimes I drove like a bat out of hell, sometimes I just crept the car along, cursing my parents and praying to God for help all in one breath.

Driving by the nursing home my granny was in; I prayed that she could hear my cries for help. Passing by my dad's old tool and die business, I spat on the front door cursing every day I had worked there.

Four hours later, I had calmed down enough to go back to my office.

But once I got inside of that racing museum and saw all those trophies and racing photographs along the wall, I lost it again. Grabbing a broom leaning beside the door, I began beating the hell out everything—smashing National trophies in a thousand pieces, raking all the memorabilia off onto the floor. For what seemed like minutes but was actually only seconds, I was going berserk. Then, thankfully, I realized what I was doing and threw the battered broom onto the floor. Weeping like a broken child, I stared at the destruction of that once beautiful room.

For two days, I went through a series of emotional fits and absolute lows, from thoughts of killing myself to thoughts of killing everyone else. To make matters worse I didn't have a soul to talk to. For sure, I was not calling Doctor Battles, for fear he would pull back his letter of recommendation. In fact, if he knew how I was feeling right then, he would probably put me in the insane ward to keep me from hurting myself.

After seeing the craziness and the destruction down in my office, my mom knew that this depression I was in was more dangerous than before. She went to my dad and threatened his life with bodily harm if he didn't give me the money for the surgery.

"We'd rather have a daughter who's alive," she told him, "than a child who's dead. We'd regret it the rest of our lives."

Three days of hell later, Dad relented and gave me the cash. I felt like I was taking blood money. We were all still raw from the struggle and Dad wasn't speaking to me. But I was just as angry at him as he was with me.

Two weeks later, one week before Christmas, I was set for the surgery on March 8, 1994.

That Christmas was not going to be warm and fuzzy. Granny was in serious condition in the nursing home, and Dad, was drinking more and more. I was stressed out, Mom had a lot on her shoulders and I knew she was just about at her wits' end with Dad. We all needed a break!

Usually we spent Christmas Eve at my Aunt Vera's up on Pick Wick Lake about 20 miles up the road. My aunt Vera was my favorite, she had halfway raised me and Christmas at her house had always been magical and some of the fondest memories I had. This year, Mom had decided that first we would do a dinner at the nursing home with Granny and then head on to my aunt's place. However, the atmosphere at the lake, where all my aunts, uncles and cousins, lived was not so friendly to me anymore. They were all pissed off at me, saying that I was embarrassing my parents and hurting my dad's business, that it was my fault that my dad had a drinking problem. Not one of them was concerned for my welfare. So once again I decided not to spend Christmas Eve in that toxic atmosphere.

My dad and I smarted off at each other over my not going to the lake. They'd assumed that I'd be driving them home because of my dad's drinking. The way I saw it, Mom could drive his drunk ass back.

I sniped at Dad saying, "So what, you left me laying in the gutter crying my eyes out when I was in California."

He sniped back, "Well, I'm paying for it now, I probably always will. You and your mom will never let me forget it."

So, I spent Christmas Eve with Granny at the nursing home and on Christmas day, I hightailed it over to my friend Michael's in Memphis where no one would be judging me. I could not help but wonder over those holidays—was this the way it would be from now on?

Here I am with dark hair hanging out with my best friend Kathy and our buddy Ben only one month before my surgery.

The Last Race

Into the first months of 1994, I had my attorney change my last name from Hayes to my granny's last name—O'Connell. I wanted a clean slate and a new surname would give me some well-deserved anonymity. I was now Terri Leigh O'Connell instead of Terri Leigh Hayes. It felt right!

Time was running out on my driving career.

That was something that Doctor Battles and I had talked about over the years. Could I really walk away from my beloved sport? After all, this had been my all-consuming life since I could open my eyes as a baby. Driving a racecar was hard-core macho stuff that gets into your blood and stays there until the day you die. Being a female most likely was not going to fill that void of kicking some bad ass at 150 miles per hour. Everyone has to make choices in life that are not easy. Could my ego take it?

The Saturday before I was to leave for Colorado, there was one last race to run: a midget race in Memphis, the last indoor race of the year. There was a lot to reflect on. I had had a good run—a blue-collar kid from Mississippi with a dream and a point to prove. Well, I had made my point, and now it was time to get on with my life.

Meantime, I needed to take full advantage of this last moment on the track, and take it all in.

On that Saturday morning, I was packed and ready to go to Colorado. All the comforts I'd need for the next few weeks – several new pairs of new pajamas, plenty of magazines for a girl to read, *Cosmo, Glamour,* and *People* magazines . . . and of course some *Road & Track* and *Racer* magazines too! You could say I like gas pedals and glamour too. Meanwhile the truck and trailer was packed with the race cars and all the gear and ready to go. Dad, Dexter and Dewayne were already in the truck and waiting on me to quit fussing with my hair.

Finally I got in the truck and we headed for Memphis—for the most important race of my life.

But, no one knew that but me. Those guys had no idea that the next day I would take a journey of no return, a journey I had dreamed of most every day of my life . . . All they wanted to talk about was how much they hated Bill Clinton and who had won the NASCAR race the week before. Total guy stuff and I hated it. Dewayne was driving, I was riding shotgun, Dexter was sitting right behind Dewayne. Dad was right behind me, still not speaking to me. The silence was only felt by me, because he was shooting the shit with Dexter and Dewayne just like always.

For the entire one-hour drive, I never said a word to any of them and they never said a word to me. It was like being in solitary confinement.

Once we were at the track, I went through my regular routine of unloading the race car, warming the engine up and double-checking everything. The first practice run went off without a hitch and within the hour, I had won my qualifying heat which would let me start the main event on the inside of the front row.

Through all of that, I didn't speak once to Dexter and Dewayne or my dad. Our race hauler was full of racers coming by to grab a bowl of Dexter's homemade chili, which he always cooked up for the late winter indoor races. But I just stayed outside tinkering with my car and reflecting on my life. Several people came by to chat with me but I wasn't really in the mood.

The early March evening air was chilly and by 10:00 p.m., time for the main event, you could clearly see your breath as you exhaled the thick Memphis air filled with exotic exhaust fumes. I caught myself actually shivering from the cold as I rolled my car down from our pit area.

That's when it struck me—the place was packed with competitors and race fans, and I virtually knew every damn one of them from all my years of racing. Seeing all those familiar faces almost took my breath away as I rolled my blue and white racing machine into the arena and gazed through the bright lights and up into the grand stands. These fans had cheered me on and patted me on my back and ask me for my autograph as I stood in victory lane. Racing had kept me alive. Within these arenas and in my racecars I had felt the only peace of my entire life. The moment was surreal because of where I had been and where I was headed. But no one knew that but me.

My focus was intense; I was seeing, hearing and smelling everything in that arena as if all my senses had been super-charged times ten thousand. I was soaking it all up, storing all the sights and smells in my memory bank as if they would have to last me a lifetime. Most likely they would.

Then, the pit steward yelled out, "Get strapped into your cars!"

I tied my long hair into a pony tail and then slowly picked up my red, white and blue carbon-fiber helmet that Bill Vukovich Jr., son of the legendary and late Indy 500 winner Bill Vukovich, had given me back in 1991. His late son Billy Vukovich III had been a friend of mine and I briefly wondered if he could have won the Indy 500 like his granddad if only he had not been killed in that sprint car race out in Baskerville in 1991. Then I pulled on the helmet as I had done thousands of times before.

As I fastened its buckle under my chin, I casually glanced up into the stands and noticed all of my crew standing around chit chatting with one another, including my dad, and none of them were looking my way. Any other time they would all be there with me helping me to get strapped in… but not tonight. They had ignored me all night and it struck me as being incredibly arrogant on their part but I didn't have time to worry about a bunch of ass holes who did not approve of my life choices.

Once I was strapped into the car, I inspected the steering wheel and dash to make sure everything was okay, and a reel of daunting memories came rushing through my mind. I had built every single part on this car with tender loving care and creative ingenuity. Hundreds of hours had made this racer a winner, a hundred times over. I was re-running every race I had taken in that cockpit. All of the wins, and even the crashes were right there playing like a movie in my helmet visor and scarred into the paint and body work there in front of me. It was almost like having an out of body experience.

Suddenly a slap on the top of my helmet snapped me back to the moment. It was an old friend, Sonny Ray, from my sprint car days in West Memphis. He gave me a big thumbs up.

Then the push car came up behind me for the warm up laps. It was time to go, one last time.

When the flagman dropped the green flag I stood on the gas like never before. I ran every lap at full speed… and even drove several laps one handed as if to show off to the fans, my enemies and to my dad that I was the best they had ever seen. I had vengeance in my heart as I drove that race, I was obsessed, racing like a mad woman, because I needed to get it out of my system once and for all. I didn't want it to end.

Then, in the blink of an eye, the flagman threw the checkered flag and it was over. I had won by a full lap.

Just for good measure, I took one more hard-ass lap. The stands stood up on their feet and cheered like crazy. I had dazzled them and I had even dazzled myself . . . what a frikin' deal.

Then it was all over. I exited the arena and drove straight up to our race hauler, got out of the car, walked over behind the hauler and fell to my knees and began to weep. The emotion of my entire life was rushing through my eyes, cleansing my soul with every tear.

A few minutes later, the crew was methodically loading everything into the hauler. None of them said a word to me, not good job, not that was amazing, not anything. While they worked, I sat in a lawn chair and gazed back down the hill to the arena, which was dark by then. All the fans were on their way back to their warm homes. It was cold as hell and I was wanting the guys to finish loading so we could get the hell out of there.

Suddenly a profound and sad thought ran through my head that almost made me dizzy. *Was that it?* Was this the end of a career that had taken me from a go-kart track in Tupelo, Mississippi to a NASCAR Winston Cup Race in Rockingham, North Carolina? I had won 500 races. I had competed against the best in America, including Richard Petty, Darrell Waltrip and Dale Earnhart. I knew some cool people, and got to do things that some people only dream of doing. It had damn near killed me more than once and I had the aches, pains and scars to prove it. But now, here I sat in Memphis, Tennessee with a bunch of guys who didn't really like me and I was leaving in the morning to have gender realignment surgery, and I had just run my last race . . . but no one there knew that but my dad, and me.

The moment left me with an ache of what could have been if I had continued on with my NASCAR aspirations. But, thinking like that was not productive. I was moving on to the next leg of my earth journey with excitement and hope for the future. If the next leg was anything like the first one, it was going to be one hell of a ride. I just hoped I could find the strength and the courage to survive it.

The trip back home flew by. As usual, I had taken the wheel of the truck and race hauler, while Dad and the other guys passed out from drinking too much beer. I just cranked up the radio to an all-night talk station based there in Memphis, and hauled our butts down highway 72 to Corinth. The windshield was like a movie screen with the bio pic of my life playing there before me. I remember thinking, those Hollywood types would have a field day with my story.

Once we got home at 1:30 a.m., the other guys left for their homes. Dad staggered into the house without speaking. Alone I pulled the huge back door of the hauler down, and unloaded my racer. We would be selling that little jewel and I owed her some tender loving care. When I was done cleaning her up, I felt the incredible urge to sit back down inside that kick- ass car. One last feel of the steering wheel, one last look over the hood.

The questions came whizzing at me one last time. Do you really want to give all this up? Can you actually make it on your own as a female? Can you actually walk away from your family?

Finally I casually lifted myself out of the racer's cockpit, wiped the arena dust off the seat, then turned, and walked away. I closed the race shop door and went into the house without looking back. I had to reach into my soul and find my courage. My courage, Terri's courage . . . not JT's courage. I was absolutely sure with my decision. There was no other choice for me.

The next morning at 8 a.m. Mom was getting ready to head to the nursing home to check on granny, then go to church. Dad was dead asleep on the couch—he hadn't made it to bed. For 45 minutes I made ten trips past the couch getting my stuff loaded up. I had said my good byes to Granny the day before. All that time, my mom never spoke or looked at me and my dad never moved a muscle. The silent treatment was starting to piss me off . . . but it was no time for a fight.

Finally I grabbed the last travel bag. Just as I opened the back door, I quietly said, "Mom, I'm leaving, I'll call you when I get there."

She never said goodbye…be careful…or I love you. She just stood there washing the dishes and looking down.

I wasn't surprised by this. My heart broke for their lost dreams, the fact that they would never have a grandchild and didn't know how they were going to explain this to the neighbors. My mom was suffering over my grandmothers failing health. She had to be feeling as if she was losing the two most precious people in her life. In the end though, mom had not done her homework concerning my gender issue, so she had no educated perspective on how to make this easier for her and my dad.

But this time I wasn't falling for the emotional blackmail.

So I got into my silver Miata, and headed for Colorado.

CHAPTER 18

Feminine Snapshots – Get on With It

When I got to Memphis, I spotted a Star Bucks just a few blocks from interstate 40 so I whipped in to the parking lot to grab myself a Grande to go. After I got my coffee, I walked outside and took a seat on the curb just to collect my thoughts before I hit the interstate. The irony in that was I was only three minutes from the arena I had race in only a few hours earlier. I could almost smell the burnt racing fuel still filtering into the air as I sat there sipping on my coffee. Just as I got ready to ease on over to my car and hit the road, a nice middle aged salt and peppered man came strolling up and I caught him checking me out. He smiled very gentlemanly, almost sexually, opened the door and went inside the coffee shop. I loved it; he was flirting with me, that was a very good sign. As I made my way to my car I casually glanced back to see if he was checking me out and, he was. Confidently, I got into my car, buckled my seat belt, fired that bay up, dropped the clutch and did a burn out as I left the parking lot. I had to wonder as I hit ole interstate 40 what all of those people back at the Star Bucks thought when this skinny ass chick, looking an awful lot like Marlo Thomas took off out of there like a bat out hell. It was priceless.

During that drive to Colorado, I often felt very lonely. Memory after memory came shooting at me, like the white lines in the middle of the highway. I had driven at racetracks all along this old and bumpy interstate highway – Memphis, Little Rock, Oklahoma City. Sometime I just couldn't turn the memory machine off and the tears ran down my cheeks from all the emotion. Those were all good times and I enjoyed reliving those moments but that was the past, and it was time to move on.

So I just reached over and cranked up my radio and kept on driving down I-40. I had to get to Trinidad that night, and the clock was ticking.

At one in the morning, the lights of Trinidad loomed ahead of me. Checking into my motel, I climbed right into bed for some needed sleep. Suddenly I was bone-tired from the trip, and from the months leading up to it. My eyes fell shut in an instant.

The next morning, at 10 a.m., I met my surgeon face to face for the first time.

Dr. Bieber looked after all the fine citizens there in that small Southern Colorado town. His office, on the second floor over one of the banks, was classic vintage, as was he – a bit worn and not so very fancy. I was intrigued by his rugged sandy-haired looks, his cowboy boots, his stocky build and air of confidence. He wore his elitist Johns Hopkins fraternity emblem on his sleeve, yet he had that down-home feel about him that only good ole country folk in the rural USA. His second job was his cattle ranch, and pictures of its good cow herd and beautiful landscape were hanging along his office wall.

Best of all, Dr. Bieber was a gentle man, and he really made me feel as if he had my best interest not only in his hands but in his heart as well. He knew that I was feeling lonely and emotional, not to mention nervous about what was ahead. He and his nurses there at the San Rafel Hospital, just about mile outside of town made damn sure they made me feel at home, and thank God they did cause I needed it.

"You look good," he said, smiling.

"Thanks," I managed.

"I'm actually amazed at how feminine you look. I had these snapshots you sent…" He opened my file and pointed at them. "…But I didn't quite believe them. Sometimes the girls photoshop their photos to look more feminine than they really are. And I do understand why they do that. But we have to deal with the reality when they get here."

Dr. Bieber took a few Polaroids of me to add to his file. Then he gave me a big hug and sent me on my way.

"Remember," he said. "Check into the hospital tomorrow by 3 p.m."

I had a day and a half to kill, so I took off to the mountains for some sightseeing. But it was hard to keep my mind on all that awesome natural beauty.

The Day of Days

It was Tuesday, March 7th – the day I'd lived for through so many dark years. At 1:30 p.m., feeling a little nervous but not enough for a panic attack, I packed my suitcase and headed over to the San Rafael Hospital, just a mile and a half from my motel. Parking quickly, I headed inside to the administrative office to register.

A few locals were in line ahead of me, so I just signed in and took a seat in the crowded waiting area. A good-looking guy in his mid thirties with a cast on his right leg made me a bit more room, so I smiled back and took a seat near him. He and I chitchatted for a few minutes and then the head nurse called his name, so he went on back to take care of his business.

About ten minutes later the same head nurse stepped into the waiting area.

"Terri O'Connell," she called. "Come with me to sign all your papers."

I stood up, gathered my backpack and headed back to the offices. The nurse had a confused look on her face. She was double checking her file and once I was standing right in front of her, she took a few steps past me and called my name out again in the waiting area.

Almost embarrassed, I tapped her on the shoulder.

"I'm Terri O'Connell," I said.

The look on her face was priceless. I thought she was going to faint from the shock. Then she smiled and said, "You've got to be kidding . . . Oh my God, I thought you were with that guy with the broken leg. . . I thought you were his girlfriend or his wife. I mean, I see girls going through this every week, and I have to tell you, you're the very first one that I did not know was here to have the surgery. Count your blessings girl, you're very fortunate."

I was shocked, to say the least, and also flattered.

"Yes, I know I'm very lucky to look like I do," I said, "but it's also been hard looking like this and having to live as a boy. It didn't play well in my part of the world."

Still looking me over in amazement, the nurse said, "I can't imagine what you had to put up with. People can be so hurtful over nothing. Didn't your parents have a clue that you were physically different than the other boys?" Without waiting for me to answer that question, she rushed on. "Well, we can't worry about the past, can we? You're here now and this will fix everything. We're glad to have you, sweetie."

Less than an hour later, I had all the admittance papers filled out and was in my room unpacking my suit case and getting acquainted with my roommate Sarah, a New York girl in her mid thirties who had had her surgery only three days before.

A few minutes later, a middle-aged guy in a white lab coat stuck his head in the door to check on Sarah. He introduced himself as Dr. Carr, the in house anesthesiologist. After chatting for a few seconds, he went on his way. I didn't give him a second thought, but ten minutes later he was back, standing in the doorway with a portable swing that you sat in so they could weigh you. He had a set of files in his hand and a confounded look on his face, as if he was in the wrong room or something. Then he left again.

I looked at Sarah lying there in her bed and we both laughed at the comical moment with Dr. Carr. Then, about 30 seconds later, he reappeared.

"Have you seen the other pre-op who is supposed to be in this room?" he asked.

"Who are you looking for?" I asked.

He double checked his chart and replied, "Uh . . . I'm looking for Terri O'Connell. I need to get her weight and check her blood pressure."

Oh no, I thought to myself, not twice within an hour in the same hospital. With a grin on my face, I raised my hand as if I was in high school and sheepishly said, "Terri O'Connell, that would be me and if you need proof, I do have my driver's license in my backpack. You have found your weigh in victim."

The look on his face was more priceless than the nurse's an hour before. After howling with laughter for a minute, he got his composure and said, "I'm around the gender identity issue every day and I always can tell that the patient is part of the gender community. But not this time. I'm impressed. You're going to be able to mix in to society without a trace of you past." Then he paused and frowned. "Are you sure you're Terri. Is Dr. Bieber playing a trick on me just to test me? He would do that, you know."

Once I had assured him that I was definitely Terri, he had me take off my shoes and sit in his swing. That would be all 117 pounds of me. He recorded my weight and blood pressure, and told me that he would see me at 7:00 tomorrow morning. He gave me a quick pat on the back and left the room, still shaking his head in disbelief.

Soon I was into my brand new PJ's bought at the Corinth Wal-Mart and climbing into my bed, which was positioned by the window. In the distance the entire town of Trinidad was appeared out of no were. This would be my home for the next two weeks. The view was beautiful, but I still missed my folks . . . this was a hell of a situation to be going through all alone.

A Vase of Flowers

The next day the Bieber team had me up bright and early, prepped and ready for surgery. They wheeled me into the OR where each person in the team came by to give me a hug and to assure me that they would be taking very good care of me. I said a quiet prayer for God to look after me and to take me into the next stage of my life with love and compassion.

Then my anesthesiologist plugged the sleep potion into my veins. Within 30 seconds I was out like a light.

Fortunately, after four hours of intense and intricate work, the surgery went through without a hitch. I spent the rest of that day and the next full day sleeping like a baby.

When I awoke, I was groggy and a bit unsure about where I was. Finally, when my senses cleared, I noticed a greeting card laying on my bed right beside my hand. It said "For Terri!" A big vase of flowers was on my food stand with a note "Get Well Soon, Girl." I was still so sleepy that it didn't sink in at first. Finally I fumblingly opened up the greeting and realized that the flowers and card were from Lake and Rice' Speed.

Then, like a moment out of the twilight zone, my phone rang. Lo and behold, it was Lake and Rice' calling. They were in Atlanta where Lake was competing in the Atlanta 500. It had been snowing down there and they were holed up in their hotel room.

"Are you all right?" they wanted to know. "Are you in good spirits?"

"I am absolutely okay," I assured them.

I needed that call. Their hearts were good and I appreciated their love and their interest in my soul. We talked for a few minutes, till I got tired.

"We'll check back in a few days," they said. "Stay strong."

Most of the next day, I slept.

But on Friday, two days after my surgery, I woke up bright-eyed and bushy-tailed, ready to take on the world …and crazy to see my newfound body. But I was flat on my back and the nurses had orders to keep me there for the next five days. So all I could do was lift my head up just a wee bit to look toward my feet. I couldn't see a damn thing. That was good. But I knew my lifelong dreams had come to be, and had a peace in my heart much like I had when I had first become a Christian almost twenty years before. The feeling is hard to explain, but I just knew that everything now fit together the way it should. I now had a physical body that fit my spirit in every detail. It was just that simple, I was very, very happy.

But one thing was missing: my folks were not there. It was a little bit of a hollow victory—having my heartfelt dreams come true but not having the most important people in my life there to share it with me. That was how most of my life had been—the most important accomplishments had always come at an emotional cost.

In fact I never heard a word from my mom until that Saturday, four days after my surgery. Her indifference hurt my feelings, especially considering that she knew my body's poor track record on asthma attacks and reactions to anesthesia. Mom might have been calling every hour to check on me. But when she did call, she was brusque and impersonal, and left me wondering why she even called at all.

In hindsight, I realize Mom was going through a grieving process of her own over losing her only son. So I had to give her a break.

The next ten days passed in that hospital bed, healing my body and bonding with my nurses who were absolute angels.

These ladies looked after me like nobody's business. With hospital food being what it is, those girls realized that I needed to eat something tasty, so they scammed me some tasty cheeseburgers every night. They were always coming in to chitchat and making sure I had anything I needed. They knew I was there all alone and wanted me to feel that they were my family. Thank God for that.

When I was finally able to get out of bed and see my new-found womanhood, you might think that I wanted to run through the hospital shouting to the top of my lungs, "Look what I have! Please, everyone, look at what I have! Isn't this the coolest thing you've ever seen!" But it didn't happen that way at all. It isn't in my nature to react like that. So when I was finally able to take a peek at my new girl-ness, it seemed as if I had been born that way – that this was exactly what I was supposed to look like. I took it in stride and never got into dramatizing how damn extraordinary this little episode in my life this really was.

It did occur to me that the tabloids would have a field day with this if they ever found out.

The two weeks in Trinidad flew by, and finally it was time for the next journey in my life. Who knew where it would lead me? It was time to go back home and live my life as Terri O'Connell, a 5'6", 117-lb. 34/24/34 female, and never look back – never wishing I could have experienced my most heartfelt dreams and desires as a race-car driver. This was my chosen destiny and I intended to live it to the fullest extent. It would not be a cakewalk, but I would never have to question my gender again. My feminine spirit was complete.

So I packed up my Miata and said my goodbyes to Dr. Bieber and all the wonderful nurses there at the San Rafael Hospital.

Then I got into my little car. Instead of dropping the clutch and spinning out of the parking lot, the way JT always did, I gently eased her into gear and slowly cruised onto the interstate.

Worried about Granny

Back in Corinth for a few days, I was taking it easy, still needing to heal from my surgery. Sad to say, my mom and dad were not accepting this fact with open arms. In fact I was afraid that my dad was going to hurt me. So I was staying out of his way.

Lake and Rice' were urging me to move back up to Charlotte and re-start my life there with their help. I could have moved to Memphis but didn't think it was far enough away to escape the prejudices of Corinth. It was time to get my job life together, and I was wasting time by hanging out in Corinth! I did not want to move where I'd end up alone—I knew my weakness – my need for mature compassionate people in my life. But I did hesitate – till one day, about five weeks after the surgery, heaven sent me a clear message.

That morning I had gotten up early to visit Granny at the nursing home. On the way back home, I stopped at a convenience store to get gas and grab a quick cup of coffee. That's when I ran into Gary, a local bookie and gambler, also an old friend I used to socialize with, around nine years back. I had not seen him in a few years and he actually didn't recognize me till the cashier called me by my name. Gary had heard all the rumors about my change, and now he actually spoke some words of support and friendship.

"You really look good!" he said warmly.

Gary's reaction was a little hard to believe. Some of the guys he did business with had been some of my worst critics. It wouldn't take long before he would be on their bandwagon of Terri-bashing.

However, just two days later, the phone began to ring . . . I almost didn't answer the damn thing but I finally relented and picked up the receiver. To my amazement, it was Gary.

"Terri, is that you? Hey, girl, it's Gary. Uh, what are you up to right at this moment? I've got a fresh pot of coffee on and I would love to have you come over and share a cup and fill me in on what's been going with you. I consider you to be a good friend and, uh, I'm just fascinated by your life."

At first I was taken aback by his enthusiasm. He and I had not had any contact since back in 1985. My first thought was – he had some sort of fetish and was giving me the PR treatment. Then I thought, what the hell, it's just ole Gary, so what's the big deal?

"I'd love to have a coffee with you," I said. "But I can only stay an hour – I've got some errands to run for my grand-mother."

He gave quick directions to his house and I was on my way.

When I got there, he was the perfect gentleman. He gave me a hug and quickly got me a cup of java. We took a seat on his couch and began to catch up on the last nine years. Every-thing was going along like any normal conversation between two old friends . . . How's your family, how's the business, etcetera, etcetera.

Then, out of nowhere, he looked me dead in the eye, took my hand and ask me to go to bed with him!

I could not believe my ears and asked him in a surprised tone if he was serious.

"Yeah, baby, I am serious," he said. "I think you're the cutest thing I've seen in a while and this whole sex change thing gets me all hot and bothered. I don't want you to think I'm being disrespectful, but you really turn me on."

At this, I slid away from him and looked right back in his eyes.

"I'm flattered you think I'm hot," I said. "But you have obviously misunderstood something. I didn't go through all this just so I could have sex . . . There is more to this than sex. Plus I don't sleep around just for the hell of it, no matter what anyone in this hellhole of a town says. Never have and never will."

Boiling inside, I got up off the couch, put my coffee cup on the counter and walked out of the house. He didn't get a chance to say one more word. I just jumped in my car, and got the hell out of there.

What an idiot! I thought. I'd just had surgery four weeks earlier and couldn't have sex yet if I wanted to!

Then, as I drove back to my house, another thought hit me. Gary wouldn't be the only one in Corinth who thought that all people in my situation went through the bullshit so we could have sex with men. I felt sickened—Gary had violated my dignity as a human being. I had endured too damn much to have to put up with that kind of attitude. So what in the hell was I doing hanging around Corinth? The town could be as dangerous for me now as it ever was in the past. The surgery was behind me now, and was able to blend into society anywhere I went.

My thoughts raced on to Dad, who was drinking more than ever. These days he slouched around the house churning with alcoholic rage and couldn't even look at me. It gave me cold chill bumps down the middle of my back. That favorite old pistol of his was handy somewhere in the house – would he lose control, and grab it and take a pot shot at me?

My mom was treating me much better than my dad was, but she was patronizing at every turn.

My mind was made up. When I got home, I called Rice'.

"Can I come up for a few days?" I asked her. "Clear my head…possibly find a place to live?"

"Pack your bags and get on up here," she said.

It did not take me twenty minutes to load my car with the essentials. I wrote my mom a quick note about where I had gone and when I might be back, left it on the kitchen table, then drove out to the nursing home where my granny was living to see her for a few minutes. Granny had accepted the new me, and we had a moment of deep and loving warmth. But there was a deep sense of finality that I would never see her again and it ripped my heart to shreds as I left.

Then I hit the road for Charlotte. It was 10:00 a.m.—if I only stopped to get gas and hit the ladies' room, I would be in Charlotte by 9:00 that night. Even sooner if I fudged on the speed limit!

If I could find any possible glimpse of opportunity for housing and employment there, Charlotte would be my new home. Three things were going for me there. I had Lake and Rice's love and support. I had a warm, friendly and industrious personality and…I had total and complete anonymity.

Behind me, the roofs and treetops of my home town faded in the rear-view mirror, that silhouette of Corinth – the land that time forgot.

To have a chance, you take a chance

Lake and Rice' were eager to help me get my life in order.

With their support, I found a cool apartment in a beautiful old colonial home surrounded by towering old oaks, right in the heart of Charlotte's historical district. Lake and Rice' felt that Charlotte would be a good place to get back on track— they could keep a parental eye on me which I clearly needed. They knew the seriousness of this transition, the need for ano-nymity, the frailty of my heart and my physical being.

After putting down a deposit on the rent, I took a deep breath and rushed back to Corinth to get the rest of my stuff.

After a bit of coaxing, a home-town friend, John, agreed to help me haul my possessions up to Charlotte. He was a six-foot, 180-lb sandy- haired country boy and a kamikaze race-car driver who wrecked more times than he finished. John's day job and claim to fame was that he was the bus driver for the country music super-group "Brooks and Dun." He had just pulled an all-nighter by driving their tour bus five hours into Nashville from Talladega where they had been the guest of their good buddy Dale Earnhardt during the Talladega 500. Then he drove four hours back to Corinth without sleeping

Now he said he'd drive my parent's van pulling a U-haul trailer filled with my bedroom suite, many of my racing trophies that had had survived my destructive meltdown with the broom handle that day... and as much of the rest of my life I could cram into that 12-foot trailer.

So John drove twelve more hours up to Charlotte . . . while I tagged behind in my 1994 silver Miata.

There was no way I could have moved my stuff without his help, yet he was not altogether friendly to me – which surprised me, because all through my two years of transition, he had been extremely supportive and looked after me when most other men had treated me with disrespect . His two small boys, Brandon and Dustin, loved me like crazy and I had given them some of my trophies as souvenirs. Plus I had helped him make his race car run fast when no one else would. We had all felt like family.

But it appeared that the finality of my surgery had affected John in much the same way it had affected my dad. He tolerated me long enough to help me move but at times, to my amazement, he didn't even speak to me.

In the end, John was a macho good ole boy from Mississippi, not the philanthropic free thinker I wanted him to be.

In fact, when we drove past Lake's race shop on the way to my apartment, John said casually, "That's where you need to be working. Hell, you could end up being Lake's crew chief if you want to."

His words shocked me. Clearly he didn't get it that I was a girl now—that I was starting my life over. Just like most people in my home town, he would never see me as a girl, even though everyone outside of Corinth only saw me as a woman. Oh well, beggars can't be choosers!

John and I hurriedly unloaded the van and the U-Haul trailer with him actually doing the heavy lifting because of my surgery. He set up my bed in the only bedroom, and piled everything else in the middle of the den floor.

Then, in a flash, he was on his way back to Corinth.

It was Monday morning, the last week of April 1994, with spring blooming in the Carolinas and the surgery six weeks behind me. It seemed as if I was back in the spring of my time on this planet. But there was no time to enjoy the flowers and freshness. I had to attack the future now, just like I had attacked the racing competition. But it scared me beyond words.

Start your engines, girl! Get your skinny ass out of bed and find a job!

The disorganized pile of stuff in the den confronted me. I didn't have a lot of stuff, but it was lost in a maze of boxes and duct tape. I had packed things in a rage of anger and fear—just slammed them anywhere they would fit. So I didn't have a clue where anything was packed. But at least I had a roof over my head.

That morning, as I wrestled with the boxes, I was asking myself, "Now what?"

For sure my guardian angels had always looked after me and now they would have to work overtime for me to survive this next little adventure. I was willing to bet that God had them strap on their crash helmets this time!

I'd been a professional race-car driver virtually every day of my life. And now, after paying my rent, utilities and telephone hook-up, I had the grand total of $236.85 left in my bank account . . . and no job. My body was still fragile from the surgery and I had to be careful not to injure myself with too much physical activity. But the rent would roll around again in thirty days and there would be no help from my family.

I had many talents to draw from when I was a male—engineer, tool maker, welder, professional driver. There was always an opportunity for JT Hayes to find work no matter where he was. But Terri O'Connell, the 5'6", 117 pound strawberry-blonde girl, was unemployed, with a blank page for a resume. What was she going to put on her job application for past job experiences?

"Well, Miss O'Connell, let's see…it says here that you are a former National Champion race car driver . . . and a NASCAR Winston Cup driver too, and a first-class machinist too. And . . . you're applying for a position in our cosmetics department?"

"Umm . . . yes, Mr. Human Resources Supervisor, sir, that's right. And I—believe that my past experience fully qualifies me to sell your best cosmetics."

I had to have a plan, a really good plan. In reality, there was a lot more going for me than I first realized. I looked pretty damn good or so I had been told. My personality was perky and friendly. I could sell Godzilla as a petite pigmy instead of a huge gorilla. And I had solid retail experience from my high-school and college days. Plus I possessed a God-given talent for art, especially motorsports art . . . after all, I was living in NASCAR country.

However, I would have to be careful about hanging out in the racing community. Too many people knew me there, and

I didn't want to lose my new-found and precious anonymity. There had to be something here in Charlotte that Terri O' could do. I just had to build up my confidence, get the local newspaper, and read the want ads. Who's hiring?

I spent the next few days going to all the local department stores—Dillard's, JC Penny's, Belk's, etc.—filling out job applications.

The personal shock of how hard it would be was deeper than I thought. There I was, a woman who as a former male racing star had signed autographs for admiring fans, who was viewed as a hero by grown men, and now I was filling out applications for jobs that paid $8.00 an hour.

Worse, none of the stores were calling me back. Doubt and terror was running through my head at 200 miles per hour. Did I look okay? Was I feminine enough? Did I have my bases covered well enough with personal references, just in case the stores did check me out? Lake and Rice' had allowed me to use them as local references. So had Mrs. Hammond, a wonderful lady who owned the upscale clothing store I had worked at during my college days – she was in on my little secret. I knew they would give me an "A" plus rating if any one called to check up on me. I was banking on it. Plus, officially I *was* Terri Leigh O'Connell, and all my legal affairs were in order so that would not be a problem.

But why weren't they calling me back? Didn't they know I was desperate here? What in the heck would I do if no one called me back? Beg? Wind up homeless?

Then, on Tuesday at 4:00 p.m., as I was scurrying around trying to organize my apartment, just 24 hours after I filled out my 15th job application, the phone rang . . . with the shrill of a five-alarm fire bell. It was my very first phone call at the apartment, and it scared the holy bo Jesus out of me. It had to be either Lake and Rice' or some department store, because no one else had my phone number!

I raced across the bedroom as if it was the last lap of a 500 mile race and Dale Earnhardt was right on my tail. Just as I grabbed the receiver and said hello, I stumbled over a stack of fashion magazines and fell flat on my back with a crash, almost ripping out my surgery. But I was a veteran of crashes, so I managed to hold onto the phone as I hit the floor, and caught my breath in an instant.

"Yes?" I gasped.

"Miss O'Connell, this is Mrs. Thomas at Dillard's department store. I wanted to let you know that we would like to hire you. Could you begin your training program at 10:00 AM tomorrow?"

"Yes, of course," I croaked.

The simple things are the most important and have the most meaning. That phone call was one of those simple things—a blessing from God and I knew to be thankful.

After Mrs. Thomas hung up, I just lay there unable to move, with the tears welling, suddenly overwhelmed by the sum total of all the dangerous curves I had handled throughout my life, both on the race track and away from it. The past two years, not to mention the last twenty years, had been a wind tunnel of unbelievable circumstances and obstacles. I had walked away from a million-dollar racing career, endured the most outrageous rumors and prejudice throughout the racing community, and now here I lay, alone and crying like a baby, thankful and humbled for actually surviving the whole damn mess.

Then, like a scene out of a Hitchcock movie, a rush of reality ran through my soul as I stared upwards at that old ceiling fan slowly going around and around. It was as if I was seeing the turning wheels of my life slowly coming to a halt . . . wheels that once sped through life undaunted and driven to win the race, to compete in order to survive. The next turns in my life would not be a fifty-lap sprint car race out in Chico, California. I was now in the grimmest race of all, the race of mere economic survival. Did I really have it in my heart to meet this life test? That $8.00-an-hour job was pennies compared my former $100,000.00 a year income but at least it would provide food, shelter and transportation . . . and self-esteem ! This was as important as winning my National Championship. I finally had a complete life where body and soul had finally found one another and no amount of money or racing wins could buy that.

Meanwhile $8.00 an hour would be just fine, thank you very much . . . at least for now.

My guardian angels were looking after me, with their crash helmets strapped on.

CHAPTER 19

Get to Charlotte –
Birth of a Businesswoman

Hello Congress

Shortly before my birth day in July, I got the shock of my life. My mother called and said she was flying in to spend a few day with me. Her birth day along with grannies and mine were on a few days apart so I just figured she wanted to be together on or birth days. On the way back to my apartment after I had picked her up at the airport, she just casually told me that Granny had died over a month ago.

"I didn't want to upset you," she told me. "I knew how fragile you were."

Right on the heels of shock, outrage boiled up in me. I tried to not rage out at her and I did hold my temper pretty darn well. But I got my two cents in.

"That's a load of small town crap," I said. "You and Dad just didn't want me at the funeral. You didn't want me embarrassing the family. That's all right, I get it, but that was real damn disrespectful." We made it through the weekend without killing one another, in fact even after the shocking news about granny, I was glad to see my mom. I had missed her.

Losing my granny hurt like crazy and I worked on forgiving them every day for keeping that news from me... and for everything else they had put me through. The thought occurred to me, that I was having to learn how to forgive people for thinking they had to forgive me. That ain't easy! They were clearly feeling guilty over what they did, and I had lost some respect for them – they were still treating me like I was 10 years old. I mean, it's easy for parents to lie to a 10 year old about a death in the family.

I had started keeping a diary, and wrote in August 1994:

"I'm not sleeping with all the lights on any more . . . I'm down to just sleeping with the bathroom light on to keep me safe, but it has been a test of my will to live like never before. I miss my parents like crazy but I would not call them at this point for one million dollars. I'm putting myself on a time table. If I don't have my act together by Christmas, I'm killing myself . . . there just seems to be no other way to get rid of the pain."

The old emotional pain was back, but it had nothing to do regretting having my surgery. I would never go back to being a boy. Now the pain was all about the relationship with my family. But killing myself was a bad and long-term solution to a short-term problem.

Fortunately, about that time, I found a new group of Charlotte friends to hang with, and was able to start putting the death of my grandmother in perspective. A couple of cute guys from Lake Speed's race team were chasing me around. I had yet to be late to work which is a huge accomplishment. Last but not least, I'd gotten quite good at stretching that $8.00 an hour – but I'd been thinking about doing better for myself...about getting back in the racing game. I missed the thrill, the pageantry and especially the competition. But these days, "competition" would have to mean my artistic talents, not my driving talents.

A cool idea was bouncing around in my head on how to create a Gap-apparel approach in NASCAR. In my spare time, I was doing sketches, and now had 10 or 12 different designs for a concept that would fit nicely into the motorsports marketing arena. Of course, I'd been bending my best friend Rice's ear every chance I got on how this idea might work and she was just as sure as I was that it could be successful. The only thing missing was how to finance the concept.

No matter how I cut it, on the track or off it, it always came down to money.

By the end of August I was worn out from the daily grind at Dillard's. My still-fragile ankle, as well as my hip and my neck, were about to kill me from being on my feet all day long, Plus the daily 25- mile commute had become something I dreaded. Once again, the time to make a change had arrived. So Rice' and I got busy trying to find financing.

Self-esteem boost

When I got to Charlotte, my self esteem had been in the pits. Then one Saturday afternoon as I tried to sell a handbag or two at Dillard's my confidence got a real boost. It was a busy day there at the store and I was making a few good sales and thinking about taking a mid-afternoon break. when I noticed my friend Marcia Parsons and her husband Phil coming down the escalator. They were good friends with Lake and Rice, and Phil was a current star on the NASCAR Cup circuit. They were among the handful of trusted local people who knew my life story. Marcia had been very supportive of my life-changing decision.

They made their way on over to speak to me.

Marcia grabbed my hand, looked me right in my eye and said, "Terri, you're one of the best looking girls in this entire mall and you're only getting better with every day. Don't let anyone tell you any different, just hang in there and your life will work out for you."

I almost burst into tears. The timing could not have been better.

On Saturday morning a week before Labor Day, I was over at Lake and Rice's eating breakfast. Lake was in Darlington preparing for the Transouth 500, which he had actually won several years earlier. The kids were outside in the yard playing, and Rice' and I were drinking coffee and brainstorming on my apparel idea.

We were getting pretty worked up about how we could capture the female audience if only we could find someone who would finance this adventure. We knew it had to be just the right person. Not everyone up there in those male dominated marketing groups was going to get it. At that time, the NASCAR attitude towards women was, let's say, less than respectful when it came to having ideas and impacting the sport. But I knew from my own personal experiences and vision that the women's movement in motorsports was gaining momentum.

Rice' had just began to put the dishes from breakfast in the dish washer, which was a regular occurrence around the Speed household, when I could tell from the expression on her face that she just had a major idea explode in her brain.

She looked over at me with her eyes bugged out of her head and said with a sense of excitement and confidence:

"I've got the perfect person to finance this… if he will do it. He's busy with politics but he has the money and the connections in the apparel community. In fact, you've met him. He's Lake's best friend, Robin Hayes. He is part of the Cannon mills family. You know, Cannon towels, the ones in all the department stores around the world!"

Yes indeed, I did know Robin Hayes. I'd had the pleasure of meeting him and several of Lake's big-time money buddies on two occasions, once in 1991 when I was J.T. hanging out in Lake's pit stall during the Coca-Cola 600, and once more three years later as Terri. This was just a few months ago in April, right after my surgery. He and his daughter Winslow had traveled over to Wilksborough, North Carolina with Lake, Rice' and myself to watch Lake race in NASCAR's Holly Farms 500. Robin hadn't recognized me in the least.

A right-wing Republican, Robin was a state representative in North Carolina, and had aspirations to be governor or even U. S. Senator. Clearly, he was capable of financing the apparel adventure—but would he have the time to focus on something like this?

Rice' makes the call

First thing Monday morning, Rice' called Robin before he left his house to go down to his hosiery mill and office ten miles away in Mount Pleasant. She made a passionate sales pitch on my idea.

At around 9:20 that morning, just as I was ready to head off to work, my phone rang. I was running a little late so I almost decided not to answer but then, I had a feeling it might be Rice' so I dropped my purse, rushed into the den, and grabbed the call.

"Hello, Terri... look, I won't keep you long but I have good news, Robin is interested in hearing what you have to say!"

"Really . . . wow, you're not kidding me are you".

"No, he wants to see you tomorrow morning at 10:00. Come by after work and we will go over everything he said."

I couldn't believe what I was hearing...and raced off to work so I wouldn't be late.

At Dillard's, I schmoozed the floor manager Robert about changing my work schedule so I could make it to the meeting with Robin the next morning. Robert hated changing schedules. But I had never asked for much, and I had never been late. Plus I offered to work that coming Sunday. Robert knew I had him!

That afternoon, when I got off of work, I made a beeline over to Lake and Rice's house to talk over details. Among other things, I wanted to discuss how to handle my past with Robin. This man was their friend and someone I was going to ask to be my business partner. I didn't want it to come up later . . . especially if the media found out, this could hurt Robin's political career. But Lake and Rice' agreed with me that what lay in the past needed to stay there.

The ten-minute trip to the Mt. Pleasant Hosiery Mill and Robin's office took me into the rolling hills of the North Carolina countryside, past beautiful tall oaks and stately houses with flower gardens and people mowing their yards. The region reminded me of the rural roads within a mile or two of my mom and dad's house, making me feel like this was where I was supposed to be. Just past the Mt. Pleasant city limits I passed a local diner, What-A-Burger, whose parking lot was jam-packed with 4-wheel drives and good ole boys standing around and surely talking about the price of tobacco and who was going to win the NASCAR race that coming weekend. It looked as if every farmer with in twenty miles was hanging out and drinking coffee and I figured that this bunch of hard legs were here bright and early every morning.

As I stopped at the light, Robin's hosiery mill was directly across the street—a big red brick building that was reminiscent of an American industrial complex from back in the '30s and '40s, when North Carolina was the center of the universe for textile manufacturing. It reminded me of Berry Hydraulics, an industrial corner stone back in Corinth where my dad had worked as a foreman for years . . . in a flash my mind took me back to when I was five years old . . . my mom and I were sitting in my dad's office while he ate the home-cooked meal she had brought him on his supper break. I could smell the country-fried steak and see the steam rising over the brown gravy and homemade rolls while the industrial machines hummed in the background. I could see all my dads' buddies and their faces as they stuck their heads through the door to pick at me and praise my mom's cooking. It left me with a sense of loneliness and a thought of what could have been if things would have only been different.

A farm truck honked behind me – the light had changed. I dumped the clutch and spun the tires as I pulled into the gravel parking lot, slinging rocks like crazy.

When the farmer boy drove on by, he stuck his mullet out of the side window, spat out a chew of Redman chewing tobacco, and yelled at me, "Frikin' women drivers!"

I wanted to flip him off but I had bigger fish to fry, so I went inside.

"Hello, I'm Terri O'Connell . . . I have a 10:00 meeting with Mr. Hayes," I told the little red-haired receptionist. She stared at me in an unfriendly fashion, but called Robin on the intercom.

Robin's office was only a few paces off the lobby floor. I straightened out my dress, grabbed my briefcase and carrying bag full of my apparel designs, took a deep breath and went in.

Robin made me feel at ease as he extended his hand to greet me with a good ole Southern handshake.

"Rice' says you have a great idea that's going make all of us a lot of money," he said.

"Yes, I do," I said.

"I like that," he grinned, "but how much is it going to cost me to make all that money? You know it takes two million to make a million in racing, ha, ha, ha!"

We both laughed. I knew exactly what he was talking about . . . any thing you do in motorsports is expensive and I could tell that he wanted no part of a losing proposition even if his good buddy's wife was putting on the pressure.

So I took a seat in one of his two big leather chairs and started pulling all of my designs and samples. To my surprise, he was impressed and summoned everyone in the office as well as the shipping and receiving department to check out my concept. They lit up, and clearly what they saw. But I was a little overwhelmed and thought the entire escapade was a bit non-professional. Finally his people returned to their work stations, and Robin and I got down to discussing my vision on a hip and mainstream approach that would service the 40% female NASCAR audience as well as the higher income males.

"NASCAR is set to explode into the mainstream," I said. "This concept could explode with it, into mainstream retailing."

"You still need a solid business plan," he said. "And financing."

"Mr. Hayes," I said, "I truly value your interest and your integrity and I didn't come down here to ask for a hand out. What I want out of this is for someone to partner up with me, so we can develop a creative and innovative company that we can be proud of, create well-needed jobs for people in this area and provide an income for myself. Right now I earn $8.00 an hour, so if I work at this full time I going to have to find a way to keep my bills paid or I'm going to have to live with you!"

Amazingly, he really didn't ask any questions, which left me wondering if he was impressed enough to even call me back. But when I wrapped up my pitch he said, "Would you mind if I kept a few pieces to show some of my friends and family for a few days?"

"Keep all of them if you like," I said. "And show them to anyone except…some marketing groups . . . I don't want anyone to steal my ideas."

He reassured me that he fully understood what I was talking about. Plus, he knew that Rice' would kill him if anything happened to me.

"I'll get back to you on Friday about this," he said.

As I drove on to work, it struck me that Robin Hayes was not such a pinhead after all. He'd had all those people come into his office because he wanted to see how people with nothing to gain or lose were going to react to something new. That personal connection to people had served him well in politics. Plus, he had put me to the test—he wanted to see if I could handle myself in a stressful situation.

Pins and needles

On Thursday, after work, I was laying on my couch with my ankle elevated, taking a quick power nap, when the phone rang. The conversation went like this:

"Hello, oh hi, Mr. Hayes, how are you? . . . Yeah, absolutely. So you think we can get something going? That is really good news. Yes sir, I would love to meet you for a cup of coffee tomorrow morning . . . 7:00 a.m. would be fine. Oh yeah, I know where the What-A-Burger is, I will see you there. Thank you so much!"

Damn, I thought. Why couldn't Robin have wanted to meet at Hardee's or Mickey D's, anywhere but What-A-Burger in Mt. Pleasant with all those country boys? Hell, I would need a spotter to let me know how close those boys were to my back bumper... just like when I was out on the track.

Friday, 7 a.m. Just as I thought, What-A-Burger was packed with the biggest bunch of country boys I ever saw. I was the cute chick with big boobs pulling up in a hot little sports car . . . alone. Inside, feeling everyone's eyes on me, I looked for Robin, trying not to look as nervous as I felt. He was in a booth in the back. I grabbed a cup of coffee from the order window and we got right down to business. Obviously, he had done his research, and I suspected that he had talked to Rice'.

"I'm prepared to finance the project," he said. "I want to go slow and develop this in a clear and precise manner. Meanwhile I'll pay you $6 an hour until we got the company up and running, if you're willing to help out at the hosiery mill during the morning hours . . . at least until the company needed more attention. If you're willing, then you and I will be fifty - fifty partners in the company."

My heart sank a little. I had hoped that he'd pay me more than Dillard's. $6 an hour was hardly more than minimum wage. Could I even pay my bills on $6 an hour? But then I pulled myself together, telling myself that I damn sure was not going to wreck the opportunity over food and shelter. I was going to be his partner, and my chance for an executive salary would come! Meanwhile I'd give Dillard's my notice, and Robin and Rice' would just have to feed me when I was starving to death.

The Winston Cup race at Charlotte was the first of October—if we pushed we might have something to showcase by then.

Monday morning, I was at my office in the hosiery mill, and hit the ground running. The receptionist was still giving mc a hostile vibe, but I paid no attention. We needed five solid embroidery concepts that we could incorporate into ten or fifteen apparel pieces. The designs had to be sharp, smart and simple. I had one design finished—five cute little cartoon-type stock cars racing up a shirt – that one was ready to go. The other designs still needed some work. My creativity was in high gear, much like when I was designing race cars . . . it felt good to have a goal.

Since Lake was a superstar in NASCAR, I asked him and Rice' if they could get us in the Charlotte Speedway's door to make a presentation to their apparel buyers. Heck, Rice' knew everyone and gave me the phone number for Wanda Edwards, executive director of the Speedway Club, the most exclusive country club in sports. It was housed on the fifth floor of the speedway's high-rise executive office complex overlooking the track itself. This was a cool highbrow place where the local and racing big shots handled their socializing and business. Wanda had created a clubhouse type situation around her five-star restaurant and bar, which sold upscale apparel and souvenirs for all the hospitality and executive seating during the racing events. This could prove to be just the niche we were looking for.

So I called Wanda and gave her my pitch about a product line designed for women and upscale motorsports clientele. To my astonishment, she wanted to meet the very next day!

There was irony in me doing business with the Speedway Club. I had been to the speedway lots of times as JT Hayes. Just five years back, various boosters had put me on the Speedway Club guest list four or five times when I was trying to get my NASCAR career up and going. I couldn't wait to get back

Let's do lunch . . .

The next morning I slipped into my best business suit, packed my briefcase, and drove the ten minutes out to the speedway. I actually had to pinch myself once I stepped off the elevator. The Speedway Club could rival the Waldorf Astoria for atmosphere and elegance. As I walked down the hallway to Wanda's office, past murals of great motorsports events and memorabilia, I was struck by the flurry of activity. The place oozed with aggressiveness . . . people were alive and in the game here and I liked it.

Inside, Wanda's secretary, Margaret, remembered me from phone conversations. She was a "fine and refined" Southern lady in her mid-sixties and I knew from looking at her that she had lots of spunk and would be one of my buddies.

Wanda came in.

"I can't wait to see what you have to show me," she said. "I've been wanting to include more things for the girls here. I'm starving, shall we go have a bite of lunch?"

Our lunch turned out to be the beginning of a solid professional relationship as well as friendship. I found her to be one of the finest people I had ever met, a woman in perfect control of her environment. Like me, she was a schmoozer . . . she had to be. This was absolutely the Alpha den for male movers and shakers in auto racing. Miss Wanda, who was one of a very few women at the corporate level in motorsports, handled those men with absolute professionalism and grace.

After our lunch, we headed back to her office and got down to business. The Speedway Club's chance to sell apparel came around twice a year, during NASCAR's Coca Cola 600 in May and the Oak Wood Homes 500 in October. Both these events were two-week affairs that packed in over 200,000 crazy fans with The Speedway Club playing host to the corporate and white-collar crowd and their guests. She wanted to step up her apparel program so my timing could not have been more perfect. She liked the way I captured the sport with clean and simple designs that lent themselves to corporate taste, especially women.

We plunged right into sketching, and came up with a jazzed-up Club logo on a pair of paisley or plaid boxers, matched up with a quality Tee shirt with the same logo embroidered on the chest. This was perfect for their pro shop and it could be sold to men and women. She gave me a $2,000.00 order right off the bat.

I couldn't believe I was taking our first order. We didn't even have a name for the company, let alone business cards or a DBA.

"What's your company name?" she asked.

Instinctively I grabbed at a name I had been thinking about for a while. "Speedsters," I said.

"Sounds good," she said.

Even though I had not consulted with Robin on what we would call the company, I knew he would be OK with what I had come up with.

As I was putting my presentation pieces back in their bag, I asked Wanda if she had a working relationship with the souvenir store on the lower level of the Speedway. This was where the average fan bought their racing apparel. I could do some high-volume business there if they bought some of my other designs.

Quietly Wanda picked up her phone and dialed Doug Stafford, one of Charlotte Motor Speedway's upper-management big wigs.

"Doug, this is Wanda Edwards, I have a young lady down here who you need to talk to. She's good friends with Lake Speed and she has a cool apparel concept put together that I believe your guys down in the souvenir shop would like."

When she hung up, she looked over at me with a grin and said Doug would see me right now if I had the time.

I grabbed my samples and headed up to the seventh floor. The 20-minute meeting with Doug Stafford went very well and he put me in touch with their apparel buyer down in the souvenir store…where I promptly sold them $1,000.00 worth of novelty boxers and tee shirts with their Charlotte Speedway logo.

I couldn't wait to tell Robin about our good fortune.

Office politics

But things weren't going so well on Robin's end. While the company was getting up and running, he'd wanted me to work in the mill in the mornings, helping in shipping or whatever. It was a terrible idea but he had me over a barrel so I did as he wished. Right off the bat, the two office girls begin to politick Robin against me. They were jealous that Robin had taken in this new gal and backed her company. Who does she think she is? Robin belongs to us and don't you forget it. After a morning of packing boxes, it really pissed them off when I put on my power clothes and headed off to a lunch at the Speedway Club.

I tried to ignore their hostility, and got busy trying to get those orders filled at the speedway. By Speed Week in Daytona in February we would be selling our product to that huge NASCAR fan base.

In the meantime, I began to nurture a NASCAR licensing agreement with the Winston Cup Wives Auxiliary that raised money for several charities within the NASCAR community. It was the perfect organization to work with, considering that Speedsters was selling apparel specifically for the female race fan. Of course, the fact that my best friend Rice' was the organization's Vice President did not hurt our opportunities to work with that great charity. Patty Petty, Richard Petty's daughter in law, was the president so Rice' told her how cool our company was. Within a week of starting at the mill, I had my first meeting with Patty Petty and Rice.'

Over the next few weeks, I met several times with the ladies up in NASCAR Sprint Cup team owner Felix Sabatas's condo overlooking the first turn at Lowes Speedway and things were looking pretty good that they would license our product. Patty's husband Kyle drove for Felix so this was why we had access to his luxury condo. This was a very big deal, I was moving and shaking with the big dogs and I was impressed. I wasn't letting my head swell up, but I knew that this could turn into something very special if I just stayed focused. I always filled Robin in. He always just told me that I was doing a good job! In the meantime, he was putting together his political team that would run him for Governor of North Carolina!

During this period I became a mainstay at the Speedway Club, and Wanda helped me develop my confidence as a businesswoman.

But around the first of October, Robin was getting uncooperative. I ask Rice' if he had said anything to her. She stunned me when she told me that Robin thought I was slacking on the job. It seemed that he believed the lies started by the two secretaries, that I never worked in the mill in the mornings. He was away from the office constantly, getting his campaign in gear, so he is never around to see how damn hard I was working every single day of the week.

The Monday before the Oakwood Homes 500, Robin called me into his office and scolded me over not working in the mill. I stood up for myself, telling him that I had already delivered the Speedway Club's orders and we were ready to go. But he hurt my feelings over the working-in-the- mill situation. Plus he was skeptical about the licensing agreement with the Racing Wives—he wasn't sure it was a real possibility.

When I left his office, I drove around for 30 minutes cursing and crying over how he had treated me. Here I thought I'd left all the jealous politics back at the sprint car races!

That next weekend Wanda reported that our produce sold well at the speedway. Now we needed to be in Daytona in February with our product ready for a very big NASCAR audience.

In the meantime, two weeks after the Charlotte race I had a power meeting with Trone Advertising over in High Point to talk to them about handling marketing and advertising for our company. I managed to talk Robin into going with me just to impress the Trone executives. The meeting went well – they were excited to hear that the NASCAR Winston Cup Wives might be linking with our company. They knew full well that any type of licensing agreement with NASCAR is a big winner.

But, on the ride home, Robin was distant. I had my suspicions that those winches back at the office were working him over about me.

By now, we were three months into this deal and I was running out of money. I realized I'd made a stupid deal with Robin about my income, but a deal is a deal. At least I was a 50/50 partner in a company with a million-dollar potential. For that I could put up with a little bit of shit.

By November 1st, I was getting worried about getting to Daytona in February. Robin's campaign was heating up, and it looked like he really had a chance at being a Republican Governor of North Carolina.

Then, the very next week and right out of left field, Robin backed out of our deal, leaving me crushed.

For a solid month, I struggled onward alone. The licensing agreement with The NASCAR Winston Cup Wives was just about finalized. I was having to smile and be upbeat but inside, I was worried like crazy that I would lose everything I had been working on. Just like back in the '80s, my tears were flowing on a regular basis. I was one month behind on my rent and on the verge of having to call my mom for money and I couldn't bare facing that defeat. I knew better than to smart off to Lake that I felt Robin had given me the screws, and just kept my mouth shut.

Dillard's wouldn't rehire me, and when I sent out resumes, no other store called me back either.

I felt humiliated over what I had allowed Robin and his bunch of small-minded office cronies to do to me.

Twilight zone

One Wednesday afternoon, when I came rolling into Lake's office like I did virtually every day, his secretary Harpo had a look on her face just like she had seen a ghost. Harpo had become a friend and buddy of mine.

"Terri," she said in a hush-hush voice, "you're not going to believe what I found in Lake's phone book while I was updating his phone list. When you came up with your new last name . . . didn't you say it was because of your grandmother's Irish descent?"

"Yeah," I answered back. "Why?"

Looking bewildered, she pushed Lake's phone book over to my side of her desk, and pointed to my old name in the book. There it was,—"JT Hayes" and right beside it was the name of Don O'Connell.

"Who was Don O'Connell?" she asked me.

For a moment, I was as confused as she was. Just like Harpo, I was thinking it was real spooky that the name O'Connell had been written down beside my old name way back in 1988. Then, it dawned on me that the name Don O'Connell should have been written as Don O'Brian, my friend and ex racing backer from San Francisco. It was obvious that Lake's secretary from back in that period, Debbie, had written Don's name beside mine so Lake would know who this guy was whenever he called up to check on our racing situation. But, she had accidentally written down his last name wrong.

Harpo looked at me and sang the "Twilight Zone" jingle. Then she said, "See Terri? God already knew what was going to happen to you . . . you being a girl was just meant to be . . . this is definitely a sign."

Just then Lake came rushing through the door and Harpo lit into him about the phone book. He took a quick look and grinned.

"Yeah, some things are meant to be," he said, then went on into his office as if nothing was strange. But Harpo and I were still reeling from the Twilight Zone moment.

Diary Notebook

November 25 . . . Thanksgiving . . .

I am really struggling now. . . I had to borrow money from my mom to pay the rent . . . that sucked the life out of me . . . I called Lake and Rice' at 1:00 in the morning on the verge of killing myself. . .at least I had the common sense to call someone . . .I haven't told Wanda about Robin backing out as of yet, I feel bad about not telling her . . . I'm too proud . . . the racing wives are wanting to know what I'm up to . . . I'm going to have to tell them next week that I've lost my backing . . . it looks as if my stupid deadline of killing myself by Christmas is going to become a reality . . ..

On December 15, as I was on at the brink of being evicted from my apartment, Robin called me up.

"I want to get back in," he said. "Let's see if we can make this deal work."

I was mad as hell at him, but so desperate that I accepted his olive branch. "But only if we can get aggressive with marketing and sales," I told him. "And I want to work full time on the business. No more mornings at the mill."

The next morning we met at the What-A-Burger. While the good old boys gawked at my boobs, Robin and I talked over how we were going to re- group. He wanted his daughter Winslow, to look after his end of the business and without hesitation I agree to the partnership. I had met her a couple of times and figured I wouldn't have any problem working with her. He had come up with the idea of going to the Daytona 500 in February and showcase the product. Duh... I had been telling him that for four months. Isn't that just like a man to steal your idea? Now, we only had five weeks to do four months' worth of work.

As we finished our sausage and eggs, Robin asked me, "Is there anything I can do in the meantime to help you out?"

Without blinking an eye, I said, "Yes. Can you loan me some money to pay my rent and get home for Christmas? I'll pay you back once we get up and running in January."

He pulled out his checkbook and wrote me a check for five hundred dollars. As he handed me the check, he said:

"Don't worry about paying me back, Terri. I believe were going to be successful here, so consider it a Christmas bonus . . . I'll see you in a few weeks and we will get ready for Daytona."

I realized that the only reason Robin was back in was that he wanted to give his daughter something to do. Winslow had just graduated from Duke with a marketing and public-relations degree, and she needed a job. She had a huge trust fund but I knew he wanted her to work at something... so why not start a company for her. Hell, it made sense to me.

When I told Rice the good news, she already knew because Robin had actually talked the whole ordeal over with she and Lake a few days earlier. They had told Robin that he should do the business with me, that it was a solid idea and all I needed was a little help in running the company. Once again, Rice' came to my rescue . . . I was very thankful!

Racing towards a deadline

On January 7, Robin, Winslow and I met at the mill to focus on Daytona. They were surprised to see that I had already organized our game plan, which included renting space at the mall across from the speedway, finalizing the licensing agreement with the Winston Cup Wives and a hundred other things. I was used to deadlines and pressure—motorsports is always about deadlines and pressure—but I could tell that they were not. During that meeting we all agreed to continue paying me $6.00 an hour until the company got on its feet.

After that, I really got busy! Ordering apparel blanks, embroidery tapes, screen prints, promotional material, art for NASCAR Wives logo, hang tags, apparel labels, packaging, finalize licensing agreement, art for our logo, de stringing embroidery designs and a hundred other things.

Winslow was supposed to be booking the mall space in Daytona, getting NASCAR credentials, securing our Visa Master Card system, and putting together a press release about our new company that will go out just before the Daytona 500. But as the month went along, Winslow was not getting the jobs done. With one week to go, we still didn't have our Visa Master Card program in place.

I was getting pissed. Plus I was broke again and having a hard time paying my bills. So I asked Robin to give me a slight bump in my paycheck. He and Winslow decided that instead of giving me a raise, they would just not take income tax and Social Security out of my check. I never will forget the look on Robin's face when I told him that I didn't have anything to fall back on if I got sick.

He looked right at me and said, "Oh...so you're one of those forty five million who doesn't have health insurance."

That statement sent cold chills down my spine. Here was a North Carolina state congressional representative who was in full swing for governor, yet he was clueless to the plight of so many Americans.

The next week, just as we were heading into a meeting, Winslow gave me my next check, but it was the same amount as before. To say that I was pissed off would be an understatement. I handed the check back to her, and said, "I'm not taking it until you change it to the amount we agreed on."

"Dad and I decided not to change it till the next pay period," she said.

I could hardly contain my rage. "Winslow, I only have one dollar in my purse and I need that check, but I'm not taking it until you make it right. You know that I'm not living above my means so, I expect you to fix this check this afternoon."

Not thirty minutes after the meeting, she brought me the new check with the right amount on it.

It also occurred to me that Robin and Winslow still hadn't worked out their written partnership contract with me. That little check affair was a red flag, but I just passed it off as them wanting to be frugal with our budget.

Women need to stay home

The next day Winslow and I had a meeting with a marketing group in Charlotte to talk about putting a souvenir trailer with our apparel out on the racing circuit. Up-and-coming female race driver Shanna Robertson was with us—she would be wearing our apparel designs. During the meeting, group director Bob had his team of guys sitting around a big conference table listening to our spill on how fabulous our concept was. When we finished, Bob ask his team for their views. One by one, they shared their positive responses.

Then John, an older crusty macho, lit into us. He thought that women should be at home raising babies, not getting into racing.

"Now, girls," he said, "don't get your feelings hurt. But I have twenty years experience in the sport and no one cares about buying cute girl stuff at the track."

Well, you could have heard a pin drop in the room. Bob had turned three colors of red. Shanna looked over at me and rolled her eyes into the back of her head and Winslow had a look of absolute horror on her face.

At that point we all calmly stood up, shook hands and left the room. Once we all got outside, Bob could not apologize enough.

"Don't worry about it," Shanna told him. "I'm used to it. I hear that kind of chauvinistic crap every day."

I told Bob we would give him a call after Daytona to let him know what we had decided, knowing that I would never call him again.

That encounter gave me a wake-up call about what we were up against there in NASCAR land where the male vibrato ruled. Yes, there were things available for women on the trailers, but they were all skimpy and trashy . . . they wouldn't appeal to the newer upper-class race fan. I knew we had a good idea.

One week before Daytona, we finally got the licensing agreement worked out. I had to help Winslow finish almost everything she was supposed to be doing. Shanna Robertson would be trying to qualify for the Daytona 500, and she would be wearing our new apparel during Speed Weeks, so we had to capitalize on that opportunity. Then Winslow was having trouble getting our rooms booked, not to mention our Industrial Observer licenses so we could access all the NASCAR events.

Ultimately, I got on the phone and did her jobs, including the public relations stuff. All the while I kissed her millionaire trust-fund ass.

Anxiety about sales

When we finally headed out to Daytona 500, I was exhausted.

During the drive to Florida, Winslow and I seemed to be getting along okay. But toward the end, I asked Winslow if we had received a copy of the licensing agreement from Winston Cup Wives and what about our business license for Daytona. I had not seen or signed anything since Robin and I had talked to their attorney over a week ago.

"Oh," she said breezily, "Dad and I already signed it and mailed it back. It's all taken care of."

My stomach sank. They had signed it without me! I knew I had just been screwed. But if I confronted her about it now, we'd be fighting about it for days. So I decided to keep my mouth shut till we returned to Charlotte.

The next morning we got to the mall and set up our kiosk. Fortunately, we got a good spot next to where former NASCAR veteran driver Benny Parsons was going to host his live radio show all during Speed Weeks. As the day passed, Winslow was antsy that we were not selling a lot of merchandise.

"Look," I said, "the big rush of race fans isn't here yet. They get here for the Budweiser Shootout. Things will kick into gear then."

Finally on Thursday, the day before Bud Shootout qualifying, the fans began to roll into town and our merchandise started selling. That weekend we banked some good sales. "When next weekend comes, and more fans come for the Daytona 500, we'll pick up twice as much."

In fact we had made a deal with drivers Lake, Todd Bodine and Kyle Petty through the auxiliary to do a photo op at the kiosk that would run in the Winston Cup Scene newspaper . . . if they could break away from testing and preparing for the 500. However, it turned out that the three drivers were working overtime over at the Speedway trying to get up to speed. Each of them were having trouble with their cars. So they couldn't help us out.

Winslow smarted off about it. "Who do they think they are standing us up . . . they told us they would be here, they just can't do that to us, we had an agreement."

I listened open-mouthed as she rattled on, saying, "Terri, it's your entire fault . . . if you had been more organized, we could have gotten those drivers over here. You and I are going to have a talk when we get back to the Hotel. My dad is going to be really mad at you. You're a slacker just like his secretaries said you are. You need to start taking some direction from me ... and if you don't your going to get fired."

I was furious at this undeserved criticism.

"What in the hell is wrong with you, Winslow? It's not my fault that their cars aren't running good. Besides, getting them over here was your job, not mine. If it weren't for my working my tail off and picking up your slack, we wouldn't even be here. Fire me? I think not. This company is as much mine as it is yours. Now hot shot, you run this frikin' kiosk by yourself for a little while...I'm going to go get a cup of coffee."

As I headed off for a coffee shop, Winslow stood there red-faced and stunned that I had stood up to her. That night, as we were driving back to the hotel, she lit into me once again. This time she got very personal, and wound up screaming, "When we get back to Charlotte, things are going to change."

I didn't back down one inch. "Winslow, you can go screw yourself. Your dad's money doesn't give you the right to run over me because things didn't go the way you wanted. Do... not...ever...yell at me again. This ain't high school, little girl, you need to grow your ass up."

She stormed off to our room.

I called Rice' Speed who was staying in a condo about two miles south of our hotel and told her the whole sorry tale, including the fact that my name was not on the Winston Cup Wives licensing agreement. Hopefully Rice' would have some words of wisdom.

To my surprise, Rice' gave me this humiliating speech about being thankful for the opportunity that Robin was giving me. In her opinion, I should just put the argument behind me and move on.

I felt alone and used and thought, What have I gotten myself into?

The next morning, I was prepared to put on a happy face. But to my surprise Winslow was packing. At first I thought she was moving to another room. When I asked her if she was going somewhere, she dropped the bombshell.

"I'm taking a plane back to Charlotte to go to a basketball game with my boyfriend," she said.

It turned out that this little return trip was something she had planned before we ever left Charlotte. She had bought her airline ticket over two weeks ago. The next day there would be over 200,000 more people in Daytona, with five days to go. The mall would be flooded with crazy race fans and I would be there by myself. In addition, I had two big PR events to do—including the annual Winston Cup Wives breakfast banquet at the Daytona Country Club. This was a huge event and every VIP in the sport would be there. There would be no one to run the kiosk.

I made an emergency call to my mom and dad. They leaped in their car and made the 14-hour drive to Daytona, getting there in time to help me out. My dad was outraged at Winslow and Robin's treatment of me – he had never had any respect for big shots.

Result: we sold everything and wrote $5,000.00 worth of orders. Having Shanna Robertson wear our apparel was a good move—the media followed her around for two weeks. Meanwhile I had schmoozed like crazy—met the PR people at the Nashville Network who broadcast NASCAR races (they wanted to promote our company), spoke at the Racing Wives banquet, and ate breakfast with legendary CBS sports analyst Ken Squire at the Daytona Country Club. Things were starting to happen.

Bring me $30,000

When I got back to Charlotte, I was even more worn out than before.

However, I did set up a meeting with Robin and Winslow the next day. Robin tried to make sure Winslow and I had buried the hatchet. I was biting the bullet, wanting to wait till Robin and I were alone before I confronted him over the contract situation. But later on in the meeting, Robin sensed that I wasn't happy.

Arrogantly, leaning back in his leather chair behind his big desk, he drawled, "Miss O'Connell, it seems that you have something on your mind."

The timing wasn't what I was looking for, but he had opened the door. Slowly I got up out my own leather chair, which was low and made me look up at him, and sat on the arm so I could look at him eye to eye.

"Robin," I said, "I feel that we need to define our roles and percentages in the company better. I don't know how much of this company I own, if any. Your name and Winslow's name are all over everything, including the licensing agreement with the racing wives, so I am not sure where my future lies. Actually, I'm just a $6 an hour employee in a company I designed, that I'm running. I'm not comfortable with that."

Mr. Hayes promptly pulled his bifocals down on his nose.

"Well now," he said, "If you can come up with $30,000, I will make you a 33% partner in the company." He didn't even blink!

I couldn't believe what I was hearing. I had sacrificed everything I had, thinking that I owned 50% of this company, yet I didn't own any part of it. I had just gotten screwed big time and they did not care! Tears almost welled up, but I choked them back. By God, Winslow was not going to see me cry. Instead I calmly put my notepad back in my briefcase, stood up and looked them directly in the eye.

"In that case, I quit," I said.

Then I turned and left the room.

Driving straight out to the Speedway Club, I vented my frustrations to Wanda Edwards. Margaret, Wanda's secretary, overheard our conversation and yelped aloud, "I wanted to tell you the first time I heard you were in business with Winslow, she is a royal bitch . . . she runs over everyone!"

For a solid month, Lake and Rice' wondered where I was. They were Robin's friends, but all I ever heard from them once they knew that Winslow and I were having trouble was to suck it up. I was angrier than I'd ever been in my life, and avoided everyone except my new friend Wanda at the speedway. My mom mailed me $500.00 to pay rent and to eat. The wives' auxiliary was on my tail wanting to know what was going on with the company. Rice' left me 20 phone messages and Robin left just as many. He and Winslow were in a panic—they couldn't run the company without me!

One Thursday afternoon, I was having lunch at TJ's deli when out of the corner of my eye I saw Rice' come in. Quickly I got up and rushed out the back, still so angry that I wanted to avoid her. When I got out to my car I realized that she had blocked me in.

"Terri, Robin wants to talk to you," she said. "You have to work this out with him."

"No, Rice,' I don't . . . he can go to hell and take Winslow with him!"

But after a few minutes of Rice' putting on the charm, with tears rolling down both of our faces, I relented.

The next day, I met with Robin and Winslow for 15 minutes. They agree to let me buy them out. Robin told me, "I'm going to let you have this."

But as usual there was a catch. Like an idiot I agreed to pay him back for what he had invested over the last eight months, including my salary . . . But that was the only way he would sign over the NASCAR licensing agreement to me. Adding to the drama, Winslow sat there snorting and groaning and rolling her eyes back as Robin and I haggled!

The day we finalized the deal, he and I got on the phone with the racing wives' attorney Jeff Howard of the prestigious Winston Salem law firm Petree Stockton and finalized every detail, then faxed him Robin's letter in which he and Winslow relinquished the license. It seemed like the entire nightmare was over.

Leaving Robin's office, I drove straight out to the speedway and the NASCAR Winston Cup Wives office to meet with their executive director, Diane Huff and to work out the details on their new agreement with me. When I walked into Diane's office, she put her finger over her mouth to signal me to be quiet, then put on her speakerphone so I could hear the conversation. To my surprise, she was talking to Robin—he was trying to convince her that the auxiliary should reconsider their decision and go with him and Winslow instead of with me.

He was backstabbing me again!

"We had no intention of doing business with you on any level," Diane told him coldly. "We always wanted to do the deal with Terri. Besides, you're running for political office, and it would look pretty bad if you were being sued for taking advantage of a girl in a shaky business deal."

Robin lost no time agreeing with her and hung up.

Then Diane and I went down to the infield where the annual car show was going on, and set up a booth to promote the company.

I was glad to have that nightmare behind me but the cold hard facts were—someone else had to help finance my company. Finding that help was not going to be easy, but the licensing agreement would be my best bargaining chip.

CHAPTER 20

Word Gets Around – I Need a Partner

Playing With the Big Boys

It was April 1995. Every day from then on, I was beating the bushes for new investors.

Lunch was spent at the Speedway Club, networking my idea and making new friends. Wanda Edwards helped as much as possible because she didn't like how Robin Hayes had treated me. She helped me get through the depression and fear I was feeling.

By this time Charlotte Motor Speedway President H. A. "Humpy" Wheeler had discovered my art designs and he liked what he saw. In all likelihood Humpy is one of the top three most powerful men in motorsports. On several occasions, he made it a point to sit with Wanda and me during lunch and comment on my designs, which blew everybody away because he never did that with anyone.

On one occasion, he asked me pointblank, "What's in it for me when I make you famous?"

When he said that, Wanda raised her eyebrow with amazement and I just about choked on my desert.

I would go home at night and have to pinch myself; it was hard to believe that I had been this damn lucky. To put that into perspective, having Mr. Wheeler sit with me at lunch and give me words of encouragement and help was equal to being an up-and-coming film director having Steven Spielberg sit with you at lunch at the Ivy in Los Angeles with all the media staring in disbelief. Mr. Wheeler gave me credibility by just sitting with me—I was still broke and had yet to find a backer for Speedsters.

By this time, word had gotten around the NASCAR community that my little company had a lucrative licensing agreement with The Winston Cup Racing Wives Auxiliary. NASCAR superstar driver Ernie Irvin's business manager, Bret Nelson, and a business associate, Dixon Johnson, contacted me about possibly getting involved. We had a little power lunch at a Burger King near the speedway to talk about their investing in my company. Something about Dixon didn't set well with me, but we did talk.

During this time, Robert Yates Racing, one of the top three NASCAR teams, for whom Ernie Irvin was driving, called me up and wanted me to design a few embroidery pieces for them to sell on their souvenir trailer that traveled the NASCAR circuit. Carolyn Yates, a blond haired beauty and the wife of team renowned NASCAR team owner Robert Yates and a member of the Wives Auxiliary, had seen my designs down in Daytona and wanted something similar for their female fans.

So I put on my best business suit, hightailed over to their corporate offices in downtown Charlotte, and met with Carolyn to see what she had in mind. She was a savvy businesswoman —headed up their multi-million-dollar souvenir program for their two drivers, Dale Jarrett and Ernie Ervin. The meeting lasted about 30 minutes. She loved my ideas and bought two of them, which would ease my financial woes just enough to pay my rent.

Like many in the NASCAR family, Carolyn had also heard that I was looking for an investor. "How is that coming along?" she asked.

I wondered if she might be interested in investing herself, so I said, "Well, Bret Nelson and I are talking, for one thing."

I was thinking that would be a feather in my cap since he was their superstar driver's business manager.

But Carolyn suddenly turned cold and distant and told me point blank, "I'm not interested in doing business with you if you're connected with Mr. Nelson on any level."

It turned that Carolyn and Bret were in heated contract negotiations over Ernie's driving and personal contract. She scared the hell out of me . . . I was broke and barely able to eat.

So I did a double backstroke and assured her, "Look, you're my number one focus. I have no agreement with Bret – he and I just talked, that's all."

That was a lesson in big-time politics in the world of NAS-CAR, and I learned not to drop names without knowing who hated whom.

On the personal front, a few guys around the NASCAR community had their eyes on me, including two of Lake's crew members and a nice gent named Rick whom I'd met at the Speedway Club. He was an event promoter and damn good-looking but I wasn't quite ready to jump in the deep end with him.

As a brand-new woman, I was learning to figure out each new situation. Were these guys just being friendly, or were they trying to pick me up? I had an open and friendly personality so I had to be careful not to have these guys think I was coming on to them when I was just showing some Southern hospitality. One guy who refused to get my message that I wasn't interested was Joe Folice, my friend Jodie Folice's dad. Joe was on my heels all the time to go out with him, and sleep with him.

However, I began to casually socialize with Lake's former PR representative Bret. We went to movies and dinner and hung out around the apartment. He knew my story, but also knew that Lake would cut his throat if he didn't keep it quiet. He didn't have a problem with my situation—in fact, he had been approached by several of Lake's crew guys to get my phone number. I suspected he got interest up for me once he realized some other guys were interested in me. He kept my secret and was a real prince about it all. I also hunt to Mr. Brit because he was a real computer whiz. He helped me put together presentations and promotional material.

Bret was cute, and I could tell that he wanted to have sex. But again, I wasn't ready for that yet.

Slowly I was getting my sea legs as a woman, and I liked it. Before, I had always been able to turn on the feminine charm on my weekends as Terri. But now it was different. Living and working as a woman 24/7, I had come to see first-hand that men really want to be in charge of the situation. At times, that was hard for my ego, so I was having to adjust. After all, I was a champion racecar driver who had been in charge of every aspect of my career. I had even designed and built most of the cars I had driven. Women had been throwing themselves at me since I was in junior high. So giving up some of that control was a big adjustment. But I was working on it.

I had to keep reminding myself, "Remember honey, you're a girl and boys don't like girls challenging them."

Invest in me . . . it will set you free

By April first, after sweating some big bullets, I had found investors up in Greensborough. Dixon Johnson had introduced these guys to me and I liked them. Aaron Johns and his sidekick and all-around ladies' man, Angelo Meyer, knew full well that if you could develop a NASCAR connection to promote your company, the possibilities were endless. They had the manufacturing capabilities and cash, and I had the designs and the Racing Wives licensing agreement. So it made sense to get together.

The Racing Wives were breathing down my neck to get going. The spring race in Charlotte was coming up on Memorial Day and I needed to have something to sell.

Aaron and Angelo agreed to bankroll Speedsters and pay me $1,500.00 a month. It would be 49/51 with me holding the biggest percentage. Aaron would handle all the financial affairs. Angelo and I would handle the sales and marketing, but I had no control over the money. That was fine with me because I did have creative control and my vision for the company was intact. We signed a contract and got busy designing a brochure to hand out at NASCAR events. We had two weeks to get it all done and I was feeling the pressure.

In the meantime, Mr. Angelo had his eyes on me, which actually I found rather charming. He was a charismatic good-looking Italian with a good sense of humor. But Aaron had threatened his life if he messed with me—at least for six months.

So we got busy on the brochure. With the help of Diane Huff we put together a photo shoot with several Winston Cup NASCAR wives—Rice' Speed, Andrea Nemicheck, Lynn Bodine, Marsha Parsons, Susan Brewer and my buddy Jodie Follice. The photo backdrop was Charlotte Motor Speedway.

By then, the Memorial Day race was just two weeks away. It was going to be close!

Publicity, please

We still needed to crank up the marketing and media exposure without spending a pile of money, so Angelo and I were always brainstorming.

I had a connection with the PR representative at the Nashville Network through our relationship with the Wives auxiliary and through giving them some shirts in Rockingham a few months back. Robin had grumbled when I comped the shirts. Now we needed some television exposure so I took a chance and got on the phone with Nancy Neil, head of public relations at the Network, to see if she would help us out during the upcoming Speed Weeks.

Luckily, Nancy loved the idea that we were doing something cool for the female race fans. It didn't take five minutes to put together a deal that would allow Rice' Speed to go on air to promote our apparel line while The Nashville Network was doing its daily broadcast from the Speedway Club on their program hosted by Katie Hass.

Then, in a stroke of incredible luck, and because of our affiliation with the Racing Wives and since Patty Petty was their president, Richard Petty's souvenir and merchandising company offered to let us use one of their 40- foot souvenir trailers to sell our product at the Speedway, out on souvenir row during the Charlotte event. That was kind of like Tom Cruise saying, "Hey, I want to help you out with your movie."

Aaron was not a big race fan, so the fact that "Richard Petty's people" were helping us almost went over his head. But he soon caught on and we got busy making enough apparel pieces to supply the trailer.

Three weeks before the race, Wanda Edwards decided she wanted to place a huge $10,000 order for The Speedway Club. She and I developed several new designs.

Now Aaron and I were really under the gun. We had to have the brochures ready to hand out during Charlotte Speed Weeks and especially to showcase on the upcoming TNN broadcast. Once the broadcast aired and they gave out our phone number, we would need the full order to mail to customers.

Five days before the race, the brochures were still not ready. Aaron's hippie screen printer screwed up some shirts and I had to re-draw the design. After pulling an all-nighter as intense as getting a car ready for a race, I had the shirts done in time. But the brochures still hadn't arrived.

A little black dress

In the middle of all this stress, Wanda Edwards had gotten me invited to the Union 76 awards ceremony two nights before the 500 in the banquet hall in the Speedway Club. This awards ceremony was a big, big deal—all the big shots in motorsports would be there on that night. The honoree was the previous winner of the Memorial Day event, Jeff Gordon.

I didn't have anything upscale to wear, so I decided to buy a little black cocktail dress. I asked Wanda, "Any suggestions on where I can pick up the right dress without breaking the bank?"

She sent me to a friend of hers who owned a formal and bridal store up at Lake Norman. Buying that cocktail dress validated me as a woman; it made me feel as if I had been voted into the coolest sorority on campus. As I admired myself in the store mirror, the dress fit me like a glove. I had let my hair grow past my shoulders and had become a redhead, which dramatically changed my appearance.

That night at the gala, as I walked into the club, I bumped into a photographer, almost knocking him down. It embarrassed me because I was trying to be so cool. Don was the lead photographer for *The Winston Cup Scene*, the official newspaper for NASCAR, and friend with Lake and Rice'. I had gotten to know him at the races every weekend since Daytona. He had been catching my eye for a few months now and I was wondering what his deal was. Was he married? If not, was he dating anyone, and if not did I have a chance at catching his eye? I had been attracted to men before, but there was something about Don that got my hormones going. He was tall, dark and handsome and a very nice guy, just my type.

We laughed over me stepping on his foot and did a little flirting for a minute or so. "Your dress and your hair look really great," he said.

Then Don headed on into the crowd of VIP's to do his job.

I took off looking for Wanda. When I walked back to the bar to get a glass of Merlot, Humpy Wheeler was standing at the end of the bar. As I glanced over at him to say hi, I realized that he and half the men in the room were staring a hole in me.

Three minutes later Wanda came over, leaned into my ear and said, "Your dress is a big hit . . . Mr. Wheeler and all his boys have already noticed."

I wanted to shout with joy but kept my poker face on and gave Wanda a wink. I was now a hot babe and, a business-woman . . . it didn't get any better than this.

I remember wishing that my mom and dad could have been there to enjoy this. Then I looked up to the heavens and told my grandmother to tell God, thanks for letting me do this—it was something I had needed for virtually every day of my life. I would sleep very well on this night!

Next day at 1:00 p.m., it was time to go on the air with the Nashville Network . . . but where were the damn brochures? With one minute to go, the delivery guy rushed into the Club with a case of brochures. I grabbed one and rushed onto the set where I quickly handed Rice' the brochure and they went right on the air. Rice' did a fabulous job promoting our apparel company. Afterwards, when she joined me and Lee Spencer who was helping me do some public relations work at our booth to watch the rest of the show, we realized that the printer had put the wrong phone number on the brochure . . . and had printed 25,000 of them.

What in the hell were we going to do with those 25,000 screwed-up brochures? I was getting madder by the second as I called Aaron over in Greensborough. They had watched the broadcast and were trying to get a hold of the printer as we spoke.

Fortunately, we rushed Rice' back on to the set and they graciously allowed us to broadcast the correct phone number. Our switchboard back at the office immediately lit up with race fans from all over America wanting a brochure and information about the product! It looked as if we had a hit on our hands, and my stress level went down a few notches.

I asked Aaron, "Who's going to pay for reprinting the brochures?"

Now, we are really running behind – we needed corrected brochures in three days when our trailer will be set up outside the Speedway.

But Angelo intervened, and his Italian charm did the trick with the printer. We got the corrected brochures in two days instead of three.

The next day after the television broadcast, there was a big event for Kyle Petty's annual charity motorcycle ride over at the Sandwich Construction just a mile up the road from the Speedway. The Sandwich Construction was where all the cool NASCAR VIP's and media types hung out when they were not out on the racing circuit doing their jobs.

I was sitting in the VIP area, watching the festivities when someone comes up behind me and a man's voice softly whispered into my ear.

"I know your story and I'm very proud of you," he said. "You don't have to worry, your secret is safe with me . . . you have obviously made the right choice."

When I looked around to see who had almost outed me at the worst possible time in my life, I was shocked to see Rev. Max Helton, the Motor Racing Outreach minister and executive director.

I knew him fairly well, through Lake and Rice' and worshiping at his chapel on Sunday mornings before the NASCAR races. Rice' had told him to look after me and to never reveal my secret! I was at a loss for words and could only nod my head yes to acknowledge his caring.

He was in a rush to get out of there but paused to say, "You're welcome to come by my office at the Speedway to talk, any time you want."

Somehow I felt that my secret was safe with him. It wasn't the minister thing—I just trusted him. I also knew I might need his guidance sometime down the road. As good as things were looking at the moment, it could all blow up and disintegrate.

That weekend, during the race, Aaron and Angelo and I worked our tails off at the souvenir trailer. Our promotion went very well—we gave out over 10,000 brochures and did about $10,000 in sales at the trailer alone. Adding that to what we had sold to the Speedway Club, the weekend had been a success.

We were all totally exhausted, and I needed a few days off to regroup.

The next day was Memorial Day and my friend Jodie Folice and her dad had invited me to NASCAR star driver Randy Lajoie's house for an afternoon barbeque. I highly suspected I was supposed to be her dad's pseudo date and that was okay.

I had decided he was harmless. Plus he always kept you laughing. He had a potty mouth, as did most of those hard core racing guys, so you had to be ready for that when you were with them.

Joe Folice was persistent and worked all the angles, but he wasn't going to get what he wanted from me.

A call from Indy

Starting the following week, Angelo and I got busy promoting Speedsters more intensely. Into the summer, I hit as many NASCAR events as possible, including the Daytona 400 and Louden 400 in July and the Talladega 500 and the Brickyard 400 at Indy in August. I was a mainstay at the tracks and became buddies with several NASCAR officials as well as several guys in the media.

I began to hang out with Carryon Myers, the wife of Chocolate Myers, the famous crewmember on the Dale Earnhardt team. And of course, I was considered to be part of the Lake Speed team. Most people thought Rice' and I were sisters, and on more than one occasion when I was looking after Lake and Rice's kids, people thought their kids were mine. I dined with them almost every weekend, as well as doing lunch with them over at Lake's shop. We all did Bible study once a week out in the brake room, eating pizza or sub sandwiches.

Once a day I dropped by Lake's race shop to just see what was going on. Michael "Fat Back" McSwane, Lake's crew chief, was always nudging me to get Lake to be more aggressive out on the track.

"He needs to rub on those guys, nudge 'em out of the way," Michael was always saying. "You can get him to do it. Just work on him."

I knew better than to tell Lake anything like that. To be honest, I thought Lake was doing just fine. He wasn't going to wreck anyone to pass them like some of the other assholes.

During this time, I had a few closed meetings with Brother Max at the Speedway, just venting my frustrations to him about my crazy life, and it took the edge off my hectic and stressful life.

When at the track, I was becoming such a familiar face that, when I wanted to bring someone into the NASCAR garage who did not have credentials, Bruce the main man in charge of garage passes would motion us over and give my guest their passes. I was hanging out at NASCAR'S big red trailer, their traveling headquarters at each event, drinking coffee and eating doughnuts during race mornings while they aggravated me trying to get free T- shirts! Phone numbers were slipped to me from crew members of other teams, not to mention one secret phone number from a former Daytona 500 winner. I was flattered but held my ground on moral fortitude.

I was still a virgin, but Bret and I had been getting pretty flirty. By late July, I was thinking about doing the deed with him.

One afternoon I got a phone call that made me take notice.

"Hello, is this Terri? This is Mary Lu Beaudry with the Championship Auto Racing Wives Auxiliary up in Indy . . ."

I had met her down in Daytona back in February. She had been impressed with our little company, and now she was interested in having me develop the same type of concept for their auxiliary, which serviced the Indy- car community.

My mom was in town visiting me for a week or so, so she and I loaded up the SUV and we took off to Indy to meet with Mary Lu and her board.

The meeting went well—we brainstormed on several approaches they had in mind. Then Mom and I headed back to Charlotte. I could see that the opportunities to take Speedsters to the next level were already gathering. I had a good vision for the sport, and the sport was beginning to boom. But to reach our peak, to become the Disney store for motorsports, we needed to look farther into the future on marketing, sales and distribution.

Amid on the circuit, I took one of my coolest embroidery designs, and incorporated it onto the work uniforms for Lake's crewmembers. They were cool and colorful and a big hit in the garage area with all the other race teams and the media. To my amazement, big photos of the team wearing my designs on their uniforms made the racing trade papers. This was a big feather in my company's cap. The Petty Enterprises merchandising company, headed up by Little Bud More, started selling our designs on Petty's souvenir trailers. We were putting our own traveling rig out on the circuit in '96, starting with the Daytona 500 in February.

Right after the Talladega 500, I headed up to Indy and the Brickyard 400, where I was doing a bigger promotion at the Petty souvenir trailer.

That weekend was surreal. Mary Lu Beaudry who I came to find out was best friends with INDY 500 icon and one of my child hood hero's was gracious enough to let me stay at her house, only five minutes from the famed speedway with its old brick track, where the history of international motorsports lived. I had always dreamed of racing at the Brickyard. But at the moment, just walking around inside Gasoline Alley was like being in heaven.

Then that Sunday, on race morning while at the MRO church services, I was sitting with Lake and Rice' right behind Jeff and Brooke Gordon listening to Brother Max give his sermon, when I caught a glimpse out of the corner of my right eye of a couple I knew. A cold chill ran down my spine. It was my old friends Don and Nancy from out in San Francisco.

Don and Nancy were looking right at me and I could tell they weren't sure whether it was me or not. What were the odds of my running into these two people in the garage area at the Indianapolis speedway?

I leaned over to Rice' and whispered, "What am I going to do about them, I think they know who I am."

Rice' looked at me with a blank stare and said, "You're going to have to talk to them. And they know it's you."

So I walked over to Don and Nancy with seeming confidence and said, "It's good to see you." However, deep in my gut, I was about to throw up from the anxiety.

They both gave me a hug, told me how good I looked and we all went over to my SUV that parked right there in Gasoline Alley and caught up on old times, like nothing had ever happened. I gave Nancy a few of my shirts and told Don that all I had on me was shirts for girls if he was up for it. We had a few laughs and then they left to take their seats in the main grandstand.

When I got back to Lake and Rice's motor coach, Rice' was just about to burst at the seams to find out how that chance meeting had gone.

"It went okay," I told her.

But seeing them in an arena where I could never let anyone know my past had just taken ten years off of my life.

I told Rice' that I needed a drink but would settle for a ham sandwich. We both laughed at the absurdity of the situation. Me being me and being where I was, a once-in-a-zillion circumstance. People would just not believe this life of mine if I told them.

About 30 minutes later, Lake and Rice' and I were walking out to driver introductions when we bumped into one of Lake's sponsors. John was an executive who ran the Hormel motorsports program. We chitchatted with him for a minute, and then, as he went to leave, he leaned over to me, put his finger through my belt loop and said, "You wear your colors very well."

Then he walked off to the VIP area.

I had been complimented on my apparel designs, which I always wore to the races, but that was a first for even little ole me. Lake didn't catch it but Rice' did and she rolled her eyes in disbelief. What was I wearing to prompt this comment? Tight-fitting bright-blue jeans, a black form-fitting scoop neck ¾ sleeve top with my retro multi-colored stock car embroidered on the upper chest, and a pair of black lace flats. The outfit fit perfectly in the context of the culture.

As cheesy as that advance was, it was good for my ego.

Two weeks later, I was back in Charlotte gearing up to go to Bristol, then down to Nashville for the "Salute to Motorsports" at Opryland. But to my surprise and horror, things were not going well at my company's office.

Someone wasn't paying the bills

One day I got a call from my friend Robin Helms, who owned the embroidery company that did work for us.

"I hate to tell you this, Terri," she said. "But Aaron hasn't paid me for the work I did back in May."

Other vendors were calling too – and the ones who were my friends were calling me instead of Aaron.

I called Aaron to see what was going on. The situation was even more complicated than I'd feared. He was pissed off at Wanda because she hadn't paid him for that big order during the 500 in Charlotte six weeks ago. The Speedway Club bill had ballooned to over $10,000 when Wanda ordered more apparel pieces. On her side, Wanda thought that Aaron had overcharged her. I was caught in the middle. To make things worse, he hadn't told me what was going on, so I had to find it out from Wanda.

Aaron and I went around and around about him paying everyone until we worked out the situation with Wanda. He refused to do it, and I recalled bitterly that I had no control over the money. Wanda and Robin were my friends and we needed them to keep our company running. This went on for a month and I was getting more pissed off by the day. My credit-card bill was out of control from traveling. I was tired and needed rest.

So one day, after Angelo pleaded for me to go and see if I could fix the situation, I bit the bullet and headed out to the Speedway Club to see Wanda and straighten things out. After I leveled with her about my dilemma with Aaron, we went over the bill piece by piece. He had over billed her by more than $1,000, which really pissed me off.

Right then, Wanda cut me a check for what she owed.

From the Speedway Club I drove straight to Lake's race shop in hopes of catching him, to get his advice on what I should do with the check. Should I turn it over to Aaron, whom I no longer trusted? Or should I deposit it in my bank, pay some vendors and personal bills, and then tell Aaron to kiss my ass?

But Lake was not there, so my old buddy Harpo and I sat around the office hashing it all out. I really needed to pay our vendors that afternoon, but I also needed to pay off my credit card bill. We decided that I should deposit the check into my personal account and pay vendors and personal bills from there.

So I drove two minutes up to my bank, deposited the check into my account and paid everyone I could including my credit-card company. There was $3000 left, and I deposited that into the company account. We still needed to pay the Winston Cup Scene but I was out of money and I figured I would let him take that $3,000.00 dollars and pay them off.

When Aaron found out what I'd done, he was furious. From that moment on, we had drawn our lines in the sand. Plus, he had not paid the Racing Wives their royalties. Aaron had no idea what screwing these people would do to our chances to make this successful. He was handsome, rich, young, and very, very dumb to the ways of the NASCAR community. They are a close-knit bunch and don't tolerate that kind of business dealings.

To relieve the stress, I was venting to Wanda and Margaret, and to Harpo instead of to Lake and Rice' because, the last thing I wanted was to have them on me too. At the time I was so fearful of being judged as a failure that I just could not bring myself to tell them what was going on. It was only a matter of time before this was going to blow up in my face.

In Nashville, the "Salute to Motorsports" presented by the Nashville Network at Opry Land was always very big deal… like the Academy Awards in Hollywood. Everyone who was anyone in motorsports was there.

I was getting short on funds, so my good friend Brit found me a place to stay in Nashville with one of his sisters friends. So I was able to spend the entire week there, out in the hot August sun working my ass off, handing out brochures and selling product. One of the PR girls at the Nashville Network, Nancy Neal, let me in on every promotion she could. I had actually met Nancy Neal back in 1990 as JT at an event that Memphis Motorsports Park was hosting. Like many others, she didn't recognize me! So being around her was a weird experience, that made me giggle a bit.

Through the Nancy connection, I got introduced to up-and-coming country singer Lisa Stewart and we decide to hang out and possibly work together on promoting my company. She was looking to nurture the NASCAR audience and I needed a high-profile pitch person to bring more attention to my product, so we decided to get together in Charlotte a few weeks later when she would be in town filming a show with the Gatlin Brothers. I wasn't sure how to get Lisa involved but she was beautiful, had the voice of an angel and she was from Mississippi too.

In the mean time, I had designed Lake a cool shirt with embroidered stock cars racing up the front, and he wore it on the "Ralf Emery Show," which is broadcast on the Nashville Network. Not five minutes after he did the show, Lake's office was bombarded with calls from fans all over America wanting to buy a shirt like that. Amazed by the reaction, I called Angelo and told him to call Harpo back at Lake's office and get messages about the shirt, then call those fans up and sell them a shirt.

Diary Notebook

Two weeks after Labor Day

Meeting Lisa Stewart was cool . . . I think she and I can get something going . . . Rice' is getting pissed at me over Robin . . . the stress is killing me, I have to figure out a way to work with Aaron. . . I'm tired, being out on the road over the summer has been hard . . . the wounds from my surgery are healing . . . I think I'm ready to have sex, but with the right person . . .

Aaron and I lock horns

Our deal was falling through. The executive director for the NASCAR Wives, Diane Huff, thought we were hiding our sales and not paying them enough royalties. This wasn't true. But to make things worse, Diane had taken a dislike to Aaron...and to my PR chick Lee Spencer. Lee who was to go on and become the kick butt NASCAR writer for Sporting News and FOX Sports, had done a great job, but she had somehow pissed off Diane, as well as Deb Williams, the executive editor of the *Winston Cup Scene*. Now Diane was telling me that I had to fire both Leigh and my business partner Aaron.

I called Leigh, and told her, "They will probably make things rough on me if I continued to use you. But I'm not going to let them run over me. You should cover youre self on this"

Only two weeks earlier Deb Williams and I had a power lunch at the Speedway Club, I wanted to bring her up to speed on my company and she was very helpful and excited that a woman was taking on this challenge. I looked up to her for being the Executive editor of NASCAR's biggest news paper and knew very well that she had put in her time dealing with all those arrogant men in the sport to get to her executive position in the sport.

She knew very well what I was up against and encouraged me to stick to my vision and to not let the boys get in the way.

I told Wanda what was going on and she said that Diane was way out of line.

To top off my stress level, I was late on paying Robin Hayes what I owed him. Rice' was getting pissed at me over that.

Up until now, I had been doing so well with my new life— had gotten my professional and social and private life running smoother than I ever thought was possible. My femininity was so natural I hardly ever thought about JT any more. I was back on good terms with my parents, which eased my personal stress a thousand points.

But this business thing was getting to me. I was trying to be focused and make good decisions, but my business partner Aaron had hung me out to dry. He had paid all of his own contacts and vendors but let mine slide. Diane Huff was right on one account—I did need to find someone to buy out Aaron's contract. But who would that be?

One afternoon, I casually told Little Bud More, owner at the Petty camp's merchandising program, that Aaron's part of the company could be bought if he was handled just right. Bud perked up at the possibility and we decided to let it simmer for a week or two and see what we could work out.

By the third week of September I was back to living on my credit card and eating for free at the Speedway Club virtually every weekday. There was a little spot back by the kitchen where most of the Speedway's office personal hung out at during lunch. It was where Wanda and I had a bite off the buffet and socialized during lunch. You might run up on anyone sitting back there catching a bite or a break, even Mr. Wheeler from time to time.

A famous sports-car racer, Elliott Forbs Robertson, popped in once a week. I always had new artwork with me, and Elliott couldn't wait to see it. I liked Elliott—he was different from the rest of those hard asses in the racing community and actually respected women. When I mentioned that raced Karts back in the '80s and would like to drive again someday, he took it seriously and never treated me like some bimbo chick trying to be cute.

The Speedway Club was my social home on Wednesday nights as well. Wanda always had a good crowd for happy hour and I had gotten to know two older gents – Fred, a textile manufacture, and Bob, a former District Attorney for Cabarrus County. I would baby-sit them while they got smashed. When I vented my business frustrations to them, they gave me some good advice on how to handle Aaron and Mr. Robin Hayes.

By then it was official, Robin was running for Governor, and he was at the Speedway every chance he got politicking, with a real shot a winning.

"It really bugs me," I told the two gents, "that I let him and Winslow blackmail me into signing that agreement."

Bob told me to tell Robin to go to hell. "Terri, don't you let him and his money get to you. They have been running over people for years around here. Don't you pay him one red cent."

But I had Lake and Rice' to look in the face if I did that.

When I had any spare time, a few friends and I boogied down at Mythos, a cool dance club. One of my new friends was Elgin, a gay man and former female impersonator who worked for Cher out in Las Vegas and had just recently been on David Letterman's "Late Show." I could tell that he had a good heart so I took a chance and told him my story. For a while he didn't believe it.

"There's no way you were ever a boy, let alone a NASCAR driver," he said. "You mustn't ever tell anyone else."

By fall, just as I had feared, Aaron and I had split up. The NASCAR Wives wanted me to invest more money into the company and put a souvenir trailer out on the circuit. Then one night at a Racing Wives banquet we all attended, Lynn Bodine, the wife of NASCAR star Todd Bodine and the newly crowned president of the Racing Wives Auxiliary, cornered me and gave me a big spill.

"Terri you're special…a creative genius and we don't want to lose you," she said. "We need to work this out."

"I appreciate your kind words," I told her. "But I have to regroup and find someone reliable to finance my company. Without money, there's no way I can ever make our deal work."

The next day, somebody told me that Lynn had been bad-mouthing me that morning to a group of the wives. I wasn't surprised—Lynn had a bit of a reputation for doing that and I was tired of their whole PTA mentality. When I told Wanda about the PTA comparison, she just rolled her eyes and grinned knowing exactly what I was talking about. It looked as if the Wives relationship was going to end.

It was early October, the Saturday before the big NASCAR race in Charlotte. My mom had flown in to hang out for the weekend, to enjoy the race and the autumn colors in the surrounding area. That beautiful morning we got up early to miss all the traffic going to the Speedway. While Mom finished putting on her make-up, I decided to make a quick trip to the ATM window just down the street from my apartment.

While I was waiting in the line of cars, my passenger door suddenly opened and Robin Hayes got into my car, holding a box of Krispy Kream donuts. In fact, he had one stuck in his mouth.

It scared the hell out of me. "I'm struggling, and I need some more time before I can pay you anything," I said.

He didn't like hearing that, but what was he going to do? So he got out of the car and went on his way.

That afternoon, things got even crazier. With half of the race already run, Mom and I went down to the Speedway's garage area and pit road to visit behind the scenes. When we headed back to the Speedway Club to finish out the race, I turned onto the little service road that led to the tunnel under the racetrack...and couldn't believe my eyes. There was Winslow Hayes, Robin's daughter, walking on the side of the road. Was I going to drive on by like I never saw her, or offer her a ride to her car? What I really felt like doing was gunning the SUV and running her over.

"Get in," I said, as I stopped beside her.

She was just as shocked as I was. But she was also hot, tired and out of breath. As we drove on, she and I didn't say much to one another, which was a wise choice. I took her to her car across the street and let her out.

When Mom and I got back up to the Speedway Club, I ran into one of Wanda's friends, Kenny Marion, who ran the Speedway Children's Charities for Bruton Smith.

"I've been looking for you all afternoon," Kenny said. "I know you've been looking for an investor, and I have just the guy."

Right away he took me over to meet an older gentleman, Bill, who ran the financial portfolio for Speedway Motorsports, the financial arm for Charlotte, Atlanta, Texas and Las Vegas Speedways, all of which Bruton Smith owned. Bill was also an old friend of the late NASCAR superstar driver Tim Richmond, the biggest playboy in NASCAR history, who had died of AIDS back in 1989.

Bill seemed nice and fatherly and interested in my ideas. So we sat down in Wanda's office and had a nice chat about my vision for the company. I showed him some of the apparel pieces that Wanda was selling there at the Club. We both agreed the concept would connect to the growing 40% NASCAR female demographic and their kids.

The following Tuesday, over at his office at Bruton's Ford Dealership "Country Ford", we met again and brainstormed on how we could finance my project. For the first time since starting this project over a year ago, I felt like I actually had someone who could take Speedsters in the right direction.

Bill invited me down to the Atlanta 500 to ink the deal.

For a moment, I hesitated. I had $75 to my name and my credit card was maxed…and I didn't want him to know I was broke. Fortunately he offered to have Kenny book me a room at the airport Hilton in Atlanta where they were all staying.

A Room for the Night

On November 1, I got to the Atlanta Hilton at around 6:30 p.m. and met Bill and Kenny at a new club, Daytona's. The place was packed with racing VIPs. After hanging out there for a few hours, we decided to go back to the Hilton for a few drinks before turning in for the night. Bill and I, along with General Sadler, a retired general and executive director of the Speedway Children's Charities, as well as Doug Rice, the guy who headed up the PRN radio network at all of Speedway Motorsports' tracks, all jumped into Sadler's rental car.

Back at the Hilton, we all walked down to the bar, ordered a few drinks and everyone began to socialize. Syndicated radio personalities John Boy and Billy were there, and General Sadler who was a regular on their morning show, went over to hang out with them. So Bill and I grabbed a table in a corner and began discussing how we would make our business relationship work. After all, that was what I came down there for, not to party. Bill seemed fired up and ready to bankroll the project.

However, I noticed that the drinks kept coming—there were three fresh margaritas sitting in front of me but, I kept sipping on my first because I wanted to be professional and in control. My tolerance for liquor was low because I did not drink much at all, so I had to be careful. I did not want Bill to think I was some bimbo.

Suddenly I realized that it was 12:00 midnight and I hadn't checked into my room yet. So I told Bill that I would be right back and walked over to the front desk. There I told the clerk that Speedway Motorsports had booked me a room, then waited for her to get my key. However, the clerk told me there was no reservation in my name. I wondered if Kenny and Bill had forgotten to book me the room. I was not in a panic just yet, but I walked back to our table.

"There's been a mistake in the reservations," I told him. "I don't have a room."

Bill then walked over to the front desk to see what the situation was, while I waited, feeling like a child waiting for daddy to straighten things out. Soon he returned with bad news. The hotel was booked solid because of the NASCAR race, and I had no room.

What in the name of Jesus was I going to do? I had fifty bucks to my name, and had to put gas in my car before heading back to Charlotte. It was 25 degrees outside, so I couldn't sleep in my car. I was not driving the 20 minutes back to the Speedway where Lake and Rice' had their motor coach parked and wake them up at one in the morning. I did not need the lecture.

For a moment, tears almost welled into my eyes but I was determined to not let Bill see me cry.

"Hey, I've got an idea," Bill said. "Why don't you stay with me? I've got plenty of space. You'll be safe there."

Right off the bat, I didn't think that was a good idea. But like the naive idiot I was, I went out to my car where it was crazy cold and got my bags, then met him in the lobby. We rode up in the elevator with NASCAR driver Rick Mast. Bill and I got off on the tenth floor and walked on down to the room. My knees were shaking. What the hell, he seemed like a nice man and I was sure he was looking after me. But a little part of my brain was wondering if this could be a casting-couch situation. After all he was part of that clan that ran around with the late notorious womanizer Tim Richmond.

When he unlocked the door, I noticed right away that there was no couch—only one bed. Maybe I could sleep on the floor. While he ducked into the bathroom to relieve himself of all those drinks he had consumed down in the bar, I just stood there frozen, holding my bag. What had I gotten myself into?

When he came out, he was being really nice.

"Just put your toiletries away in the bathroom," he said, "and make yourself at home."

So I quickly rushed into the bathroom, slamming the door, feeling as if I was running from a mugger in the worst part of Atlanta. Standing there frozen in time, I stared at myself in the mirror, reliving the night's activities and trying to convince myself that I was making myself crazy over nothing. Finally I figured I needed to get back out there and face the moment as best I could. That old fear and fearlessness thing was working on me.

When I opened the door, to my astonishment, he was standing right there in the doorway waiting on me. He immediately grabbed me, put his arms around my back and began kissing me on my neck.

"Terri, I've wanted to make love to you since the first time I met you out at the speedway," he growled.

He was very aggressive and I was frightened out of my mind not knowing how I was going to deter the advances of this powerful man whom I'd wanted to finance my business. I was broke and virtually homeless . . . and my dreams were falling to pieces second by second. My body and hands were trembling like crazy. Soon he maneuvered me over to the bed and was laying on top of me, fondling my breast and working his way down to my pants. I was so frightened that I had lost all of my strength—weak, sick, beaten, and angry all in one emotion.

By the time he got my pants unbuttoned, I had relented myself to his power over me on every level. He took control of me physically, mentally and professionally . . . he was now inside my body and I was so sunk into submission that I couldn't stop him. My mind was spinning out of control from the guilt and humiliation. The worst part of this sexual obliteration of my heart and soul was, this was my first time to have sex with a man. Was I being raped, was I consenting somehow, fact was I had no idea what was going on at the time. Just that I did not want to be there with him on top of me. He was a powerful executive who could make me or break me in motorsports in the blink of an eye. But I was just a roll in the hay for him.

He had stolen my virginity and I now realized that he had no interest in financing my apparel company.

The only good thing about this abuse by his sexual and professional power was, it did not take him long to finish his manly business!

Defeated and used

The rest of the night, I lay right on the very edge of the bed rolled up in a petite little ball with my back turned to him and as far away from him as I could get. I never slept a wink, as my mind went wild with thinking.

Since March of 1986, I had been celibate—had dreamed of having sex for the first time as a woman with someone I had picked, someone strong yet gentle, someone who genuinely cared about me. Not in a hotel room in Atlanta with an older man I would never have slept with anywhere at any time. In this crucial moment of my life, I had been betrayed by my lack of experience in living as a female. I had just been getting my sea legs as a woman. If I had already spent a lifetime as a woman, I might have seen the danger coming and avoided it with all the skill of a seasoned fighter on the battlefields of sex.

As it was, I hated myself for what had just happened. All I could think about was, I wanted to go home to my parents. I wanted my dad to kick this s.o.b.'s ass for me. I wanted Lake Speed to run over his sorry ass with his racecar. I wanted to run down the hotel hallway, shouting to the top of my lungs that Bill had abused me, that he had stolen my most precious dream. A dream I had held in my heart for over twenty years, a dream that I had waited to share with the right person at the right moment. I would never have that magical and loving first time I had so desperately held deep in my heart and soul for most of my life.

The next morning, Bill had to be out at the track very early, he was taking a helicopter over to the speedway with his boss, Atlanta Motor Speedway owner Burton Smith.

"Stay in the room as long as you want," he said. "Just remember to lock the door when you leave."

Clearly he was clueless that he had abused me in ways he could never imagine. He had no emotion other than, he had to go, he was late. I just looked at him with a blank stare and nodded my head yes.

Right after he walked out the door, the phone rang. Answering it was a reflex action. Bruton Smith was on the line.

"Where's Bill? He's late. We're going to leave him if does not get his ass in gear." Then… "Who is this? Did ole Bill get lucky last night?"

Bruton never knew that it was I on the phone. I just told him, "Bill got luckier than you could ever imagine."

CHAPTER 21

Life Goes on – But for how long?

Lost Innocence

Pulling myself together, I left the hotel at around 11:00 am and drove straight to the speedway.

At Lake's motor coach I checked in with Rice', trying to be positive and upbeat, but she was all pissy over the Racing Wives deal and my not paying Robin Hayes yet. Right-wing Christian child psychologist Dr. James Dobson, whom Rice' listened to on the radio daily, was really into the tough love thing so Rice' was giving it to me with both feet, and I was tired of it. I was not a child, and I did not need tough love—I needed support. She had me in tears.

Just as she was winding down her lecture, Marcia Parsons came to visit, so I quietly left the motor coach without saying a word. I was sick to my stomach and my hands were trembling so hard I could barely hold on to my purse.

At that point, the only person I knew who would give positive support was my good friend Bret. So I went to the garage area to look for him. Instead, I ran into Kenny Marion and he asked me if I was coming to his fundraiser that night.

"No, Kenny, I'm going back to Charlotte," I said. "Bill showed his true colors last night and I have to get the hell out of here."

He looked confused and said, "Well, what else is new? You didn't know that Bill had his special ways?"

At first, I didn't understand what he was saying. Then it dawned on me that if ole Bill had his special ways, why had I not been told?

I finally found Bret at Lake's race hauler and immediately told him I needed to borrow $20.00 so I could get back to Charlotte. He could tell from my red eyes that something was not right. I was so embarrassed that I could only tell him that Rice' had given me a lecture.

He answered, "Well, get in line, I know how you feel."

He gave me a hug and $40.00, told me to be careful. I got the hell out of there as fast as I could.

It seemed as if I cried the entire four hours back to Charlotte. What had I done to lead Bill to think he could do that to me? Was it my fault? Why didn't I just stand my ground and say no?

About halfway to Charlotte, in a moment of desperation, I darn near turned around to head back to Corinth and the comfort of my mom and dad's house. However, I just kept on driving like hell. If I was lucky, my own apartment would be warm and comforting, though I hadn't paid my gas bill. My life was falling apart again, second by second. If I did not get something working that would give me a sense of purpose for my career, I was not going to survive! I was looking up to God and begging for His touch.

First thing Monday morning I made a beeline out to the Speedway Club. I needed Wanda's advice on what I should do about Bill and my company.

She was shocked at my story, but believed every word of it.

"Bill has a reputation," she said.

By now, I had calmed down, and was getting a grasp on what Bill's professional power meant for me now. Wanda and I both agreed that this was clearly a he-said she-said situation. I had to be careful about pressing rape or sexual abuse charges, or it could backfire on me. What Wanda did not know was this: if I did decide to press charges, then my past would surely come up and all hell would break loose. Bill and his lawyers would go after me with all their might. So for now I had to find other ways to handle my hurt and anger.

As our meeting was wrapping up, I told Wanda, "I need to find some kind of work—something that would let me continue to develop my apparel company. Is there any possibility that I could work for you here at the Speedway Club?"

"Yes," she said without hesitation. "I can find you something part time."

Wanda also offered to personally invest in my company, knowing full well that this apparel idea had gold written all over it.

By Thanksgiving I was working overtime every day, trying to make sense of it all but by Thanksgiving, I was deeply depressed. The hotel experience had hurt me deeply. I was praying every day for something to change the deadly course that I was heading down.

Diary Notebook
The second week of November . . .

Lake called and wants me to come by and see him . . . I know what he wants, I ain't going! I finally get my personal life under control and my professional life falls to pieces . . .here at night, I just can't seem to stand being by myself . . . why can't I sleep with the lights turned off? . . . I need a relationship...can I deal with that responsibility? . . . I just need to be a woman at times . . . not a woman in business . . . have I bitten off more than I can chew up here? . . . I don't know . . . last night, I wanted to kill myself ten times . . . I fought through and made it to morning . . . I don't want to give up . . . I've come too far . . .

Alpha males

The week before Thanksgiving, I had been over at the South Park mall recharging my emotional batteries with my friend Elgin during one of his breaks. After Elgin went back to work, I took a quick stroll through the mall, just checking out the latest fashions and getting a wish list together for Christmas, when I felt some one tap me on my shoulder.

A 6'2" slender handsome hunk of a man was standing there, handing me a business card.

"Hi," he said. "My name is Randy Mottsinger. I own a modeling and talent agency here in town and I'm looking for people to do local and regional modeling and promotional work. I need people over twenty-five and people who can work corporate conventions. I need good looking soccer moms and I would love to have you on our team if you are interested."

His interest made my self-esteem blossom on the spot. I reached out, took his card.

"I'm flattered that you find me interesting," I said. "But I have no experience in that line of work, and I don't think I'm tall enough."

He smiled. "This kind of work doesn't require a 6' blonde – just real and beautiful people. You fit that bill."

I was a bit suspicious having heard horror stories about modeling agencies running scams on people.

"Thanks," I said, "I'll give you a call in a week or so."

As I walked off, however, I had no intention of calling him. It just didn't feel right. But it clearly was good for my ego.

Over the next hour or so I continued roaming through the mall, just thinking about my life. It seemed like I was star-crossed—just when I would have everything going for me the bottom would fall out my life again. The past year had been a mirror image of my entire life—something good and fantastic followed by something devastating and tragic. Had I moved too soon to break out on my own and start this apparel company? Should I have waited a year or so and become more comfortable in my new skin? I was naive to how men treated women in everyday life and especially in the hard-core business world of NASCAR. I hated the chauvinistic attitudes, but I loved being a woman beyond any words. It meant everything to me to be who I was—there was no way in hell I would ever go back to being a male. The very thought repulsed me. I had to find some way to bounce back from that night in Atlanta.

I thought about going back to Corinth for Thanksgiving. A trip back home would recharge my batteries. But Wanda wanted me to help at the Speedway Club on Thanksgiving Day so it would be Christmas before I could see my parents. I also knew that I needed to get into counseling, maybe talk to Brother Max, and that really scared the hell out of me!

As the holidays came on, I continued to be struck by how womanizing all these men are. One afternoon, about two weeks before Christmas, I was at the Speedway Club and had an encounter with a public-relations executive who worked for Football Hall of Fame coach Joe Gibbs, who was also involved with NASCAR.

This good-looking alpha male had seen me standing with Wanda inside the restaurant area overlooking the Speedway. I recognized him because I had interviewed with him about a job only a month after my surgery, when I was thinking of moving to Charlotte. I was thinking he had recognized me too, from the NASCAR garage area sometime during the past year.

Now, as the PR executive and his corporate boys were leaving, he spotted me standing by myself near the elevators overlooking the fifth-floor ballroom. As the other men paid their bill, he casually strolled over to approach me and I could tell by the look and grin on his face he was trying to impress me. But neither one of these situations was the case, he was interested in me from a sexual point of view.

"Hey," he said, "I really like those pants you're wearing. Those silver zippers are sharp."

Then he dared to reach out and took hold of one of the zippers that ran diagonally across the pants pockets, and pulled it open and shut. He never even blinked.

I thought to myself—this s.o.b. has a big set of balls to be doing this right here in the Speedway Club. Especially a few feet from his fellow executives. So I grinned and stuck out my own right hand.

"Let me re-introduce myself, Larry, I'm Terri O'Connell, Lake and Rice' Speed's friend. I don't think you remember me because my hair was dark and a lot shorter then. But I interviewed with you a year or so back concerning a public-relations job."

Right away he jerked his hand back, turned white as a sheet and stuttered, "Uh . . . I do remember you, UH . . . how is Lake and Rice'. . . uh, well, I got to run. My guys are calling me. It was nice seeing you again."

The irony was, this friend of Lake and Rice's was a right-wing married Christian, and he had just been clocked playing around. The other irony was that his boss, Coach Joe Gibbs, was also an ultra right-wing Christian and would have blown a gasket if had seen his number one PR guy philandering.

I made a beeline back to Wanda's office to give her the details on this repulsive advance. She laughed and said, "Terri, you have an eighteen-year-old's figure with boobs, you have eyelashes out to here. These guys can't help themselves!"

What was up with these married men thinking they could get away with this behavior? I loved being with men, and longed to have a real relationship but since Atlanta I had grown suspicious and wary, and withdrawn from men's advances. I knew I had to get over my fear.

On top of all the emotional and spiritual stresses, I had an excruciating urinary tract infection. Fortunately, Wanda hooked me up with some little red pills that knocked out the infection in a week or so.

Better yet, Wanda invested in Speedsters and convinced one of her friends, Jennie, who was a crack sales guru, to get involved as well. By Christmas there was new life in the apparel company and I had caught up on my bills.

We also had been approached by a group of buyers from a new company hired to develop a retail chain called NAS-CAR Thunder. They were in search of new and innovative apparel and art pieces to put in the stores, set to be located in malls across the southeast. The meeting and presentation was scheduled for the first week after New Years at the Speedway Club. Wanda, Jennie and I were pumped up about the opportunity and we decided that my new cartoon series would be a great fit.

I had also contacted a counselor in Charlotte, A professional was needed to help me work my way out of this mess. I thought about going to see Brother Max at the speedway but couldn't bring myself to tell him about that night in Atlanta. He was close friends with Lake and Rice' and might somehow let his friendship with them cloud his view of me.

I knew I needed to sit down with Wanda and tell her my life story. She was genuinely interested in my success and had invested in my company. I owed it to her. Sometimes you have to take a risk and let people know your past. Most of the time, however, you can never tell people because you know that they will not protect you no matter what. But Wanda was different. Finding the right time to tell her would have to come after Christmas. I needed the holidays to work out in my head and heart all that could happen to me in the future if things did not turn around.

About that time, I started rethinking about writing my autobiography. Over the years, doctors and friends had encouraged me to do it so many times – when was I going to get going?

Meanwhile, all the drama aside, I had to find a cool dress to wear to that Speedway Club fundraiser . . . and I needed a date!

That's me promoting my Cartoon designs in 1995. Carryon Myers, wife of famous Dale Earnhardt crew member "Chocolate Myers took the photo.

Home for Christmas

As I lay my lipstick case down upon the dressing table, I glanced into the lighted mirror and gazed in disbelief at the woman who stared back at me. My eyes, a liquid green, perfectly shadowed and framed by my long thick lashes. My strawberry hair falling gently about my face. My cheekbones, high and defiant. My lips, full and richly colored. My shoulders, soft and creamy against the black velvet evening gown bought specially for tonight. I had never felt so feminine, so natural. The woman who stared back at me was a triumph of strength and will, of courage and perseverance. I felt honored to be her, to be a woman.

Fighting back the emotions that had lived inside of me for most of my life, I looked down at my hands, petite and graceful. Hands whose skin had once been cut by sharp tools, whose nails had been torn by rough machinery, hands that had built high-speed vehicles from design to finish, and that had gripped the steering wheel around curves at 180 mph.

Only one year ago, I babysat for my friends, Lake and Rice' while they attended this event. I had helped Rice' find her perfect dress and, the whole time we shopped, I wistfully wondered what it must feel like to attend such an affair. Through my mind flashed the images of another lifetime, so distant now, yet still so mysteriously near. Memories of the track, hot asphalt and cheering fans, the smell of gas and oil, the pain of my journey—all were reflected in my knowing and somehow vulnerable expression. I knew I had made the right choice.

A buzzing sense of shock seemed to pass through my body as the reality of my new personae reconciled itself with my past in the mirror before me. Tonight I would enjoy myself as only a woman could . . . the glamour of a celebrity gala, the arm of a handsome executive, my beauty admired, my presence sought after by strangers in the crowd, the effect of my perfume on those I casually passed . . . my mind reeled in fantasy until it was interrupted by a knock at my door.

As I opened the door, the chill of the evening, carrying the scent of the holidays and a frosty mist, sent a quick chill over me. It was just before Christmas, my favorite time of the year, and the festive spirit filled my heart, forcing the twelve months of business and personal nightmares from my memory.

Before me stood my escort—a tall and handsome man: mature, with salt-and-pepper hair, and immaculately dressed in his tuxedo. The power of this position as the VP of a Fortune 500 company seemed to surround Jack like an aura. In the drive beyond him, his limousine was humming gently as if it was Cinderella's carriage waiting to take her to the ball.

His approving and slightly mischievous smile told me that he was as pleased with my appearance, as I was with his.

Our date, for the Head Injury Foundation Benefit Gala, hosted by Jim Brady and his wife, had been arranged by some higher-ups in the motorsports community. The fund-raiser was the major event in Charlotte, attended by politicians, activists, and celebrity figures from all over the country. This was Terri's debut into national society, and I felt every bit the debutante. I wished that all those self-righteous naysayers back in my home-town could see me now.

Earlier that day I had dropped off a donation piece, one of my own cartoon designs that Wanda and I had encased in a multicolored frame, to be sold during the event's silent auction.

I needed this night, this event. I was on the edge of a nervous breakdown and I knew it – searching for the energy to just get out of bed in the morning. I needed something positive tonight . . . reaffirmation as a woman... pretty and glamorous and appreciated . . . not aggressive and competitive and trying to always sell myself.

Jack gave me a quick kiss on the cheek and help into the limo, and we were on our way.

Stepping out of the limousine at the entrance of the gala and taking my date's hand, I felt as glamorous as any Hollywood Star. As far as I was concerned, this was the Oscars. . . I had James Bond at my side. On the elevator up the Speedway Club, we were in the company of actor and activist and head-injury survivor Gary Busey. He was impressive standing there in his tuxedo and I caught him checking me out. In a mischievous moment, I wondered how he'd feel if he knew he was riding with the once J.T. Hayes, former National Racing Champion and serious crash survivor.

As the elevator doors parted to reveal the lavish ballroom and brilliantly attired guests, I stood tall with dignity in the knowledge of all I had been, and all I was at that moment. There before me were movie stars, soap opera stars, racing legends, local celebrities, famous politicians, and everyone whom was anyone, all laughing and chatting together as if they had known each other for years.

My date and I made an impressive pair as we mingled artfully through the animated crowd, the soft tinkling of glasses, and the music of the string quartet playing in the background. I was aware of appreciative glances by those I knew, and from strangers. However, I was a bit nervous about running into

Robin Hayes and his daughter Winslow—they were probably there somewhere.

Eventually we made our way to the silent auction display. There among the many valuable items was my own art piece. I felt proud, and my date seemed delighted over it.

Soon, we were in the banquet room, seated at huge round tables that elaborately set and decorated with elegant flower centerpieces. Gary Busey was sitting at a table just across from me, and Senator Orin Hatch was at a table just to our right.

As the staff began to serve dinner, I prepared to enjoy the elegant conversations – but shortly I noticed that they were to take on a certain flavor of their own.

At first, I was mildly amused by some of the off-color stories that were being good-naturedly tossed about. But as dinner proceeded, jokes became racial slurs, anecdotes became bigoted attacks. Soon I felt a hot rush from my chest all the way to my forehead as I found myself the inadvertent buff of an ignorant remark about gay men. Then the jokes progressed to a new level of low. Suddenly a balding man sitting across from me, who had obviously had too much to drink, told a joke about transsexuals and Jerry Springer. The entire table laughed out loud and continued to trash the diversity community, making it clear how much they hated those people.

Calmly, I looked down at my plate; demurely, I smiled— anything to disguise the growing offense welling up inside me. To my disappointment, Jack went along with the distasteful conversations, even expecting me to join in.

Suddenly all the hopeful preparation I had put into the evening, all the fantasies of glamour, seemed to melt around me like thawing slush on the pavement outside. Here were some of the country's most respected people—people I wanted to look up to and associate with—speaking and acting in ways that I couldn't abide. I wanted to stand up and shout to the entire banquet hall… "HEY, you firkin' idiots, I'm one of those people."

But at that moment, I couldn't find the courage. Would I still be accepted as I had so graciously been all evening? I had already lost my anonymity once, back in my home town, with devastating results for me and my parents. For people in my situation, anonymity is precious. When it's lost, people never see you the same way again.

I had heard these kinds of jokes all my life around the racetracks and coffee shops of the rural South. What made them sting more now?

As the evening progressed, I hardly touched my meal, feeling as if anything I ate would come back up again.

After dessert, I made a bee-line to the ladies room to try and collect myself. There, in the mirror, the warm lights of my bedroom had been replaced by a harsh fluorescent glow. My face looked as drawn as I felt inside. What I was doing in this place and among these people?

I thought to myself, "Be careful what you wish for . . . you might get more than you bargain for!"

The ride home was spent mostly in silence. I felt let down by my date, and even by myself for what seemed now like silly expectations. As my date walked me to my door, his well-aimed kiss landed firmly on my cheek as I turned my head to avoid his lips. I said goodnight and went inside.

Life Goes on - But for how long?
Lost Innocence

559

The reality of Cinderella and her wicked stepsisters seemed all too real.

Dreaming of Christmas

Next day, during the twelve-hour drive home to Corinth for Christmas, I had plenty of time to brace myself. What kind of welcome was I going to get this time?

To my surprise, it was everything I'd hoped for. My parent's house was decorated with all the old familiar ornaments and lights and smelling deliciously of my mother's baking, especially her oyster dressing. My dad had finally come around on my surgery—he completely accepted me as his daughter in every way.

By this time most of my hometown seemed to have adjusted to "Terri." I started seeing old friends, and sharing some things that I felt I could share – including the fact that I was thinking of writing my autobiography. But I wasn't foolish to think that everyone in Corinth would accept me. After all, it was a small town in the South, duh! The trick to enjoying the holidays in Corinth was to avoid the assholes at all cost.

Our family tradition was to open presents late on Christmas Eve in the family room. The three of us – Mom, Dad and I in our pajamas and robes—gathered around the Christmas tree in the glow of the old bulbs that always reminded me of candy and cakes left out for Santa. I remember Nat King Cole singing the Christmas song in the background as well as the Marty Robbins Christmas CD. I felt warm, safe and comfortable.

My dad and I shared a blanket, and he put his arm around me and gave me a hug, as he did when I was a kid. I felt like I had already received the greatest gift in the world—my family.

Then, one by one, we exchanged and opened gifts. Finally there was just one little package left under the tree. It was from my mother.

When I finally opened it, and realized what it was, what it meant my heartfelt too big for my chest, and my eyes filled with tears. In a tiny velvet box, my mother had given me a simple opal ring. All the words I had ever wanted to hear from her had just been spoken in that one gesture . . . she had accepted me as her daughter. I tried to hold back my tears but I just couldn't. I had waited a life time to experience a moment like this, and would have traded every trophy and award I had ever won for this ring.

Hearts are much more important than gold and awards . . . most times we just can't see that, we are too busy trying to impress everyone, trying to be successful, too caught up in life to embrace the little things.

Later that night after my parents had gone to bed, I went back to the living room to sit and watch the Christmas-tree lights. As I sat there curled up on the couch, the lucent glitter from my opal ring reminded me of a crystal ball and I began to reflect on how far we had come as a family. I thought about how far I'd come as a person and a woman—how far I'd pushed them as Southern Baptist parents; and how much they must have loved their son to accept him as their daughter. It had not been easy on any of us, but somehow, in the glow of that Christmas tree I had the feeling it was going to be all right.

Even the presence of my grandmother was there with me . . . there was a feeling of her arm around my shoulders. I still missed her almost daily, especially her wisdom and unconditional love. From this night on my heart had a rebirth, a reconnection to my past and to my future . . . a future filled with a family's love and support, that would never be driven apart by other people's arrogance and meanness.

Trouble

By the day after Christmas, all my friends who had either come home to Corinth, or who still lived there, were stir crazy to get out of the house. Nine or ten of us agreed to meet at a local restaurant and bar called AG'S.

I was reluctant to join them at first, but we had all been going there for at least 15 years and AG's was known for some hot Southern Rock. Why not take the chance to have a good time like we used to, only better, because now I felt completely comfortable in my own skin?

Admittedly the thought of running into some people whom I hadn't seen in years gave me a certain mischievous thrill, as well as a fearful hesitance. That fear and fearlessness thing was eating at me once again. However, I knew I'd be among friends, and didn't really expect any trouble.

At AG's, we settled into a large booth near the band and began catching up on the past few years. Who got married, who got divorced, and more importantly, who was doing who was the baseline of our highly intelligent conversations.

I'd noticed a group of men in a corner that gave me pause. They were obviously a little drunk, a little loud, nothing out of the ordinary. I recognized one of them as an old high-school friend, David. He was now a used car salesman with a seedy reputation. I pretended not to see him but heard my name tossed up in their boisterous conversation. As their tone grew sharper, there was an ugly sense of trouble in the air.

After fortifying himself with the right number of beers, David swaggered over to our table. His eyes were bright with drink, his hair rumpled, his stance was confrontational.

"I hear you've been working on a book about your life," he growled.

Clearly word had already gotten around. But I had not said anything about David. At that time, I hadn't planned to mention him, other than peripherally. There was a funny story involving him—about how I had gone from doing Terri in a gay bar in Memphis one night to playing poker as JT with a group of redneck car dealers, one of which was David, all in the same weekend.

"If you write anything about me in your damn book, I'll kill your damned ass!" David threatened. "Don't you write nothing about me, you fucking freak!" He went on raving, repeating himself and getting louder. "Look at you...you ain't nothing but a damn freak! You think you're pretty, but you're nothing but a freak! I ought to beat your ass right here!"

Frightened and humiliated out of my wits, I wondered what he was so afraid of. Suddenly I remembered a Christmas party ten years earlier. Most of the town had been there, and rumors about me had already been circulating about town. Was I gay . . . did I wear dresses . . . typical small-town bullshit talk that was impossible to squelch. As the party wound down, David asked me if I wanted to go back to his place for a few more drinks, and talk about all the crazy stuff we used to do in high school—look at annuals and old photographs. I agreed.

At his house, as we sat there on the couch, I found out that what he really wanted was a blowjob. I calmly got up and told him he must have misread me. Then I left, shaking my head in disbelief that this redneck would have the guts to ask me that. Now I knew that the possibility of me telling that story had to be what threatened him. He would never live it down.

By now my friends had stepped between us, trying to calm him down. Others in the bar started to notice as they heard the raised voices. Heads turned, some people even stood up. Those who didn't know me saw a 215-pound man abusing a 117-pound women. They didn't like it.

David retreated back to his friends, only to stir them up even further. Their drunken remarks and laughter got screechingly loud. I began to worry about a possible riot situation. My friends were no lightweights either. One of them, a biker friend, had a gun.

Finally, the alcohol-induced tempers were right at boiling point. One of my long-time male friends, Jerry, who had once been a city cop, stood up and motioned to three other of my friends. They quickly ushered me out as David and his gang of rednecks tried to follow us down the stairs to the street below.

My bodyguards rushed me over to my Ford Explorer, told me to go home, and said they would deal with David and his gang. By the look on their faces, it wouldn't be a pleasant affair . . . especially for David. In a panic, I cranked my SUV and high-tailed it out of there.

This was my first encounter with violence directed toward me simply because of who I was. My whole body was shaking and enough tears were rolling down my face to fill the mighty Mississippi River. At the next red light, I didn't even know which way to turn. After about an hour or so of driving confusedly around the town, brooding about the craziness of the whole past year, I finally made it home.

As I pulled into my parent's driveway I breathed a sigh of relief. That's when I noticed the workshop where I had spent most of my childhood and adulthood, immersed in the science of auto racing and the fine art of concealing my feelings. That building was a forgotten refuge where I had once felt safe. The cold clear night made its silver metal roof shine like a lighthouse, guiding lost ships back to the safety of a peaceful harbor. I wondered if the manger in Bethlehem had shown so brightly as it called the wise men to the baby Jesus so many Christmases ago.

Slowly I eased out of my Explorer and walked down to the door. As I entered, a serene feeling came over me as if this building had missed me as much as I had missed her. My office and trophy room was off the main floor of the shop. The chill from outside was sharp, so I lit the small gas heater to warm my chilled bones and my feeling of isolation.

By the flicker of the flames, I sat down at my old desk and looked around me, taking in every sight as if starving for my past to come and embrace me. I realized I had not sat in that chair for almost two years, not since my operation, but suddenly it felt as if I'd never left. There on the desk was a huge trophy I had won in 1976 for a National Karting title, surrounded by many other racing achievements, all glittering in the flickering flame creating the only light in the room.

Underneath my arms perched up on my desk was my day planner from 1994, with scribbled dates and notes to myself, especially March 8th . . . the date of my gender surgery.

I looked around at all the reminders of my career that I'd collected over the past 20 years. Photographs of racing days gone by, old garage passes from NASCAR events, battered racing helmets. It struck me that everything in that shop and office could be used to define me. The trophies, plaques, and awards, all hard-earned against hundreds of the best race drivers and competitors in America, said something about me that could not be said for David, or his drunken friends back at the bar. None of them had accomplished what I did, nor had they faced the incredible hardships I had felt while doing it. Why then was I letting them make me feel this way?

Who was David, who had done nothing but get into more trouble than anyone I knew, to belittle me? Hadn't I felt the same way just a week ago at the Benefit Gala? How had I let the politician steal my business, my creativity, my dignity? Why hadn't I been more forceful fighting off the sexual attack of the powerful banker? Why didn't I feel stronger against these people?

With tears still flowing from my eyes, I lay my head down on the desk and tried to find the strength that had allowed me to make the sacrifices for all the things I saw around me. The crazy oxymoron of my life was coming clear to me. I'd spent the first 30 years trying to hide my femininity and now, as Terri in Charlotte, I was afraid for anyone to find out about the masculine side of my past. In Charlotte, I had total anonymity as a woman with my feminine beauty appreciated by everyone who knew me. In Corinth, I had no anonymity and was hated for my femininity.

In short, I had traded one lie for another, and didn't know which lie was worse. Everyone has something they are hiding—that's just life. But it seemed that my issue kindled the vile rumors and gossip more than most. For the life of me, I had never understood why I was so threatening. Was God speaking to me… did He want me to be out and open about who I was?

I slowly drifted off to sleep, comforted and embraced by the room that held the secrets of my soul.

When I awoke, the sky was becoming brighter, the stars dimmer, and the 30 years of memorabilia still surrounded me on the wall of the shop. The pain I had felt only four hours earlier was not gone, but I had awoken with a better perspective for easing that pain. My life had been given and lived for much more than a shelf of trophies and a few cartoon characters. There was more to living, to my endurance than I had ever imagined. Lessons given to be shared so others might not have to live the uncertain highway I had traveled . . . one dangerous curve after another with fear and fearlessness lived as one daunting emotion with every single breath.

Maybe it was time to see if people would believe the Terri O' story, only time would tell.

Before I left town, I told my dad about what David had done to me at the bar. Later Mom said he was so pissed off that he went looking for David and took his gun.

"I tried to stop him," Mom said, "but he was hell bent on teaching ole David some respect for you."

Ole David had better count his blessings my dad could not find him.

Get Busy, Girl

Once I got back to Charlotte, the day after New Year's Eve, I knew I had to get my butt in gear.

Speedsters was still holding on by a thin thread. Wanda Edwards and I were scheduled to make a presentation at the

Speedway Club to that new retail start-up, NASCAR Thunder. Wanda and I both thought they were making a mistake by trying to sell driver merchandise and souvenirs at malls when race fans could get the same merchandise at the track. We thought they would be better served to develop an in-house brand. I had ten cool cartoon characters that played off one another very much like the Disney cartoons, that we thought could be that brand. The clothes really looked creative, original and professional.

I pulled an all-nighter making storyboards that showed our characters interacting with one another in a motorsports story line.

By 9:00 the next morning we were at the Speedway Club setting up our presentation. Wanda had booked us a conference room up on the sixth floor just around the corner from her office. We thought we had a good chance for a sale.

The meeting went well, and we made a sharp, professional presentation. But in the end, the buyers were only interested in putting driver merchandise in their stores. We knew that their concept was not going to work.

NASCAR Thunder went belly up after a few years.

Down to Daytona for the 500

By February 1996, I was still trying to figure out how to keep the bills paid. The part-time work for Wanda was not enough. I had applied for jobs at most of the department stores in Charlotte but this was their off season and no one was calling me back. If I could get rid of my apartment and just rent a room, I could cut my monthly bills in half.

My friend Jodie Folice's dad Joe had a big farm 15 minutes from the Speedway and offered to rent me a room for $200 a month. That was exactly what I needed—except Joe had the hots for me. Three weeks before Valentine's Day, I moved in with Joe with a threat that if he tried anything funny, he would wake up missing a few of his male parts.

The next week Rice' asked me if I wanted to come down to Daytona with her and Lake for the 500. She needed me to help out with the kids. Lake had a lot of sponsor commitments during Speed Weeks that would keep them jumping and she knew I could use the extra cash for babysitting the kids. Plus, being in Daytona for the 500 would help me nurture possible investors for my apparel company. Rice' still believed that I could keep Speedsters float if the right opportunity presented itself.

Plus, Robin Hayes had been nagging her about me paying him what I owed him, so Rice' was trying to do both of us a favor.

I was always amazed at how people saw me sometimes. The morning before the Daytona 500, as Lake, Rice,' the kids and I headed to chapel service in the Daytona Speedway garage, Mary Lou Beaudry, the national director for Championship Auto Racing Auxiliary that I'd met before, tapped me on the shoulder as we all tried to find our seats.

"Why, hello, Terri," she whispered. "I didn't know you had all these kids. They're so cute! Is your husband here?"

Once again, the soccer mom image was out front and center. Rice' looking at me right out the corner of her eye with a silly grin on her face.

"No, the cute kids don't belong to me," I said. "I wish they did. They're the darling kids of Lake and Rice's." I introduced her, and we all had a quiet laugh about it as we took our seats. Even Lake, who was getting into his race zone by then, thought it was funny.

It was good to hear that you're not only a woman, but a good looking woman with a husband and three kids.

CHAPTER 22

Who Can be Trusted?

Chance Meeting – Country Crooners

A few weeks after the Daytona 500 we were all down in Atlanta for the Atlanta 500, and Bret threaded his way back into my life again.

The Friday night before the race, my pseudo business associate and new friend Lisa Stewart had been hired to sing at a big VIP gala and fundraiser for Burton Smith's Speedway Children's Charities at the Renaissance Hotel located at the Atlanta airport. The marketing group that headed up the Hormel sponsorship on Lake's team, International Integrated Strategies had contacted me about getting them some tickets to the gala—they wanted to bring in the CEO in charge of the Spam program and have him enjoy the exclusive event. I made a few calls and got the tickets. The Hormel group made a substantial donation to the Children's Charities and we all enjoyed the event. Lisa put on a hell of a show, while the Hormel group and I danced our tails off to Lisa and her band.

Getting those tickets put a feather in my cap and I was thinking about how I could get the Hormel guys interested in Speedsters. That night after the gala, Lisa and I and one of her best high-school girl-friends all crashed in Lisa's room. The next evening, Lisa and her girlfriend had a dinner date with Richard Childress, Dale Earnhardt's team owner. I had a quick bite with the Hormel bunch, then headed on back to the hotel room to catch some TV and some needed sleep.

At around eight o'clock, the phone rang. A familiar voice said, "Hey Lisa, it's Kenny, you want to grab a beer down in the bar?"

"This isn't Lisa," I said. "She won't be back till later. Kenny, do I know you? Your voice sounds familiar."

"Oh, I'm sorry, it's Kenny Chesney, me and Lisa are old buddies. Hey, you wanna have a beer with me and my base player? We could use the company...the bar is deserted."

I knew he was the up-and-coming country star who was in Atlanta to sing the national anthem the next day. Lisa was going to sing "Georgia on my Mind." So I freshened up and went downstairs. Kenny and his band member and I chit chatted about the music industry and about how popular NAS-CAR had become over the past few years.

The next day, we all headed to the track bright and early to miss the traffic, Lisa did some appearances, and I hung out with Lake and Rice' in their motor coach until driver introductions. Later I hung out with Lisa and Kenny. When they belted out their songs in front of about a hundred thousand people and millions on national television I was standing only ten feet away in the roped-off VIP area.

Afterwards, as we were all walking over to Burton Smith's hospitality suite, my good buddy Bret spotted me and yelled out that he had never seen anyone who could hang out with VIPs like I could. He came over and gave me a hug.

"You look great," he said. "Are you doing okay?"

"Oh, I've still been struggling," I shrugged.

"Call me when you get back to Charlotte, and we'll have dinner."

At Burton's hospitality suite, everybody settled in to enjoy the race with platters of giant prawns and other gourmet food, plus VIP's and a few big-time politicians. My worst nightmare, Mr. Bill, was there. It made me sick to my stomach to see him, and I avoided him. I was in the middle of a mine field that could get me blown up at any second. I was keeping my distance.

Anyway, the weekend was fun, and I had the Hormel gang on the hook with Speedsters, and my ideas about how they could enhance the Hormel Brand in the NASCAR community.

Hearts of gold

Back in Charlotte, my good buddy Bret was helping me put together a marketing presentation focused on the Hormel brand. He had also helped me put together a new business plan for my apparel company to present to a potential investor.

One Saturday, after Bret and I had been working for the better part of the afternoon, he and I decided to kick up our heels just a bit. He was putting his own NASCAR Nextel Cup team together, and was stressed out like I was. I called up my friend Elgin Kena and his posse, and they were up for whatever would be fun.

By eight o'clock we already had a spot locked down at the Adams Mark Hotel Bar and Club. They always had a kick-ass

R&B band that you could dance to. By eleven, we were feeling no pain and wearing the dance floor out. Bret and I were sneaking kisses and not letting our friendship or my past (which he knew everything about) get in the way. He was a great kisser and he had my hormones all stirred up... and I had his hormones going too. After we left the club, we all headed out to Elgin's house for a nightcap and once we got there Bret and I were ready to jump one another's bones.

Elgin was laughing his ass off at the both of us. "Go catch my guest room," he said. "The two of you shouldn't be driving home."

That was all Bret and I needed to hear. When we hit that guest room, we shed our clothes and attacked each another with pent-up attraction that had been building quietly for a long time. For the better part of the night, he made passionate and unyielding love to me. That was my first time to have a real relationship with a man—and it was with a man whom I would have chosen anytime, anywhere. He was not only a good lover, but took me to a place emotionally and physically that I had only imagined before now. It was heavenly and finally made me feel wholly appreciated for being a woman. I returned that passionate love to Bret—he had filled my deepest and most heartfelt dreams on that night.

The next morning, when we woke up, I felt my femininity was glowing. Bret was laying there beside me smiling.

Neither one of us had any regrets, we accepted the night's lovemaking for what it was—two lonely people coming together in the middle of some big sexual attraction, and enjoying each another with no boundaries or expectations that we needed to carry it any father.

The next day, I called him up.

"I really enjoyed last evening," I said. "But have you had time to realize just what we did?"

Being sly, he said," I don't know what you're talking about. We danced, we had some fun and now, we have to just go forward."

I laughed. "Well, Lake and Rice' will kill us if they ever find out."

"I'm not telling if you're not telling," he said.

Bret and I never talked about it again. We both knew we did not need to be intimately involved. He was starting his own race team and needed to stay focused. And I knew he did not need the possibility of a rumor about us following him around if my story ever got out.

In the end, making love to my bud Bret helped me move forward from the hotel disaster in Atlanta.

An unlikely pair

Two weeks later, I met a cool guy named Ray at a dance club there in Charlotte.

Ray and I were an unlikely pair, but who cared. He had a bit of a biker look—about six feet tall, stocky, with a fu manchu and a pony tail. He wasn't really my type—I liked the executive type. But Ray pursued me at the club, and I liked him, so I agreed to go out with him.

Like me, Ray was an artist, so we had that connection. He was the art director for a specialty t-shirt company that provided graphic design and unique shirt concepts for many of the nation's department stores. He was smart, talented and had a heart of gold. By the end of May we were inseparable. I took him out to the Speedway Club, introduced him to Wanda and the gang, hauled him over to Lake and Rice's and showed him off, and made sure Bret knew that I had a boy friend.

Ray was good for me, he settled my nerves, he helped me with my apparel company and gave me amazing back and neck rubs. We never talked about my past. To him it was just what it was. He let me vent my frustrations over how Robin Hayes and his daughter had treated me, and he always caught my back no matter what.

I was glad to have him in my life; he came along just at the right time.

When the month of May rolled around, Ray and I had settled into a pretty comfortable relationship and I was beginning to get my act back together. The Stock Car Café had made a deal to sell some of my t-shirts during Charlotte Speed Weeks coming up at the end of the month. Plus the Café, which was owned by my friends Dan Duvall and Sandra Thomas over at Group Five Marketing, were already selling some of my Speedsters Apparel. I wasn't getting rich but I was keeping the bills paid.

On Memorial Day weekend, Lisa Stewart came in for the races and the Speed Street Celebration in downtown Charlotte. Her good buddy and writing partner, country music star Mark Collie was headlining the entertainment bill for the big downtown celebration and Lisa was going to perform a few songs as well.

This was how I met Larry Franks, high-powered owner of East Entertainment, who had booked Mark Collie for the celebration. Larry was a good-looking middle-aged guy with a beard, very attractive, very much the executive type that I liked, and we briefly exchanged a look. I could tell that he was hot on my trail. But I was really only interested in Ray, so the moment passed.

Lisa has some regretful news for me.

"I can't be involved with Speedsters any longer," she told me. "My manager is on my case – he thinks I'm putting too much time into this. He wants me to focus on my music career."

I hated to lose her support, but what could I do? I told her I appreciated all her support over the past year. We were still friends.

Over the next month, Ray and I got closer with each day. While he played softball with his working buddies, I sat with the other players' girl friends and wives, supporting Ray as his team fought hard for their wins. He and I continued to make my cartoons and apparel line better and better.

Meanwhile I made daily visits to the Speedway Club and Lake and Rice's house. Lake and Rice were riding me a bit about my payments to Robin, who was running for Governor of North Carolina by now. But I was just barely paying my bills, so paying thousands of dollars to Robin was not possible at the moment.

Who is that cute little ole girl?

For the Fourth of July, Ray and I took a trip to Corinth and spent a few days with my folks. They had already met Ray a month earlier, so they were comfortable with me having a boyfriend. In fact, surprisingly, Dad had taken to Ray, which really eased the tension.

One day Ray and I were over at the big house of my friend Ernie Welch's mom and dad. We were lounging around at the pool, having a few cool beverages; socializing with friends I had known for most of my life and just having a wonderful fourth of July afternoon. Ray was mingling with the guys and I was in my swimsuit with four or five of my girlfriends dangling our feet in the pool.

At about mid afternoon Ernie's dad, Dr. Carl, who was my current home-town doctor, and his beautiful wife Jennie came out of the house and joined the party. They said hi to everyone, had a beer or two and then wished us a happy Fourth and went back in the house. Not five minutes later we heard Dr Carl laughing as he came down the stairs and back out to the pool. There he made a bee line over to me. He leaned down and said, grinning, "Well, Terri, you have made it, girl."

"What do you mean?" I said.

"My wife just asked me who that cute little ole girl with the perfect figure and the long blonde hair was...that she had never seen her around before. I told her, Honey, you have known her for most of her life. She used to be Terri Hayes, she is Terri O'Connell now. Just wanted to let you know girl. You have made it and we are all proud of you."

He gave me a big hug and laughed his way back into the house.

All of us had a great laugh about it. This was the ultimate compliment, coming from a true Southern gentleman and his lovely wife.

The next day I hung out with my mom, while Ray and my dad hit a few junkyards looking for some old car parts

Ray needed to help fix one of his cousin's vintage cars back in North Carolina. Ray and my dad were doing some real male bonding—something me and my dad had done a hundred times before, back in the day.

Time to move on

On Labor Day weekend, the biggest apparel mart in America was scheduled for Las Vegas. Ray's t-shirt and graphic-design company had always attended the Magic Mart, and this year Ray had convinced me that I needed to go as well and just walk the floor—meet buyers and investors and see if I could jump start my apparel company on a larger scale. Ray included me on his flight and room arrangements and we headed out to Vegas.

I was excited about the opportunity but not so excited to be going with Ray. Ever since the trip to Corinth, we had been growing apart. We liked each other, but in the end he was not my type and it seemed as if he was feeling my distance.

During the week in Vegas, he went his way and I went mine. One night he never even came back to the room, he and his buds stayed out all night chasing strippers and who knows what else and it pissed me off.

By the time Ray and I boarded the plane to head back to Charlotte, I knew that Ray and I were over.

I was sad about it all. Ray had been a good friend to me, but it was time to move on.

It was also time to start looking for a new place to live. Out at the Joe Folice farm, Joe had turned out to be a pain in the ass, always hitting on me. I had been late on my rent a few times and he wanted me to have sex with him to pay it off. Plus I wanted to get closer into town, closer to the Speedway or even see if I could find a place over in Charlotte.

When I woke up one morning shocked to find Joe lying beside me in my bed, I totally freaked out. He and his bud Ivan Baldwin and a whole host of bad boys had been partying most of the night and somehow in the middle of the party, Joe thought it would be cute if he just snuck in there and got in the bed with me. I immediately called and told Ray what had happened. He told me to get my butt out of there ASAP. I was more than ready, I told him, "I'm going to find me a Gay guy to live with. At least he won't be hitting on me or sleeping with me. I've had it with good ole boys who are always trying to get into my pants."

I drove over to the Caribou Coffee on East Avenue to check out their community bulletin board. Lucky for me, a card was posted with the names of two gay guys looking for a room-mate. Brian and Berry had bought a new house in a subdivision only a mile from the Speedway and wanted a girl to rent part of the house. The next day, I went to see them, and made a deal with them.

Ray helped me move my things.

I needed to have a more pleasant and open living environment…to not constantly be living in the witness protection plan. So I told Brian and Berry my life story. Surely I could trust two gay guys, who would know how important it was to keep secrets like that. At first their jaws dropped on the ground. Then they got over it and welcomed me to the neighborhood.

Over the next few months I continued to do art work for Wanda. My good friend Carryon Myers, who was a journal-

ist as well as the wife of famed Dale Earnhardt crew member
Danny "Chocolate" Myers, began to pal around with me a bit.
I was working on a few t-shirt designs for her and Chocolate
to promote his ever growing popularity. I made a dozen trips
up to their house in Lexington, and a few trips over to Richard
Childress Race shop where Earnhardt's cars were kept. Meanwhile, every week I went out to see Lake and Rice.'

In the middle of all this, I was trying to avoid Brian and
Berry as much as possible. Living at their place was okay—it
was close to the Speedway, closer to Charlotte and all the coffee shops I loved. But they were turning out to be a bit weird.
Brian, who taught music at a Methodist day school, was extro-
verted and pushy while Brian, who worked for the IRS, was
introverted and had a mother complex. When his mother said
jump, he asked her how high.

I was still keeping my graphic design work going, but I
needed extra cash, so I got a job at Calico Corners, a high-end
fabric retail store, and worked there three days a week. I told
the manager that I was just divorced, had a nine year old kid
and really needed a job, I hated doing that, but I was back into
a financial spot at the time and hoped a little sympathy from
the store manager would get me the job. It did... but in the
end all I was doing was making my witness protection plan that
much harder to keep up.

During this period I began to think more about writing
my autobiography. I didn't know where to start. I had tried to
jump-start that process with my diary, but got completely lost
in the process.

So, a week or so after New Years, I took a chance and contacted a lady named Jane who wrote for Arts and Entertainment newspaper there in Charlotte to see if she might be up

for co-writing a kick-ass book about my life. She jumped at the opportunity.

So we began to hang out. Jane took some notes and I attended a few parties at her home in the historical district of Charlotte. It was a wonderful big house that reminded of our historic neighborhoods in Corinth. One part of her house was vacant and she was looking for a renter. I told her that I'd like to rent from her if the space was still available when my lease with the two guys was up in two months. Plus it would allow us to work on the book more closely.

We agreed to wait and find out how it all played out.

What rumors?

The first week of February, on a cold and rainy Thursday afternoon, I went to the Speedway Club to give Wanda some promotional art work I had done for her for her annual Valentine's Day gala. As I left Wanda's office, Carryon was waiting for me. She had a look of hurt on her face that I had never seen before.

"What's bothering you?" I asked.

She motioned for me to walk over to a more private area. We sat down in a corner. She grabbed me by the hand and said, "Your roommates are being mean…they're spreading rumors about you."

"What rumors?" I said, with my stomach turning over.

"They are telling everyone who calls over there wanting to talk to you that you're not being honest with everyone…that you were once a boy. If it's true, you need to be careful, even

Kenny had heard the rumor. Please tell me the truth, Terri. You can trust me and I'll help you with this."

I was slammed to the ground by hearing this. It conjured up all of those old memories …when I had been outed in my home town years ago …when OJ had read my diary and blabbed it to the racing community ten years back. I had no idea what I was going to tell Carryon. Could I trust her? She was a journalist, her job was getting the story. But we were friends, and if she wanted to, her journalistic experience would help me get to the bottom of this little outing party by two assholes.

In spite the panic I was feeling, I decided to trust her.

"It's true," I said. "All of it."

She seemed most relieved. "Do Lake and Rice' know?"

"They know everything. They've known for years. In fact, they've protected me and supported me all along."

Carryon drew herself up. "Terri," she said, "you have to confront those two guys. They need their ass kicked and if you want, we will get Chocolate to do it. He will take pleasure in it."

My heart was beating so fast, I was almost ready to faint. "Who else has heard the rumor?"

"Kenny and Wanda and I know. But who knows who else they've talked to?"

I knew then that I was in big trouble. If Kenny knew it, most of the people at the speedway knew it… especially Bruton and Humpy.

Was it possible to do any damage control? Physically and legally there was no way to know my past. Not only was I one of the most feminine chicks around the Speedway, I was also legally and physically a female. But a rumor like that is just too damn good to not spread.

For an hour, Carryon and I sat there hashing it over. She promised me she had my back, and we agreed that I had to get the hell out of that house right now. That night, I gave Jane a call and asked if her rental was still available. It was.

The next day I put on a bland face and told the guys that, since my lease was up and they were trying to sell their house, I would start looking for a new place to live. They were all lovey-dovey and told me that they would give me a letter of recommendation. The next morning Brian had typed me up a letter that said I was a fabulous renter. That weekend, I moved my stuff over to Jane's.

Monday afternoon, I left their key in the mail box. By then Carryon had told me that the two guys were thinking about reporting me to the IRS because they knew I was not paying taxes on the art work I was doing for her and the Speedway. Here I was…barely paying my bills, making less than $5000 the year before, and they were going to turn me in.

My guns were loaded for them. I had done battle over the years with some of the meanest s.o.b.'s in America, so these two airheads had another think coming if they thought I was taking this off them.

That night I gave them a call.

Brian answered the phone and I lit into him about what they'd done, right down to the IRS threat.

"What in hell," I asked him, "makes you think it's all right to do me this way?"

Brian had the gall to snipe at me, "We think you should be honest with everyone about your past."

I sniped right back.

"Tell you what," I said. "I'm going over to your Methodist Day School tomorrow and tell them that you're a pissy little gay boy. You will have some big-time explaining to do to the church folks. Then I'm going over to Berry's office and let all his conservative IRS buddies know that he has a boyfriend. We'll see how you guys feel about that."

"You wouldn't dare!" he screamed.

"It's not your business to out me," I yelled back, "especially here in this right-wing city. Damn it, Brian, you're an idiot. You could get me killed!"

Brian went silent. Clearly this had not occurred to them.

I hung up on him.

Sitting there in deep shock and disgust, I realized I'd been the idiot. Whatever made me think I could trust those two with my secret, even though they had life-and-death secrets of their own? It was almost worse than what Bill had done to me in Atlanta.

What about that modeling agent guy?

Over the next few weeks, Carryon and I waited and waited to see where the rumors would go, while I just tried to re-group. I hated my job at Calico Corners and started looking for something better.

A few days later one of my new neighbors told me that I should contact a friend of his who owned a modeling and talent agency there in town, called Carolina Talent.

Jimmy said, "I'll give Randy Mottsinger a call and set you up."

Ironically that was the guy I had met at the mall, I already had his business card.

Within two weeks I was doing promotions at new car dealerships and a few conventions around town. The money was better, I had more free time for Speedsters – and Randy was actually becoming a good friend of mine.

By the end of March, I was feeling better about myself and paying my bills. One Friday night, I agreed to meet a friend, Kathy, at the Adams Mark Hotel lounge for a few drinks. The place had the best R&B music this side of Memphis and I got there a little early, ordered a cosmos and shot the bull with the bartender Alex. Not five minutes after I sat down at the bar, somebody tapped me on the shoulder.

I turned around, thinking it was Kathy. It was Larry Franks, the guy who owned a major entertainment booking agency on the East coast and who had booked Mark Collie and Jo Dee Macenna for Speed Weeks that past May. I hadn't seen him since then, but I could tell right off he was still hot on my trail.

"Hey, Larry, what are you up to?" I asked.

"I booked the band that's here tonight," he said. "I want to hear a few sets to make sure they're up for my gig."

For the next hour, we sat there getting to know one another, Kathy finally made it. I introduced her to Larry. He and I danced a few dances, had one more drink and he told me he had to get back to his office to finish up on some pressing bookings. Would I like to have lunch that Monday? I told him I'd love to, and we traded a kiss.

Over the next month Larry and I dated several times a week. He treated me like a queen, and I was beginning to think I could have a real relationship with him. Then, one Wednesday he called and wanted to meet for a quick bite—he had something important to tell me.

At the restaurant, as we ordered our food, I could tell that he was really nervous. He hemmed and hawed and made small talk.

Finally I just asked him, "OK Larry, what is it? Spill the beans."

He reached over, grabbed my hands. "Well, Terri, I don't know how to say this except to... just say it. I have feelings for you. You're beautiful, fun to be with and I want to spend more time with you. However . . . Uh, I'm married. Me and my wife are not close. We have an agreement that we don't want to get divorced because of the kids, but I have the right to see other people. And, I would like to see you only more. If you're comfortable with it, I'd like you to be my mistress."

My stomach sank. I pulled my hands back over to my lap, and said, "Larry, you have to be kidding. You're a nice guy...

but I don't sleep with married men. If you want to divorce your wife, then call me and we might have something. Till then, I'm off limits."

It dawned on me that I hadn't told Larry my life history either.

By now, Carryon Myers told me that several in the motor-sports media had heard the rumors—they had even asked Lake about it. It was only a matter of time before the media asked me if it was true. To make things worse, the political climate was taking a dramatic right-wing dive around Charlotte. The city council was up in arms about government funding of the arts and had condemned the play "Angels in America" that was playing there in Charlotte. This distressed me—Charlotte wasn't just NASCAR, it was also all about religion and bank-ing. Some diverse and talented people also lived there.

So I decided to tell my modeling agent and now good friend Randy Mottsinger about my past life. He would be a good ally and help me process what we should do about the rumors at the speedway. We had to figure out how to get ahead of the press somehow.

More than that, I had to figure out what I was going to do with the rest of my life. Speedsters was dead in the water. With the rumors floating around, no one around would invest in my company and most likely what little art work I was getting would dry up. I needed to kick that autobiog-raphy plan into a higher gear. That could turn everything around, get the facts out and maybe put some major cash in my pocket. However, that could also backfire on me and cause such an uproar that I would have no place to hide. I damn sure did not intend on living underground for the rest of my life.

And I was not comfortable living my entire life in the GLBT community, I wanted to be a straight chick. That was my dream. and I had been living that dream over the past few years. In spite of all the crap, I liked it. I just wanted to have a normal life, and a normal family but, it just did not look as if that was in my cards.

"You raced *what?*"

Two days later, I got my courage up and told Randy my life story. I needed to be free of the deceit once and for all, I needed out of the witness protection program. Or at least out of the one I was currently in.

We were sitting in his office. He was lounging behind his desk, and started out by smiling, almost laughing out loud.

"There is no way in hell you was once a boy," he said. "No way. You're too pretty, too damn small. You're all chick."

I assured him I was not kidding, and kept talking.

"You raced *what?*" he said in disbelief. "Come on Terri, you've got a story better than that. I'm going to kick your ass if you're kidding me."

By this time I had begun to cry. Ever since Carryon had confronted me out at the speedway about the two gay boys outing me. I had kept my hurt locked down. Now it spilled out.

Slowly my reality sank in with Randy.

"My god," he said. "You're not kidding. You raced sprint cars…you…my god."

Randy got up and locked his door so other people in the office could not see me cry. Then he did his best to console me. After about 30 minutes, I pulled myself together. The question was now before us. Should I write my book? Should I end my anonymity for good?

"Let's give it a few days to sink in," he said, "and think how we can go ahead with your book project."

That was a start. I went home, got in my bed and slept for two days.

A few days later Randy and I got together with Jane, my potential co-writer, and started brainstorming on the negatives and positives of telling my story. We knew we needed to keep as much control of the story as possible, but we also knew this story had legs.

There were VIPs and powerful people who would have some explaining to do once my story hit the press. Just having been seen with me could be potentially detrimental to their career and their social status. Robin Hayes, who had lost the Governor's race that past fall, was now getting ready to run for the U.S. Congress. The fact that he'd been business partners with me might come up during the election. Hell, on race weekend mornings, some of the NASCAR officials gave me neck rubs as I sat on their big red steps eating doughnuts and drinking coffee with the guys. I had dined with Humpy Wheeler at the Speedway Club. I had socialized in Bruton's hospitality suites, always filled with Fortune 500 Executives and big time politicians. There was hardly anybody in the sport whom my life hadn't touched.

Most likely a publisher would want to do a book, but was it worth the risk? By going public, I would create a firestorm. The

NASCAR community was going to go nuts. This was not the Ladies Tennis Association Board, trying to keep Renee Richards off the court. This was hard core, right wing stuff—high powered international executives who played rough with anyone who rocked the boat.

However, I always had handled myself with class and dignity in the racing community, I had good friends there, and many would support me. In the end, it was a 50-50 crap shoot on how people would react.

CHAPTER 23

Breaking the Story – Pivot Point #4

By July, Randy, Jane and I had decided to go with a story in the press, Jane wrote a column for the local Art and Entertainment Paper there in Charlotte so she had a secret meeting with the publisher. He wanted to break the story, and would let us have the cover and control of the content and. The story would break in late August, so I had five weeks to get ready.

I had quietly talked it over with motorsports friends who I knew would be honest with me. Going public would definitely change my life. They all supported me, but told me to be careful—that some in the community would not be happy about it. One friend told me I might need to get a bodyguard that my life might be in danger.

However, I felt it was the right thing to do. We would beat the motorsports press and the tabloids to the punch. I would get my own say about my life. Hopefully I could dispel the awful stereotypical images of "gender" on most of the tabloid TV shows. I despised and loathed those images that Springer, Sally Jessie and Jenny Jones were portraying. They made the world a more dangerous place for anyone suffering from gender-related issues. I wanted to do this for not only for myself, but for the moms and dads out in Kansas, the brothers and sisters down in Birmingham and the friends and cousins up in Ohio who had to deal with this issue.

The first week of July, I drove down to Daytona where I met my mom and dad for vacation, it would probably be the last time I could go down there with total anonymity, and I wanted to enjoy it.

No, I'm not Kathy Lee . . . yes, I'm sure!

Whenever we were in Daytona, Dad and Mom and I always loved going to a cool seafood shack called the Oyster Deck, located right on the Halifax River leading out to the Atlantic Ocean. All the racers and crew hang out there during race weekends and the food there is killer. So we hadn't been in Daytona 30 minutes before we headed over there to eat some boiled shrimp and raw oysters.

While I parked the van, Mom and Dad grabbed us a picnic table right next to the water. As I headed to the counter to place our orders, I noticed that all the girls working the order window were rubber- necking me and whispering. I thought to myself, what the hell is going on here, is my boob hanging out, are my shorts unzipped? But when I checked myself out, everything was in place.

At the window, the girl taking the orders yelled, "Are you Kathy Lee Gifford? Oh my God, you are!"

I was taken back. Most people thought I looked like Jane Fonda or Teri Garr.

"No, I'm not Kathy Lee Gifford," I told her.

"Are you sure? You look like her!"

"Yes, I'm sure," I said patiently. "If I was, I'd know."

It took some real denying to get her to take our order. Afterwards she kept on pointing to me and my folks, the entire time we dined. When my mom and dad heard what the girl had said, they both burst out laughing.

I made it a point to enjoy our vacation, I needed the time away from the emotional storm over whether to go public with my story or not.

One night, I was walking on the Daytona beach pondering my future, knowing that my world be changing in about a month. As I strolled down that moonlit shore with the waves gently washing the sand – that shore where the history of stock-car racing first started—I challenged myself on my decision to out myself so dramatically. Would it be better if I moved to Nashville and started over again and keep my anonymity? I had friends in Nashville, it was close to Corinth and my parents. I could nurture my old connections with the music industry… start an apparel and design company there just like I had in the NASCAR community.

Hell, I could get a job at a department store, like I did when I first moved to Charlotte, to get my life back on track.

I knew what losing my anonymity would mean. I had already lost it in my hometown. After the surgery, when I restarted my life in Charlotte, I had realized how precious anonymity can be. I cherished it and now, I was about to throw it away. Plus, my cachet as a cute, talented and personable woman would be gone the moment that article hit the newsstands.

My femininity was my entire essence and now I was getting ready to let it be put on trial. Some people would never view me again as a natural woman. They would see me as being flawed, less than a woman. The thought ran chill bumps down my back because to me, my femininity felt as natural as to any woman on this earth. On the other hand, I had a life story that would reset the bar for the gender issue. I was proud of who I was and what I had accomplished.

Now, facing the moon across those quiet dark waters, I felt I had made the right decision to tell my story. But things could get messy once the story was out. I had to find courage to withstand the scrutiny. Thank God I had my new best friend Randy catching my back.

Still, in the back of my mind, as I walked back to the hotel, I was asking myself, "Am I fooling myself about how it's all going to come out?"

I was about to learn another strange thing about people. Once they find out your past history, they start saying things about you that make no sense at all.

The Terri Watch

About three days before my story broke in the media I went out on the town one last time. Once the story hit, most of those local good ole boys were not going to get it. So going out to dance clubs and hanging at the local heterosexual hot spots was going to be over for a while. The fact that I was cute was not going to matter to those hard legs; their brains were going to calculate me as the former male racecar driver.

There in Charlotte, a cool nightclub kicked out R&B music and a crowd was always there dancing every night of the week. My friends and I liked going there—it was our kind of place. Adding to the excitement of the music, there were always plenty of hot studs to dance with, but I always played it cool and never left with anyone but my friends. So three days before the article was to break I got all dolled up and headed over to the club to hang out and maybe dance a few steps.

I hadn't been there ten minutes before a tall good-looking guy in his mid-thirties casually slid a chair beside me and started up a conversation . . . what's your name, are you married, do you have a boyfriend, all the standard pick-up lines. He was actually a nice guy so I went along with the program, and we danced our tails off for the entire evening. When it was closing time, he tried his best to get me to go home with him.

I wasn't tempted, but he was so determined that I gave him a little test. "Here's my phone number," I smiled. "Call me toward the end of the next week. I might be up to going out with him that next weekend."

He jumped at the opportunity.

As I headed back to my apartment, somehow I didn't figure this guy would be calling me back once the newspaper article hit the stands.

Terri Watch started the next Wednesday, when the story appeared. It made a hurricane sweep through the Charlotte area, and especially the NASCAR community, with my name in the eye of the storm. To hear people talk, you would have thought I was the devil's girlfriend.

"How on earth could it be? How could this little girl, who once was a male, who raced in our top series and was dating some of our people and socializing with us at the most exclusive parties, have ever been in our midst?" was the rallying call.

The NASCAR gang ran for the hills and separated themselves from me as if I had the world's most contagious disease. I was hiding out in my bed with the covers over my head, depressed and sick to my stomach and wondering what in the hell had I done. I had no idea that this community would react in a manner that was even more mean-spirited than I'd imagined in my worst moments. But now I had to learn to live with it.

Two days after the news broke, at about two in the afternoon my phone rang. After about 20 rings I reluctantly answered it, thinking it might be my mom. Instead there was a deep and sexy voice that I immediately recognized as the guy I had given my phone number to. By the way he said hello, I could tell he had a quirky smirk on his face.

"Hey there, girl," he said. "I read all about you in the paper. Wow, you've had quite a life."

"You don't know the half of it," I countered.

We chitchatted for a few minutes about how he would have never known my past had he had not read that article.

Then he asked me, "Are you sure you not making all this up just to get someone to sponsor your racing? I mean, this is pretty crazy stuff, most of my buds don't believe it's true."

I was blown away at his belief that "crazy stuff" like mine would bring in racing sponsors.

"Well, it's true," I said. "Every bit of it."

"Then I guess I know why you were driving that big ole truck . . . You like that kind of guy stuff because you used to be a guy."

What an idiot. He had just stereotyped me.

"You've got to be kidding," I snapped. "Last weekend you thought I was the hottest chick in the room. If I had given in, you would have had sex with me right there and then. Now you decide something is weird because I drive a Ford Explorer… which if you took a poll you would find out that 90% of the soccer moms in Charlotte are driving. You owe me an apology … I'm as much of a woman as any other woman in this town."

He began to chuckle.

"Damn girl, I touched a nerve didn't I? . . . You're right, I just felt like I had to get at you for leading me on… which you really didn't do. Damn, you're cute. I just can't believe you used to race those stock cars. Wow, you're going to make a lot of people crazy over this. I'm sorry if I hurt your feelings. Maybe I can buy you a cocktail sometime and we can have a long conversation about your life. This is really fascinating."

I finally got down off my high horse.

"I appreciate your apology," I told him. "And I would love to have a drink with you. But if we happen to drive somewhere, I'm going to do all the driving."

He laughed like a madman. "No way are you driving me anywhere. I wear the pants and you wear the dresses. You can drive my car anytime but I'm still going to wear the pants."

I chuckled back. "That's a fair trade-off," I said. "I look good wearing a dress, and you look good wearing the pants."

I never heard from him again.

The venom spewing from the NASCAR community was shocking. The sport's morning-show DJs, specifically Paul Schat, went after me tooth and nail on their shows. Paul had never met me but accused me of making the story up for publicity to help me find a sponsor for my racing. Oh yeah, that was a really good idea.

Meanwhile, 90% of the notoriety was not positive and I was already regretting my decision to go public.

Then, on the eighth day of Terri Watch, I got a call from my friend Carryon Myers. She had just gotten off of the phone with NASCAR President Mike Helton, and he was trying to figure out who in the hell I was. He knew I had been hanging around in the garage area for a few years but he couldn't put my face with the story. He had quizzed Carryon over and over. Was I the brunette, was I the short-haired blonde, was I the tall hard-looking chick? He never guessed on his own, so finally Carryon told him I was the cute skinny strawberry blonde who was friends with Lake Speed.

He accused her of bullshitting him. "That chick had to be a real chick," he said. He just couldn't believe that I had ever been a guy let alone raced in the cup series.

Finally he told Carryon that if she knew what was good for her that she would not write about my story, making the point that NASCAR controlled whether or not she got credentials to cover the NASCAR events.

It was hard to believe Helton had strong-armed her like that—she was married to a NASCAR legend. But there was worse.

"Everyone is <u>really</u> up in arms," Carryon said, "that you want to get back into racing."

After all, they were negotiating a four-billion-dollar TV deal that would catapult NASCAR into the next stratosphere for worldwide media exposure. According to those guys, my timing could not have been worse!

Their reaction seemed incredible. But the more we talked, the more I realized that she was telling the truth. It scared the hell out me. Up until that point in my life I had had nothing but the utmost regard for NASCAR. But I had also seen what had happened to Tim Richmond. They played hardball with him to protect their image.

But I did have one thing going for me that could keep them from completely destroying *my* image. By now, the national media was ringing my phone off the hook. I didn't have any skeletons in my closet that hadn't already been dragged out. My life was an open book and I knew that many of the NASCAR notables could not withstand a media blitzkrieg into their own personal lives.

I wanted to find the next journalist I could and tell them what Carryon had told me. But soon I calmed down, and decided to keep my mouth shut for the time being. Besides, I was a NASCAR fan. My family and I had been going to NAS-CAR Cup races in Daytona and Talladega since I was born. I loved stock cars and NASCAR had done one hell of a job getting themselves to this point in American sports. I had nothing but admiration for the France family.

The Cannonball Run

Over the next few months, my life took on a whole new tone. Every media source and talk show in the world wanted to do interviews. They included *Inside Edition, Extra, Hard Copy,* the *New York Times,* and many other newspapers.

In the meantime, since I couldn't race professionally, I had cooked up a publicity stunt to get me a seat…any seat. I would drive in that crazy-ass cross country-road race called the Cannonball Run. Yeah, this was the same one, named after the great NASCAR driver Erwin "Cannonball" Baker, that Burt Reynolds turned into a movie back in the 1970s. I had never liked the movie, feeling it was a silly and unrealistic portrait of the sport. In reality, the race itself was a pretty cool road rally that ran from coast to coast and back in seven days.

All winter I worked my tail off trying to find sponsors. At the 11th hour, Volkswagen gave me a new Beetle, and several local businesses in the Charlotte area who were still friendly to me offered to pay some of my expenses. I was still short the cash to cover all the rally expenses, so I called Louis Forman, a young entrepreneur I had met, who had made millions in the NASCAR screen-printing industry. He was a wee bit reluctant at first but finally committed 144 t-shirts with a design I did that commemorated this historical race. I got busy selling those shirts for $15.00 a pop.

I had talked a girlfriend into going with me as co-driver. Amy was a gorgeous model who worked for Randy's agency. She would be the perfect traveling partner, she was just about as crazy as I was.

On the marketing front, I had put together a good little media package to promote the new Volkswagen Beetle with *People Magazine, Inside Edition, Hard Copy, Extra* and daily live call-ins to the nationally syndicated "Bob & Sheri" radio show. In addition I made a marketing deal with the Fashion Café in New York and the national hip shoe brand, Candies. I also had sweet talked Carryon Myers into helping run the PR logistics while I was out on the road so everything looked good at the start.

But nothing ever comes easy for me; there is always some last minute drama.

On the way to the start at Watkins Glen in New York, we stopped at a convenience store to fill up our gas tank and grab a bite of breakfast to go. By the time I had eaten my egg sandwich and was down the road about 20 miles I began to get sick at my stomach. In another 10 minutes I was on the side of the road throwing up. It was a full blown case of food poising and I was sick as a dog by the time we got to Watkins Glen. If it hadn't been for Amy stepping in to drive, I would have had to cancel the race.

Once we got to our motel at 12:00 midnight I was seriously dehydrated. Amy said, "I'm taking you to the emergency room to get some fluids."

But a reporter from *Inside Edition* was outside the lobby waiting beside the new bright yellow Beetle that Volkswagen had left there for us. He was poised like a hawk going after his prey. I pleaded with him to let me have an hour at the hospital but he was on deadline so I gave in and gave him a quick five-minute interview just to get him off of my back. The emergency room fluids brought me back to life and I managed to get about four hours of sleep before I had to get our car ready for the race.

When I walked out of the motel room, the film crew from *Extra* was waiting there. They followed me around all day as I got our Beetle through race inspection and put our multi-colored daisy decals on the car. By the end of the day I was on the verge of collapsing. That night Amy and I and a nice guy, John from New Hampshire, who was doing the race for the tenth time had a nice dinner together, and then we got some badly needed rest.

The Cannonball Run experience was amazing. Of course, even before we started, most of the other racers figured out who I was. *Time Magazine* had done a little story a day or two before the race. *The New York Times* had published a full one-page story the week before. Most of the guys in the race were curious but respectful—in fact several of those hard tails were chasing me around until they figured out why the media was chasing me.

But a pack of three guys took a special interest in Amy and me right from the start. Eddie was the leader—the editor for *Acura Driver* and *Elegant Bride Magazines*. He and his bunch looked after me and Amy like we were their daughters . . . they pumped our gas, paid for our motel rooms and in general looked after our tails while we were out on the road in the middle of the night.

By the time we had run about 75% of the race it dawned on me that they did not know my story. When we went through Memphis, I told Amy that I thought I should tell those guys, just so they didn't get blindsided by the media at some point. She agreed.

So I took Eddie aside and told him my story. At first he was shocked.

"Are you trying to pull a joke on me and my buds?" he blazed at me.

I finally managed to convince him. To my surprise he took hold of my hand, kissed it and then gave me a big ole bear hug, and said, "Your past like doesn't affect my respect and friendship for you in any way."

He told his buds, and they both reacted as Ed had. In fact all three of them pulled me aside on the last morning of the race and told me I completely changed the way the way they viewed this issue, that they only say me as a girl and a damn pretty one at that. Their support and acceptance warmed my heart , those bunch of hard legs in NASCAR could have taken a lesson in life from those Gentlemen.

Meanwhile, in the Cannonball, we did pretty damn good during the speed events at tracks, even outrunning some Corvettes and Porsches at some of the smaller and tighter venues. We were in a show-room stock Volkswagen Beetle so outrunning anyone out on the track was a real stretch. But at times, I wowed everyone with my road-racing skills especially in Memphis and Greenville, South Carolina.

All in all, while we met some assholes on the trip, 90 percent of everyone in the cross-country adventure were just great to me and Amy. However, I did think that the Cannonball promoters were not pleased that I was giving their iconic event so much media exposure; they really wanted to keep it as an underground classic. Oh well!

After the Cannonball ended at Watkins Glen, Amy and I headed down to New York City to do some promotional events at the Fashion Café in Rockefeller Center. We parked our little ole yellow Beetle with all the Cannonball decals and road grunge right in front of the Café. That car was the hit of Rockefeller Center for two days while Amy and I did our events, including an appearance on the Howard Stern Radio Show.

Of course Howard did ask to see our breasts. And of course we graciously declined that incredible opportunity. But he did treat us with respect.

"I'll catch your back," he said, " if anyone out there in the big bad motorsports world messes with you."

Me and the little yellow Beetle during the Memphis leg of the famous "Cannon Ball Run".

Here Amy and I stand looking good outside the Fashion Café up in NYC during our after Cannon Ball media blitz.

Things get out of hand

By now the media were worked into a fever pitch over me. The very day I got back to Charlotte, there were ten calls wanting interviews, including *20/20* on ABC and a production company that produced pieces for A & E and the Biography Channel. It was all a little overwhelming, but I returned their calls.

"I need a few days to think your offer over," I told each of them.

Indecision gnawed me on whether to take my story to the next level. The media themselves had been incredibly fair with me, but the conservative racing community had circled the wagons and were even working to destroy my reputation. My former adversarial business partner, Robin Hayes, who had just been elected to the United States Congress, was one of those who unleashed the Republican PR attack dogs on my story.

It was a bad moment for me to be short of funds. At that point I could not pay anyone in Charlotte to hire me . . . I had $500 a month coming in from my trust fund and that was it. Plus one of the girls from the modeling agency had let me use her credit card on the Cannonball Run to take care of gas and food and I was having a hard time paying her back because – guess what—all my Cannonball sponsors there in Charlotte were suddenly and mysteriously slow in paying me.

To top everything off, my rent was due, and my landlady was pissed off at me because I had gone public. "If you want to continue to live here," she told me, "you have to tone it down."

Next my landlady and I had a disagreement over her standard poodle, who had chewed up and destroyed that precious black cocktail dress of mine, along with five pairs of my shoes. I told my landlady that I would just trade her my rent for the amount it took to replace my clothes. But she refused to make that deal, and hinted that she wanted me to move out…which suited me just fine except I didn't have any money to rent another place.

My modeling agent and I were developing my autobiography but we were so far from having a book to sell, that depending on income from that was not do-able at the time. So I was just trying to buy time, in hopes of getting paid by my sponsors.

Two weeks after the Cannonball Run, I gave in and committed to doing the *20/20* and A & E interviews. Then, the day before I was to fly to Memphis to film the race-track scene, I went by Randy's agency to try and scrape together the money to pay my back rent before leaving town. By then my landlord had gotten wind of the 20/20 deal. She retaliated by throwing all my stuff out on the street. When I got back to my place, my clothes and other personal possessions were strewn all over the lawn. I spent the rest of the day gathering up my clothes, putting them into garbage bags and storing them at Randy's modeling agency.

During the trip to Memphis to film at the sprint-car races, and my sit- down interview there at the Peabody Hotel, and then on to Daytona to film at the NASCAR race, I wore a happy face for the cameras, and kept thinking to myself, "These media people have no idea that I'm homeless." The shoot at the sprint car-races was especially humiliating—those hard ankles were the ones who had run my reputation through the wringer for most of my professional racing career. Now there I was, right back in the middle of their hornet's nest, exposing my personal life to their world.

To me the experience of having the public know my past was turning out to be not only humiliating, but senseless. In fact, I was now realizing how much I had underestimated the damage that could be done to a person's life by publicity. Overnight I had lost my feminine cachet—had become a media image of a girl who was once a boy, or as the media played it a woman who was once a "MAN". It all made me sick to my stomach. Thank God, my parents were hanging in there with me. Without them I would have been an emotional mess.

Fortunately Judy Tygard, the *20/20* producer, had treated me with the utmost respect. If not for her, I would have pulled the plug on the interview and just gone underground right then.

Congressman Bob from Ohio

After I got back from Daytona, my modeling agent and manager Randy had me move in with him and his roommate and model, Hank Fields. Randy was seeing the madness engulf my life and vowed to not let anyone else run over me. Thank God he did because when I got off the plane from Daytona I have no place to live. All my clothes were stored in garbage bags in a closet at his office, and I had no idea what I was going to do.

At that moment, an offer came along that might have tempted me to give up my independence.

"Terri," Randy said, "you have a call from this guy who says he wants to fly down and meet you. He has called three times today; he says he used to be a congressman up in Ohio."

What did he want? I returned the call.

"Hello . . . hi, Terri... is that you? Oh my God I can't believe I'm actually talking to you. My name is Bob Doyle, not Bob Dole . . . ha, ha. I just think you are terrific, I saw your story on television and in *People Magazine* and I would really like to come down to Charlotte to meet you and maybe take you out for a date."

What in the hell was this guy up to? If he was really a former congressman and wanted to date me, he was either nuts or had not yet realized my gender identity. But I listened to his spill about his background. According to him he now had a successful lobbying business in Washington DC. He was not trying to harm me—he just thought I was beautiful and he wanted to take me out.

I was at a loss for words and had Randy quietly pick up the connecting line so he could listen to this line of bullshit.

By the time we hung up, Congressman Bob had wiggled enough room out of me for me to let him send me information about his life and his successful company. When we all hung up, Randy just howled out loud.

A few days later, a package came with Bob's propaganda and to be honest, it was quite impressive. He had been a state Republican Congressman from Ohio and he did have a successful company that lobbied Capitol Hill on a daily basis.

The next day, Congressman Bob called me up.

"Hey Terri," he said, " I would like to come down to Charlotte to take you to dinner. No strings attached...just a fine meal at a five-star restaurant."

So, what's a girl to do? It was really tempting, even though he was considerably older than I was.

"Well, Bob, if you want to do that, my birthday is next weekend. If you want to come down and take to dinner on my birthday, I'm up for that. But that's all. I understand?"

When I hung up I looked at Randy and said, "Am I really this stupid?"

The afternoon Bob arrived in Charlotte, he came by the modeling agency for our first meeting. I was keeping it safe—if he was a serial killer he was doing it in the midst of my entire modeling-agency posse. Later that afternoon, we had coffee at his hotel restaurant over in South Park. To be honest, old Bob didn't seem so bad. He was a nice guy, he was clean and smelled good. Even though he was not Brad Pitt, he was good to look at. Since he knew he was on probation, he was on his best behavior.

That night at around seven, I drove over to his hotel because I did not want him knowing where I lived just yet. We met in the lounge for a glass of wine, then took a limo over to Chops, a five-star restaurant down town Charlotte. The meal—steak for him and salmon for me—was just fantastic. After a few hours of getting to know one another better, we headed back to his hotel to have a quick nightcap in the lounge.

As we were driving, he launched into a passionate tirade that he wanted me to move up to Columbus to live with him.

"I'll take care of you like no one else," he said. "You'll be living at my house at the country club…driving a Mercedes…"

Tempting, very tempting, to a gal who was broke. I wondered if he was bullshitting me. He was still very convincing.

"…And I have a birthday present for you," he said. He looked like he was just about to burst into flames about the present.

When we got to the hotel, instead of heading us the lounge for our nightcap, he said he had chilled wine waiting up in his room. He wanted to give me my present in private.

Right away my guard was up, and he sensed it.

"Don't worry, Terri," he said, "I'm not going to do anything crazy baby, I just think it would be a nicer moment to give you your birthday present there, and we can continue our conversation from dinner without being bothered by people."

I was suspicious. This was not going to be a repeat of the Mr. Bill episode down in Atlanta. I was not getting hoodooed by his Yankee ass on this night. However, I thought what the hell, I had my game together now, I could handle myself.

So I told him, "Okay, I'll come up… but only to get the present and to have one small glass of wine."

I figured he wanted to get a little smooching for all his efforts and that would not hurt anything.

When we got to the room, he poured two glasses of Chardonnay and gave me two beautifully wrapped packages. Inside the first was a beautiful white satin negligee, very expensive, that any woman would love to have. It was clear what he was up to, but I went along.

"It's beautiful…but you shouldn't have been so generous," I purred.

"I can't wait to see you in it, baby, you're going to look so sexy. Please, open up your other present, you're going to love it even more."

Inside the second box were three pairs of sexy panties from Victoria's Secret. He had a big grin on his face.

I was getting madder by the minute. But I kept my cool and just thanked him once again, took a sip of my wine and worked up my courage to say no to this possible offer of the good life—of "being cared for" when I was homeless and had no professional future at the moment.

He leaned over, gave me a kiss and proceeded to get fairly aggressive.

I pushed him back. "I just met you, for God's sake. And I don't sleep around."

Now he was pissed off and said, "Terri, we are both adults. What's wrong with a little adult fun? We both know what the score is here."

At this, I saw red. "Bob, you have radically misunderstood who I am, I told you I would only have dinner with you last week before you came here. Just because my gender issue is out there and open does not mean I'm some fire-crotch who will sleep with anyone anywhere. I'm out of here… and don't call me again."

I did grab the presents as I stormed out the door. He followed me forlornly down the corridor, trying to assure me that he meant me no harm.

Over the next month ole Bob tried to mend fences. He called me weekly—even asked me to go to Hilton Head with him on a golfing weekend… "to get back on track," he said.

Of course I declined, and he finally quit calling.

It was one more example of people imagining that my gender-identity crisis had made me more sexual than other women.

Quarantined in Charlotte

Over the next six months I finished the *20/20* and A & E interviews, flew to Argentina to do the #1 talk show in South America, and made a little money for my efforts. Still living with Randy, I changed my professional name and booked some modeling jobs in the area including a supermarket commercial. But my opportunities to make money in the Charlotte area were now very slim. The racing community continued to blacklist me and I couldn't sell them a piece of t-shirt art for love nor money. It hurt me to think I was so beloved by them only a year earlier.

By October, the media appearances were flowing so steadily that my anonymity was in question anywhere I went. This gender-identity stuff wrapped around a NASCAR theme had people tuned into my story like no other gender-related story in American history.

To my surprise, unlike other celebrities in American sports who continued to be recognized and revered for their iconic accomplishments even though they'd done something controversial, I found that I was being stigmatized by the Springerization of gender issues by the tabloids. So all of a sudden, my national championships in America's most popular sport didn't seem to count any more.

Right there in NASCAR, fans continued to respect the memory of super-star driver Tim Richmond, though he had been a notorious womanizer before he died of AIDS. Indy 500 winner Al Unser Jr. was a chronic alcoholic, arrested for numerous DUIs, not to mention an arrest for battering his girlfriend, yet he was put in an INDY 500 car by A.J. Foyt after he finished rehab. On other fronts, Martina Navratilova finally came out as a lesbian, but the controversy didn't diminish the high international regard that she enjoyed as a professional tennis champion. Probably the most glaring example was heavyweight boxing champion Mike Tyson, now a convicted felon who did three years in prison for raping a beauty-pageant contestant in 1992. But after he got out in 1995, he was still revered and respected for his achievements in the fight game, and even allowed to make a comeback.

But me, a former national champion, winner of over 500 races…I couldn't get a seat in any motor sport now – all because my gender transition was viewed as badder than being a felon.

"My gawd, Terri," a Fox producer told me, "you're more controversial than Snoop Dogg."

This remark left me speechless. Snoop Dogg had a record as long as your arm—dozens of arrests for drug and weapons possession, plus being banned from the UK and Australia because of acting up. Generally in those days, this iconic rapper was viewed by many people as one of America's baddest "bad boys." Yet he continued to be revered by many as a pioneering music artist.

So I was more controversial than Snoop, even though I'd never been arrested once in my life, had no sexual escapades and had basically behaved myself in every way my entire life and my issue was clearly biological? No one was giving me the benefit of the doubt or a chance, just judging me to the high heavens.

Anywhere I went in Charlotte, people would stare and gawk. Of course a few people around the city still hung in there with me. But for the most part, I felt alone and quarantined there in Charlotte, and really missed my old friends out at the Speedway, especially Wanda and Margaret, whom I hadn't dared to go see for some time.

Just before the *20/20* interview was to run, the week of the Coke 600, I finally got the courage to go out to the Speedway Club. It had been a year since my story had first ran like wildfire through the racing community and I had not had the guts to go there for fear that someone would ask me to leave.

When I first got off the elevator to enter the Speedway Club, my knees were shaking so bad I could barely walk through the doors. But once I got to the restaurant, everyone was acting like they always had before my story broke in the press. The first two people I saw were two sisters who worked there as servers and had always been my good buddies. As soon as Doris and Betty spotted me they came running over.

Doris said, "Where have you been, Terri? Damn, we have been worried about you. You're way too skinny…get yourself a plate and load it up. Has Wanda seen you yet?"

After I filled my plate at the buffet, I headed back to where the employees and racing celebrities hide out to enjoy their lunch. Soon Wanda came by, between meetings, and we chit chatted for a few minutes.

"I support you 100 percent," she said. "Don't let your situation keep you from coming out to the club. You're always welcome here… we love ya, and we are worried about you. We want you to be happy, and safe."

Giving me a hug, Wanda rushed off to her next meeting.

But the next encounter, there at the Speedway Club, was more disheartening. Another of my old lunch buddies came meandering over to greet me. Elliott, in his late forties, was a world-renowned sports car racer who had moved to Charlotte to open up a racing parts business. I had had lunch with him at least once a week over the past few years. Now he shook my hand and we talked about the upcoming race at the Speedway. He seemed perfectly comfortable with me, even though he now knew my story. So I asked him if he'd help me get back into racing.

"I'd love to race in the 24 Hours of Daytona with you in February," I said.

Elliott looked shocked and confused. Finally he said, "How are you going to do that? I mean, how can you handle the forces of the physical sport? You had all this surgery—your shoulders narrowed up and your ribs removed to create your womanly waist...."

Now I was the one in shock. Elliott was a good guy but he was really misinformed on what I had done to my body. I searched for just the right words not to offend him.

"Hey, look, Elliott... I haven't had any surgery to my body to make me more womanly. I'm the same size I have always been, including my shoulders and my 23- inch waist. I was born a physical girl with a weird chromosome count. Sorry to disappoint you and all your racing buddies, because I know you've been discussing me for months. But I've always been built like a chick."

He stood there stunned for a minute, then grinned and apologized.

"Hey Terri, I did not intend to offend you. We're just a bunch of racers, we have a lot to learn about all of this. I've got you back from now on...you'll have no worries from me."

He gave me a light hug and headed back to work.

The next day, a phone call came from my old buddy Bret. "Hey, Terri, do you have any apparel designs we can use in a silent auction?"

He and a few others were doing a fundraiser for the Racing Wives Auxiliary at the Hilton next day, but they needed more merchandise and memorabilia to auction. I was shocked that he would ask me to do something with the Wives Auxiliary because of my stormy past with them.

"I do have a few denim shirts and t-shirts I could let you have," I said.

"Great," he said. "Would you like to come to the event with me and my friends? You need to get your ass out of the house and back in the racing scene."

"Bret, you're kidding! Those girls don't like me. Through the grapevine I know that their director has been badmouthing me ever since my story broke. They will have a cow if I show up."

"Damn it, Terri, don't let them get to you. Go with us and get back in the game. No one is going to mess with you, I guarantee it."

When I got to the Hilton, I was nervous as a cat on the hot roof of a car. I walked down to the banquet room, and gave Bret the shirts. Soon enough the room crowded with notables. As we headed for the buffet line, I notice that one of the racing wives, Lynn Bodine, was giving me the eagle eye, but I acted like I never saw her. Then, lo and behold, when I got to the buffet line, standing in front of me was my radio nemesis, Paul Schat.

Not only did ole Paul not recognize me, but as we made our way along the tables, filling our plates, he was warming up to me. I did look sharp in a black Ann Taylor suit and a pair of sharp-toed suede boots, and my hair was perfect. I was having a little fiendish fun letting him check me out.

When we got to the end of the line he was flirting with me and put a slice of chocolate pie on my tray.

I said, "How did you know I wanted that chocolate pie?"

He just grinned. "My name is Paul Schat, and I just knew you probably like chocolate. All women do."

As I stuck out my hand, I had a gleam in my own eye. "Hi, Paul, it's great to meet ya. I'm Terri O'Connell . . . I believe you've heard about me."

He turned fifteen colors of red and damn near dropped his tray, then got the hell out of there.

Bret was watching nearby, shaking his head in disbelief. When we sat down at our table, he leaned over to me and whispered, "Priceless."

Hollywood to Buenos Aires

A few weeks later my parents went down to Daytona for the Cup races, which had been postponed from summer because of the wildfires.

The *20/20* piece had run just a few days before, so many people recognized me. I signed autographs for a lot of race fans and realized that they actually liked me, especially the female fans. What a change from the response of the power players!

A month later A & E aired the profile (it was turned into a Biography Channel profile later), taking my media profile up another notch. By now, the tabloids had discovered my story too, and were wearing me out. I have to give them credit—they actually got the story right and ran some great photos. Hell, even *Playboy* put me up on their website with an eight-page profile that millions read all around the world.

It still made me uncomfortable to be so out there in the "A" list media. Randy and I had discussions about me being safe while out in public. I couldn't afford a bodyguard, but I did change my hair color a few shades in a vain effort to recapture a little anonymity.

On the positive side, a few Hollywood producers and production companies were calling up. At first Randy was fielding those calls, trying to get a sense for who was legit and who was not. Finally one of the big agencies took me on as a client.

It was a big surprise to start learning how Hollywood business really worked. I had always heard that people with big stories got paid big money. But not in my case. Everybody who contacted us was trying to lowball me, to hedge their bets.

"Your story is very controversial, very risky," they said. Yeah, right. More controversial than Snoop Dogg.

So the typical offer I got was a free option for many years, meaning nothing up front that would give me a bare living from my story. The option period could last for a year or two, before they actually paid me for the film rights. And even that purchase amount would be peanuts, compared to the big prices being paid for controversial stories that everybody reads about in the entertainment media.

A typical story was one well-known independent producer who even refused to talk to my agent. "I only want to deal directly with you," he said. I guess he thought I was a babe in the woods.

So I let his weenie offer (no option payment, $60,000 for the rights to the story) sit on the table while I talked to other people.

Finally the guy called. "You've had my offer for two weeks now."

"I'm talking to other people," I said. "Your offer isn't very impressive so far. I'm not going to just give my story away."

"You'd better make up your mind in the next 24 hours," he said.

I told him I didn't like his car-salesman pressure tactics, and we hung up on each other.

The next day he called again. When he found out I was still not ready to deal, he said he was withdrawing the offer.

"That's okay by me," I said. "It's a nothing offer."

Two days later, this Hollywood good ole boy was on the phone again, all sweetness and light, trying to mend fences and talk up the same nothing little deal as before. Who could figure these people out?

With no movie deal in sight yet, my ability to earn a living was drying up. I had reconnected with the marketing firm I had worked with back in the day in Charlotte. We repackaged the cartoons, and made a pitch to some big-time motorsports investors… only to be shot down when one of the investors recognized my art. He stood up in a meeting and bellowed, "Anyone using that art, it's gonna come back to haunt them, because of this individual's past life as a boy."

After the meeting, my marketing guy cornered the investor in the back of the room and read him the riot act about his own personal life.

"How dare you talk so bad about Terri," he said, "when everybody at this meeting, including me, knows you're having sex with your 16-year-old babysitter?"

In the end, though, that guy was just one of many so-called VIP moneymen who were trashing my life. I was basically screwed.

Then, just as my bank account ran dry, a Miami agent booked me for the *Tonight* show down in Argentina (*Hello Suzzanna*). It paid three grand. So I quickly got a passport, and Randy and I headed out to Buenos Aires. The week before Gloria Estafan had been on the show. They loved having racing personalities on—Argentina had a huge motorsports base.

The next day, when Randy and I went sightseeing around the capital, people recognized me everywhere. And no one was mean to us. Go figure.

What's up with Dad?

Soon after Argentina, I headed to Corinth for Christmas.

During the holidays, Mom and I noticed that something was up with Dad. He was quiet and barely ate a bite the entire week I was home. After New Year's, as I was loading up to head back to Charlotte, I told Mom, "You need to get him to the doctor."

"I know," she said.

The next day Mom told Dad that she was calling Dr Sweat and getting him an appointment.

To her surprise, he admitted that this was probably a good idea. He was 72, had smoked since he was ten, and worked in the machine shop and tool-and-die business for 50 years, breathing welding smoke and grinding dust. "Plus I drank up all the liquor this side of the Mississippi," he told her. "So I gotta get checked out."

A week later, my mom called me.

"Terri, I have some bad news," she said.

Feeling a wave of dread wash over me, I braced myself.

"Your dad has lung cancer," she went on. "Dr, Sweat doesn't think there is anything he can do. Except maybe blood transfusions to build him up a little. Your dad is going to start his treatments on Monday. I don't want you to worry and I don't think you need to come home just yet. Let me see how it goes after his first treatments and he responds."

I wasn't crying yet but my heart was right in my mouth and my stomach was churning almost out of control. The thing about my mom is that she can be overly dramatic or completely myopic. On this occasion she was being myopic, so that damn phone call that virtually confirmed my dad's death sentence was very impersonal and strange.

The second week of March, Mom called and asked me to come home.

"Your dad is in the hospital," she said. "They're trying to get his blood count and his strength back up. I've got the flu… Dr. Sweat made me go to bed."

So I jumped in my Explorer and rushed back to Corinth. My dad was in worse shape than Mom had led me to believe. It broke my heart to see him in the hospital. It was all I could do to look him in the eye without bursting into tears. But I just sucked it up and put on a happy face and tried to keep his spirits up.

One thing was for sure, though—Dad had plenty of company. All his old buds made a daily pilgrimage out to Magnolia Regional Hospital to visit with him. Every one of them loved my dad and it was pay-back time for all he had done for them over the years. Finally, after a week, Dr Sweat had gotten Dad to feeling better and sent him back home. We were all hopeful that maybe Dad could pull himself through.

During the next few days, Dad and I hung out there at the house, catching all the NASCAR stuff on the tube that we could. Both of us went out of our way to be nice to each another. Over the past few years we had gotten back to where we were when I was a kid, but we both knew that we had tried each another's patience. The gender ordeal had pushed us to the brink of destruction time and time again over the past twenty years. Now, our time was running out and in our hearts we both knew it. We wanted to make amends as much as possible before it was too late.

For a few weeks, everything seemed to be going along pretty smoothly but just like clockwork, that cancerous demon showed back up.

That day, Dad had been feeling a bit rundown and slept most of the afternoon. At supper he didn't swallow more than two bites of the soft scrambled eggs Mom had fixed him. We got him to drink a glass of Ensure, and all of us watched *Larry King Live* together.

Afterwards Dad felt tired, so we helped him back to his bedroom and he tried to get some sleep. Mom and I were thinking that it might be time for Dr Sweat to give him another blood transfusion to get his energy back up. At around eleven o'clock, I was laying on the couch in the den watching TV when I heard my dad yelling out almost in a panic for my mom. He was trying to walk down the hallway staggering against the wall as he frantically tried to make it into the kitchen.

Rushing over, I helped him to the dining table where he basically fell into the chair. He was shaken and having difficulty catching his breath. He laid his head down on the table to rest while Mom and I called 911. As we waited for the ambulance, Dad mumbled, "I'm freezing." So Mom pressed a warm bath rag against his face, while I wrapped a blanket around him.

Suddenly, with his head laying on his crossed arms, Dad started saying, over and over, "I never thought this would happen to me...I just never thought it would end up like this . . . I just never thought this would happen to me." My mom started bawling like a child.

Hearing Dad make that cry, seeing him so broken, was devastating. He had been the fearless leader of our lives, the hero, the kamikaze pilot, the bedrock of confidence—even through all his drinking issues. Now he was suddenly frightened and helpless. There would come a time when the blood transfusions would no longer help. For him, at that moment, in the house that he and Mom had built back in the Fifties and worked their fingers to the bone to pay for, it was all coming to a close. My dad's era, his time on this earth, had now run its course. It was such a sobering and prophetic moment that I knew it would live with me until my own time came to leave this earth.

Thirty days later, my dad's life did end. He died in his own house, in his own bed, on his own terms. In the end, he gave his heart to God, and visited with all his buds one last time. And he and I had one last moment of that love and respect that we took for granted when I was a kid starting out in go-karts.

The day of the funeral, one of my parents' best friends said to me, "Terri, I want to give you a hug. You're probably not going to get many this weekend."

The friend was Betty Nelms, a true-blue salt-of-the-earth human being I had known her virtually all of my life. She had seen the obscenity of how people in my hometown had treated me over the years. So when she told me that and folded me in her arms, I broke down and bawled.

The funeral was huge. The funeral home couldn't hold all of the flowers that friends sent from all over America – they spilled onto the lawn. My dad was so beloved that half of the town turned out to tell him good bye. He was going to be missed tremendously and fervently by everyone. I knew that as much as I wanted him all to myself through the years, he actually belonged to everyone he ever touched. He was a one-of-a-kind human being, warts and all.

Betty was right about the hugs. The usual suspects from back in the day—a few of my dad's buds—had the courage to shake my hand. But giving me hug was out of the question. Dewayne, the two Larry's and ole Dexter could barely acknowledge me, let alone tell me they were sorry. Support came from Randy and all my friends at the modeling agency up in Charlotte, as well as Lake and Rice', who kept tabs on me with regular phone calls. My best bud Nathan came by the funeral home.

But, in the end, as Mom and I stood in the cemetery with the flower-draped casket and the big crowd around us, and the Baptist preacher saying his typical thing over the open grave, I was pretty much on my own.

I knew where I stood there in Corinth, but it still hurt my feelings that people were so aloof. It was if they no longer considered me a human being, with human feelings. I had to let all those negative feelings go. The funeral was for my dad, not for me.

That weekend, through all my sorrow and tears, I tried to focus on the positive memories of Dad. The ones that always came rushing back were from when I was a kid. I could see him down in his little ole shop behind the house, squatting beside his race car, tinkering on the next speed secret that would take him to victory lane. Or fine tuning my first Sears and Roebuck go-kart he had bought after my appendix ruptured when I was only three years old. I could see him winning in his purple-and-white midget racer up in Nashville at the Ewing Lane Speedway, and then downing a BC headache powder with a short bottle of Coke to ease the tension after the races were over. As the fans gathered around him, he was decked out in his starched black pants and polo shirt, adjusting his black warfare sunglasses so they fit on his face just perfectly. In his youth, in his 20s and 30s and on into his 40s, Jimmie Hayes was movie-star beautiful and wore his good looks with grace and indelible confidence that made everyone who met him feel that all was right with the world as long as he was around.

Now, as I loaded my Explorer to leave town one more time, I wondered just how right the world would be, now that Dad was gone.

He had left an amazing legacy. At last I knew that I had to stop trying to make his legacy mine. No matter what I did, that would not be possible, ever. It was time to make my own legacy.

The Big Apple

One week later I was in New York City meeting with several publishers about publishing my autobiography.

Maer Roshan, the deputy editor of *New York Magazine,* had teamed up with former Details editor Joe Dolce had teamed up. They gave me a cocktail party at a hip new restaurant called the Globe, which—ironically – was managed by Margie Ensile, the girl who was managing the Fashion Café when we did the Volkswagen and Candies Shoes PR event the year before. Maer had most of the cool hip journalists in NYC there at the party, doing a meet and greet with me. Even ole Roy Blunt, a Southern literary icon, came by to share a few drinks and buddy up with the media.

The next day most all the media did pieces, including the *New York Post* where I made "Page Six."

But when we started sending my book manuscript around town, all the literary publishers shot it down. One well-known female literary icon, who we actually thought would be perfect to publish the book, rejected it flat out, calling me white trash from Mississippi that no one cared about.

The myopia and mean-spirited attitude really blind-sided us. Even Maer and Joe were confounded by it all. It seemed that everything we had going for us—a life story chomped full of amazing experiences, the world's number-one spectator sport and me being the most controversial person in it—should have been a slam dunk. But the New York literary community, especially the ones at the top, were turned off by it all. The NASCAR and Southern thing actually offended them. Most of them seemed to think that all motorsports fans are booger-eatin' morons, so they looked down on my achievements and first-in-world-history racing story. One editor wondered if anyone in NASCAR knew how to read. When we reminded him about the book advance Jeff Gordon had just gotten, he guaranteed that Jeff's book would fail.

The literary community couldn't fit me into their box. I was not stereotypical within the accepted "gender identity theme." They said my story was either too emotional… or not emotional enough. I had either had too much media exposure… or not enough media exposure. Too much sex, or not enough sex.

Ironically, the next Christmas, I was back to New York and attended a cocktail party where I accidentally ran into the female publisher who had—without meeting me—called me white trash. I engaged her in a long and sophisticated political conversation, never telling her my first name and trying my damnedest to hide my Southern accent. Then, as I was leaving the cocktail party I went back to her, introduced myself by my full name.

She stared me up and down. There I stood wearing a burgundy size-four satin Calvin Klein suit, with open-toed Jimmy Choo heels and my blonde hair flowing down my back.

"It's been great to meet you," I said, looking her in the eye. "And by the way, I know you said I'm white trash."

As Bret would have said, the look on her face was priceless.

CHAPTER 24

The Next Dangerous Curves – The Media

Home Again

That next spring Randy and I got serious about me getting back in the NASCAR drivers seat or in any other professional racing series.

My marketing friend Dan Duval at Group Five Marketing in Charlotte was helping chase down some sponsors as well as car owners who had enough guts to put me in their race car. We finally got world-renowned sports-car team owner Dick Barbour out of Atlanta to give me a shot and sent out at least 50 proposals to sponsor me and Dick in the American LeMans series driving one of his factory Porsches.

At first no one was biting. Then I found a guy named Norm out in California who put stock-option deals together and sold the stocks for advertising. I pumped him about my racing efforts. Maer at *New York Magazine* hooked me up with Kevin Gray, a kick-ass freelance writer friend of his, and Kevin had *George Magazine* on board to do a major article about my life.

Kevin was a well-buffed 5'10" Northeast boy who wore his New York journalistic attitude on his sleeve, Kevin had game. He made a trip down to Charlotte to attend the May NASCAR

Cup race at Lowe's Speedway to research the article. When he got there he had a hell of a time with NASCAR over his press credentials because he told them he was doing a piece on me. While he was there, we attended the World of Outlaw Sprint Car races at the half mile dirt oval across the street. Kevin had never in his life seen anything to compare with twenty-four 900-horse-powered sprint cars screaming around a tiny dirt track at 130 miles per hour.

As we were leaving the races that night, Kevin told me, "I can't believe your girly ass used to race those damn things. Hockey ain't shit compared to this crazy stuff."

Dan Duval and his partner Sandra Thomas, Dick and myself worked our asses off nurturing that sponsorship with Norm. He made us jump through more hoops than a circus dog, and his asshole attorney was the one who made the hoops. There were morals clauses in the contract that even Mother Theresa couldn't live up to. But because of my life history and America's Springerizing of the gender issue, they wanted to make sure I would not be running naked in the streets and having nasty sex while wearing their company logo on my back.

The next fall, after almost nine months of negotiating with them, we finally got a commitment. Kevin Gray mentioned the sponsorship commitment in the *George* piece and we all thought we would be racing in 2001.

Adding to my stress at the time, Kevin Gray had questioned Congressman Hayes about our business relationship. His representative blandly responded that I was nothing more than an artist and Mr. Hayes could have found an artist anywhere to provide designs for the company.

When Kevin told me that, I went crazy with anger. The truth was—and Kevin knew it, because he had done his homework—that the company named Speedsters, which Congressman Hayes and I was suppose to own together with his daughter, was a company that I had conceived, designed and had been running, I had birth that baby on every level. Kevin actually caught an associate with the racing auxiliary changing a date on a key Speedsters document, in an effort to protect the Congressman.

Kevin also found out that Bill had been telling many in the motorsports community that he was actually having an affair with me back in '95—that he had sex with me at his Speedway office. Of course, Bill did not have an office at the speedway. His office was at Bruton's car dealership down in Charlotte. Bill's allegations planted a seed of doubt in Kevin's mind, and he and I actually had words over it, before he finally realized that I was telling the truth.

Meanwhile, when the *George* piece hit the newsstands, Norm backed out and the sponsorship fell through.

I was devastated. Dan and Sandra had spent $15,000 in attorney fees getting the contract written, and Dick Barbour had been taken in a side deal with those guys that might cost him a new Porsche to get out of the deal. Kevin shared my outrage over how it went down, but there was no way to fight it.

Two weeks later, Kevin called and told me that Candice Bergen had contacted him. She wanted me to come out to Los Angeles to be on her new talk show "Exhale" on the newly formed Oxygen Network, which was owned by Oprah herself. Three weeks later, I was in L.A. filming the show. Thank God, that was a paying job.

Ironically, the day after filming the interview, I was over at Barney's checking out the latest fashions when my cell phone rang. Lo and behold, it was ole Norm.

He schmoozed me up for a few minutes, then finally said, "Look, I want to get back in and sponsor you at the 24 Hours of Daytona this coming January."

"Damn it, Norm," I told him, "if you mess us around this time, I'm sending my mom out there to hunt you down."

So Dick Barbour sent Norm the budget for Daytona, and we went through the same hoop-jumping as before. Three weeks before the race, Norm backed out again.

Dick Barbour had given me a firm commitment to put me in his cars, but I was beginning to wonder if sponsorship would ever be possible.

Meanwhile, that summer, my best friend Kathy Dixon passed away. She had been one of the ones who hung in there with me from day one —but she had struggled for two years to beat lung cancer, and now she had left this world to join her fallen husband Victor in the cosmos. I knew she was in a better place, but I would miss her like crazy, much as I was still missing my dad.

Emotionally I was worn out from all the media exposure, the criticizing of my life and working on putting sponsorship together to get me back on the track. I felt like I was suffering from post traumatic stress syndrome and Randy knew it. I had begun to cry at the drop of a hat once again.

"At Christmas," I told Randy, "I need to take a break...go back to Corinth to re-group for a while. I need to be around my old office and all of my trophies and the hometown friends who had been there for me through all of my troubles."

Going back to Corinth would be touchy. Not only would the redneck faction give me hell, but my mom and I still had our differences. Those differences had been set in stone from the time I was a kid. But we still loved each another and she was all the family I had now, we would work it out, that is what family does. So I packed my clothes and got ready to move.

The day before I headed back to Corinth, Randy and I ran all over Charlotte, doing Christmas shopping and having a great time. I loved being around him—he could be a big ole goof-ass and get way too obsessed over Christopher Radco Christmas ornaments. At dinner that night he brought up something that I had been wondering about myself.

"Hey, Terri O," he wondered out loud, "where in the hell is the GLBT media?" He sounded bewildered. "Why aren't they covering your story? Especially the political organizations that should be catching your back when all these shock jocks are ripping you up. I mean, most of the mainstream media and the tabloids have covered your story… but there hasn't been a peep out of the GLBT media."

I shrugged my shoulders.

"I'm amazed too," I said. "When the story first broke, even the GLBT media right there in Charlotte didn't call me. You know, a few regional GLBT newspapers did little cute blips about me which I thought were a bit demeaning. They basically trivialized the story with some cute remarks."

"Well," he said, "maybe it's best that we just stay mainstream. That's who you are anyway. You're not in that box. Your story, your life is so different. Plus, the words transsexual, transgender and especially gender bender have nothing to do with your situation. You were really born a woman. You've been a woman all along. We need to get the media straightened out about that somehow."

Randy wasn't just being ironic by asking this question. We had submitted our book proposal to the biggest GLBT publisher, having struck out with all the New York boys. A junior staffer sent back a snotty rejection letter, saying that the editors believed I had made most of the story up. He added that I had "only" finished 38th in my NASCAR race any way. So what was the big deal?

I fired back an email telling them they were a bunch of ignorant literary snobs plus a whole lot more.

I probably shouldn't have done that, but they were clueless about the facts. Luck and circumstance plays a huge part in where you finish in motorsports. You can be leading till the final turn, and suddenly crash out of the race because of a blown tire and finish dead last. The results in news papers the next day says you finished dead last, not that you could have won if not for that tire. Four times NASCAR Cup Champion Jeff Gordon and most of NASCARS super stars past and present had finished worse off in their first Cup race than I did. Oh, I admit that I got arrogant and patronizing as I explained to the knot head little gay editors that I had run only 90 testing and training laps before the Goodwrench 500, on a $25,000 budget for the race without a highly skilled team engineer or a crew chief, and never drove a full-bodied stock car before that race. On the other hand, Jeff Gordon had raced stock cars for a solid year before his first race, plus he had thousands of testing and training laps, and a $200,000 budget for his race. He had highly skilled engineers and one of the sports most renowned crew chiefs at his disposal. For me, it was like playing at Wimbledon with no practice, against Martina Navratilova or John McEnroe with only one tennis shoe and a tennis racquet missing half the strings. Not mention having to sleep in my car because I did not have enough money for a hotel room. It did not matter that I had won hundreds of professional races especially in other professional series, specifically sprint cars against some of the same drivers in NASCAR to these pinheads.

Recently, two time NASCAR Sprint Cup champion and all around bad boy Tony Stewart made the statement on his weekly *Sirius* radio show that the hardest thing he ever had to do in auto racing was learn how to drive a winged sprint car. Well, I won over 150 of those babies over the years, set a whole host of track records and fast times so, what does that say about my driving ability. But those urban idiots rejecting my book and demeaning my ability had no idea about the sport and in the end, they did not want to know. My national championships, my broken bones, my extreme sacrifices that took me to victory lane over five hundred times in my career meant nothing to these superficial disco queens.

Just the fact that I had made world history, and was taking risks like never before by going public with this story just went straight over their heads. I had more media and fan interest in my story than most of the literary communities bestselling authors combined. The fact that I was the most media covered gender identity story in history and the first person in professional motorsports to go through this just blew right by them. All of my interviews presented me as being articulate, extremely feminine and not a booger eat'n moron from the deep South at all. But these urban GLBT geniuses as well as many in the literary community chose to be mean and trite instead of informed and aware, go figure.

In the end, though, Randy and I both agreed that many in the GLBT media just weren't interested in my sport, though it was America's biggest and the most popular spectator sport. They had the idea that race car drivers and race fans are a bunch of redneck morons. They actually had it backwards on the moron front.

The irony was, I had a lot of personal friends in the GLBT community. But for the most part that "community" had been silent and non- supportive.

Later on, in a moment of frustration after the GLBT press had been falling all over an openly gay race car driver who's racing career entailed minor success in SCCA amateur sports car racing, I damn near lost my cool.

The uninformed GLBT press was elevating this guy to rock star and Jeff Gordon status simply because he was gay and cute, not because he had a comprehensive professional driving resume. This guy had never raced in any NASCAR series at any level, in fact he had never even been to a NASCAR race and had no interest in NASCAR. But he was being touted as the "Gay NASCAR Driver", who was bold and courageous by being out and open about his sexuality.

I went into a rant and told Maer Roshan now the executive editor at Radar Magazine, "Damn it Mare, what is it with these people, here I am, the one who has actually won national championships and actually raced in NASCARS top series and many of the other professional racing series here in America. I'm the one the power players in the sport are trying to silence, not his ass. I'm the one taking the social heat out here in Middle America where I live but no one is catching my back. This guy lives and socializes in the gay community where no one cares about his social status. Let him go public with is story up in Charlotte like I did instead of down in Miami where no one gives a rats ass what your gender or sexuality is. By being out and open and in the media like I am here in Middle America, every one cares about my social status and I'm basically un employable and homeless over it. These disco divas are all up his jock strap and he has no pro wins in any racing series and I have hundreds. You know what, I get more respect and support from a bigoted Baptist preacher in rural Mississippi than I get from most of the GLBT press. Damn it Maer, I don't have any-thing against this guy, I actually like him and hope he makes it big time out on the sports car circuit, but these gay media types need to get their facts straight. They don't have any problem fact checking my skinny white ass to the high heavens, so why don't they fact check his ass."

I hated being pissy like that, never in my life had I com-plained about anyone having it better than I did in the sport or in life, but I had worked my tail off looking for sponsors and putting a positive face on this issue all to have someone show up without one tenth of one percent of my professional resume and all of a sudden be touted as the next best thing. All these gay boys were worshiping at his feet.

It pissed me off, not only was it disrespectful to me, it was disrespectful to all the men and women in the sport who had sacrificed everything they owned including their lives to make the sport what it is today. Being cute and gay trumped talent and experience in that camp, the GLBT press was solidifying the old stereotypes that Middle America and the motorsports community had about the GLBT community being trite, triv-ial and more consumed with cuteness than accomplishment.

However I was beginning to get it, the hard core gay com-munity really had some major issues with the gender identity issue. I was kidding myself if I thought I was ever going to get

The Terri O'Connell Story

their full support! I had this girl thing going on, the boys just were not interested in a chick being cute, feminine and a kick ass athlete. They were all in to the male stud stuff. I should have known that. I just had to stay focused on what I was doing, stay main stream with my life and story and not worry about the disco divas. I knew the main stream press and especially the motorsports media would weed out the bull shit, they would look at the record and cover my story and racing quest accordingly. I wasn't gay, I did not need to align myself or even worry about the GLBT agenda if I ever wanted to get back to NASCAR. I talked all of this over with several of my motorsports friends just making sure I wasn't over reacting and every one of them, including one who was a player in the motorsports media agreed with me 100%. In fact, every one of them was more pissed off about it than I was.

To my amazement, Maer actually agreed with me, though he was a die in the wool New York boy, and an openly urban gay man in the media himself.

Then out of thin air, a few months later – I was offered the opportunity to be in a leading GLBT magazine but there was a catch. They wanted me to do the photo shoot with the gay race driver because of his bold courage for being out in NASCAR. I could not believe my ears, I quickly reminded them that this guy was not a NASCAR driver which they had failed to fact check – they did apologize for their mistake trying to schmoose me. I declined the offer to appear in their magazine. There was no way in hell I was doing that, he had not earned the right to elevate his status to mine in the sport simply because he was gay. My story stood alone, once again the GLBT press failed to get it. I truly felt slighted and disrespected over the offer. I wondered if the GLBT press just wasn't getting it right out of their own ignorance about motorsports or if the race driver was leading them down that NASCAR path knowing that would get him some press. I did not think he was misleading the press, at least I was hoping he was not. If he was, it would come back to bite him in the ass if the main stream ever did cover his racing efforts. However he did not have any problem throwing my name around during some of his interviews getting him some additional press he would not otherwise received.

When the leading GLBT magazine found out about their competitors offer through a friend of mine, they wanted to do a center spread story on me for their fortieth anniversary issue. That was not without drama though, they wanted an exclusive and were adamant about me not doing their competitors magazine or all bets were off. That did piss me off a bit, no one in the main stream press had ever handled me that way, not *20/20*, not *A&E* or any one, after all I wasn't getting paid for the interview. However, because I liked and respected their editor, I accepted the opportunity. I was actually flattered they wanted the story that badly. They did a great job, the photo was great, the story was good and I totally appreciated their efforts but they failed to mention my hard won National Championships and my artistic talents. It left me and all of my racing friends wondering why they left that bit of important info out of the article. Then, a few months later, Daniel Kent a writer who wrote for a GLBT news paper in Nashville did a really good story based on the legacy issues I felt trying to live up my dads bigger than life image. I had met Daniel during a personal appearance at Tribe, one of the hottest night clubs in Nashville my friend Bud East managed. Daniel and I ended up being friends and since then, he has actually helped out with some of my public relation needs.

Indeed, there were some in the GLBT media who were getting it, kinda. I had to take my hat off to them for actually doing a pretty good job covering my story. In the end though, as

I said before, I wasn't gay and I did not fit into the traditional Transgender box on any level, I was a skinny Middle American chick. So, I had to ask myself the question, <u>why</u> was I getting so worked up and whiney about all of this any way.

As one of my motorsports media friends Roger said, "Your letting a group of people who are minor players in the grand scheme of things get under your skin, you're a winner and someone who is a proven pro. These people have no living experiences or the capacity to understand you talent, your commitment or your accomplishments. The main stream media and the majority of Americans have a fascination and respect for you, so don't let anyone get you off of your goal. Don't elevate them to them to a higher level. Get back to racing and stick it in their ear. Besides Terri O', you're a chick, they ant in to chicks. Remember this, having the GLBT community compare the gay racer to you is like comparing a local bicycle rider to Lance Armstrong. You're Lance Armstrong, not the gay racer guy. We get it, they don't, move on."

He was right, I did not need to get into that box. Even one of my friends and a business leader in my home town whom I used as a sounding board echoed Roger almost to the word on what I should do. I had to stop my bitching, get back to my like minded people who appreciate my accomplishments, find a marketing partner for my racing efforts and get over it.

I made sure from that point forward that I listened to their sound common sense based advice.

Here is Randy and me clowning around at his modeling agency in Charlotte.

That's me helping out at the modeling agency and looking very serious. I had just done the A&E interview two day earlier.

*Looking oh so sexy during a fashion and promotional
shoot in Charlotte.*

Another Daunting Loss

Just when you think you're getting your head high enough out of the mud to see ahead, life smacks you down again. At times, even though I knew I had a great life, and a brighter future, I still felt star-crossed.

Being in Corinth did bring some healing. It was good to settle into my old race office and remodel it a bit.

I re-connected with old home-town friends—like Wanda Lilly, Wanda Hannie and Lynn Martin. We gathered at our old watering hole, the Alley Galley, and made frequent trips over to BB King's blues and dance hall in Memphis. We hung out at friends houses, listened to our old buddies Neal, Ernie and the Smoke House Band pick and jam every chance we got, just getting back in the swing of things around Corinth. I also re-kindled my friendship with Jan Roland. Back in the early '90s I had driven sprint cars for Jan and her ex-husband—it was her race car that I wrecked on the fateful night in Little Rock that changed my life forever. Jan was still the gorgeous Jill St John look-alike, and kept me informed on all the bullshit about my life that was still spewing out of the Memphis racing bunch.

But living in Corinth had stirred things up again. That old rumor about me working as a prostitute at the Tupelo Mall was swirling around—one prominent citizen actually called me up and asked me to make a X- rated video that he could give to one of his buddies for his birthday. The irony was that all these people who were trashing my reputation lived in great big glass houses. Some were having affairs with the babysitter, some were car thieves, and another up in Charlotte who was being pissy once had a scandalous affair with a Baptist preacher. All of them were the biggest bunch of Harper Valley Hypocrites you've ever seen. There was even a stupid completely false rumor going around that Jan and I were having a salacious lesbian affair.

Topping off the hypocrisy, a couple of the Corinth Casanovas were calling me to try and schedule a secret sexual rendezvous, and yes—they were both married men. The gall of these guys amazed me.

I hung in there and tried to ignore all the bullshit. A few times I did get pissed off enough to contact an attorney about suing someone for slander. But in the end, it would be too expensive and stir the town up even more. You had to hand it to them – that little bunch of right-wingers and rednecks were good at their hypocrisy, and relentless about pursuing it.

At least once a week, I called Randy in Charlotte to stay in touch. I had been redesigning Speedsters, and was beginning to think about going back there for the NASCAR races that coming May to try and re- introduce the company.

Right after Easter, I called his agency one afternoon and one of his bookers said, "Randy's home at his condo…sick with a stomach virus."

When I dialed his home number, it rang 20 times before he picked up the phone. His voice was frail, and he could hardly speak. Finally he began to cry.

"I'm scared, Terri," he said. "I'm really sick…I think something more is wrong with me than just being sick at my stomach."

Quickly calling his agency back, I told his best booker and friend Scott that he needed to check on Randy ASAP. Scott took off in a flash. What Randy had not told me was that they had already taken him to the emergency room the night before, but the doctors had sent him home dismissing his illness as a 24-hour bug. When Scott got to the condo, he and Randy's new roommate Robert rushed him to the hospital once again.

One week later, Randy died of meningitis.

Just like that, my buddy and the one person who had stood by me through all the media mess was gone.

As the months passed and his loss sank in with me, I became very reflective about my life. It seemed as if I had spent most of it on the verge of tears, always in the narrows, trying to transition into the next positive phase of my life, trying to escape the lesions my destined life was giving me. Now, within three years I had lost three of the most important people in my life. It took me a solid year to get back to somewhat of a normal life after Randy died. His death manifested all the raw emotion I had locked up inside since I had first moved up to Charlotte back in '94. Now, I had to regroup once again and escape the narrow tunnel of depression and loss. This crap was getting old.

It was during this period that I briefly entertained the idea of getting a prescription for antidepressants, to take the edge off my life. That was a bit ironic considering I had never ever done drugs. Hell, I didn't even drink much. My Guardian Angels had kept me safe from these vices and life-numbing agents. I had just always dug deep and got through things. This time was no different.

Countless times I went out to the Corinth cemetery where my granny was buried and cried my eyes out for her to please help me get through the loss I was feeling, and give me some understanding of what I was going through. Each time I felt better—as if she had sat beside me holding my hand. Little by little, prayer by prayer, I managed to get my joy back and to realize that I had God's grace. Granny's spirit comforted my heart ache and lifted my bruised self esteem which had all but disappeared. I leaned on her strength to not only find resolution in losing my loved ones but to find the strength to endure the hurt and heart ache I felt over my social status there in Corinth. I knew at some point, to have any sort of peace and anonymity, to ever fully enjoy and have my femininity appreciated, I would have to leave Corinth once again, there just did not seem to be any other resolution. Ironically, I was damned and determined to not let anyone know I was going through these tough times, I was not going to let anyone there, not my family, not my friends and especially not my enemies see me hurting. I just could not bare the thought of letting them see me in such a venerable state. I know that was stupid, but at the time that was where my head was because, I could have used a hug or two just to get me through the day. In fact, I could have used a lot of them.

Hello, Hollywood

That summer, Hollywood came calling again. The producers of the *Grumpy Old Men* movies wanted to option my story. So I took off to L.A. to meet those cats. The meetings went great. They brought in a team of writers and other support people to assure me they would make a good movie about my life. As usual, when they met me in person, they saw that I was completely different that what they expected. My ultra-feminine appearance got them even more anxious to make a deal.

I had already met casting director Paul Weber, an old friend of Randy's. Paul, who by now had become like a brother helped me look over the offer and we both thought my story was worth much more than the few thousand bucks they were offering. Once I got my book written, the value of my story would surely be worth even more. So I said no.

On the positive side, I met some Hollywood people who became great friends. A literary agent at CAA introduced me to a Beverly Hills coffee shop at the top of Mulholland Drive that's a favorite with industry people. There I hung out with comic Mort Sahl and documentary filmmaker Gil Toff, who today is one of my best friends and someone I totally lean on and look up to. My make-up artist friend Robert Wilford and his partner Mark became my L.A. hang-out buddies. When the pressure in Corinth became too much, I piled up at Robert and Mark's for months at a time.

I even had a short fling with one of the nation's top restaurant and night club entrepreneur's when we met by chance at a popular LA Hotel Lounge. It did not go anywhere for very long but did not pass me by what would happen if the tabloids or the paparazzi had spotted us, There would had to be some major explaining to do.

I had been working on my autobiography and getting Speedsters back up and running, designing hundreds of new cutting-edge art pieces to print and embroider on high quality shirts. While promoting my new line VLU500 in LA, I met Bianca Jagger through her friend and my new friend Debbie Kanifinie, the ex- wife of Yasser Arafat's finance minister. I needed a place to stay, and Debbie graciously allowed me her couch at her apartment. Bianca had her own room there, so we palled around for a month while I worked on my deals. Because Bianca doesn't drive, I made sure she got where she needed to go.

Yet another Hollywood new friend was Donzeleigh Abernathy, a beautiful and accomplished actress who had starred in the successful TV series "Any Day Now" and the Southern epic "Gods and Generals." When Paul Weber introduced us and she found out I was a race-car driver she flipped out; when she heard the rest of the story she flipped out even more.

Over cups of Joe at the coffee shop, Donzeleigh shared stories of her own amazing life. She was the daughter of Dr. Ralf David Abernathy, who was Martin Luther King's best friend and partner in the civil-rights movement. So, she had lived through it all – the marches, the bombings, the death threats. The first time I saw her speak at a public function I could swear that I was listening to a female version of Dr. King and her dad themselves. She blew me away. I wound up loving her like a sister and appreciating the gift of awareness she allowed me to have about her amazing life.

And so it went. The meetings with famous and amazing people just happened as I went along.

Back in the seat . . . and beyond

I'd been back in Corinth a few weeks and was in my office cleaning and doing a bit of remodeling. Dad had a lot of machinist tools packed away there, so I was going through them, sorting out what I wanted to keep, what I wanted to sell and what I wanted to give away to his friends.

One Wednesday afternoon an old racing buddy, Dan, came over to see what I had that he might want. We both did a little bench racing, laughed at some of the crazy-ass stunts my dad had pulled, especially that one down in Talladega that time.

All of a sudden, out of nowhere, Dan said, "Hey, you want to take my car down to Tupelo and race it Friday night? Your red driving suit is hanging right there on the wall. We could kick those country boys' asses and have some fun."

A bit stunned, I didn't know if he was serious or not. But, from the way Dan was looking at me, he was dead serious. After about 30 seconds of me pondering the thought of getting back in the seat of a midget racer, I said, "Why the hell not? I need a racing fix really bad."

To be honest, it actually gave me a bit of pause but by that Friday, I was over the jitters. It was time to go racing!

When we got to the track, the local fans didn't know it was me buckling into that purple-and-white midget racer. I had entered under my middle name Leigh, and my old last name Hayes. No one but a few of my fellow racers had any idea I was there, and they really didn't care one way or the other. I didn't want the media finding out I was racing, so I tried to keep that night as incognito as I could. The big news splash was better saved for when I got back in a stock car or an Indy car.

At first it seemed like running the race was not that big a deal. . . I was just having some fun. The juices were still flowing, and I actually won the main event—barely. After the races, Dan took me for some breakfast just like we had done a thousand times before, over the past 20 years.

However, as I was driving back to Corinth, I found myself wishing sadly that my dad could have been with us to enjoy the night . . . to see that things had come full circle. These days I wasn't driving for the money or the fame. I was back driving simply out of passion for the sport. For me being back around the racing culture, the lingo and especially the competitive spirit was something I had missed desperately since going public with my story. Just the fact that someone there knew what I was talking about when I said the car was loose, or that we need to change the stagger and did not make a smart ass and trite remark about it was indeed very refreshing. The more frivolous and superficial social atmosphere I had been thrust into since then, and especially when I was involved with the modeling agency had left me missing motorsports more than ever. I hated the revved up politics involved with high level professional motorsports, but I loved the sport, I loved the fans and I needed to be around people who got it not only about racing, but about life in general. I had missed the common sense.

What men need to do

But racing was not the happy ending to my story. The happy ending was when I had the surgery back in 1994. Getting back in the seat of a race car again was just a nice little bow tied around the trilogy of my life.

Everything that came after my surgery was a gift – a luxury. Even the tough spots were worth the pain and suffering— because now, my gender and my body were finally at peace with one another. I had made the right decision to stop trying to be a male and let my true self as a woman shine… as it should have from day one.

My spirit couldn't have been more at peace.

Don't get me wrong—living in the feminine sorority is not all perfect. I don't like it when some people are mean and disrespectful to me after they discover my past. I don't like the way women are treated by many men socially, especially in a professional setting that is definitely a man's world.

Certain men out there need to get more humble and start respecting women as equal partners in life. Men and women are definitely different species, but different does not mean better than or less than, just different! But changing the superior and demeaning attitudes that many males have toward females—or towards anyone who shows femininity—is going to be difficult. It's going to take a huge commitment by parents, by schools and more importantly by the religious communities. Little boys need to have it hammered into their heads that girls are just as important as they are.

One of my biggest heroes, Sarah Ofilia Cannon (aka Minnie Pearl) was once asked, "What drew you to your husband… what made you love him so much?" Her answer was quick and crystal clear. She said, "I fell in love with him over the way he treated other people . . . he treated everyone he met with equal respect, no matter if they were a famous celebrity or a janitor."

In spite of America's 40 years of "women's liberation," during which the women's movement has supposedly softened the country up a little, the fact is—a lack of respect toward the feminine gender has manifested itself all over again into virtually every crevice of our society. All you have to do is turn on your television set to see the box that women are shoved into. For all the positive role models and positive professional images that get portrayed in the media, women have to constantly deal with those bimbo, needy, clingy and oversexed images that are also crowding the TV screen. The media and advertisers just love to present the sexes in extreme rolls, men are promoted as confident heroes and women are presented as mommy types mopping floors or scantily clad cheerleaders rooting for the big confident football hero when we all know that in reality, gender lines are so much more blurred than just the extremes.

Those images prevent women from getting the same respect as their male counterparts, whether it's in politics, sports or Fortune 500 ventures.

Just because a guy is a macho jock who is good at sports does not make him more important than a physically fragile girl who is best at academics and modeling. When a coach tells his male players, "Hey knuckle heads, you're throwing like a girl. You're playing like a bunch of girls, act like men and get your heads in the game." The message the coach is sending is that males are superior to women – the message is plain and simple. Just recently, after a more aggressive finish to a NAS-CAR Nationwide event, two drivers got into a verbal smash down match on who was at fault for the wreck. When one of the drivers in the wreck was ask by the ESPN reporter about his point of view on what happened in the accident, he responded by saying, "Oh hell, he tried to blame the wreck on me, he is just acting and whining like a little girl, if he can't take it, he needs to go play with the girls." The ESPN reporter stood there looking back at him a bit in shock and smiling like a big goober knowing full well that women all over America were probably going to be sending this idiot an e mail the next day calling him a pin head with a little weenie. If they didn't, they should have.

Last time I checked, the male species is the one raping and abusing women, not the other way around. Men are the ones who are creating most of the violence on this earth—starting and maintaining the deadly wars that will end up destroying all of us at some point.

In my opinion, the "boys will be boys" syndrome is the most ridiculous thought process in history, it's letting them off the hook for bad behavior. Sometimes the "boys" need to be taken down a notch or two and get that testosterone under control.

Making boys more aware, more compassionate and less aggressive in a social setting is not going to feminize them – it will just make them better, well-rounded men. If they want to beat each others' brains out on the football field or the race track while expressing their machismo, let them have at it. But they have to learn to leave the aggression there, not bring it home to their wives and girlfriends. Men need to realize that having physical power and emotional intimidation over a female does not get them love and respect in return. Crushing the spirit or knocking the hell out of a loving and nurturing human being is just stupid. That is trying to generate love and respect out of fear. That is what the Taliban does to people, it's wrong on every human level.

That training process needs to start on Day One, as moms and dads raise them up to be aware and balanced men. Dads, especially, have to take responsibility for keeping their sons straightened out on respect for women. Just recently, I was at a well-known downtown nightclub in Memphis. On this night, I was there under the radar – just another cute chick to some of the patrons – and was being pursued by a former NBA star who had become a successful college coach. This man and his two 20-something sons, along with their entourage, were sitting at a table having some big-time fun. The coach asked me to dance, and as we walked out onto the dance floor, his youngest son actually reached out and grabbed my butt. To my surprise, his dad—instead of telling his son to knock it off—just laughed about it and let it go.

This kind of negative example by a dad is how we wind up with so many adult men who are clueless when it comes to women not only socially, but especially in a professional environment. I can tell you without any doubt that I can tell by how a male treats me once my story is known to him on whether or not he will treat all women with respect. However, we are making some progress thanks to many fine and courageous women throughout the world. Women are getting there on the equality front but we all still have a long way to go, it's time to get on with it and loose all of those old sexist stereotypes toward women.

But hey...I don't want to rag on all men...on all rednecks and bubbas. The ones who went after me were big, bad and loud, for sure, and they made my life a living hell. But they're also my people. I'm a Southerner born and bred...first, last and always! I've never understood the elitist attitude that so many Americans have, that makes them think they have the right to make fun of rednecks and bubbas. In fact, I'm tired of people who try to make me feel like I should apologize for being from Mississippi. Those guys may be SOBs, but they're <u>my</u> SOBs... *So don't mess with them! Some of my best friends are men, rednecks and bubbas. Most men are perfect gentlemen and those Talladega NASCAR fans are the best, so don't think I can't hang with the bubbas just like I do with the wine and cheesers out in California, because I can and love every second of it.*

I don't rag on everything about my hometown either. Over all, there are many fine people in Corinth, where I lived through so much pain...and where I finally found my way to the highway of life that is truly mine.

In fact, all over America overwhelmingly there are more fine people who love me, support me and make damn sure I'm looked after than do not. A lot of these fine people are men. So I don't want to spoil the entire barrel by saying there's a few bad apples in it.

What Women Need to Do

However, women have to share the responsibility in this re-educational process too. When girls appear in those obscene "Girls Gone Wild" videos, or try to persuade some rock star to pick them over some other over-sexed chick on a salacious TV dating show, or when they take Paris Hilton and Pamela Anderson as role models, it sets all women up be seen as non-thinking sex objects. Hey, the guys love it, but that image just destroys the ability of women to have an equal footing with men in the professional work place and in their private lives.

Being sexy and beautiful is cool, but when it gets exploited, women pay a terrible price. Ironically, there are some powerful women role models around. Some female athletes are drop-dead gorgeous and can kick most guys' asses at most of the stick-and-ball sports as well as in motorsports. There are thousands of successful businesswomen, politicians and other worthy female role models to look up to. As women we need to start doing a better job of bringing those dynamic feminine lives into the spotlight instead of letting the Victoria's Secret fashion shop and over-sexed images be the benchmark for feminine goals and success.

Parents of little girls have to start raising their daughters to be strong, independent and self reliant, not needy, whiney and little shrinking violets who are always deferring to the male specie. By doing so, these girls will grow into positive women who can control their own destiny instead of relying on men to support and affirm them as human beings. It does not make you less feminine to be strong and independent, those traits will only make you a more aware and productive woman. A woman's feminine beauty and nature will shine no matter what, it's in a woman's DNA to do so. Victoria's Secret is just fine, but cannot be a woman's total identity. Mother Nature is still in control so girls, don't worry about losing your femininity to being strong and accretive, that is not going to erase your God given feminine beauty and soul. The guys will adapt, they will have too if they want to cuddle up next to you on a cold winters night sitting in front of cozy fire while sipping a glass of well aged merlot, and hoping for a little bedroom rendezvous. Remember ladies, it's your body and your life ... you own it, he doesn't. You're a girl, enjoy it, but don't sell yourself short, use the brains, gifts and common sense God gave you to be all you can be, it's not a man's decision on whether or not you can or cannot do anything you want, it's all yours.

In my years as a card-carrying member of the most macho and exclusive fraternity on this earth, I've heard a lot of demeaning things said about women. I've listened to boyfriends and husbands – men who are revered and respected in their communities—trash-talking their wives and girlfriends when in the midst of their fellow fraternity brothers. This is another way that the bad attitude gets passed on to impressionable sons.

The men who do that trash-talking are milking the bad old attitude for all it's worth. If a female has multiple sex partners, they call her a whore. But if a guy is sleeping around, they call him a stud. In business, when a woman is strong, smart, confident and decisive, she is called cold, uncaring and a bitch, whereas when a man is strong, confident and decisive he is called a man's man who is a strong leader. No matter that in a lot of cases the man is dumber than mud and has run the company into the ground. But when a woman complains about those attitudes, she is called a whiner and hard to get along with.

When many men deal with my story, they actually feel threatened. Why? Because I left their almighty fraternity to join the much less important sorority, and I'm cute, which makes them have to reevaluate their sexual attraction to me. Who in their right mind (these men ask themselves) would ever want to leave the most important fraternity? "That just ain't right" is what many men say to themselves. But I was a female, it was in my DNA so staying in the fraternity would have been a stupid thing to do, so their sexual attraction to me is a natural, not made up and unnatural. Yes, a normal male would not want to, or should do what I did to fix my life, that is just common sense.

What in the hell is wrong with being a woman, anyway? Without women, men would be in a real pickle. I can just see some of those right- wing politicians sending one another flowers with sweet little hand-written cards on them. Come to think of it, making men do our jobs is not a bad idea. Forget helping with the dishes or changing diapers. Every man on earth should have to live as a woman full-time for one year, so they can learn to get it!

We have to find a balance between the genders that lets everyone shine with equal billing. If we can do this, the natural order of male and female will find its way into place and every one will be happy.

Being Blacklisted

I have few regrets for my life adventure. I've had one hell of a life. No one else that I know of has walked down—or raced down—the same road that I have, for better or worse.

My one regret is – I shouldn't have gone public with my story when I did. Instead, I should have waited at least 20 years, and put in some serious living as a woman before I took on that heavy load. Going public took away some of my feminine cachet in certain circles. It opened my life up to some monster-size scrutiny and criticism that I could have lived without.

Even though most of the media were overwhelmingly fair and got the story right, some did not and they caused me some undue hardships. I didn't have a team of publicists and managers catching my back during the media storms, so for the most part, I had to figure out the best strategies on my own.

As I look back to when the two gay boys in Charlotte outed me, I should have had some one big and bad kick their asses, then just packed my bags, cut my losses and re-started my life in anonymity in some other city once again. I could have done that without any real trouble at all.

While all the coverage about me was swirling through the airways and into the racing communities, it also hurt my ability to earn a living. I realized that I was being blacklisted in a way that few controversial athletes in other sports are ever done. And that blacklisting wasn't just limited to the motorsports scene. I had good reason to suspect that the motorsports power players kept me from getting a publishing deal for a book as well as getting the door slammed at two of the most prestigious talent and literary agencies in New York and Los Angeles. Then there was the TV reality-show deal that was all but signed with one of the big networks but then fell through mysteriously. In my hometown of Corinth, blacklisting meant that I could not do business there under any circumstances.

I tried to get my urban friends in New York and L.A. to understand what I was up against, but they had never lived through anything similar, so they were clueless. It seemed that the motorsports community and my hometown just wanted me to go away and never come back, to just go and spray perfume at a mall and get over it. Problem was, that was not in my business plan. They wouldn't get to run me off any more—I was learning how to fight better. And I had to make sure the mainstream media knew the score and caught my back.

At one point, I actually stumbled into a minor friendship with a relative of the person who had negotiated NASCAR's four billion dollar contract package for television. When my new friend found out who I was, he told his relative about knowing me. He reported back to me that his family member knew everything there was to know about me, right down to my home address. That really got my attention.

I told him, "NASCAR was nervous about what I was up to when my story first broke in the press in '98."

He looked at me quizzically and said, "Well, do you blame them? They were protecting their four billion dollars. In their minds you were the enemy. You weren't the kind of image they like to sell."

Hearing that really pissed me off. I had not only socialized with most of those boys, I had dated some of them. They sure liked my cute-ass image then.

There has been—and continues to be—some major criticizing of my life going on. That race-car driving stuff really gets some people all worked up. The way they talk on certain blogs and bulletin boards and radio shows, you'd think I killed their grandmothers. At times I have felt a bit like the Dixie Chicks must have felt at the height of their public chastising. Unlike the Dixie Chicks, though, I didn't have a million dollars in the bank and a high- powered team of professionals watching my back. The irony in that is these people who rip me up with their opinions about my life and looks would not know me if I walked into the room in a thousand years. Just like ole Paul Shat back in Charlotte and the arrogant literary editor in New York.

But...what are you going to do except to stay true to your dreams? I just have to put all the negativity behind me and get on with my life the best way I can. I'm careful to surround myself with friends who will catch my back no matter what.

Common sense and God's grace will get me through a lot.

I make no apologies for being from the South, or being a part of the motorsports culture. I love the South for its heart and friendly spirit. Yes, the South has its flaws but so does every other part of the United States. I will not tolerate it when someone from somewhere else goes to belittle me and my friends simply because we come from the South.

The same goes for the sport of auto racing, the world's number one spectator sport and one hell of a thing to do. Snobs might as well not waste their time turning their noses up at me because I love and participate in this kick-ass sport. It takes really smart and courageous people to compete and win in this sport. In fact, these days, damn near every hotshot celebrity in America is clamoring to get a garage pass and VIP seating at NASCAR, Indy Car and NHRA races any time they can.

Fear and fearlessness revisited

Today, at 5'6," 117 pounds and 34-24-34 measurements, and looking like my mom when she was thirty, I have an exclusive membership in the coolest sorority in the world. God blessed me with natural feminine attributes and it warms my heart and fills my life with joy to be included in that club. As far as men go, I can handle the bad boys, I know their game now. I learned my lesson with ole Bill back in '95.

Hell, for me, having the surgery and living out my dreams as a woman was like winning the Indy and Daytona 500s all on the same day. If I never race again at the highest level of motorsports, I can't complain. I've had one hell of a drive while here on this big green planet. I'm so much luckier than 90% of most people on Earth because I've had that ride, and have gotten a strong perspective on the things I've had to endure. I count my blessings every single day that I am who I am – that I had the opportunities to experience the amazing and unique things in my life. Of course the media continues to call; they just can't seem to get enough of my story. It's always risky doing television, so I don't always accept invitations to appear on talk shows, it kills my anonymity and I don't do panels with other gender related or unrelated stories. But when the producers called from *Larry King Live*, I accepted their offer and just recently, *Newsweek* and one of Hearst Publishing's women's magazine, *Quick and Simple*, a spinoff of their *Better Homes and Gardens* publication did a feature story which was written and presented with great skill and taste. Now, with the internet explosion and the Wild West atmosphere involved with that media medium I have a whole new set of obstacles I have to navigate trying to keep control of my Middle American life. Some on the web do a great job writing about my life, and of course just like all other athletes and celebrities I have to deal with the negative aspects that hurt and demean my life and my image this lighting fast medium offers up.

Some people out there just think they have to attach themselves to your life, they throw you up on their personal web sites with all kinds of things and people I would never be associated with in a million years, pop it up on Google as far up on the list as they can get it and act as if they are a legitimate news source. They all know because of my celebrity and the motorsports connection that attaching themselves to my name will bring web traffic to their sites they would not otherwise have, get them hits and for some, make money for them. This gets me stereotyped and hurts my image.

Adding to the Wild West internet outlaws and my stress level, there are those who grab published and copyright material by professional journalist along with my personal copyrighted photographs, put it on their personal sites without permission and just think no one will call them on it. Then they get pissy when you ask them to take you off of their sites claiming first amendment rights. Of course the first amendment does not protect them, but they will fight you tooth and nail over it. I do not care what others put on their own personal sites, that is their right to do so, just do not include me.

When I do an interview with a legitimate news source, I do so with my eyes wide open, I know the personal consequences by putting myself out in the open with my story and I have to be willing to live with those results. Some people mean well by including me on their sites, but some only want to use me to get what they want. But when non legitimate sources throw me up on their sites, sites with sexual over tones and with those "T" words, with people I don't know and stereotypical images that hurt my image and don't represent me in any way, that is just not right. There have been some on the web who manipulate my photos and television images to make me look bad just to get at me. It seems that some people just can't let me be who I am, they somehow feel as if they have to crush my femininity. That diminishes my brand, my Middle American heart and really pisses me and my attorney off. We will be fearless in going after these internet outlaws.

There are times I truly consider walking away from all of the media, just forget about the book and all of my goals. If I did, I clearly would not have to deal with all the media scrutiny, having people trying to attach themselves to my story and always having to fight like hell to explain my life. I could be married to a well to do banker up in the mid west or out in California having a nice little life in total anonymity. But because I want to get back to racing, tell my story and set the record straight, I just keep on digging at getting my racing interest out there in the media. So, I have to deal with the bad side of this if I want to reach my goals. But it always amazes me just how far people will go to get in on my story or to criticize me. More importantly though, it's not in my DNA to let the bad people win, so I just keep on plugging away trying to make this gender identity issue a better under stood medical condition.

I don't like or want to be associated with anything or any web site that uses the words Transsexual, Transgender, Trannie, Gender Bender or Queer and Fag. I've never been comfortable with those terms and since my story broke in the press, to my absolute horror, I've come to realize those words are too broad and diverse. Those words are hurtful and in my and all of my friends opinions both in my home town and in the racing community, they are as bad and hurtful as the "N" or "B" words are to other humans in our society. Those words marginalize people and put them in a box that once you're in there, it's virtually impossible to get out. It seems as if people want a one size fits all box to put everyone in. A bald headed fat man wearing a string of pearls and a pair of red pumps and lipstick gets slammed into the Transgender box along with a salacious Trans prostitute out in West Hollywood or an exposed pregnant belly in one of the hard core tabloids completely blurring the line of common sense and the facts on what this is actually all about. Middle Americans are offended by these images and so am I. I'm not going to be put in a salacious box that broad and diverse, it's just insane that people even think that is ok to do. Those words have been hijacked by the Springer Nation, they have salacious over tones and prevent people from getting jobs, being safe and having a good life. The sad part is, most of the so called experts, hospitals and psychologist throw those words around at the drop at a hat. It's time to find and use new words along with integrity and awareness when analyzing and describing this issue.

My issue is about Gender Identity, or from a more analytical stand point, it's about Gender Realization. It's about biology and a life time of daunting heart felt living experiences. My story is about applying common sense in fixing and dealing with a damn difficult biological life challenge, not about partying, sexual escapades, hooking up or networking with in the shadow underground under a false name.

I'm trying to make this world a better and safer place for people caught up in a really misunderstood medical quagmire. Those internet divas don't help the cause on any level, they send the wrong messages to Middle Americans and more importantly to the ultra hard core conservatives who work like crazy to make this a mental disorder. These internet sites just put fuel on the fire. I want moms and dads, aunts and uncles and kids throughout the heart land to have a story, a personality they can relate to and not be offended by because of salacious sexual and hip urban over tones. So when I'm attached to those unauthorized web sites it diminishes the story, hurts the cause and prevents people who would otherwise be open to listening to the medical issues that would allow them in turn to deal with their loved one in a more open and compassionate way. I don't want kids hurt, abused or thrown into some reprogramming camp to try and make them normal. I don't want this to come down to someone cramming a pill down a kids throat trying to re program their brains just because mother nature did not give parents the child they or the church wanted. I want compassionate, aware and common sense based approaches in dealing with kids who have any social or biological issue to confront. I want to be a role model that kids and their parents can look to as an example of how to, and how not to deal with this issue of Gender Realization. That's pretty plain and simple, it's just a matter of using the good sense that God gave you instead of listening to people who don't have a clue on what their talking about or have a political or religious agenda they are trying to sell. *I do have to say one more thing here on the mental disorder bull that the ultra conservatives try to play. The truth of the matter is they think that everyone who does not agree with them on politics and religion or is not male, has mental disorders. So you have to take their point of view with a grain of salt, it is what it is.*

For me, I live and work in the heart land, not in urban settings where everything goes, I have a completely different set of social circumstances I have to live with. My profession is Auto Racing and the motorsports and female apparel business, not doing cabaret shows in the Village or out on the Sunset Strip with people stuffing dollar bills down my bra. I've all ways had pretty thick skin, being a race car driver, going eye ball to eye ball with those racing rattle snakes you better have thick skin, but this internet thing and the people involved takes on a whole new set of thick skin skills that I haven't quite gotten down pat just yet. But I'm learning – I've also found myself a very good attorney to help catch my back. So if you don't see me on a legitimate news source web site, or on one of my own authorized sites, you will know that someone has illegally used my name and image to gain exposure for their own personal gain.

What if?

From time to time, people ask me this: if I had been raised as a girl from day one, would I have wanted to race? Would my mom and dad have even let me race? I don't know for sure the answer to that question. But there is one thing I do know for sure. In this life, I am both a woman *and* a race car driver. No one who ever saw me drive, who got their tail beat by me and saw me stand in victory lane, or saw me in person as a woman, can ever deny those facts. God clearly made me that way.

And I can *still* get the job done driving a race car.

Stay tuned, you just might see me in a victory lane near you!

Today we hear a lot about "boxes." As a society we have to get out of all the boxes of bigotry and prejudice that we've stuffed ourselves into, and kept ourselves cramped inside of, for so many centuries. We have to rethink our human interactions across the board. It we do this, we can transition our human planet into a more aware and successful cosmic ball! We have to stop letting our fear of the unknown, or fear of someone's difference, get in control of our reactions to others. If I had listened to some of my detractors throughout my life, I would have never driven past the city limit sign to win my national championships, or ended up in California wining sprint car races or have built that kick ass cutting edge little blue midget that I won in virtually every time I drove it. More than that, I would have never gotten up out that gutter out in California, made my way back East hurt and emotionally bruised to race in NASCARS top series Sprint Cup, with in the year. I only found success when I listened to my inner voice and took control of my life, my career and my heart. I always knew who I was, and what I wanted to do, I just had to reach down inside of my soul, stop listening to all the negativity and get on with it. The trophy's and awards on my office walls along with my apparel and art concepts are proof in the pudding that I had a pretty good idea I knew what I was doing. God gave me intelligence and talent, and the common sense on how to apply it – I wasn't letting anything or anyone get in the way and keep me from living my dreams.

For me, it comes down to fear and fearlessness on a higher plane than the race track. We can be fearless in our quest to be better and more aware human beings. We can manage to feel respect for everyone, no matter who they are. We can be fearless in lifting people up instead of tearing them down. We can take the awareness that we've learned from living and turn it into a vision for the future that allows all people on this Earth to be everything they can be, without prejudice and malice!

Fear doesn't make us better human beings, it will leave you shallow and lost if you don't confront it. If we brake too hard for those dangerous curves, fear can control us – can turn our lives into mangled, smoking wrecks. So the secret is to take that fear, no matter what it is, and channel it in a positive way then stand on the gas with it—drive it into victory lane. Our fears can actually push us to greatness, inspire us to do great and amazing things. When someone tries to put their own personal fears into us by telling us that we can't do something out of their own personal fears and ignorance, we can simply drive away from those unwelcome fears of theirs…like a speeding race car driving away from the competition to win the race. You can't win it, unless you're in it, that not only pertains to competing out on the track, but all aspects of life. When you do fail, get back up off of the matt, dust yourself off, regroup and get a better plan going forward. Plan "B" has to be a better and revised plan "A". Learn from your mistakes and get on with it. However, to me, the most important thing to remember and the thing I most live my life by is – to finish first, first you must finish. So get in life, and finish it with guts and gusto and you will finish first. When you do that, your life will be full and productive no matter what others say and do. Be smart and aware, use the common sense God gave you and never ever let anyone hold you back. Be brave, don't have a faint heart …always dream big and never ever stop dreaming.

Yeah, let's go racing…after our dreams.

Different Divisions of Auto Racing

Because auto racing is so diverse and complex, we have included several different types of auto racing descriptions in this section of the book. These are the different types of car described in this book. Of course feel free to just Google each different division of this amazing sport to find out more … rev it up!

Race Karts

If you think one can go down to the local Wal-Mart and pick up one of these little fire crackers, you are badly mistaken, not even close. Race Karts, not go-carts, are high tech finely tuned engineering marvels designed by really smart people and their computers. Their dyno-developed two cycle and four cycle engines jet out so much horse power that their eight inch wide super grip racing tires bellow smoke as they charge around specially built racing tracks all over the world. Whether on an asphalt road course or on a dirt oval, these little fire breathing machines are the training ground for all of professional motorsports. Oh yeah, they race at speeds on some tracks at over 120 miles per hour!

Horse Power – 75 Price - $3,500.00 Weight – 350lbs. Top Speed – 120 MPH

Karting is an entire industry all around the world. In Europe and Asia Kart racers have rock star status and here in America, most of the top drivers in Indy Cars and in NASCAR have all graduated from the Karting ranks. Even after drivers make the leap up to the bigger series including Formula One and NASCAR, these drivers continue to drive Race Karts to keep their racing reflexes sharp!

worldkartingassociation.com   internationalkartfederation. com

Midgets

You could call them bumble bees on steroids . . . Back in the day, Midgets gained their fame throughout America as these little H-Bombs were used to showcase and develop the driving talents of the best race drivers competing in the Indy 500. Today, these little miniature exotic racing machines eat drivers like sharks eat fish, they are like a Volkswagen Passat with three V-8 engines racing around quarter and half mile dirt and asphalt ovals throughout America and Australia. There are several different variations of the midget racer but all are exotic and very, very fast and fans flock to watch these brave drivers man handle these amazing little machines. You can check them out on most of the sports channels but before you do, be sure to install seat belts on your favorite recliner, you're going to need them. Enjoy the bad ass ride!

Horse Power – 300 Price - $15K to$40,000.00 Weight – 750 Lbs. Top Speed – 140 MPH

Today, the nation's top drivers, including NASCARS top guns, Tony Stewart and Casey Kane own and race Midgets many times during the racing season! Midgets are where NAS-CARS "Golden Boy" Jeff Gordon made his mark leading him to his hall of fame NASCAR career!

Just Google Midget Racers to learn more about these amazing cars.

Sprint Cars

I've seen 200 pound macho manly men who drive Sprint Cars throw up over a case of the Hee – Bee – Gee – Bee's before the start of a Sprint Car race. If you are not brave beyond reason don't apply for a license to race a Sprint Car. These crazy ass racing machines have more power than any human being or extra terrestrial should be allowed to play with. With engines pumping out over 900 hundred horse power and weighing less than a golf cart, let your imagine be your guide if you can think that far outside the box on just how fast and crazy these racing machines really are. Just think about 30 mad as hell bulls in a Rodeo arena going 140 miles per hour all trying to buck their riders off their backs and then ramming their horns right through the riders spine . . . all at the same time and not for just eight seconds, but for thirty minutes. THAT, is a sprint car race on a quarter mile or a half mile dirt or asphalt oval any where USA. No smoked salmon or a glass of Merlot here. Any Questions, if so give ole Ben Hur a call, he will get you up to speed on just how damn crazy Sprint Car racing really is!

Horse power – 900 Price - $40,000.00 Weight – 1300 Lbs. Top Speed 160 MPH +

To learn more log on to www.worldofoutlaws.com or just Google Sprint Cars to see how incredible this sport is.

NASCAR Stock Cars

If you compare a NASCAR Sprint Cup stock car to let's say, a car that you can buy off the show room floor or any car lot in the world, most people would be totally shocked to realize that a NASCAR stock car is not remotely similar to a regular car that people drive daily. NASCAR Stock Cars are $250,000.00 high tech 200 miles per hour rocket ships designed and built from the ground up by the smartest engineers and fabricators the world has to offer. Over 150 million race fans in the US alone are mesmerized by the skill and drama NASCAR Stock Cars generate every weekend at billion dollar speedways and on the major Television Networks. The worlds # one spectator sport is now as Americana as Base Ball and Foot Ball with every NASCAR Sprint Cup actually being bigger than the Super

Bowl for fan fair and people in the seats. It's hard to imagine 43 of these engineering marvels racing around Daytona at 200 miles per hour only inches apart for 500 miles. The tension is thicker than when NASA launches the Space Shuttle. This is wild and crazy stuff, this is out of control, this is Led Zeppelin on steroids!

Horse Power – 800 Price - $250.000.00 Weight – 3,400 Lbs. Top Speed – 220 MPH +

By the way, the top NASCAR teams employ over 400 employees trying to make these cars perform out on the track. To learn more log on to www.nascar.com or Google NASCAR and you will be amazed at how cool this sport is.

More Info on Terri O'

You can check more incredible information and see a full gallery of photographs chronicling Terri O'Connell's extraordinary life @ **www.goterrio.com**. News updates, personal appearances, video reels and info all about her racing career past and present are readily available on the **goterrio.com site**.

Apparel

Terri O' also has many great apparel designs and concepts for the entire family with the Dangerous Curves theme in addition to her hip and urban designs that are so popular today. Log on to **goterrio.com** to find a link or just go directly to **oterstore.com** and catch the hot fashions.

New Projects

Keep an eye out for Terri O's upcoming projects, she is currently writing her follow up book to Dangerous Curves, **"Getting Out of the Box"**, due out early 2010. She also has a cool and hip reality based motorsports program that will be launched and ready for some kick butt action on **MYDANGEROUSCURVES.TV** – This fan participation and interactive program looks to be on the track and running in the spring of 2009. Terri O' will also be launching her long awaited **Go Terri O' Driving Experience** geared to anyone who wants a full tilt driving and entertainment experience in the Summer of 2009.

These projects are brought to you by GKA Management Group in association with O'ter International and My Dangerous Curves Inc.

goterrio.com dangerouscurvesthebook.com oterstore.com

Terri O'

Made in the USA